RURAL DEVELOPMENT IN TRANSITIONAL CHINA

THE LIBRARY OF PEASANT STUDIES

RURAL DEVELOPMENT IN TRANSITIONAL CHINA

The New Agriculture

Edited by

PETER HO
JACOB EYFERTH
EDUARD B. VERMEER

FRANK CASS
LONDON • PORTLAND, OR

First published in 2004 in Great Britain by
FRANK CASS PUBLISHERS
Crown House, 47 Chase Side, Southgate, London N14 5BP, England

and in the United States of America by
FRANK CASS PUBLISHERS
c/o ISBS, 920 NE 58th Avenue, Suite 300
Portland, Oregon 97213-3786

Website http://www.frankcass.com

British Library Cataloguing in Publication Data

European Conference on Agriculture and Rural Development in China
(6th : Leiden University)
    Rural development in transitional China : the new agriculture. –
(The library of peasant studies ; no. 22)
1.Rural development – China – Congresses 2.Rural development –
China – Sociological aspects – Congresses 3.Agriculture and state
– China – Congresses 4.China – Rural conditions – Congresses
I. Title II.Ho, Peter III.Eyferth, Jacob IV.Vermeer, Eduard B.
307.1′412′0951

ISBN 0 7146 5549 X (cloth)
ISBN 0 7146 8432 5 (paper)
ISSN 1462-219X

Library of Congress Cataloging-in-Publication Data

Rural development in transitional China : the new agriculture / edited
by Peter Ho, Jacob Eyferth, Eduard B. Vermeer.
    p. cm.
Includes bibliographical references (p.) and index
    ISBN 0-7146-5549-X (hardback) — ISBN 0-7146-8432-5 (paperback)
    1. Agriculture–Economic aspects–China–Congresses. 2. Rural
development–China–Congresses. 3. China–Rural conditions–Congresses.
4. Peasantry–China–Congresses. 5. China–Economic
conditions–Congresses. I. Ho, Peter, 1968- II. Eyferth, Jan Jacob
Karl, 1962- III. Vermeer, E. B. (Eduard B.) IV. Title.
    HD2097.R84 2003
    330.951′009173′4–dc21
                                                    2003011126

This group of studies first appeared in 'Rural Development in Transitional China: The New
Agriculture' a special issue of *The Journal of Peasant Studies* (ISSN 0306 6150),
Vol.30/3&4 (April/July 2003) published by Frank Cass and Co. Ltd.

Printed in Great Britain by MPG Books Ltd., Bodmin, Cornwall

Contents

Acknowledgements

The editors are indebted to many people for their support in the gestation of this edited volume. These are the participants at the Sixth European Conference on Agriculture and Rural Development in China (ECARDC) hosted at Leiden University; Anthony J. Saich; Willem Vogelsang; Wim Stokhof and Marieke de Booij. We would also like to thank Tom Brass for his continuous support in bringing out this publication. We gratefully acknowledge the financial support for the conference by the following organizations: the Ford Foundation (Beijing), the CNWS Research School for Asian, African and Amerindian Studies (Leiden), the International Institute of Asian Studies (Leiden), and the Dutch Royal Academy of Arts and Sciences (Amsterdam).

Explanatory Notes

In the articles Chinese (traditional) units are used:
1 *mu* equals around 1/15 ha
1 Rmb or *yuan* equals around 1/8 US$ (in 2002)

For a good understanding of the articles, it is necessary to give some explanation of the administrative organization of the state and the collective. The Chinese state is divided into two echelons: a national and a local level. The local level includes the province, the municipality or prefecture, and the county. The term 'collective' or 'rural collective' refers to the successor of the so-called people's commune that was established in 1958 and disbanded in the mid-1980s. Apart from regional variations, the people's commune generally consisted of three levels: the commune, the production brigade and the production team. After decollectivization, these were replaced respectively by the township, the administrative village and the natural village or villagers' group (see figure below).

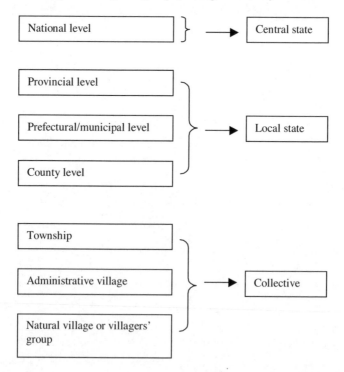

Introduction:
The Opening-Up of China's Countryside

JACOB EYFERTH, PETER HO
and EDUARD B. VERMEER

The Plenum of the 11th Central Committee of the Communist Party in December 1978 marked the beginning of the economic reforms and the close of collectivism in the People's Republic of China. With this, China had embarked on one of world history's largest experiments in social engineering. The mere size of the country and its population (9.6 million km^2 and almost 1.26 billion people in 2000) automatically imply a wide regional diversity in sociological, economic, political, ecological and ethnic terms. In addition, China's rural development had to start from a weak resource base: the average amount of farmland per capita is only one-third of the world average, while its agrarian society features high hidden unemployment, low levels of education and healthcare, rural poverty, and large shortages in water and energy.

When the people's communes were dismantled in the mid-1980s, this was trumpeted as the 'second land reform' as opposed to the 'first land reform' during the early years of the People's Republic. After more than three decades, the use right to rural land was once more returned to the tiller through lease. The lease system, termed the Household Contract Responsibility System, was no policy imposed from above, but sprang from the grassroots of rural society. It was the outcome of regional experiments borne out of dire need in the poverty-ridden county of Fengyang in Anhui province. The people's commune had definitely failed as an economic and

Peter Ho is Assistant Professor at the Environmental Policy Group of Wageningen University. He has published widely on issues of environment, rural development, institutional change and property rights in China, and is currently working on a monograph entitled *Institutions in Transition: Land Ownership, Property Rights and Social Conflict in China*.

Jacob Eyferth is Assistant Professor for Modern Chinese History at Simon Frazer University, Vancouver. He has been a Postdoctoral Research Fellow at the Fairbank Center for East Asian Studies at Harvard University and at the Center for Historical Analysis, Rutgers University.

Eduard B. Vermeer is Senior Lecturer at the Sinological Institute of Leiden University and Head of the Documentation and Research Centre for Contemporary China. He is a member of several academic advisory committees on China, including the board of the European China Academic Network at the School of Oriental and African Studies (SOAS), London University.

administrative unit. In the last four years before the economic reforms in 1978, grain production had stagnated at a level of around 280 million tons [*State Statistical Bureau*, 1990: 12]. By allowing private lease, the state hoped to stimulate farmers' incentives that had been dampened by years of collectivism. Shortly after the dismantling of the commune system, the grain harvest reached an all-time record of 400 million tons in 1984. The land lease system replaced the commandist and centralist commune system and privatized agricultural operation.[1]

It is no overstatement to say that the past two decades in China have witnessed the fastest change ever and anywhere of a rural economy and society. Over 200 million rural inhabitants have been lifted out of absolute poverty, and tens of millions have become wealthier than the average urban resident. Agricultural output has been growing at a much faster pace than food demand, leaving the Chinese population healthier and better fed than in the past. The impressive growth figures of the Chinese economy were, certainly in the 1990s, to a great extent propelled by the rural (industrial) economy. From 1991 until 1998 the average annual growth rate in GDP was 10.8 per cent, with an average of 20.6 per cent coming from the primary industry [*State Statistical Bureau*, 1999: 21 and 56]. One indicator of the great changes that took place in Chinese agrarian society is the proportion of income produced in the agricultural sector. Between 1952 and 1998, the share of agriculture in GDP declined (from 50.5 to 18.4 per cent) [*State Statistical Bureau*, 1999: 56]. Scholars seeking an explanation for China's extraordinary agrarian change found it in its rural industries.

'LOCAL STATE CORPORATISM': A CHINESE RURAL
DEVELOPMENT MODEL?

Rural industry has been the fastest growing sector of the entire Chinese economy, with an average annual growth rate of about 30 per cent. Eventually, at the end of the twentieth century, the main problems for the Chinese farming sector had become similar to those in most countries. Overproduction resulted in falling prices and declining income from crop cultivation[2] and the costs and environmental risks of energy-intensive agriculture kept rising. Rural households suffered from a weakening demand for rural products and cutbacks in employment in the urban sector. To the growing burdens imposed by local government were added the rising costs of education and healthcare, which were less and less subsidized. At the same time about 50 million households, or six per cent of the rural population, mostly living in remote areas without access to markets, remained extremely poor even by Chinese official standards – if international standards were applied, their number would be far higher.

FIGURE 1

ADMINISTRATION MAP OF CHINA

Source: Provided courtesy of The General Libraries, The University of Texas at Austin.

Growth has slowed down considerably, and the rural industrial sector – flagship of the reforms and engine of rural growth – has seen a declining performance for the last few years.[3]

For nearly 20 years, it looked as if China had found – by chance rather than by design – a uniquely successful development model, with rural industrialization at its core. Its uniqueness was mainly due to the fact that to some extent it could remedy the market and institutional constraints produced by China's urban–rural segmentation. Moreover, it capitalized on existing differential treatments of state-owned, collective and private enterprises. The phenomenon was captured under the term 'local state corporatism' [*Oi*, 1998]. In other words, the local state treats the enterprises under its jurisdiction as components of a larger corporate whole. The whole functions as a business corporation with local officials acting as the equivalent of a board of directors or CEO. Such a relationship is one of mutual dependence, with the local state controlling enterprises through the allocation of labour, capital and land resources, while the enterprises in return adhere to local corporate interests and turn over substantial portions of their revenues to the local state.

Another unique feature of Chinese society is the formal institutionalization of a rural–urban divide through the household registration or *hukou* system – a remnant of the Soviet state. Through the *hukou* system the state strictly controlled rural–urban migration. Those with a rural *hukou* were excluded from the urban job market, social welfare, housing and education. The rural–urban divide also ensured that only the members of rural collectives enjoyed access to agricultural land. This exclusion of urban entrepreneurs, officials and citizens prevented the rise of a class of impoverished, landless peasants. As the agricultural reforms freed a substantial portion of rural labour from the land, millions of migrant farmers started to look for alternative employment opportunities, which they eventually found: in the township and village enterprises.

The medium- and small-scale township and village enterprises (TVEs) provided employment for 140 million workers – virtually one-third of the rural labour force! In 1997, out of 214 million economically active rural households, those engaged both in agricultural and non-agricultural activities reached 34.4 per cent and another 9.7 per cent were employed entirely outside the farming sector.[4] The TVEs not only provided employment, but also earned incomes for local governments and individual entrepreneurs. The higher income led to increased and diversified demand, and facilitated by improved transportation and processing facilities, farming could be directed towards a swift expansion and technological upgrading of meat, fish, fruit and other labour-intensive and high-value products. The income gap between the urban and rural population was reduced at first, then stabilized for a decade at about 2.5 to 1, a major achievement for a country with the size and rapidly developing economy of China.

As more and more labour was absorbed into rural industry and services, the pressure on land and other resources was eased in certain regions. In the most advanced areas, land was consolidated into large fields, and farming delegated to specialists who supplied enough grain to feed the community and meet tax quotas. For example, in Jianli county (Hubei province) the number of farmers working off the farm reached 220,000 people in 2001, or 49 per cent of the total rural labour force. They vacated 520,000 *mu* (35,000 ha) – one-third of the county's total area of arable land – which was subsequently subleased to fewer migrant farmers who could thus operate on a larger scale. It is notable that the original lessee in most cases had to pay the new tenant a fee to work his land. This fee could amount to 300 Rmb per *mu* [*Huang*, 2001: 1]. Like industrialization, migration not only generated income but also eased constraints on agriculture and served as another escape route from rural poverty. In 1994, 37 million rural migrants sent an average of 2,000 *yuan* to their home communities, particularly in the wealthier coastal provinces such as Zhejiang, Fujian and Guangdong.[5]

RETHINKING CHINA'S RURAL DEVELOPMENT

By the turn of the century, however, it looked as if rural economic growth was running out of steam. Some of the most significant advances have been one-off events. The restoration of household production in the early 1980s produced rapid output and income growth in agriculture, but during the 1990s higher output gave diminishing returns. The phenomenal growth of rural industries in the 1980s was largely due to pent-up demand after decades of underconsumption, and to the fact that state-owned enterprises were fettered by state plans and burdened with social welfare costs. By the mid-1990s, most of the early gains were exhausted. China is no longer a shortage economy; both agriculture and rural industry are plagued by excess capacities. Cotton output was scaled back after 1995, and, under the pressure of giant stocks, finally also grain. The reform model, like the earlier Stalinist model, excelled at generating double-digit growth driven by resource mobilization. In industrial but also some agricultural sectors, local governments selected a promising 'project' (which was easy enough in the 1980s) and mobilized the resources at their command: land, labour, capital and administrative connections. Once the project started making profits, these were ploughed back to generate further growth. Resource mobilization through government channels still works, but its usefulness in industry has diminished. Local industrial policies have aggravated the current investment duplication and overcapacities, and it would be a mistake to think that industrialization is the answer to problems in agriculture.

Some economists in China ask themselves whether reform of the TVE sector is worth the effort. In the words of critics, TVEs 'have become just like state-owned enterprises, characterised by poor property rights, soft budget constraints, and perverse incentives. Public support should not assist their revitalisation or institutional restructuring [...]. Privatisation merely legitimates asset stripping and programs to support the transition to new ownership forms is just another way to get access to government or bank funds.'[6] While this observation may be true, the real question is not whether institutional and financial state support should be provided to reforms – there never was much of that, and the initiative was usually local and private. Different regions have emerged with 'diametrically opposed property rights regimes ... some only marginally different from that of the Mao years, and other ones with wholly new forms of private household and foreign-funded enterprise' [*Oi and Walder*, 1999: 20].

More important is whether rural communities will be able to maintain some control over and protect themselves against newly risen interest groups of rent-seeking, often corrupt cadres and capitalist managers. Without political reform resulting in greater transparency and accountability of local government and more public participation in politics there is little hope that corruptive trends will stop. Supported by central and local policies of the Chinese Communist Party (CCP), privatization of TVEs has made rapid progress in recent years. The restructuring of the sector is accompanied by a declining propensity to create jobs. In contrast to collective enterprises, which were often founded with the explicit aim of creating jobs, private enterprises are more likely to put profit first and lay off underemployed staff – something local politicians would find hard to do. In fact, this is seen as one of the main motives for leasing or selling off collectively owned TVEs [*Chen*, 2000]. Total employment in the sector has been falling, even in years when output grew. Migration, the other major outlet for surplus rural labour, is also unlikely to provide much new employment in the coming years. The rapid rise in urban unemployment, caused by the restructuring of the state-owned sector, puts pressure on urban governments to reserve remaining jobs for the urban underemployed. So there is a continuous need to secure gainful employment in agriculture.

This brings us to the need for more investment in agriculture and human development. Agriculture-related investments have declined continuously in terms of percentage of agricultural GDP, even if *public* investment in fixed assets and R&D went up considerably since 1990. Farmers failed to invest for many reasons: a tradition of reliance on government, uncertainty over land use rights, and blurred contractual relations with government. Most importantly, private investment in agriculture and particularly crop growing had much lower returns than in industry or services [*Fan*, 1997: 131–40]. Chinese data about rural investments, savings, fixed assets and farm animals are rather unreliable and do not allow firm conclusions about the agricultural capital stock. When the data of the First National Agricultural Census held in 1997 were published in 1999, provincial aggregates showed enormous discrepancies with all previous (and unfortunately, also most subsequent) official statistics and State Statistical Bureau (SSB) sample surveys of the 1990s. Apparently, particularly in the northern agricultural provinces local cadres had vested interests in over- or underreporting and the SSB survey samples are biased [*Vermeer*, 2001]. It is clear though that most villages need better access to education, health, drinking water, electricity and other amenities, all of which need considerable government investment. Without them, their youth will have little chance to develop and compete with the coastal and suburban advanced regions.

In short, the development strategy that has produced such extraordinary results during the last 20 years seems to be approaching the end of its useful life. The problems of post-Deng China are not unique; many of them are shared with other developing nations. What is unique about China is the diversity of the problems, from absolute poverty and environmental degradation in the interior parts to the new burdens of affluence in some coastal areas. Some of these problems are best described as the social and environmental costs of development: pollution, environmental degradation, increasing income disparities within and between regions. Others are related to the weakness and thinness of institutions, whose growth has not kept pace with the growth of the economy. The low level of taxation (China's revenue-to-GDP ratio is one of the lowest in the world) is a severe handicap for redistribution of funds and investments between rich and poor regions and economic sectors. Moreover, the fiscal system is decentralized and regressive, all of which leave the poorest areas starved for funds. Other problems include rural-to-urban fiscal flows and pressures on local governments to invest in revenue-producing industry, even where infrastructural investment would do more to raise local incomes. What all these issues have in common is that they require a different kind of government intervention: from developmental and command-and-control to more targeted, decentralized and consensual approaches. Instead of an entrepreneurial, fiscally self-sufficient local state, one needs a variety of different agencies (not all of them necessarily governmental) that regulate economic activity, build infrastructure and institutions, and redistribute income to reduce extreme poverty. In different ways, the articles in this volume reflect these changing functions and priorities, and the beginnings of a new agriculture.

THE CONTRIBUTIONS

The 1997 Census is a landmark, and its data will be of great significance for future studies of rural employment, infrastructure, facilities, use of land and agricultural technologies, housing and many other aspects of rural economy and society. In their careful analysis on the geographical aspects of the 1997 First National Agricultural Census, Roberto Fanfani and Cristina Brasili show how different types of counties (ranging from poor and mountainous to rich and peri-urban) are distributed within and among provinces. Data of this kind (and more fine-grained, down to the township level) are needed to deal efficiently with rural poverty, public investment, development of infrastructure and other government concerns. Their analysis demonstrates that there is a decreasing importance of persons active in agriculture, according to the economic development of the different provinces. The number of persons engaged in agriculture in total in the main municipalities is less than 40 per cent (Shanghai and Beijing), and less than 60 per cent in most provinces of the eastern part. In these provinces, there are now many households whose revenue is mainly coming from non-agricultural activities, and only 55 per cent of total households are pure agriculture households. The data available from the 1997 Census also show that the official classification of Chinese provinces into six geographical regions or three main economic–geographical regions (west, middle and east) is insufficient to describe a composite reality of Chinese agriculture. In most cases, the largest differences emerge from the western and middle provinces, on the one hand, and the eastern provinces on the other hand. The authors, however, found statistically relevant differences inside these larger geographical areas, at both the provincial and the county level.

The problems of farmers are compounded by local tax burdens. Li Xiande presents a detailed analysis of the so-called peasant burden, since 1990 a highly politicized problem, which commands great attention by both scholars and politicians.[7] National regulations of 1991 and 1993 have failed to stop the perception of predatory local fees and burdens, resulting in widespread rural discontent. Li uses the example of one village in Hubei province, where he found that in 1997, families paid nearly 13 per cent of their net income as all kinds of charges to village and township government. However, only the three per cent paid in official charges (the so-called three *tiliu* and five *tongchou*) are included in the official definition of the 'peasant burden', for which government has set a ceiling of five per cent. Agricultural and special agricultural product taxes and the water/electricity fee amounted to over one-third of the total contribution of 202 *yuan* per capita in this village. Administrative fees, the common production fee, the education supplement and converted corvée money were other main items. The combined total is presented as a contracted sum (*hetongkuan*) to the villagers, and subsequently deducted from their quota sales of grain. The distribution of revenues between state, township and village, and their management has become more decentralized and departmentalized, with detailed definitions of their uses and functions. Li sees the swollen staffs of local bureaucracies and lack of alternative revenues of county government as major reasons for the worsening peasant burden. Besides economic growth, only greater administrative efficiency and democratic control of the use of public funds might solve the problem.

Jacob Eyferth contrasts the failing TVEs in Chenyan village, Jiajiang county, Sichuan, with the traditional household papermaking industry. After decollectivization it took the papermaking households only a few years before they re-established their industry, and on the basis of special skills, a strong market orientation and specialization they managed to expand their sales throughout China. The TVEs depended on local government support for their establishment and financing, and most were ill conceived. Collective factories of paper, acetylene, calcium carbonate and ceramic tiles all failed, for reasons of lack of research into market demand, too large size, and low level of technology. Apparently, village cadres badly wanted to have a large-scale factory to run, and were prepared to sink considerable village funds into ventures, often just copying the examples of existing enterprises. In a situation of full employment and higher wages in the traditional handicraft sector, the low-skilled jobs in the TVEs were not attractive to most villagers. Only the clerical and managerial positions, no more than two dozen, provided new and rewarding employment. Eyferth concludes that since the early 1990s, the TVEs made a negative contribution to the local economy. Even if their turnover was about equal to that of the paper handicraft sector, the latter earned profits of 10–20 per cent, while the former hardly earned any. Statistics from other townships in Jiajiang systematically undervalue household industries (many of which are classified as 'sidelines' or unreported to escape taxation) and overvalue TVEs. In contrast to the entrepreneurs of the household industries, local factory workers are regarded as a class that work at a leisurely pace but does not command high wages.

Issues of income distribution, welfare and social security are central to several other articles in this volume. Here, too, there is a need for more detailed knowledge. Eduard Vermeer's analysis of the determinants of wage incomes in 22 villages in Wuxi and Qingyuan (Hebei) provides crucial information. Since property and non-wage incomes from farm and household businesses are relatively evenly distributed, wage income plays a crucial role in social differentiation. Vermeer found vast differences in the proportion of wage income to total household income, stemming largely from different degrees of wage labour participation between localities. Other important findings concern returns to education and age and gender differences. Interestingly, better education had different effects in the two localities: in rich and industrialized Wuxi, education increased the chances of finding paid employment much more dramatically than in Qingyuan. Moreover, education translated more effectively into higher wages in Wuxi than in Qingyuan. In both places, men benefited from education more than women did. Political affiliation, if corrected for age, education and gender, showed different effects on wage income in the two localities.

A critical issue in the development of agrarian China concerns land tenure security. Here the scholarly studies probe into the relation between land tenure and use (in terms of cultivation, management and investment). Following the introduction of the Household Contract Responsibility System for rural land lease in the early 1980s, wide academic attention focused on the question: Can the present land tenure system – under conditions of socio-economic and demographic change, and strong control by the rural collective – stimulate the farmers' economic incentives to ensure sustained economic growth? At present, many problems still haunt the rural land lease system. Owing to the unclear property structure and a low legal awareness, villagers are uncertain about the rights they enjoy to land property. A major concern of the Chinese authorities and scholars is the powerful control of the lessor over land rights. The contract is often but a 'paper agreement' because collectives can appropriate and redistribute leased land whenever deemed necessary. On the other hand, redistribution of land is often a bare necessity in response to demographic change. In land-scarce regions the collective faces strong social pressure from the community to uphold a more egalitarian land allocation, which leads to frequent readjustment of the land lease.[8] The rural land tenure issue has been intensely debated by Chinese and Western scholars [*Kung and Liu*, 1997: 33–64; *Liu* et al., 1998: 1789–806].[9] It is, however, certain that the problem can never be resolved without the transfer of surplus rural labour to the non-agricultural sector. In 1998 China had an official urban unemployment rate of three per cent (5.71 million people) [*State Statistical Bureau*, 1999: 892]. To date there are no reliable figures for the rate of rural unemployment, and estimates for it remain no more than an educated guess. Chinese farmers are "earthbound" – in the words of the renowned Chinese sociologist Fei Xiaotong – and to some extent this situation still obtains today. A senior official at the Ministry of Agriculture once said: 'The future problem of China will not be the laying-off (*xiagang*) of urban workers, but that of its huge population of farmers.'[10]

In this volume, this issue is not directly addressed but it features as the backdrop for problems of environmental degradation and rural poverty. The articles by Peter Ho and Rita Merkle demonstrate the impossibility of improving the environment and relieving poverty if the question of rural unemployment is not simultaneously dealt with. A second strand of thought that links the two articles is their focus on the nerve tips of the state: how do governments assess complex local situations? How do they weigh different needs in situations where no ideal solutions exist, and every gain implies a loss for somebody else? In all cases, there are trade-offs between income and the environment: short-term measures to improve local livelihood will result in long-term environmental degradation.

Peter Ho examines a new stage in China's land reform: the auction of wasteland to individual farmers in the northwest of China. In an effort to deal with rural poverty alleviation while tapping into the undeveloped resources of wasteland, local authorities launched the 'Four Wastelands Auction Policy' in the mid-1990s. The policy was hailed as a breakthrough in soil and water conservation through the sale of use rights to the highest bidder. Not only would good stewardship of the land be stimulated as farmers themselves would be responsible for the land, but the policy would also tackle the critical issues of rural unemployment and environmental protection. The development of wasteland for afforestation and animal husbandry would give farmers alternative income-generating activities, while simultaneously improving soil and water conservation. The article argues that the Wastelands Policy signals a dual break with the past. First, the formulation process of the policy is an example of the space opened up by the reforms, which allows lower administrative levels (county and below) to initiate and shape policies that are normally considered too sensitive or innovative. Second, the policy entails the potential for great socio-economic changes because it removes the so-called rural–urban divide of the *hukou* system. The Wastelands Policy permits 'open auctions' in which not only farmers, but also cadres, urban entrepreneurs, and legal entities such as mass organizations and companies are allowed to participate and, more importantly, gain access to rural land. However, the lesson to be learnt from the auction policy is that China is still characterized by command-and-control, and campaign-style policy implementation. It leads to frequent policy failure, and ultimately even risks the rise of a new class of landless peasants as the weak and poor cannot compete on an even footing with the wealthier farmers in the open auctions.

Staying in the northwest, Rita Merkle's article also deals with this combination of resource constraints, rural poverty and environmental degradation through a study of a large-scale resettlement programme. Like most of China's poorest areas, southern Ningxia is remote, mountainous, resource poor, and has a substantial minority population. Areas like these have been unable to capitalize on the opportunities created by the reforms. Being deficient in subsistence crops, they do not benefit from farm product price increases; neither do they have the resources and market access to generate off-farm income. To the contrary, investment in off-farm activities in such areas is often driven by revenue considerations and diverts scarce funds away from where they are most needed [*Park* et al., 1996: 751–78]. Alleviation measures begin with targeting the needy, and this is, as Merkle shows, by no means easy. Poverty is defined in territorial terms: the poor are those who live in counties officially designated as poor – including the non-poor in these counties, and excluding the poor elsewhere. Merkle's main focus is on a large-scale (250,000 persons) voluntary programme in which poor households are resettled on newly opened land. This is a measure of last resort, but one that China's leaders intend to use more often in their efforts to stamp out poverty within the next few years. Project implementation was initially poor but improved over time. One of the most interesting findings is that relief targeting remained imperfect and that administrators reluctantly accepted that aid went not to the most needy, but to people who were well equipped to make use of it. In all these cases, short-term gain must be balanced against the long-term ecological consequences. Interpretations differ and statistical data are hard to come by, but there can be little doubt that the reform period has witnessed increasing pressure on the environment, from air and water pollution to soil erosion and desertification.

Many scholars and politicians were concerned that China's land scarcity would not only cause environmental pressure, but would also endanger food security. In 1995 Lester Brown shocked the Chinese government with his prediction that the People's Republic would face critical food shortages in the future [*Brown*, 1995]. Despite substantial agricultural growth generated predominantly by increased use of chemical fertilizers, land is still one of the basic inputs to farm production. From the viewpoint of the government, the average area of farmland per capita is low: only one-third of the world average. The situation is aggravated by substantial losses in arable land owing to rapid urbanization, industrialization and environmental problems (soil erosion and desertification) [*Ash and Edmonds*, 1998: 838]. There is a strong economic case for regional agricultural specialization and cashcrop cultivation to enable higher grain imports. But the government is committed to grain self-sufficiency out of strategic considerations. Most experts now consider Brown's thesis untenable because it does not address the issue of the capacity of land for increased agricultural productivity, while the greater part of China's land actually produces well below its potential.

Zhang Xiaoyong's contribution builds on the debate sparked by Brown's thesis. She presents a comparison of projection models for China's food demand and supply. As Zhang shows, widely divergent projections hinge on apparently arcane details: relatively small differences in the feed–meat conversion rate make all the difference between feast and famine in projections. Zhang cautiously refrains from pronouncing on the issue of food security. She shows that the margins of error are too wide to be confident about any long-term prediction. Moreover, the official data on cultivated land and pork production and consumption are known to be wrong. None of the models she discusses supports alarmist predictions that China's future food demand could not be met by domestic and international supply (China exports over twice as much food and food products as it imports). Partly because of protection measures for arable land, China has no problems in meeting its target of (almost) complete grain self-sufficiency. This is essentially a political decision with substantial economic costs: the comparative advantage of a land-short, labour-rich country like China lies in labour-intensive horticulture and livestock industries, not in production of wheat or maize. One of the most pressing questions is how to protect the interests of grain farmers (about three-quarters of farmland being devoted to grain, and even more in poverty areas) while simultaneously shifting resources to more viable sectors. As China's subsidization of farm products conflicts with World Trade Organization (WTO) requirements, and by early 2001 this was a major remaining obstacle to China's accession to the WTO, China must devise new subsidy policies based on direct income support instead of price support. This means the government should direct its subsidies to poverty areas and poor farm households, and establish more direct links with the latter.

Rural welfare reform would make it easier to untie the knot that ties land to people and people to their land. As China evolves from a subsistence-oriented agrarian economy to an increasingly affluent industrial economy, also the basis of social welfare needs to change. Traditionally, the costs of welfare in rural China were borne by the income-sharing household and/or collective and secured by control over land. As we have seen above, the link between land and social security has been a perennial problem for property rights reforms. Large numbers of rural wage earners no longer rely on land. Yet people who are no longer farmers in any meaningful sense of the word hang on to their allotments, partly because regulations require them to deliver grain quotas, partly because land is their only subsistence guarantee if they lose their jobs. In the absence of other guarantees, land needs to be periodically reallocated to ensure minimum subsistence for all. Government and academic studies have shown that the majority of farmers, in fact, favour such redistributions.[11] In a wide-ranging article, Jutta Hebel discusses how social welfare depends on a complex nexus of households, communities, social networks and the state. Hebel presents a multilevel approach for the analysis of social welfare – which is understood in the broad sense including income, value generation, services in kind, state subsidies, and so forth. The objective of this analysis is to combine the levels of institutions that determine welfare arrangements at the household level. For this purpose, Hebel draws on three scholarly views to the social welfare problem: the 'security approach', the 'rural developmental approach', and the 'family approach'.

The links between community and welfare are further explored in Heather Xiaoquan Zhang's chapter on gender differences in inheritance rights. Like Hebel, she sees welfare as consisting of more than pensions and insurance payments. Most welfare transactions in most societies take place within families, through aid and financial support for the needy, elderly or ill. Such support is typically mirrored by intergenerational transfers: gifts, bequests and inheritance. In China, and not only there, these exchanges are slanted against daughters, who provide much of the social support but get less than their fair share of the inheritance. As Heather Zhang shows, such discrimination derives from the prevalent practice of virilocal residence. Upon marriage, women leave their natal family and village, and the share of the family patrimony that is theirs by law. This is not only condoned but also openly encouraged by village leaders who want to prevent resources from flowing out of the (agnatically defined) community. The facts are well known, but the complete disjunction between formal law (which guarantees equal inheritance rights for daughters) and common practice (which all over China denies them their rights) deserves much more attention than it has hitherto received.

Environmental degradation, gender discrimination, income differentiation – all these are issues that cut across administrative boundaries. Above, we argued that local governments are in the process redefining their functions. This is not to say that the developmental local state and the managerial township, which were highlighted in previous studies, are no longer active [*Christiansen and Zhang*, 1998]. Maria Edin gives us a spirited defence of the local state, and a new perspective on its inner workings. The usual answer to 'what drives local development' is brief: the need for fiscal revenue. This, Edin argues, is theoretically unconvincing and empirically untrue. Many local governments successfully transformed themselves from owners of collective firms to facilitators of private enterprise. This transformation is guided by non-economic incentives, primarily by the cadre assessment system. Routinized censure and praise, fines and bonuses, demotions and promotions within the bureaucratic hierarchy ensure that development is led into the right channels. Since the early 1980s, the cadre management system introduced both individual and collective performance contracts for leading and medium-level township cadres, which were not unlike those given to enterprise managers. Subsequently, they were integrated within the civil servants' evaluation system, which became a powerful tool of governance, at least in the developed areas of China. Leading township cadres are evaluated by the county on the basis of their performance contracts, which include a hierarchy of soft, hard and priority targets. Nationwide, family planning and maintenance of social order are priority targets. Local targets differ and reflect local priorities. Edin describes various incentives and political rewards for target fulfilment. Evaluation procedures vary, but a significant degree of 'mass participation' is realized by the use of complaint letters and appraisal meetings of medium-level cadres. A major element of local economic success is the selection and preferential treatment of local private industrial enterprises. By contrast, township government performance may be quite defective in poor areas, which lack economic incentives for good performance. A question Edin raises but does not answer is why this system works so well in some regions while it failed in others. A possible answer is that it requires an exceptional level of bureaucratic expertise to run such a system, which is less likely to be found in poor inland regions.

This volume lays emphasis on rural and agricultural problems in the inland provinces, and has relatively little to say on rural industrialization and the coastal areas. This may appear paradoxical: despite recent setbacks, China is becoming more affluent, more industrial and more urban. The position of agriculture in the national economy has changed, probably for good. It is no longer the workhorse that subsidizes the urban sector with cheap grain and other inputs and helps the nation realize industrialization. China can no longer guarantee that the rural unemployed and poor will not burden the socialist state or crowd its modern cities. Domestic terms of trade, long set against the farmers, changed in their favour in the 1980s and only in the past few years the government has reverted to less generous prices and limitations to guaranteed purchases of grain, cotton and oil crops. If China were to meet WTO conditions of accession, many of its farmers will in the future become net recipients of income subsidies – objects of protection rather than extraction, like their European colleagues – as the sector as a whole will be exposed to world market prices. Because of comparative disadvantages, producers of cotton, wheat, maize, wool, beef and dairy products are likely to suffer most. In 1998, an official Chinese study of the effects of WTO entry calculated that by 2010 its net effect would be positive (+4.6 per cent) on urban income but negative (–2.1 per cent) on rural income [Yu, 2000: 66–72]. Sheer numbers make it impossible that most farmers will be absorbed into industry, services or become producers for international markets. Nonetheless, the problems of rural China have become smaller, more localized and more manageable – and perhaps also more easily neglected. The shift of focus in this volume is a measure of the magnitude of these changes: this much has been achieved, this much still needs to be done.

NOTES

1. Initially the national government allowed farm households a land lease period of five years, which was extended to 15 in 1984. To safeguard stable tenure, the lease term was extended with another 30 years on top of the original contract in 1993 [Cheng and Tsang, 1995: 44].
2. In 1998, 1999 and 2000 per capita net income from crop cultivation declined by 6, 45 and 98 yuan, respectively [State Statistical Bureau, 2000].
3. In 2000, collectively owned industries had a lower growth rate than shareholding companies or state-owned industries, namely 7.4 per cent vs. 14.5 per cent and 10.1 per cent [State Statistical Bureau, 2000].

4. Another 12 million rural households were non-productive [*National Agricultural Census Office of China*, 1999: 16].
5. Data based on 23 large cities [*Nyberg and Rozelle*, 1999: 101].
6. Quoted in Li *et al.* [2000].
7. A recent article calls the peasant burden 'a reflection of systemic weaknesses in the political and administrative system as a whole' and stresses the burden on the poor owing to the regressive character of taxes [*Bernstein and Lu*, 2000: 742–63].
8. Based on research in Sichuan province, Pennarz observed a more even distribution of resources, stricter land use regulations and a stronger commitment to strive for common interests in land-scarce regions (with high population pressure) as opposed to land-abundant regions [*Pennarz*, 1996].
9. The research on urban land touches on a similar topic: the relation between property rights and the construction industry. See Walker [1991]; Chen and Wills [1999].
10. Li Sheng, oral communication, 2000.
11. The 1997 survey of the Central Policy Research Office indicates that 62.8 per cent of the sample villages still advocate land redistribution. Of the 36.1 per cent that opposed land redistributions, 46.7 per cent thought their villagers' committee could safeguard a policy of stable land lease, 22.9 per cent said that land was abundant and uneven land distribution would not incite social conflict, 17.1 per cent said that income from land was no longer important because of alternative employment opportunities, and 13.3 per cent stated that land distribution was too cumbersome and they were unwilling to redistribute after the first time. See Wang [1998: 56–7]. In a survey of 800 households in four provinces done by Kung and Liu it was found that 62 per cent of the respondents preferred the village policy 'that periodically reassigns land among farm families in response to changes in the composition of their families' [*Kung and Liu*, 1997: 34].

REFERENCES

Ash, Robert F. and Richard L. Edmonds, 1998, 'China's Land Resources, Environment and Agricultural Production', *The China Quarterly*, No.156 (Dec.), p.838.

Bernstein, Thomas P. and Lu Xiaobo, 2000, 'Taxation without Representation: Peasants, the Central and the Local States in Reform China', *The China Quarterly*, No.163 (Sept.), pp.742–63.

Brown, Lester, 1995, *Who Will Feed China? Wake-up Call for a Small Planet*, New York: W.W. Norton.

Chen, Hongyi, 2000, *The Institutional Transition of China's Township and Village Enterprises: Market Liberalization, Contractual Form Innovation and Privatization*, Aldershot: Ashgate.

Chen, Jean, and David Wills, 1999, *The Impact of China's Economic Reforms upon Land Property and Construction*, Aldershot: Ashgate.

Cheng, Tiejun and Mark Selden, 1994, 'The Origins and Social Consequences of China's Hukou System', *The China Quarterly*, No.139 (Sept.), pp.644–69.

Cheng, Yuk-shing and Tsang Shu-ki, 1995, 'Agricultural Land Reform in a Mixed System: The Chinese Experience of 1984–1994', *China Information*, Vol.10, Nos.3/4, pp.23–44.

Christiansen, F. and Zhang Junzuo (eds.), 1998, *Village Inc.: Chinese Rural Society in the 1990s*, Richmond, Surrey: Curzon Press.

Fan, Shenggen, 1997, 'Public Investment in Rural China: Historical Trends and Policy Issues', in *Agricultural Policies in China*, Paris: OECD, pp.131–40.

Huang, Guangming, 2001, 'Xin tudi geming' (The new land revolution), *Nanfang zhoumo*, 14 June, p.1.

Kung, James Kai-sing and Liu Shouying, 1997, 'Farmers' Preferences Regarding Ownership and Land Tenure in Post-Mao China: Unexpected Evidence from Eight Counties', *The China Journal*, No.38 (July), pp.33–64.

Li, Hongbin, Scott Rozelle and Loren Brandt, 2000, 'To Save or Limit Rural Industry: An Analysis of Privatisation and Efficiency in China', in *The Agro-Food Processing Sector in China*, Paris: OECD.

Liu, Shouying, Michael R. Carter and Yao Yang, 1998, 'Dimensions and Diversity of Property

Rights in Rural China: Dilemmas on the Road to Further Reform', *World Development*, Vol.26, No.10, pp.1789–1806.

National Agricultural Census Office of China, 1998, *Abstract of the First National Agricultural Census in China*, Beijing: China Statistics Press.

Nyberg, Albert and Scott Rozelle, 1999, *Accelerating China's Rural Transition*, Washington, DC: World Bank.

Oi, Jean C., 1998, 'The Collective Foundation for Rapid Rural Industrialization', in E.B. Vermeer, F. Pieke and W.L. Chong (eds.), *Cooperative and Collective in China's Rural Development: Between State and Private Interests*, New York: M.E. Sharpe.

Oi, Jean C. and Andrew G. Walder (eds.), 1999, *Property Rights and Economic Reform in China*, Stanford: Stanford University Press.

Park, Albert, Scott Rozelle, Christine Wong and Ren Changqing, 1996, 'Distributional Consequences of Reforming Local Public Finance in China', *The China Quarterly*, No.147 (Sept.), pp.751–78.

Pennarz, Johanna, 1996, 'Collective Land Ownership and Sustainable Agriculture: Perspectives on the Diversity of Land Use Rights in China', Room Document No.2, Workshop on Agricultural Policies in China, OECD Headquarters, 12–13 Dec.

State Statistical Bureau (ed.), 1990, *Quanguo gesheng, zizhiqu, zhixiashi, lishi tongji ziliao huibian – 1949–1989* (A compilation of historical statistics of all provinces, autonomous regions and municipalities – 1949–1989), Beijing: Zhongguo tongji chubanshe.

State Statistical Bureau (ed.), 1999, *China Statistical Yearbook 1999*, Beijing: China Statistics Press.

State Statistical Bureau, 2000, *SSB Bulletin on China's Economic and Social Development in 2000*, d.d. 28 Feb. 2001, www.stats.gov.cn.

Vermeer, Eduard B., 2001, 'Determinants of Agricultural Productivity in China: A Comparison of the New Provincial Census Data with Official Figures, and some Implications', *International Seminar on China Agricultural Census Results*, FAO (Food and Agriculture Organization (UN)), Beijing; China Statistics Press.

Walker, Anthony, 1991, *Land, Property and Construction in the PRC*, Hong Kong: Hong Kong University Press, 1991.

Wang, Huimin, 1998, 'Dangqian nongcun tudi chengbao jingying guanli de xianzhuang ji wenti' (The present situation and problems facing the management and administration of rural land lease), *Zhongguo nongcun guancha*, No.5, pp.56–7.

Yu, Yongding, Zheng Bingwen and Song Hong (eds.), 2000, *Zhongguo 'rushi' yanjiu baogao: jinru wto-di zhongguo chanye* (Research report on China's entry into WTO: An analysis of China's industries entering the WTO), Beijing: Shehui kexue wenxian chubanshe, pp.66–72.

Regional Differences in Chinese Agriculture: Results from the 1997 First National Agricultural Census

ROBERTO FANFANI and CRISTINA BRASILI

RECENT DEVELOPMENTS IN CHINESE AGRICULTURE

The development of the Chinese agricultural sector and its capability to increase agricultural production is gaining a greater importance for food security and food trade on a worldwide scale. Considering the size of China, this could influence international food prices, and thus determine major problems for food-importing developing countries.

The People's Republic of China (PRC) remains predominantly a rural country, but its economy is characterized by strong macro-regional differences owing to factor endowments (human capital, resources and infrastructure) and differences in the structure of agriculture and other economic sectors. Economic development in China has registered uneven economic growth in favour of the coastal region (vs. inland and border ones), the urban areas (vs. rural areas) and the industrial sector (vs. the agricultural sector). During its transition the Chinese economic system faced strong structural changes. One of the main changes is certainly the reduction of the share of the agricultural sector in relation to total GDP and labour force. Indeed, the rural enterprises (or township and village enterprises, TVEs) are the leading and most dynamic elements in China's economy. Therefore, the integration of agricultural activities with other economic activities in the rural areas is of great importance and interest [*Biggeri, M.*, 1998; *Giovannini*, 2000].

Roberto Fanfani, Dept. of Statistics, University of Bologna, via Belle Arti, 41 – 40126 Bologna. Email: fanfani@stat.unibo.it. Tel. +39 051 2098212. Cristina Brasili, Dept. of Statistics, University of Bologna, via Belle Arti, 41 – 40126 Bologna. Email: brasili@stat.unibo.it. Tel. +39 051 2098260. Both authors share the responsibility for this article. However, Roberto Fanfani wrote the sections 'General Characteristics and Differences among Provinces' and 'The Complex Reality of Chinese Agriculture: A First Analysis at County Level', Cristina Brasili wrote the section 'The New Geography of Chinese Agriculture'. The sections 'Recent Developments in Chinese Agriculture' and 'Concluding Remarks' were written jointly. The authors thank also Mirko Bonetti for his valuable help in preparing the article.

Despite its declining relative importance, the agricultural sector has still a relevant and decisive role to play in the economic and social development of China, at least for the following three reasons. First, China is still a predominantly agricultural country. Second, Chinese agriculture should try to meet the increasing domestic food demand caused by natural population growth and by the change in food consumption patterns. Finally, the agricultural sector is important in labour force and intermediate inputs supply to China's industrial and economic development.

The Chinese government faces the problem of producing enough food in order to avoid an increase in imports (mainly cereals) and to maintain food prices accessible to urban consumers for reasons of political stability. There is a general consensus that China will import an increasing quantity of cereals in the near future. However there are two main different positions. Brown [1995] estimates a large net import of cereals (between 200 and 370 million tons) in 2030. Alexandratos [1996] estimates a net import of cereals of around 44 million tons. Brown's thesis assumes a rapid growth of food consumption, especially for livestock products, and a substantial decline by 20 per cent of cereal production. On the other hand, Alexandratos claims that the reduction of cultivated land will be lower, owing to other crop production and aquaculture, not only to urban development. The most recent projections drastically revise down previous estimates. The USDA report [2000] estimates China's net import of wheat at only 2 million tons by 2005 and, surprisingly, a net export of corn of more than 3 million tons. The (UN) Food and Agriculture Organization [*FAO*, 2000] revised its long-term projections in view of the slowdown in population growth and the decrease of the erstwhile rapid growth in food consumption in the past decade.

The development of the Chinese agricultural sector becomes relevant for its implications on the international food market. The 'definitive opening' of the PRC is something new for the international food market.

> In recent years, there has been a rather significant amount of research undertaken on China's food and agriculture prospects, and how these prospects relate to wider issues of world food trade and food security. It is no secret that such research has been hampered by uncertainties, providing opportunities for all sort of extreme positions concerning China's future role in world food trade, with some such positions verging on the outright alarmist for the food security of the world as a whole [FAO, 1998: 3–4].

The statistics are a crucial development in the empirical study of Chinese agriculture, and the results of the First National Agricultural Census, held in 1997, have played an important role recently in relation to the consideration of prospects for China's food security and for world food markets (especially for grain). In fact, the 1997 Census data suggest that China has significantly more cultivated land (30 per cent) than previously estimated by official data, and that the number of livestock is lower (–20 per cent) in comparison with previous estimates. Both these results indicate a greater potential for increases in yield and therefore in the domestic production of agriculture in China.[1]

In this article we first analyse the main results of the 1997 Census to give evidence of the differences between provinces (section 2). We then show the complex reality of agriculture with a brief analysis of some variables for the 2,300 Chinese counties (section 3). In the fourth section we will define a 'new geography' of Chinese agriculture defining first macro-agricultural areas at province level; then we analyse these areas more closely, down to county level. We mainly use cluster analysis methodology and data of the 1997 Census. Concluding remarks are reported in the last section.

GENERAL CHARACTERISTICS AND DIFFERENCES AMONG PROVINCES

The 1997 Census is considered a milestone for gaining a better understanding of the Chinese rural system and for designing adequate policies targeted to the promotion of long-term socio-economic development. From a statistical point of view, it can be considered a starting point for the revision of current and future statistical rural surveys of agricultural systems. It collected detailed data on the structure of the agricultural sector statistics as well as information on many other aspects of the rural economy.

In this section we will consider some general characteristics of agriculture in China revealed by the 1997 Census, but in particular we will emphasize the differences between provinces in order to give evidence of the different geography of agriculture in China. The *Abstract of the First National Agricultural Census in China* [National Agricultural Census Office of China, 1999] gives data aggregated by province that could be further aggregated by economic–geographical regions. Census information shows important aspects of rural and agricultural holdings (households and other holdings, purely agricultural household, etc.), the importance of the main activities of persons (agriculture and non-agriculture) and the amount of agricultural machinery and equipment.

The Census data, for instance, highlight that the number of rural households is about 214 million, with more than 193 million agricultural households. The number of persons involved is more than 873 million, with about 561 million engaged in production activities. The number of active people is much higher than the previous official statistics on the rural labour force (453 million [SSB, 1997: 363]). However, the larger size of labour force estimated by the Census could be a result, at least in part, on the different definitions used. For instance, the Census definition considers those working less than two months a year as active persons.

According to the 1997 Census, the number of persons engaged in agriculture is very high. In rural households, over 75 per cent of the population are active in agriculture, while only 25 per cent are engaged in other productive activities. It is important to underline that the current statistics report a lower proportion (less than 70 per cent) for the agricultural sector. The difference between Census data and the previous statistics on the proportion of people engaged in agricultural activities varies considerably between provinces. This variable, as we will show later, is high correlated with per capita GDP.

Census results give important information on households classification according to their prevalent activity (agricultural and non-agricultural) and the typology of agricultural households (pure agricultural, mainly agricultural, mainly non-agricultural). The main findings show that in rural areas the degree of integration of agriculture with other economic activities is an important variable characterizing the differences between provinces. In fact, of the 214 million Chinese rural households, about 193 million (more than 90 per cent) are agricultural households, accounting for more than 799 million people. The agricultural households are differentiated as follows:

- Pure agricultural households, more than 126.7 million (65.6 per cent of households) accounting for more than 500 million people (61 per cent).
- Mainly agricultural households, more than 39 million (20.2 per cent of households) accounting for more than 179 million people.
- Mainly non-agricultural households, more than 27.3 million (19 per cent of households) accounting for 120 million people.

The total cultivated land is more than 130 million hectares, according to the Census, with more than 123.3 million hectares of sown land in household holdings. The average size of all households is only 0.6 hectares of cultivated land. The household holdings have 0.64 hectares of sown land. The agricultural households under 1 hectare are more than 90 per cent of the total agricultural households, but they have about 79 per cent of the sown land. The evaluation of total cultivated land is relevant because it is much higher than the previous estimate of 95 million hectares. This result could indicate that it will be possible to increase the productivity and intensity of agricultural production, in terms of both the labour force and the amount of land worked.

FIGURE 1

CHINA AGRICULTURAL CENSUS:
PERSONS ENGAGED IN AGRICULTURAL ACTIVITIES IN RURAL HOUSEHOLDS

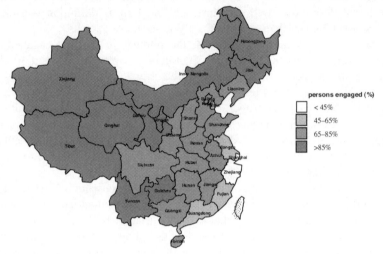

Source: Authors' elaboration, SSB [1997].

FIGURE 2

CHINA: GROSS DOMESTIC PRODUCT PER CAPITA 1996 (*YUAN*)

Source: Authors' elaboration, SSB [1997].

The results and the analysis of data of the 1997 Census, as we have seen, are important and relevant for their economic and policy implications. This is particularly true if we consider the differences between provinces and counties. Since the future development pattern of China will result in a gradual reduction of the agricultural labour force, to a different extent among macro-regions, provinces and counties, it is worthwhile to make some first analysis on the changing importance of agricultural labour force. Considering the three macro-regions, the proportion of the labour force engaged in agricultural activities is 66 per cent for the eastern area and about 80 per cent and 85 per cent for the provinces of the middle and western areas respectively (see Table 1 and Figure 1). There is also a large variation between provinces, from a minimum figure for agricultural employment in Shanghai (31 per cent) and Beijing (39 per cent), to a maximum in Tibet (95 per cent) (see Figure 1) We will see in the next section that such differences are more relevant at county level.

In order to obtain a better understanding of provincial development, we have analysed the correlation between the proportion of agricultural persons engaged in economic activities and the level of economic development for each province. We have measured such correlation using the GDP per capita (1996) as a synthetic variable for economic development for the Chinese province represented in Figure 3. The results show a very high inverse correlation between these two variables, with a high correlation coefficient (−0.81). However, the analysis demonstrates that the Chinese provinces can be divided into two main groups. One group includes the provinces characterized by a high percentage of people engaged in agricultural activities (more than 75 per cent) and by a low level of GDP per capita (less than 6,000 *yuan*). This group includes almost all the western and middle provinces, which are the main rural provinces of China (see Figure 3). The other group of provinces, with high levels of GDP per capita and lower levels of people engaged in non-agricultural activities, includes the municipalities of Shanghai and Beijing, the provinces in the eastern coast (Tianjin, Jiangsu, Zhejiang, Fujian and Guangdong). The only provinces with high levels of agricultural activities and a relatively high level of GDP per capita are Shandong and Liaoning, in the northern part of the eastern coast.

The results of this analysis show that the provinces of China have very different levels of development (in terms of GDP and share of agricultural labour). The most developed ones are those located in the eastern area. However, the eastern part of the three economic–geographical regions of China have less developed provinces, both in the north (Liaoning and Hebei) and in the south (Guangxi). Our results are also different from the six main geographic regions of China. This result clearly indicates the

TABLE 1

CHINA: NUMBER OF PERSONS ENGAGED IN AGRICULTURAL AND NON-
AGRICULTURAL PRODUCTION ACTIVITIES BY GEOGRAPHIC REGIONS

Geographic regions	Total persons	Agricultural activities		Non-agricultural activities	
		Persons	%	Persons	%
China, Total	561,479,490	424,995,487	75.7	136,484,003	24.3
North Region					
Beijing	2,195,012	855,091	39.0	1,339,921	61.0
Tianjin	2,305,319	1,246,816	58.0	1,058,503	45.9
Hebei	31,760,002	24,417,806	76.9	7,342,196	27.0
Shanxi	13,354,323	9,970,377	74.7	3,383,946	25.3
Inner Mongolia	8,367,447	7,410,471	88.6	956,976	11.4
Northeast Region					
Liaoning	14,281,809	10,976,276	76.9	3,305,533	27.0
Jilin	8,036,539	7,071,955	88.0	964,584	12.0
Heilongjiang	10,201,106	9,009,975	88.3	1,191,131	11.7
East Region					
Shanghai	2,861,042	892,583	31.2	1,968,459	68.8
Jiangsu	36,417,453	20,868,549	57.3	15,548,904	42.7
Zhejiang	22,867,225	10,232,612	44.7	12,634,613	55.3
Anhui	14,602,387	9,021,487	61.8	5,580,900	38.2
Jiangxi	19,160,861	14,112,097	73.7	5,048,764	26.3
Shandong	45,384,910	35,263,460	77.7	10,121,450	23.0
Central South Region					
Henan	47,774,836	38,553,743	80.7	9,221,093	19.3
Hubei	24,016,439	19,170,020	79.8	4,846,419	20.2
Hunan	31,932,654	24,918,200	78.0	7,014,454	22.0
Guangdong	27,556,073	15,777,116	57.3	11,778,957	42.7
Guangxi	22,328,674	18,073,078	80.9	4,255,596	19.1
Hainan	2,390,188	2,026,855	84.8	363,333	15.2
Southwest Region					
Chongqing	16,863,591	13,619,697	80.8	3,243,894	19.2
Sichuan	46,793,756	37,341,931	79.8	9,451,825	20.2
Guizhou	18,501,594	16,619,576	89.8	1,882,018	10.2
Yunnan	21,191,199	18,920,874	89.3	2,270,325	10.7
Tibet	1,217,889	1,162,910	95.5	54,979	4.5
Northwest Region					
Shaanxi	16,504,193	13,696,170	83.0	2,808,023	17.0
Gansu	12,060,126	10,521,324	87.2	1,538,802	12.8
Qinghai	2,067,124	1,871,359	90.5	195,765	9.5
Ningxia	2,219,375	1,887,506	85.0	331,869	15.0
Xinjiang	4,911,188	4,569,593	93.0	341,595	7.0

Source: Authors' processing of *Abstract of the First National Agricultural Census of China*
     [1998].

necessity for a new geography of Chinese agriculture, capable of taking into account the existence of differences within each macro-area.

There are other significant differences between the main geographic areas, in particular between the eastern provinces and the rest of China. In fact, in the provinces of the eastern area, purely agricultural households are only 57 per cent of the total, mainly agricultural households are 22 per cent, and the mainly non-agricultural households are 21 per cent. If we consider that in the eastern area there are also 15 per cent of non-agricultural households, these data emphasize the great importance that non-agricultural activities have assumed in this area. The remaining Chinese provinces, both in the middle and in the western areas, have a much lower share of mainly non-agricultural household (7.8 per cent in Southwest regions), and mainly agricultural households (19 per cent Southwest regions); see Table 2.

Another interesting aspect is the size of Chinese rural households. The average number of active people (engaged in economic activities) per rural household is six (Figure 4), which is not a high figure (similar to that of Italy for example). It reflects the fact that, on average, the size of rural families is not particularly large, owing to birth control and family planning policy. There are not big differences between provinces for this variable, with a minimum of about two persons per household (Beijing), and a maximum of three people in Tibet and Qinghai. The differences between provinces in the household dimension are strictly related to the differences of persons engaged in agriculture and in non-agricultural activities (see Figure 5).

The National Agricultural Census Office also reports data on numbers of selected types of machinery (tractors with less and more than 20 hp, harvester-threshers, thresher engines, transportation vehicles). The total

TABLE 2

CHINA: VALUES AND PERCENTAGES OF THE DIFFERENT TYPES OF
AGRICULTURAL HOUSEHOLDS, BY GEOGRAPHIC REGION

Geographic regions	Agricultural households	Agicultural households of which:					
		Pure		Mainly agricultural		Mainly non-agricultural	
	Number	Number	%	Number	%	Number	%
China, total	193,088,158	126,718,837	65.6	39,011,614	20.2	27,357,707	14.2
North	20,947,554	13,833,739	66.0	3,578,774	17.1	3,535,041	16.9
Northeast	12,282,944	9,500,555	77.3	1,632,511	13.3	1,149,878	9.4
East	56,427,802	32,026,100	56.8	12,604,790	22.3	11,796,912	20.9
Central South	52,997,596	34,249,853	64.6	11,623,203	21.9	7,124,540	13.4
Southwest	37,181,588	27,118,559	72.9	7,152,725	19.2	2,910,304	7.8
Northwest	13,250,674	9,990,031	75.4	2,419,611	18.3	841,032	6.3

Source: Authors' processing of *Abstract of the First National Agricultural Census of China* [1998].

FIGURE 3

CHINESE PROVINCES AND MUNICIPALITIES:
PERSONS ENGAGED IN AGRICULTURE (%) AND GDP PER CAPITA

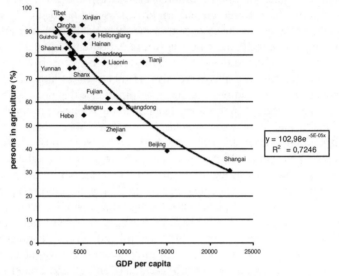

Source: Authors' elaboration of *Abstract of the First National Agricultural Census of China* [1998]. Including autonomous regions and municipalities.

FIGURE 4

PERSONS ENGAGED IN AGRICULTURAL ACTIVITIES (%) AND HOUSEHOLD
DIMENSIONS (PERSONS PER HOUSEHOLD)

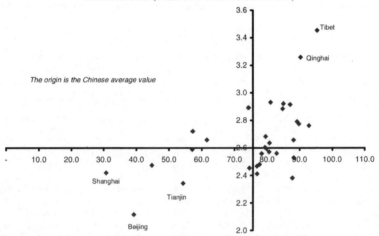

Source: Authors' processing of *Abstract of the First National Agricultural Census of China* [1998].

FIGURE 5

AVERAGE NUMBER OF PERSONS EMPLOYED PER HOUSEHOLD

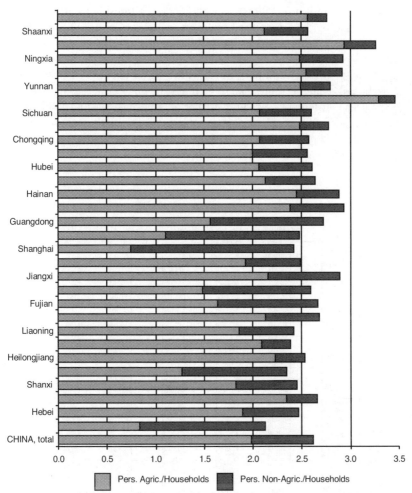

Source: Authors' processing of *Abstract of the First National Agricultural Census of China* [1998].

number for China of these selected types of machinery is about 25 million. The most common types of machinery are small tractors with 20 or more hp (less than 12 million), followed by the operated threshing machines (7.5 million), and by the agricultural transport vehicles (4.6 million). In China, there are only 126 machines per 1,000 rural households, and only 58 machines per 1,000 persons engaged in agriculture. The differences are very large, with higher numbers for eastern provinces (172 per 1,000 households), which is more than three times the number in the western area (53). These differences become greater if we consider the numbers of machines per 1,000 people engaged in agriculture, with the number for the eastern area (85 per 1,000 people), about four times that for the western area (22 per 1,000).

FIGURE 6

UNITS OF SELECTED AGRICULTURAL MACHINERY BY GEOGRAPHIC AREA

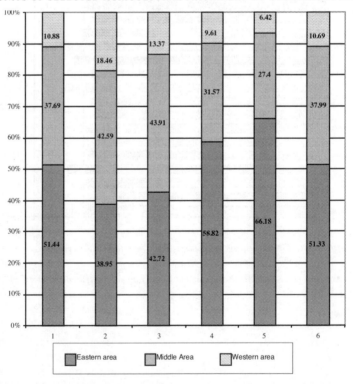

Source: Authors' processing of *Abstract of the First National Agricultural Census of China* [1998].

THE COMPLEX REALITY OF CHINESE AGRICULTURE:
A FIRST ANALYSIS AT COUNTY LEVEL

For a better understanding of the complexity of Chinese agriculture we have utilized data at county level. The *Abstract of the First National Agricultural Census in China* just shows seven maps representing data at county level. The seven variables represented in the maps are: per capita possession of cultivated land; agricultural machinery power possessed by 100 persons engaged in agricultural activities; proportion of non-agricultural households to rural households; proportion of persons engaged in agricultural activities to rural persons engaged; proportion of effectively irrigated area to agricultural land; proportion of number of towns to total number of towns and townships; educational level for rural labour force in years.

The maps presented at county level show that the reality of agriculture in China is much more diversified in comparison to that shown by data presented at province level. Thus, the analysis of data at county level could represent a great development to define a new geography for Chinese agriculture, not only at national level but also inside each province.

However, although available variables are few, a first descriptive analysis at county level (2,392 counties) allows us to make some useful consideration of Chinese agriculture.[2] In order to analyse the relationships among these seven variables, we sorted all counties by the decreasing proportion of persons engaged in agricultural activities to rural persons engaged. We used this variable to classify the counties for its strict relation with economic development, as we have shown in the previous section.

The graphical analysis highlights, first of all, that the proportion of persons engaged in agricultural activities at county level shows a range of variability much larger than that among the provinces described in the previous section. By contrast, there are numerous counties with very high numbers of persons engaged in agriculture (in some cases more than 85 per cent); but it is worth emphasizing that, on the other hand, there are also several counties with less than 40 per cent of persons engaged in agricultural activities. This result indicates that rural development in China is much less uniform than expected, and in particular there are many areas (counties) where agriculture is not the main economic sector. However, the most numerous group of counties in China have 60–85 per cent of persons engaged in agricultural activities; these counties represent the reality of the large part of rural China.

The proportion of non-agricultural households to rural households shows a clear inverse relationship with respect to the proportion of persons engaged in agricultural activities. Most counties have a proportion lower than 60 per cent, but, at the same time, there are also counties with proportions between 20 and 40 per cent. This confirms the presence in

China of a diversified situation of rural development at county level. In addition, as shown in Figure 7(b), the presence of non-rural households is characterized by a larger variability between counties with respect to the previous variable.

The analysis of the educational level of rural labour force shows an interesting relationship with the other variables. The educational level is generally high: in most of the Chinese counties rural workers have from six to eight years of education. However, when the counties have a higher proportion of persons engaged in agriculture, the educational level becomes less homogenous, with an increasing number of counties with a very low educational level (less than four years). The counties with low educational levels are not numerous. In fact the problem of ensuring an adequate level of education of the rural labour force interests several rural counties, which are mainly located in the provinces of Sichuan, Guangxi, Guizhou, Yunnan, Tibet and Gansy.

The distribution of cultivated land (per capita) among the counties is much more uniform. In most of the counties the per capita possession of cultivated land is held at constant level (1, 2 or 3 *mu*), even if we can observe higher values in the counties with a higher concentration of agricultural labour. The distribution of cultivated land among counties seems to reflect, even now, more the criteria adopted in applying agrarian reform, than the degree of development of the counties. The fast transition and change of the Chinese economy will probably lead to a substantial change in the distribution of land among households.

Also, the distribution of agricultural machinery among counties does not change according to the proportion of persons engaged in agricultural activities. In almost all counties, the agricultural machinery power is less than 100 per 100 persons engaged in agricultural activities. However we can note greater machinery power in counties with both low and high concentrations of agricultural labour. Hence, we can say that the distribution of machinery power too does not reflect completely the agricultural development of the counties.

The proportion of effectively irrigated area to total agricultural land is the variable with the largest divergence between counties. The presence of irrigated areas is relevant (or otherwise) both in the less developed counties (with lower proportions of workers in agriculture) and in the most developed ones. The distribution of this variable is related mainly to the characteristic of natural resources, and up to now has only partially influenced the general degree of rural development.

The analysis of the distribution of the variables considered at county level was carried out not only for China as a whole, but also for each Chinese province. The results of the analysis by province confirm the trends

FIGURE 7

MAIN VARIABLES FOR CHINESE COUNTIES
THE COUNTIES ARE RANKED BY VARIABLE (a)

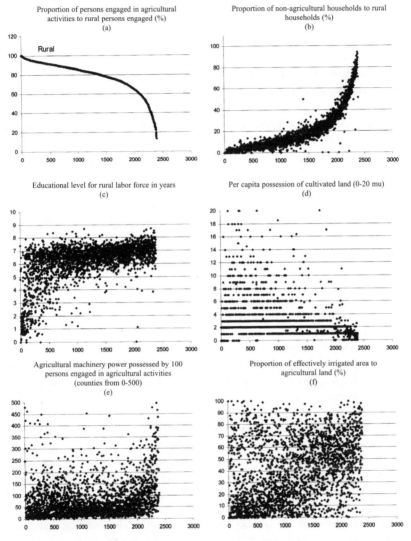

Source: Authors' processing of *Abstract of the First National Agricultural Census of China* [1998].

described for the whole of China. Obviously, the shape of the distribution of each variable among the counties slightly differs across the provinces, and with respect to the national pattern. The results of this analysis are available on request.

THE NEW GEOGRAPHY OF CHINESE AGRICULTURE

The Macro-Agricultural Areas at Province Level

The 1997 Census data give us a great opportunity to gain a better and deeper knowledge of the agricultural geography of China. The significant conclusion from the analysis in previous sections is that the economic geography of the China is very different from the agricultural geography, but these two important aspects are closely related. In fact, in section two we showed how GDP is inversely correlated to the ratio of persons engaged in agriculture. This means that we need to deepen the knowledge of the different agricultural systems in China, in order to identify those areas where the situation could be modified and those where the chances of modification are low, because the terrain can be extremely difficult.

In order to obtain a new geography of agriculture we undertook some statistical multivariate analysis. The analysis was carried out in three steps. In step one we chose 30 indicators and carried out the principal component analysis (PCA). In the second step we employed cluster analysis (CA) on data at province level, in order to identify the principal macro-agricultural areas. Finally, in the third step, we carried out a cluster analysis inside each of the four macro-areas, identified in step two. We found 15 groups of counties very similar from a social and agricultural point of view. In the following paragraphs we will review the three steps in detail and the results obtained.

In the first step we chose 30 indicators of the Chinese social and agricultural situation, as revealed by the First Agricultural Census, for the 31 Chinese provinces. We employed the following indicators from the 30 (see Table 3): percentage of persons aged 7–25 years in rural households; percentage of persons aged 36–61 in rural households; rural households – percentage of persons aged seven and over engaged in crop planting; rural households – percentage of persons aged seven and over engaged in non-agricultural activities in rural areas; rural households – percentage of persons aged seven and over engaged in economic activities in home townships; all holdings – persons engaged in non-agricultural activities/persons engaged in agricultural activities; household holdings – percentage of persons illiterate and semi-illiterate; household holdings – percentage of persons with superior educational level; household holdings – percentage of females with superior educational level; household holdings – males/females with superior educational level; household holdings – percentage of persons engaged in agricultural activities six months and over; all holdings – percentage of agricultural land (area) for cultivated land; all holdings – percentage of agricultural land (area) for woodland; all holdings – percentage of agricultural land (area) for fisheries; all holdings – percentage distribution of sown area for grain; all holdings – among cultivated land tractor ploughed area (per cent); all holdings – number of large animals for 100 persons engaged in agricultural activities; large and medium tractors/persons engaged in agricultural activities; small tractors/persons engaged in agricultural activities; all holdings – persons engaged in agricultural activities/persons engaged in economic activities.

Then, to reduce the number of indicators, we implemented the principal component analysis (PCA). From the 30 indicators we extracted five principal components, which explain together 85 per cent of the total variances. The first component explains about 46.4 per cent, the second component explains 15.6 per cent, the third component explains 11.2 per cent, the fourth component explains 6.3 per cent and the fifth component explains 5.6 per cent.

The first component, which explains a large proportion of variance, characterized the provinces in the sense of concentration of people engaged 'in agricultural or in non-agricultural activities'. In contrast, the second component is mainly linked to the level of agricultural mechanization.

In the second step we carried out a cluster analysis on the five extracted components. We chose four clusters that identify the most important Chinese agricultural macro-areas.[3] The results are represented in the map at Figure 8. The four macro-areas have very different numbers of provinces: cluster 1 (mountain area) has two provinces; cluster 2 (peripheral area) has nine provinces; cluster 3 (urban area) has four provinces and cluster 4 (principally agricultural area) has 116 provinces. The means and the variances of the 30 original indicators for each cluster are reported in Table 3. The main characteristics of the four macro-agricultural areas are as follows.

Cluster 1. It constitutes only two provinces (Qinghai and Tibet) but they have a very large area, mainly mountainous. This cluster is largely characterized by traditional agriculture (67.8 per cent in crop planting), also by animal husbandry (25 per cent of the persons over age seven) with less use of machinery. There is a large number of young people in comparison to the other clusters and there is the highest number of semi-illiterate persons (61 per cent). The holdings are large in terms of surface area. In these provinces there are no fishery activities.

Cluster 2. It includes nine provinces from the northern part of China and also from the south (Yunnan and Guizhou). It is the largest cluster in terms of surface area. It is also characterized by the largest holdings in terms of surface area (1.6 hectares). The proportion of persons engaged in agricultural activities is about 90 per cent of total persons engaged in economic activities. The level of education is not high, with 21 per cent of persons being semi-illiterate.

Cluster 3. This cluster includes four provinces and municipalities (Beijing, Jangsu, Shanghai, Tiajin). It is the smallest cluster in terms of surface area. This cluster represents the biggest urban areas of China with remarkable food consumption. This cluster shows the smallest percentage of persons engaged in agricultural activities (66.5 per cent), and the highest level of education (only about 13 per cent of persons are semi-illiterate and 7.6 per cent have superior education). The holdings have the smallest dimension. There is the highest level of mechanized agriculture: 82 per cent of tractor ploughed area, and 30 per cent of mechanically harvested area. The agricultural land for fisheries is the highest (6.7 per cent).

Cluster 4. It includes the highest number of provinces (16), all located in the southeast, middle and south parts of China. This cluster includes also Sichuan province from the southwest part of China; this is probably due to the fact that Sichuan includes the Chongquing municipality, which has a large part of cultivated land (65 per cent of agricultural area). This cluster is significant in terms of the number of persons engaged in agricultural activities (80 per cent), which is greater than the previous cluster (pink). Generally, there is a good level of education and the lowest percentage of semi-illiterate persons (12 per cent). This large cluster represents the 'core' of Chinese agriculture. The agricultural land is characterized by a large presence of woodland (43 per cent).

The four clusters emerging from our analysis are mainly ranked by the different levels of agricultural development, as shown by the different levels of persons engaged in agricultural activities, associated with the different levels of education and mechanization. The four macro-areas derived from our analysis describe a geography of Chinese agriculture that is really different from the general economic geography of China reported in the previous paragraph.

The Internal Differentiation of Macro-Agricultural Areas
(at County Level)

The third step of our analysis has the objective of further differentiating the internal situation of each of the four macro-areas described before (except

FIGURE 8
MACRO-AGRICULTURAL AREAS IN CHINA

Cluster

1. Mountain area

2. Peripheral area

3. Urban area

4. Principally agricultural area

Source: Authors' processing of *Abstract of the First National Agricultural Census of China*
[1998].

for the urban area, which is small and uniform). We have used the same approach as in step two but in this step we utilize data at county level for each macro-area. In this case there are available only seven indicators, as described and analysed in section 3.

We standardized the indicators and then we carried out the cluster analysis with hierarchical methods on the counties inside the macro-areas to choose the numbers of groups. Then we applied the non-hierarchical method and obtained the final results. The numbers for the clusters (representing groups of counties inside each macro-area) are five for cluster 1, five for cluster 2, whereas cluster 3 remains uniform. In fact, we found that each cluster has a very different numbers of counties belonging to them (as reported in Table 4).

The total number of Chinese counties is 2,392 and the mean and variances for the seven indicators used are shown in Table 5 and Figure 9.[4] This table immediately highlights the relevance of a differentiation inside each of the macro-areas previously defined. To underline the results for the most important reality of Chinese agriculture we have to note that inside the principally agricultural area there is a large homogeneous area that includes 1,050 counties. In Figure 9 these counties are represented in white. These

TABLE 3

FIRST STEP: CLUSTER ANALYSIS ON THE CHINESE PROVINCES

	Cluster 1 Mean	Cluster 1 Var.	Cluster 2 Mean	Cluster 2 Var.	Cluster 3 Mean	Cluster 3 Var.	Cluster 4 Mean	Cluster 4 Var.
1 Persons in agricultural households/persons in non-agricultural households	191.26	13785.62	36.02	184.72	2.49	2.00	14.20	35.62
2 % of persons aged 7–25 years in rural households	37.53	0.56	28.61	17.04	15.94	6.70	23.89	10.94
3 % of persons aged 36–61 years in rural households	35.39	0.42	42.78	9.06	54.26	19.28	46.69	9.60
4 Rural households: % of persons aged 7 and over engaged in crop planting	67.80	15.05	84.24	13.07	41.40	124.57	70.27	130.51
5 Rural households: % of persons aged 7 and over engaged in animal husbandry	25.00	40.72	3.11	3.57	1.54	0.35	2.52	3.14
6 Rural households: % of persons aged 7 and over engaged in non-agricultural activities in rural areas	6.99	6.17	12.21	10.35	54.60	114.64	25.61	107.53
7 Rural households: % of persons aged 7 and over engaged in non-agricultural activities in urban areas	0.78	0.01	0.92	0.08	0.33	0.01	0.91	0.17
8 Rural households: % of persons aged 7 and over engaged in economic activities in home townships	95.70	3.71	93.07	5.87	82.56	23.64	86.08	17.88
9 All holdings: persons engaged in economic activities, female/male	0.98	0.00	0.88	0.00	0.92	0.00	0.89	0.00
10 All holdings: persons engaged in non-agricultural activities/persons engaged in agricultural activities	0.07	0.00	0.12	0.00	0.51	0.01	0.25	0.01
11 Household holdings: % of persons illiterate and semi-illiterate	61.06	216.53	21.24	96.71	13.22	28.19	12.37	12.90
12 Household holdings: % of persons with educational level of primary school and junior middle school	37.40	177.30	73.86	87.68	79.16	21.28	82.17	13.92
13 Household holdings: % of persons with superior educational level	1.54	1.96	4.91	2.16	7.61	3.82	5.45	1.80
14 Household holdings: % of males with superior educational level	2.09	3.48	6.61	3.86	9.10	2.09	7.64	4.03
15 Household holdings: % of females with superior educational level	0.97	0.82	2.99	1.30	6.06	7.92	3.04	1.01
16 Household holdings: males/females with superior educational level	2.71	0.36	2.45	0.65	1.72	0.36	2.69	0.75
17 Household holdings: % of persons engaged in agricultural activities 6 months and over	82.68	6.42	75.56	104.53	50.00	17.12	66.47	128.51
18 All holdings: hectare number per rural households	1.06	0.00	1.60	0.67	0.36	0.01	0.53	0.04
19 All holdings: % of agricultural land (area) for cultivated land	24.31	22.52	48.44	441.02	82.25	33.41	47.19	332.04
20 All holdings: % of agricultural land (area) for woodland	10.84	5.31	28.59	370.58	5.68	34.66	42.92	333.36
21 All holdings: % of agricultural land (area) for grassland	64.78	6.03	21.10	787.30	0.12	0.00	3.44	80.65
22 All holdings: % of agricultural land (area) for fisheries	0.01	0.00	0.72	0.36	6.70	7.49	2.24	2.37

TABLE 3 (cont'd)

	Cluster 1		Cluster 2		Cluster 3		Cluster 4	
	Mean	Var.	Mean	Var.	Mean	Var.	Mean	Var.
23 All holdings: % distribution of sown area for grain	78.28	62.88	79.99	114.75	79.14	51.34	79.01	53.64
24 All holdings: among cultivated land tractor ploughed area (%)	20.68	163.71	39.34	830.81	82.17	6.30	27.27	451.46
25 All holdings: among cultivated land electro-mechanically irrigated area (%)	2.26	0.11	13.01	213.78	74.28	58.12	25.37	353.59
26 All holdings: among harvested area mechanically harvested area (%)	9.62	45.70	12.35	143.59	30.24	213.85	6.07	69.65
27 All holdings: number of large animals for 100 persons engaged in agricultural activities	369.21	13831.25	55.07	440.63	12.61	66.69	22.46	116.68
28 Large and medium tractor/persons engaged in agricultural activities	5.90	15.57	8.40	45.11	34.34	843.68	7.58	52.11
29 Small tractors/persons engaged in agricultural activities	4.59	5.82	4.14	4.59	3.35	1.55	1.95	2.31
30 All holdings: persons engaged in agricultural activities/persons engaged in economic activities	93.51	4.99	89.74	6.67	66.54	20.71	80.40	41.13

Source: Authors' processing of Abstract of the First National Agricultural Census of China [1998].

TABLE 4

COUNTIES CLUSTERS IN THE MACRO-AREAS

Clusters – macro-areas	Number of cluster	Number of counties inside the cluster	Total counties
Cluster 1	5	24, 16, 8, 21,46	115
Cluster 2	5	427, 206, 15, 14, 75	737
Cluster 3	1	100	100
Cluster 4	4	42, 333, 15, 1,050	1,440

Source: Authors' processing of Abstract of the First National Agricultural Census of China [1998].

counties are about 40 per cent of the total number of Chinese counties and they are characterized by a very low per capita possession of cultivated land (0.03). Further, this cluster has a high proportion of non-agricultural households to rural households (16 per cent) compared to the other macro-areas (except the urban area) but the lowest proportion in cluster 4. Also, these counties have the highest proportion of persons in agricultural activities to rural persons engaged compared to the other three clusters in the principally agricultural area (80 per cent). It has also a lower proportion of irrigated land (36 per cent of agricultural area). In these counties the number of towns is also lower. The counties included in this cluster (1,050) appear so similar that we could not produce a further differentiation, at least with the indicators available. Since this is the most important cluster of counties inside the most significant agricultural macro-area (at province level, see step two), it will be really important to have new and more indicators at county level. Only then we could make more precise groups of homogeneous counties for each macro-area or province. Inside the green macro-area there is another important cluster of 333 counties. The agriculture of this cluster seems to be less developed than that of the previous cluster. The proportion of non-agricultural households is much higher (38 per cent) and the proportion of persons engaged in agricultural activities is much lower (60 per cent). The proportion of irrigated land is high (more than 62 per cent), and the number of towns is greater.

CONCLUDING REMARKS

The results of the First National Agricultural Census of China provide a better knowledge of the structure of Chinese agriculture. The differences between provinces and counties are very large, but the potential for future growth of Chinese agriculture and other economic activities in rural areas is bigger than expected.

TABLE 5

SECOND STEP: CLUSTER ANALYSIS OF COUNTIES INSIDE THE FOUR CLUSTERS OF PROVINCES

				Per capita possession of cultivated land (ha)	Agricultural machinery power possessed by 100 persons engaged in agricultural activities	Proportion of persons engaged in agricultural activities to rural persons engaged	Proportion of non-agricultural households to rural households	Proportion of effectively irrigated area to agricultural land	Proportion of number of towns to total number of towns and townships	Educational level for rural labour force in years
		Number of counties								
Cluster 1	1	24	Mean	0.06	8.54	92.29	4.84	41.23	5.21	2.57
			Var.	0.07	1672.46	89.10	108.73	52.37	62.56	3.33
	2	16	Mean	1.16	33.48	94.06	1.72	83.16	1.76	2.18
			Var.	20.05	16801.93	14.60	8.26	221.60	16.25	3.10
	3	8	Mean	—	0.01	0.01	0.00	38.33	—	2.04
			Var.	—	—	—	—	2813.00	—	0.34
	4	21	Mean	—	0.01	93.97	2.64	61.56	3.62	2.29
			Var.	—	—	20.52	12.79	15.76	50.06	2.30
	5	46	Mean	—	—	95.54	1.93	6.90	3.37	1.81
			Var.	—	—	11.24	5.47	70.94	25.59	2.00
Total cluster 1		115								
Cluster 2	1	427	Mean	0.15	0.21	88.54	8.23	13.68	12.16	5.06
			Var.	1.58	10.13	52.07	68.47	116.24	164.48	4.71
	2	206	Mean	0.02	0.16	83.70	11.23	72.45	11.35	6.19
			Var.	0.06	4.25	132.78	200.81	338.02	179.42	3.74
	3	15	Mean	—	0.01	0.01	4.36	19.97	4.64	4.76
			Var.	—	—	—	17.76	283.54	72.35	4.10
	4	14	Mean	3.15	123.90	67.55	33.76	41.24	22.08	6.75
			Var.	1227.65	136.67	290.11	509.70	344.60	2.96	7.03
	5	75	Mean	—	0.01	83.96	13.81	16.84	55.92	5.80
			Var.	—	—	94.25	171.27	212.56	161.67	3.66

TABLE 5 (Cont'd)

		Number of counties			Per capita possession of cultivated land	Agricultural machinery power possessed by 100 persons engaged in agricultural activities	Proportion of persons engaged in agricultural activities to rural persons engaged	Proportion of non-agricultural households to rural households	Proportion of effectively irrigated area to agricultural land	Proportion of number of towns to total number of towns and townships	Educational level for rural labour force in years
Total cluster 2		737									
Cluster 3	1	100		Mean	0.19	35.84	52.49	50.78	75.83	30.18	5.82
				Var.	0.32	11772.45	405.64	651.88	1766.01	639.24	6.75
Cluster 4	1	42		Mean	0.65	123.93	51.27	53.27	51.04	24.52	7.32
				Var.	0.52	1528.34	255.75	342.15	1960.77	836.70	0.92
	2	333		Mean	0.05	1.04	60.07	38.45	62.07	49.53	6.25
				Var.	0.06	45.52	380.61	420.20	370.82	834.33	4.24
	3	15		Mean	0.50	263.76	43.36	59.58	46.47	42.07	6.43
				Var.	0.70	1136.80	105.19	171.28	186.81	595.85	3.27
	4	1050		Mean	0.03	0.55	79.95	16.04	36.49	20.71	5.76
				Var.	0.10	21.18	145.01	135.12	566.16	432.32	4.42
Total cluster 4		1440									

Source: Authors' processing of Abstract of the First National Agricultural Census of China [1998].

FIGURE 9

COUNTIES CLUSTERS INSIDE THE FOUR MACRO-AGRICULTURAL AREAS

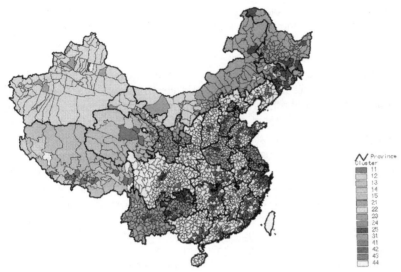

The Agricultural Census shows that there is a decreasing importance of persons active in agriculture, commensurate with the economic development of the different provinces. The proportion of persons engaged in agriculture in total in the main municipalities is less than 40 per cent (Shanghai and Beijing), and less than 60 per cent in most provinces of the eastern part. In these provinces, there are now many households whose revenue is mainly coming from non-agricultural activities, and only 55 per cent of total households are pure agriculture households. The multi-sectorial activity (or part-time) of the households is now a reality in many provinces and counties of China. The great availability of workers and mobility of people working in agricultural households (between villages and townships) could be the main impetus for future developments of non-agricultural activities in China.

The larger availability of cultivated land, but also the lower numbers of livestock (cattle, pigs, poultry) relative to previous estimates indicate the possibility for increasing the productivity and intensity of agricultural production, in terms of both the labour force and the amount of land worked.

The data available from the Agricultural Census at province level show that the differences between the provinces are relevant. The official classification of Chinese provinces into six geographical regions or three main economic–geographical regions (west, middle and east) will not be sufficient to describe a composite reality of Chinese agriculture. In most cases, the largest differences emerge from western and middle provinces, on the one hand, and the eastern provinces on the other hand. But we have found more profound differences inside this large geographical area, between provinces and counties.

The cluster analysis we have applied using variables of the 1997 Census at province and county levels confirms that the four macro-agricultural areas of China are different from the previous classification (economic areas, economic–geographical areas). Generally, the cluster analysis revealed that there are numerous provinces and counties belonging to the same group (cluster). The largest macro-agricultural area is characterized by significant agriculture and a high proportion of persons engaged in agricultural economic activities. The level of education of people is generally high while mechanization is relatively important. The other two macro-areas are mainly mountainous regions or peripheral areas, characterized by poor endowment of natural and agricultural resources. The smaller macro-area represents the specific situation of most urbanized provinces and autonomous municipalities, where the persons engaged in agricultural activities are less relevant and agriculture is more developed.

The cluster analysis carried out in respect of the previous macro-agricultural areas, exploiting the few variables available at county level, show clearly that inside each macro-area there are different groups (clusters) of counties, with different degrees of agricultural development.

The results of our analysis show a totally 'new' geography of agriculture in China. The reality of Chinese agriculture is different at province and county level. The future utilization of Census data at province and especially at county level could contribute to a better definition of the reality of Chinese agriculture. Specifically, further analysis could be done to specify the actual situation of agriculture in each Chinese province, by utilizing more data at county level. Further analysis of Chinese agriculture will be based not only on structural agricultural characteristics, but also on natural resources, human resources and on the relationship between agriculture and the general economic development. The publication of the complete results of the First National Agricultural Census of China will provide all the information needed to achieve a better understanding of Chinese agriculture. The definition of a new geography for Chinese agriculture, with appropriate aggregation of provinces and counties, will be particularly important for the policy maker in order to define appropriate strategies and policy measures for future agricultural developments.

REGIONS OF CHINA

1. Administrative Regions of China (31):
Municipalities (4): Beijing, Tianjin, Shanghai, Chongqing.
Autonomous Regions (5): Inner Mongolia, Guangxi, Tibet, Ningxia, Xinjiang.
Provinces (22): Hebei, Shanxi, Liaoning, Jilin, Heilongjiang, Jiangsu, Zhejiang, Anhui, Fujian, Jiangxi, Shandong, Henan, Hubei, Hunan, Guangdong, Hainan, Sichuan, Guizhou, Yunnan, Shaanxi, Gansu, Qinghai.

2. Geographic Regions of China (6):
North (5): Beijing, Tianjin, Hebei, Shanxi, Inner Mongolia.
Northeast (3): Liaoning, Jilin, Heilongjiang.
East (7): Shanghai, Jiangsu, Zhejiang, Anhui, Fujian, Jiangxi, Shandong.
Central South (6): Henan, Hubei, Hunan, Guangdong, Guangxi, Hainan.
Southwest (5): Chongqing, Sichuan, Guizhou, Yunnan, Tibet.
Northwest (5): Shaanxi, Gansu, Qinghai, Ningxia, Xinjiang.

3. Economic–Geographical Regions of China (3):
East (12): Beijing, Tianjin, Hebei, Liaoning, Shanghai, Jiangsu, Zhejiang, Fujian, Shandong, Guangdong, Guangxi, Hainan.
Middle (9): Shanxi, Inner Mongolia, Jilin, Heilongjiang, Anhui, Jiangxi, Henan, Hubei, Hunan.
West (10): Chongqing, Sichuan, Guizhou, Yunnan, Tibet, Shaanxi, Gansu, Qinghai, Ningxia, Xinjiang.

4. Macro-Agricultural Regions (4):
Mountain area (2): Quinghai, Tibet.
Peripheral area (9): Gansu, Ningxia, Xinjiang, Inner Mongolia, Jilin, Heilongjiang, Henan, Yunnan, Guizhou.
Urban area (4): Beijing, Tianjin, Shanghai, Jiangsu.
Principally agricultural area (16): Hebei, Liaoning, Zhejiang, Fujian, Shandong, Guangdong, Guangxi, Hainan, Shanxi, Anhui, Jiangxi, Hubei, Hunan, Chongqing, Sichuan, Shaanxi.

NOTES

1. For a description of the problem in design of the Agricultural Census and in data collection see Biggeri, L. [2001], whereas for a first comparison of the previous official statistics and the census results see Xiangdong [2001].
2. The data at county level represented by the maps in the *Abstract of the First National Agricultural Census of China* were made available courtesy of the State Statistical Bureau (SSB).

3. We have used for this elaboration the CLUSTER procedure of SAS system. We have used for this elaboration the FASTCLUS procedure of SAS system. In particular, first we used a hierarchical approach, through the Ward Minimum Variance and Average Linkage Clustering methods, in order to choose the number of groups of provinces. The results of the analysis show four or five clusters. Then we applied the non-hierarchical method – according to the statistics (pseudo F statistics and Cubic clustering criterion) – and we chose four clusters. For more details see Fanfani, R. and C. Brasili, 2000.
4. The complete representation of the 15 clusters at county level within the four main clusters at province level is shown in Figure 9.

REFERENCES

Alexandratos, Nikos, 1996, 'China's Projected Cereals Deficits in a World Context', *Agricultural Economics*, Vol.15, No.1, pp.1–16.

Biggeri, L., 2001, *China Agricultural Census Design and Data Collection: Issues and Lessons*, Proceedings of the International Seminar on China Agricultural Census Results, Beijing: China Statistics Press.

Biggeri, M., 1998, 'I fattori dello sviluppo dell'agricoltura cinese dopo le grandi riforme, analisi empiriche su un panel di dati a livello provinciale', doctoral thesis, University of Siena.

Brown, L., 1995, *Who Will Feed China? Wakeup Call for a Small Planet*, New York: W.W. Norton.

Fanfani, R. and C. Brasili, 2000, 'The New Geography of Chinese Agriculture', paper presented at the International Seminar on China Agricultural Census Results, Beijing, 19–22 Sept.

FAO, 1998, 'Technical Seminar on the First Chinese Agricultural Census Preliminary Results', Rome, 26 Feb.

FAO, 2000, 'Agriculture: Toward 2015/30, Technical Interim Report', FAO, Global Perspective Studies Unit, Rome, April.

Giovannini, E., 2000, 'The Chinese Rural Non-Agricultural Enterprises: The Evidence from the Agricultural Census', International Seminar on China Agricultural Census Results, Beijing, 19–22 Sept.

National Agricultural Census Office of China, 1999, *Abstract of the First National Agricultural Census in China*, Beijing, China Statistics Press.

SSB (State Statistical Bureau), 1997, *China Statistical Yearbook 1997*, Beijing: Beijing Agricultural University Press.

USDA, 2000, 'China WTO Accession Would Boost U.S. Agricultural Export and Farm Income', Washington, USDA Agriculture Outlook series.

Zhu, Xiangdong (ed.), 1995, *The Concise Aggregate Data of National Pilot Agricultural Census*, Beijing: Food and Agricultural Statistics Centre (FASC).

Zhu, Xiangdong, 2001, 'A Concise Analysis of the Main Results of the First National Agricultural Census in China', in *Proceedings of the International Seminar on China Agricultural Census Results*, Beijing: China Statistics Press.

Rethinking the Peasant Burden: Evidence from a Chinese Village

LI XIANDE

INTRODUCTION

Following decollectivization and the subsequent reforms in the Chinese countryside, both agricultural production and peasant incomes increased greatly. But, at least for the past decade, these gains have been partly countered by a new phenomenon, called in popular jargon and by the Chinese government the rising of the 'peasant burden' (*nongmin fudan*):[1] the increase in the charges paid by peasants to local authorities. In some places, large-scale riots have been triggered and peasants' deaths have resulted from the conflicts that occurred during the process of collecting the charges.[2] Historically, the issue of the peasant burden first arose in the late 1980s, and attracted then the attention of the central government.[3] In December 1991, a national regulation was passed, setting a five per cent ceiling on the amounts to be charged (relative to the peasant net income).[4] Since then, a number of other measures have been taken, and regulations passed, to try to tackle the problem, without much success (for example, the decision of the State Council, in 1993, cancelling some 43 varieties of contributions for reaching certain standards and planned targets (*dabiao*) and 37 fund-raising (*jizi*) items, as well as rectifying ten incorrect methods for the collection of funds from the peasants).[5]

As well indicated by its very appellation, the problem of the peasant burden has strong political connotations. It touches not only the peasants' own economic interests, but also the whole issue of the distribution of benefits between the state, the collectives and the peasants, involving the social stability of the country. Therefore, the topic of the peasant burden became highly political throughout the 1990s. The government at various levels put this issue at the top of the agenda. And, accordingly, assessments

Li Xiande, Researcher in the Institut National de la Recherche Agronomique (INRA), 63–65 Bd de Brandebourg, 94205, Ivry sur Seine, France. He would like to express his sincere thanks to Claude Aubert of INRA for his encouragement, support and help. Thanks are also due to Peter Ho and Jacob Eyferth for their constructive comments on the early version of this article. The author takes full responsibility for the opinions expressed.

and discussions about the implementation of these policies appeared in almost every year's edition of two most authoritative and influential documents of the Ministry of Agriculture, the *China Agricultural Yearbook* and the *China Agricultural Development Report*.

In the meantime, many researchers analysed this problem from different angles. Some did very detailed descriptions of the degrees of burden [*Ministry of Agriculture*, 1990; *Sun* 1998]. In their exploration into the causes of the burden, some studies proposed reforms for the separation of tax (*shui*) and fees (*fei*) [*Li*, 1995]. Lu Xiaobo argued that the distortions denoted by the 'burden' and its unintended consequences were the results of the transition from a 'redistributive-mobilization' state to a 'regulatory-developmental' state [*Lu*, 1997: 133]. Jean Oi touched also on this problem from the point of view of the financial system when she tried to analyse rural China's development [*Oi*, 1999: 20–21].

But the very basis of these discussions is often ambiguous, confusing and even misleading. For example, in the *Agricultural Yearbook*, the peasant burden is currently estimated at three to four per cent of the peasants' income [Ministry of Agriculture, 1998: 58]. If this figure were correct, the official policy would have been quite successful and there would be no more problems with the so-called peasant burden. In fact, the whole issue is still lacking precise evidence about the contents of the 'burden', its real weight in peasants' income, not to mention the roots of the phenomenon.

In this article, based on the observations made in 1997 in one village of Hubei province, we will show that if all the real charges were accounted for, the total amount 'officially' due to the village and local government represented near 13 per cent of the net income of the surveyed families, whereas the official 'charges' (*tiliu* and *tongchou*) constituted only three per cent of this income (see definition below). Moreover, if additional and unofficial payments made by the peasants towards the different kinds of local organs were to be included, this percentage would reach nearly 20 per cent.

Why do such huge differences exist? Does the government standard set at five per cent of the net income reflect the real picture of the burden shouldered by the peasants? Is the five per cent criterion an effective instrument for the policy implementation? Apart from these questions about figures, many other important related issues have been seldom studied on the basis of empirical observations, such as: How are the peasant payments determined and collected? What causes the social conflicts and tensions between the peasants and the state during the collection process? And, more fundamentally, what are the reasons behind the peasant burden?

This article will try to answer these questions. It will be organized into four parts: first, a brief description about the chosen village and families, with the corresponding data; second, the definition and measurement of the peasants' charges; third, the determination, collection of the contracted sum (*hetongkuan*) paid to the government and its consequences; fourth, the causes and origins of the peasant burden; and as a conclusion, the formulation of possible solutions and countermeasures for solving the problem.

DESCRIPTION OF THE SURVEYED LOCALITY

For a full understanding of the entire picture of the peasant burden and its significance for the peasant families, I have chosen one village of a county located in the southern part of Hubei province. About 30 peasant families in that village were surveyed and constitute the basis of reference for my observations.[6] At the county and village levels, the collected information principally concerned the basic economic situation. Official data were supplemented by personal interviews. As regards the families' sample, the survey covered almost every aspect of the family unit: production, consumption, social interactions and economic obligations towards the government, mainly the quota, the *hetongkuan* (contracted sum) and family planning, following the peasants' saying that the government's essential tasks are 'asking for money (contracted sum), grain (quota) and lives (family planning)'. For every aspect, a very detailed survey was conducted. For example, as regards the production and income-generating activities, the farmers were asked about all the crops cultivated, animals raised, the off-farm activities, and the inputs forwarded. For each product the different utilizations were measured (self-consumption, quota sales, above quota's sale, sales to the free market, stocks, etc.) and the different prices asked for each kind of utilization. Normally, a standard interview with one family took half a day, and the results were checked by informal discussions.

The studied county is a mainly agricultural county, compared to the provincial or national averages. This is quite clear from some key economic indicators for the year 1996. The cultivated land per inhabitant was 1.24 *mu* (1 *mu* = 1/15 hectare) per person, higher than the average 0.97 *mu* for the province and 1.16 *mu* for China. More rural people stayed in the countryside. The proportion of rural population within the total population reached 73 per cent, against 70 per cent for Hubei and China. Still more important, the agricultural workforce constituted 75 per cent of the total active population in the county, against only 50 to 55 per cent in the province and in China. As a consequence, agriculture produced 45 per cent of the GDP in the county, compared to 20 per cent for the whole of the province (1998). And, not surprisingly, the income per capita of rural inhabitants was only 80 per cent of the provincial average.

This low income was in contrast to the high levels of availability of agricultural products per capita. Compared to the province, this availability was 38 per cent more for grain, 123 per cent more for cotton, 113 per cent more for oilseeds (respectively 34, 4 and 23 per cent more compared to the national average). Still these figures were affected by the flooding of that year, resulting in a 25 per cent decrease in the grain production compared to 1995 (55 per cent decrease for cotton, and 7 per cent for oilseeds).

Indeed the county is one of the top producers in China for agricultural products, owing to its particular favourable natural resources. It is particularly best suited for rice production, which constitutes 95 per cent of the grain harvest, and occupies 85 per cent of the cropped surface.

With only one-quarter of its active population engaged in non-agricultural activities, the county is also very noticeable for its lack of diversification and economic development. The situation is the same in the village surveyed. There is not a single industrial enterprise there. This absence of TVEs (township and village enterprises) explains why a large part of the village labour force is forced to seek employment opportunities elsewhere to supplementing their families' incomes. In one particular natural village where the sampled families were located, no less than 30 per cent of the workers were employed permanently outside the township (mainly in big cities), working more than ten months a year, and going back to the village only for the New Year (90 per cent of the migrants being of an age between 16 and 35). They usually work in the cities as heads or employees of small familial enterprises (61 per cent), tailors (11 per cent), small traders (18 per cent), temporary workers in city factories and other activities (10 per cent). On the whole, 15 per cent of the registered families are actually absent from the village. Within the remaining 85 per cent, 59 per cent are engaged in pure agriculture, 33 per cent have mixed activities (agriculture plus trade, etc.) and 8 per cent in non-agricultural activities (teachers, etc.).

The surveyed village was well representative of this economy dominated by rice cultivation. Constituting 493 peasant families, with more than 80 per cent engaged, totally or partly, in agricultural activities (mainly crop cultivation), it had a total population of 2,157 persons. The average family therefore consisted of 4.4 persons, out of which 2.7 were workers. Each family cultivated 6.4 *mu* of arable land, of which 5.5 *mu* were of paddy fields. The quota of grain was 1,792 kg, of which 10–15 per cent was wheat and 85–90 per cent rice. For each family, the *tiliu* (all payments included, except the corvées' contribution) amounted to no less than 1,278 *yuan*, or 292 *yuan* per person. What *tiliu* exactly denotes and of what various charges the peasant burden is actually composed, will be discussed in the next section.

CONTENTS AND MEASUREMENT OF THE PEASANT BURDEN

The Tiliu

The term *tiliu* (contributions) appears frequently in the official documents of the government, referring to the peasants' financial obligations towards local governments (at village level and above). Strictly speaking, this term denotes the payment made by the peasants for the village level under the item of the 'three *tiliu*' (three contributions) and for the township level under the item of the 'five *tongchou*' (five unified planning). It is precisely this *tiliu* (three *tiliu* plus five *tongchou*), corresponding to the local legal obligations of the peasants, which, according to state regulations, cannot exceed five per cent of the peasants' net income. But, in fact, even in the local government's official demands, the required payments are larger than these two items. On the one hand they include also state taxes, and on the other hand different raised funds (*jizi*) and apportionments (*tanpai*). Altogether, the *tiliu* officially demanded from the peasants therefore constitutes four parts:

1. For the state:[7] agricultural tax, tax for the occupied (agricultural) surface area, special agricultural products tax, irrigation and electricity fees, fees for the trans-provincial and trans-county major hydraulic works.
2. For the township: the five *tongchou*, that is to say, education supplement, social help, family planning, collective transportation, and militia exercises.
3. For the village: the three *tiliu*: public accumulation fund, public welfare fund, administrative fees.
4. Different raised funds (*jizi*) and apportionments (*tanpai*), are legally assigned for various local governments as well as for different government agencies. The items included differ widely from place to place in China. And they constitute the part of the peasant burden that is most frequently referred to and criticized. In some places, the number of items has been reported to reach as high a number as more than 100. In the surveyed village, there were only ten items, covering different fields: contribution for the construction or restoration of schools, preventive medicine, corvées converted into money, common production fee, territorial development, grains quota collection etc. Some of them are to be remitted to the local government branches, others are for public services at different levels.

The detailed list of the items of the official *tiliu* assigned to the village by the township authorities in 1996 is presented in Table 1.

In 1996, the *tiliu* officially assigned to the village totalled 434,560 *yuan*, that is to say 202 *yuan* per capita or 138 *yuan* per *mu*. Out of this total, only

TABLE 1

THE VILLAGE *TILIU* ITEMS DETERMINED BY THE TOWNSHIP (YEAR 1996)

	Total (*yuan*)	Total (%)	Per capita (*yuan*)	Per *mu* (*yuan*)
Total	434,560	100.0	201.5	137.9
1) For the state	167,028	38.4	77.4	53.0
out of which Agricultural tax	101,020	23.2	46.8	32.0
Water and electricity fee	38,610	8.9	17.9	12.2
Special agricultural products tax	27,398	6.3	12.7	8.7
2) Three *tiliu*	60,627	14.0	28.1	19.2
out of which Public accumulation fund	21,079	4.9	9.8	6.7
Public welfare fund	13,038	3.6	6.0	4.1
Administrative fees	26,510	6.1	12.3	8.4
3) Five *tongchou*	42,374	9.8	19.6	13.4
out of which Education supplement	31,508	7.3	14.6	10.0
Social help (*minzheng youfu*)	3,912	0.9	1.8	1.2
Family planning	2,608	0.6	1.2	0.8
Collective roads	2,608	0.6	1.2	0.8
Militia exercises	1,738	0.4	0.8	0.6
4) Other *jizi* and *tanpai*	164,531	37.9	76.3	52.2
out of which Approved assembled funds	34,333	7.9	15.9	10.9
Administrative fee of *xiangzhen*	27,814	6.4	12.9	8.8
Common production fee	34,661	8.0	16.1	11.0
Corvées converted money (*yizidailao*)	39,114	9.0	18.1	12.4
No.1 High School of county	4,346	1.0	2.0	1.4
Preventive medicine (*xue fang*)	2,173	0.5	1.0	0.7
Animal vaccinations	8,360	1.9	3.9	2.7
Territory development	6,358	1.5	2.9	2.0
Grains quota collection	6,806	1.6	3.2	2.2
Cotton procurement	566	0.1	0.3	0.2

Source: Author's survey in 1997.

one-quarter went to the village (60,627 *yuan*, 14 per cent of the total) and to the township (42,374 *yuan*, 10 per cent), whereas the state coffers were to receive no less than 38 per cent (167,028 *yuan*). One must emphasize also the importance of the 'other' charges, *jizi* and *tanpai*, totalling also 38 per cent with 164,531 *yuan*.

The part of the state. As for the state's part, the existing studies have been mostly concerned with the agricultural tax. They all show that its relative importance has been on the decline as the central government has usually fixed the amount of the tax for a certain period of time (normally three to five years), followed by minimal readjustments, whereas the agricultural production increased more rapidly. The problem, with respect to the state's share in the peasant burden, is that the agricultural tax is only one part of the whole of state taxes. In the survey, the agricultural tax accounts for only 60 per cent of the state share in the official *tiliu*. Apart from this tax, one has to take into consideration the water and electricity fee and the special agricultural products tax.

The collection of the water and electricity fee began in 1956 in that county. At that time, the local government decided to levy this fee as a supplement to the agricultural tax, in order to fund the construction and maintenance of large-scale hydraulic works. This practice has lasted up to the present time. Within the national government's accounts, this particular fee is probably integrated into the agricultural tax as it is considered as a supplementary part of this tax, assigned for a specific utilization. But, at local government level, this water and electricity fee is added to the agricultural tax, and represents no less than 23 per cent of the state levies.

The taxation on the special agricultural products is more recent. It began in 1989 in the county, on the basis of 0.67 *yuan* per *mu*, then increased from year to year and reached 8.7 *yuan* per *mu* in 1996 (according to the village data), that is to say 13 times higher than in 1989! According to the explanation given by a responsible person of the county finance bureau, the special agricultural products tax constitutes 36.6 per cent of the agricultural tax received at the county level (equivalent to our village's 'state part'), and therefore provides 15.8 per cent of the total local financial revenue. Nominally, this tax is imposed on the special agricultural products, mainly aquatic products, hemp or flax in the county. But, in the village, where 'special products' constitute only the fruits from 20 *mu* of orchards (with a contract providing only 4,000 *yuan* to the village finances), the total paid for this tax is 27,000 *yuan*, equally distributed among all the farm families, without regard to what they really grow. In fact, this kind of situation is common all over the county, and even in most parts of China.

The part of village and township. Payments by peasants' families for the township (or commune) and village expenses existed since a long time ago, even during the period of collectivization of the 1960s and 1970s. At that time, the distribution of the collective income was undertaken in a global, direct and simple way. The total revenue minus the production costs constituted the disposable income shared between the state, the collective (people's commune, brigade and production team) and the peasants. The state took one part under the name of the agricultural tax, the collective had the public accumulation and public welfare funds, administrative fees, etc. The remaining income was distributed to the peasants.[8]

The distribution was mainly done in kind (then converted into money). Usually the production team sold the agricultural products (mainly grain) to state agencies as payment of tax. This practice was called *jiao gongliang* (remittance of the public grain). As for the collective, it set apart a portion of the agricultural products for seeds, feed, reserves, etc. As for the peasants, they got their ration of grain from the collective harvests. The final account was calculated with cash at the end of the year in order to 'distribute the profits' (*nianzhong fenhong*). So the production team acted as accounting unit, for the distribution as well as for production, while the collection of charges was done at the same level.

As regards the 'collective part' of the distribution, no detailed analysis about the sharing between commune, brigade and production team is available. In general, the grassroots level administration (production team) was responsible for the actual organization of production while the higher levels (brigade and commune) took responsibility for tasks of mobilization, regulation and command. So it seems that the main part of the collective funds were actually retained at the local levels (team and brigade). The township cadres depended principally on the financial resources assigned to their functions (salaries, administration and management fees).

After decollectivization and the subsequent reforms, the bureaucratic system at local levels and the management of resources became more decentralized, so the retaining of funds for each level became more desegregated, departmentalized, with detailed definition of uses and functions, at least nominally. We will elaborate further on this important evolution. Presently, as regards the administrative village, three kinds of funds (the so-called three *tiliu*), are kept by the village committee, with the same items which, in the collective period, were assigned to local institutions (commune, brigade and team), namely:

1. Public accumulation fund: used for the development of the village-level economy such as the basic construction of agricultural or hydraulic works, afforestation, the buying of productive fixed assets, the opening of village enterprises (if any), etc.
2. Public welfare fund: for welfare services such as provisions for the 'five-protected family' (*wu baohu*), subsidies for families in great difficulty, cooperative health and other collective welfare items.
3. Administrative fees: for the remuneration of the village cadres and administrative expenses.

For the township level, the peasants pay a fee called *xiang tongchoufei* ('expenses for the unified planning at township level', or simply the five *tongchou*). This fee must cover the following matters: schooling at township and village level, family planning, social help, militia exercises, collective roads, etc. From the surveyed locality, the expenses assigned to education account for three-quarters of the total amount of the five *tongchou*, whereas the other items represent less than ten per cent each.

The objective of these payments to village and township (three *tiliu* and five *tongchou*) is to sustain their administration, paying the salaries of their staff, and to permit them to implement certain governmental functions, developmental ones such as the building and maintenance of collective roads, supplying for the public accumulation, or administrative and political ones such as family planning, etc.

Social Charges

The official *tiliu*, as already described, not only includes the state taxes, and the *tiliu* and *tongchou* for the village and the township, but covers also different charges under the names of *jizi* and *tanpai*. Ten of them have been officially listed and entered in the *tiliu*. In practice, the burden of the peasants does not stop there. Other social charges are to be added to the previous ones, some under the form of unofficial levies, fines, or illegal financial contributions, other under the form of the (legal) corvées, not counted in the *tiliu* when delivered by the actual, non-remunerated labour of the peasants.

The corvées. There are two categories of labour corvées: the 'rural compulsory labour' (*nongcun yiwugong*) and the 'labour accumulation work' (*laodong jileigong*). The first category of corvées is used for ordinary maintenance work of public utilities: planting trees, preventing flooding, maintenance of roads, reparation of schools, etc. These works take place mainly within the village territory. The standard for these corvées is that every agricultural worker (those with an agricultural registration, *nongye hukou*, in the village, therefore with access to the land use) must contribute five to ten workdays per year, according to the rules. Because of its non-monetary nature, this kind of work is not entered into the financial accounts of the *tiliu*. But if the worker is not present in the village, and therefore does not himself deliver the work, he can pay a fellow villager to do it in place of him, and pay him at the market price (eight to ten *yuan* per day).

As regards the corvées of the labour accumulation work, they are used for the basic construction of agricultural and hydraulic works, as well as for afforestation projects above the village level. The usual standard is 10–20 workdays per labourer and per year. The rules governing this standard are flexible, and the number of workdays may be increased, so that the actual amount of work may be over 20 days. In general, these corvées are served by the manual work of peasants. But it may happen that part of the workdays are first converted into money to be paid to the township. This practice is called 'substitute the labour with capital' (*yizidailao*). In this case, the amount of money corresponding to the *yizidailao* is entered into the accounts of the *jizi* and *tanpai*.

For example, in 1996, each worker paid on average about 30 *yuan* of *yizidailao* or 18.1 *yuan* per capita (Table 1). But, not counted in the table, each worker contributed that year, only for the labour accumulation work, about 20 days for digging big ponds in the township, which planned to convert 1,000 *mu* of paddy fields into fishing ponds, apparently a promising and profitable enterprise for the township's future finances. At the rate of eight *yuan* per day, that means that each agricultural worker contributed in kind the equivalent of 160 *yuan*, or about 400 *yuan* per family and per year.

Other charges. Occasionally, but still quite often, other unofficial *jizi* and *tanpai* are also collected. Their total value, varying from village to village, is difficult to estimate. Whatever their number and amount, it is certain that the real number of these items is much higher for the village than it appears in the list presented above. According to different surveys, the actual situation is even worse in certain places, where the number of items may reach more than 100 different kinds.[9] These payments go not only to the township or higher-level government bodies, but also to the village committee.

In addition to these unofficial levies, the peasants have to pay other kinds of fees, for the village level or above, which are difficult to include in the total account of the real charges. An exhaustive list would be difficult to establish, but a few, very common, examples can be mentioned.

1. Insurance fees. The insurance company obliges (often with governmental intervention), the peasants to buy or pay for different kinds of insurance (for the children, buffalo, house, etc.), with or without the agreement of the farmers concerned. This 'compulsory' insurance is frequently badly reimbursed. In the surveyed village, a peasant had a case where his buffalo died by accident. In the region, a buffalo costs about 2,000 to 2,500 *yuan*, but the insurance company paid him only about 800 *yuan*. To get this sum of money, he had to engage the village cadres, who made an attestation. The cadres and the peasant himself went then to negotiate with the company. In the process, the peasant had to buy some gifts and to offer an invitation to a restaurant, which cost him up to 300 *yuan*. Finally, he just recovered 500 *yuan*, net of costs, only 20–25 per cent of the purchase cost of his buffalo.

2. Fine for delay in paying the *hetongkuan*. According to the local regulations, the peasants must pay their *hetongkuan* (final *tiliu*, see below) on two occasions: the first one is in June, after the summer harvest, the second one in August and October, after the early and middle rice harvest, being the remaining balance. In general, the first

part is the heaviest burden for the peasant, because, at that time, peasants are in desperate need of money for buying their inputs (fertilizers, etc.), while they have only harvested a minor part of their crops. If they cannot make this payment in full, they must pay an annual interest rate as high as 30–36 per cent for the sum due, plus a fine named *chi na jin*, literally 'fine for late payment'.

3. Fines in respect of family planning (birth outside of planning), etc. Of course, all these fines are individualized, related only to the families concerned. But they aggravate the burden of the peasants, and contribute to the coffers of the village.

So, if we take into account these other charges together with the township-designated *hetongkuan*, the peasants in the surveyed village actually paid 630,000 *yuan* of *hetongkuan* instead of the 434,560 *yuan* assigned by the township. Therefore, another 195,440 *yuan* were added to the official bill, out of which were 150,000 *yuan* for the fees of construction of a primary school in the village, and 45,000 *yuan* for covering the village's non-accounted needs and other uses.

ASSESSMENT OF THE PEASANT BURDEN

From the township-designated *hetongkuan* and the families' sample surveyed in 1997, we are now in a position to assess the real burden of the peasants in the village. According to Table 1 (which is not, as we know, the final account for the peasants), the villagers paid a total 434,560 *yuan* in 1996, or 138 *yuan* per *mu* or 202 *yuan* per capita. Out of that sum, the three *tiliu* and five *tongchou* accounted only for 103,001 *yuan*, that is to say 48 *yuan* per capita or 33 *yuan* per *mu*. If we are to take the governmental definition of the peasant burden (three *tiliu* plus five *tongchou*), this burden represented only three per cent of the peasants' net income, so well below the government ceiling of five per cent, a rather good figure to be showed off by the cadres. If we take into consideration the total sum of the official *tiliu*, the payments by the peasants accounted for 12.8 per cent of their income of the previous year, four times higher than the first measurement of the burden.

But the peasants' real payment, according to the final *hetongkuan* that each family received from the village committee, was still much higher: 292 *yuan* per capita (instead of 202 *yuan*) or 200 *yuan* per *mu* (instead of 138). This equates to no less than 18.6 per cent of the nominal net peasant income of the previous year as reported by the village.

What does this sum of money represent for the peasants in their everyday life? We can try to answer this question by taking the example of the 26 families surveyed in 1997 (data of 1996). Owing to the fact that these families, located in a natural village with more land available (and with therefore a higher share of contracted land, which is the basis for the calculation of the *tiliu*), the per capita amount of the *hetongkuan* was still higher than for the average villager. In this sample, reflecting the situation of the families mainly engaged in agriculture (and crop cultivation), the figures are quite impressive. The *tiliu*, or *hetongkuan*, represented no less than one-quarter (25.3 per cent) of their total net income, and one-third of their net monetary income (33.6 per cent).

Even if we take the more modest figures from the whole village level, with nearly 20 per cent of the total net income, the *hetongkuan*, or total financial obligations of the farmers (corvées not included) was indeed a huge burden for the peasants. On the other hand, we can see that the five per cent ceiling set by the government has not much significance as it covers only a fraction of the actual payments made by the villagers. In the *China Agricultural Yearbook 1998*, a special article discussed precisely the Hubei province's peasant burden, giving respectively for the three *tiliu* and five *tongchou* the figures of 4.45 per cent of peasants' net income for 1996, and 3.8 per cent for 1997 [Ministry of Agriculture, 1998: 58]. Clearly these official figures, indicating some kind of improvement in the peasants' situation, were simply void of any signification. In practice, a reduction in the three *tiliu* and five *tongchou*, given the present circumstances, would mean only that the *jizi* and *tanpai* and other charges, not counting the unofficial ones, would have proportionately increased.

Thus, the very incomplete official approach in measuring the peasant burden cannot enable us to capture the extent of the charges really paid by the peasants. This is the reason why, even while the government-defined part of three *tiliu* and five *tongchou* has not exceeded five per cent in the past years, the problem of the peasant burden remains acute and unsolved.

If we are to consider the peasants' final payments as a whole (630,000 *yuan* for the studied village), the portion of three *tiliu* and five *tongchou*, as defined and controlled by the government, constituted only 16 per cent of the peasants' actual paid sums. Even if we exclude from our calculation the construction fee for the school (indeed a very special and occasional charge, particular for that year), the three *tiliu* and five *tongchou* still accounted for only 21.6 per cent of the peasants' total payments, whereas the *jizi* and *tanpai* accounted for about half of the total. This result is very similar to the findings of surveys done by other researchers.[10]

The taking into account of only the peasants' payments to the collectives, excluding from the calculation of the burden not only the taxes for the state, but, moreover, the other contributions to the different government agencies (half the total of all payments), renders illusory the hope of regulating the peasant burden through the five per cent ceiling.

DETERMINATION, COLLECTION OF AND CONSEQUENCE OF HETONGKUAN

Determination of the Hetongkuan

From our description of the *tiliu*, of the different kinds of associated charges, one may realize that the issue of the peasant burden is rather complicated. The peasant payments include all kinds of items, concerning different administrative levels (state, county, township), as well as the village administration. As for the form of payment, it may be monetary or in kind. Moreover, if some payment items are legal, set and determined by the state, other parts are illegal, but nonetheless imposed by the village or other government institutions. Therefore, in order to have a clear picture of the situation, it is necessary to analyse precisely the process of the determination of the total payment to be made by the families, including the legal parts as well as the informal ones, as indicated in the yearly contract signed with the collective. This final sum, usually a single figure without any explanation or details, is named the *hetongkuan* (contracted sum).

Before a *hetongkuan* is assigned to a peasant family, it must go through certain stages. First of all, at the county level, the Rural Economy Management Bureau or the Rural Work Department is the institution concerned with the implementation of the contracted sum. According to higher level governmental demands and related regulations, it investigates the peasants' income situation, consults other government institutions and takes into account other factors as well. Then, it works out a plan for the official *tiliu* as described in Table 1 at the beginning of the year. After approval by the county government, the county government distributes the *tiliu* (otherwise called *hetongkuan* by the county officials and peasants) among the different township governments.

The township governments distribute again their assigned shares among the villages, along the same principles as in the county. At this stage, the township government considers the interests of its own branches, and may add some items to the sum determined by the county. This practice of 'adding figures at each level' (*cengceng jiama*) is quite common. The resulting *tiliu* assigned to the villages is then similar to the one described in Table 1.

The figures, as listed in Table 1, have therefore been determined at the two levels of the county and the township. In this process, the resulting *tiliu* take care of the interests of their respective institutions. One can say that the planned *tiliu* is indeed the result of interaction, discussion, consultation, bargaining between the different governmental levels and their respective institutions. But, in this way, the interest of the village government has obviously been given a lesser consideration.[11] And this is precisely why the figures of Table 1 are not the final ones that the peasants will have to pay. In the meantime, the village committee will also adjust the sums in order to address its own needs.

In fact, when the village receives its assigned items for the *tiliu*, it cannot but add its own demands (which, of course, do not appear in the official documents compiled at the township level). And it has good reasons to do that. First, the three *tiliu* as determined by the township government are not sufficient to cover the current needs of the village. For example, in Table 1, the township government set a sum of 26,510 *yuan* for administrative fees of the village in 1996. This figure was quite far from adequate. For the salaries only of the collective staff and service personnel, such as the cadres, the village school teachers, the electrician, the doctors, the village had to pay up to 53,050 *yuan* for that year, a figure double the amount assigned for all administrative expenses in the village. It goes without saying that, in this situation, no money was left even for current administrative management expenses.

Second, the village has no collective enterprises, and therefore no source of revenue for itself. For all kinds of collective affairs, even minor ones such as the maintenance of schools or roads, the village must rely on the villagers' extra contributions. For example, the public accumulation fund for the village, in 1996, was 21,079 *yuan* (Table 1). But that very year, the village had built a new school at the cost of 405,000 *yuan*. Of course, all the cost fell on the peasants' shoulders, who were obliged to pay for it within three years. For 1996, the corresponding amount was 150,000 *yuan*, seven times higher than the village officially approved accumulation fund. This amount was of course added as an extra, non-official fee, to the *tiliu* to be paid by the peasants.

In the same manner, the village therefore adds its own items for extra fees to the list communicated by the township authorities. After that, the final amount of the *hetongkuan*, really paid by the farmers, is divided among the peasant families, according to their contracted land surface area. Normally, at spring time the village committee will give each family a 'contracted charges notice' (*hetong fudanben*) in which are only indicated a few figures, such as the total to be paid, and the subtotals for some items. That is the way the final amount of money to be paid by the peasants, the *hetongkuan*, is calculated at the family level. This real *hetongkuan* is much higher than indicated in Table 1, and this is the very reason why this 'contracted sum' is dubbed all over China as the 'peasant burden'.

Apart from the official *hetongkuan*, in the course of the year, the local government may demand some more payments from the peasants for various purposes. But these payments are occasional and not included in the peasants' contracted charges notice.

Collection of the Hetongkuan

The collection of the *hetongkuan* in the county is not simply the demand for money from the peasants. In fact, it is closely related with another big issue in the countryside, the delivery of the grain quota. The system of the compulsory deliveries of grain quota in China has indeed multiple functions. On the one hand, the fulfilment of the quota implies that the state gets the grain needed for supplying the cities; on the other hand, for the local government, it means that the lion's share of the *hetongkuan* will be successfully collected. In practice, the delivery of the quota is the opportunity for the local cadres to collect the money of the *hetongkuan*, deducted from the sum due to the peasants for their sales. Actually, even the totality of the sales of the quota is not enough to pay the whole *hetongkuan*. In the surveyed village, if all the fixed quota was fulfilled, it would amount to only 86 per cent of the *tiliu*.

For a proper understanding of the way the burden is imposed on the peasants, some explanations are therefore needed regarding the quota system as it is applied in the village.

Quota. The grain quota system was designed as an important instrument for the state to ensure the supply of grain for the city inhabitants and maintain social stability. It was established in 1953 and has lasted up to the present day, despite numerous changes and attempted reforms in the past two decades.[12] Fulfilling the quota is indeed a hard task for the peasants. In the surveyed village, the peasants cultivate mainly rice. So rice is the main component of the quota to be delivered to the state. For each family, the total quota is 1,792 kg of grain, or 148 kg per *mu*. Within the quota, wheat constitutes 10–15 per cent and rice 85–90 per cent (out of which 72 per cent is fulfilled through the sales of early rice, and the remainder by those of middle-season rice, whereas the late rice is kept for human consumption or for feed). The sales of the grain quota take place just one or two weeks after the harvests.

As regards the quota, two aspects must be considered: quantity and price. The quantity varies from one place to another. Even within the county, there are big differences. For example, the quota per *mu* in the village is 31 per cent higher than the average one in the township, and no less than 96 per cent higher than in the county as a whole. This difference can be partly explained by the natural resource endowment of this particular village, with a lot of land available for each family, a high proportion of which is devoted to rice cultivation, combined to higher yields. As regards the price, the administrative price paid for the mandatory quota is usually lower than the market price. In the county, for 1995 the market price was 27–56 per cent higher than the quota one (depending on the crop). The years when, owing to excess harvests, the market price falls under the quota price are the exceptions. It happened in 1984 in the county, and again in 1997.

In fact, the difference in prices between the quota and the market was for decades the main instrument for the state for extracting at low value the countryside's surplus grain, therefore imposing on the peasants a *de facto* tax. This hidden tax should be added to the burden of the peasants that we have already described. But, owing to the theoretical difficulties involved, another article would be needed for assessing this kind of hidden taxation, so it will not be considered in the present analysis of the peasant burden.

Whatever the magnitude of this hidden taxation, it is clear that the higher the quota, the heavier will be the losses incurred by the peasants. It is therefore not surprising that the peasants are unwilling to sell their quota to the state, and delay their deliveries, obliging the local administration to intervene to speed up the process, and of course deducting from the product of the sales the sums due for the *hetongkuan*.

Collecting the quota and the hetongkuan. Theoretically, the collection of the grain quota should be a matter that involves only the peasants and the grain-purchasing agencies. In fact, collecting the grain, for the above-mentioned reasons, constitutes the core work of the year for the local cadres. It is for them a unique opportunity to get hold of the money needed for their salaries and administration. So, naturally, when the harvest arrives, almost all the staff of the local administrative bodies are mobilized to intervene in the process of the grain delivery and *hetongkuan* collection. These institutions do not act separately, but on the contrary their cadres behave as a joint team under the direction of the township government. We will take the early rice quota delivery in the village as an example (this delivery provides for more than 70 per cent of the grain quota and 60 per cent of the *hetongkuan*).

The surveyed village is difficult to access because of the poor quality of the dirt road that links it to the township. So, in this month of August 1997, the township cadres decided to go down to the village, taking advantage of several sunny weather days. The team from the township was composed of seven persons, of whom four were from the town grain station, two were from the 'administrative section' (*guanli qu*, a level of administration between the township and villages in the county) and one was from the township government. The persons from the grain station were responsible for the purchase, weighing and controlling the quality of paddy (already prepared in bags by the peasants), thereby making up the accounts for each operation of the peasants' sales. The cadres from the township and the administrative section supervised the operation, ready to intervene in case of problems, resolving possible conflicts during the delivery (actually enforcing the whole process). Still more important, the members of the village committee were also present at that time. The accountant and the cashier of the village verified the transactions made by the grain station personnel, took note of each family's sales and deducted directly their respective *hetongkuan* from the sum due for the sales. As in most cases the total value of the sales was not enough to cover the *hetongkuan*, the peasants just got nothing from the delivery of their quota sales.

Differing from this second collection in August, at the delivery of the early rice quota, the first collection of *hetongkua* takes place in June, after the harvest of wheat. For this first collection, the township officials usually do not dispatch cadres and do not intervene directly, as the wheat constitutes only a very small part of the grain harvest. Nonetheless, the amount due from the peasants to the village government during this first collection represents a sizeable part of the total *hetongkuan*, no less than 30 per cent in 1996, and 40 per cent in 1995. As it was quite impossible for the peasants to meet such an enormous sum, the village cadres took economic measures to make sure that the collection would be achieved, imposing a 30–36 per cent annual interest rate on the sums not remitted, plus a certain percentage's fine for the unpaid part. Even so, many peasants had difficulty in meeting their obligations.

In fact, the task assigned by the township to the village for this first collection could not have been achieved: in June 1997, only 60,000 *yuan* were collected of the 130,000 *yuan* asked for by the township. After these two occasions of delivery of the quota and collection of the *hetongkuan*, the sums still due are usually paid after the sales of the middle season rice sale in October. But it is not possible for all families, especially the poor ones, to satisfy their financial obligations at this time. So near the end of the year, the village cadres visit the families in debt and try to force them, by all means, to meet their obligations.

Consequences

Of course, the collection of the quota as well as of the *hetongkuan* is never easy to accomplish. Sometimes conflicts arise, and even violent incidents occur between the peasants and the state agents (local cadres and personnel of the grain station). The situation was especially tense in 1995. That year, two serious clashes happened in the village. One concerned a dispute and battle between peasants and cadres, with one cadre and one peasant wounded. The second case was about a peasant who was beaten and wounded during the collection after he refused to pay the *tanpai* demanded in the course of the year. He appealed to the court. In 1997, after two years' appeals to courts of different levels, the case was still not settled (the judgments being contradictory from one court to another). Needless to say, this unresolved dispute has not improved the general atmosphere in the village, with deepening conflicts between peasants and cadres.

The burden of the *hetongkuan* and its mode of collection also have negative effects on the agricultural production. In the surveyed village the summer is the agricultural busy season. The peasants then desperately need the money for undertaking the necessary agricultural investments, such as the purchase of fertilizers and pesticides. Our own survey shows that almost 80 per cent of the crops' cultivation expenditure take place from April to August. Within that period, from March to July, the harvest of wheat and oilseeds can bring only 12–15 per cent of the total yearly revenue, so that the peasant family budget is particularly tight. If then the peasants must pay at the same time 30–40 per cent of the *hetongkuan*, they will have no money left or will go into debt for continuing the agricultural production.

As regards the amount of money collected, the *hetongkuan* accounts for nearly 20 per cent of the peasants' net income, even 30 per cent for the poor households or those engaged only in agricultural production. Moreover, all the payments are in cash, reducing the peasants' purchasing power on the market. It is therefore no surprise that, according to national surveys, the consumption of animal products by the rural population is significantly lower than that for the city dwellers, and has not increased in recent years.

The consequences are social as well. Indeed, the very social stability in the countryside is at stake. As peasants are unwilling or sometimes refuse to pay the *hetongkuan*, local governments take administrative measures in order to fulfil the state objectives and protect the interests of their cadres. The collecting process is never an easy one. The peasants resist, paying late or paying less, even paying nothing. If the peasants are really poor, the government can take some extreme measures such as taking peasant grain reserves, pigs, or entering the household, taking away the furniture. These measures are enforced by mobilizing public security officials and representatives of the judiciary. This results in conflicts and violence, with sometimes tragic consequences for the peasants.

As a result of this difficult collection process, the relationship between the peasants and local administration gets tense. Cadres no more venture alone into the peasant households for collecting the *hetongkuan* and the grain quota. They now often act in groups, and behave in a hostile manner towards the farmers. The social situation in the countryside can be therefore characterized as conflictual.

ORIGINS OF THE PEASANT BURDEN

From the evidence described in the surveyed village, it is clear that the peasant burden is indeed an economic and social problem in the Chinese countryside. Sure enough, the central and local governments have issued a lot of decrees and regulations, trying to tackle the problem. But the problem still remains. In reality, the issue is not a simple administrative one that decrees or regulations could easily solve. The peasant burden is a result of the interaction of many factors, related to the level of development of the local economy, the fiscal and financial situation of the county, the changes in scope of the public services, the actual working and performance of the government administrations.

Low Level of Economic Development

During the period of the people's communes, the collective played the main role in organizing agricultural production and distributing the products. The peasant was then only a member, not deciding on management issues, but merely carrying out orders. At that time, though poor, but in a massive and egalitarian way, the ordinary peasants had no direct contact with higher levels of administration and had no way of knowing or controlling the distribution of the collective benefits. In contrast, after the reforms and the ensuing decollectivization, the peasant families became independent producers as well as independent accounting units. They personally pay the taxes, charges, the fines and so forth. So the farmers now receive financial demands directly from the different administrations, feel the full effect of the taxes and fees on their individual budgets, and of course react correspondingly. Knowing now the full extent of the burdens imposed on them, they cannot but complain, sometimes in a violent manner.

On the other hand, rural reforms have brought about the liberalization of the economy and the regionalization of financial resources. Liberalization of the economy has meant reduced state intervention in the process of agricultural production and in the trade of agricultural products. Regionalization means that local governments must take more financial responsibility for the affairs of their respective territories. For example, at the level of the township, education, the maintenance of roads, the building of the new public infrastructure and utilities necessary for the economic development are now essentially the responsibility of the township government. All these services or projects need money. If the villages and township have no proper collective resources, the burden will fall on the peasants' shoulders.

It is a well-established fact that in villages or townships that own thriving enterprises, and therefore plenty of financial resources, the peasant burden is no longer a problem, whereas it is prevalent in most of the poor localities. Jean C. Oi has well described the situation in these poor villages:

> Villages with a primarily agricultural economy had few sources of revenues ... The primary source of revenue for many village coffers was ad hoc surcharges, known as Tiliu, levied by the village on its members. The fiscal crisis faced by the villages was heightened by the centre's decision to shift the burden of infrastructure investment to the localities. Local governments that control a primarily agricultural, particularly grain-based, economy have few options other than to levy ad hoc surcharges and various other fees and penalties [Oi, 1999: 20–21, 191].

This description accords quite well with the situation of our surveyed township and village.[13] Among the 28 villages of the surveyed township, there was no one village with a collective enterprise. As for the township's small market town itself, there were about ten enterprises, almost all of them bankrupt. Therefore one could not count on them to help public investments, not to mention agriculture! In that situation, the funding of collective affairs depended totally on the peasants' contributions.

For the village, the collective affairs are quite numerous: improving the state of the road, the construction or maintenance of the school, the installation of public utilities such as water, electricity and telephone lines. Without the peasants' contribution, nothing could be done.

Funding all these expenses is of course a burden for the peasants who just cannot pay the required amounts. Unable to raise the necessary resources, the village committee simply goes into debt. In our surveyed village, for the one year 1996, the sum of 180,000 *yuan* of the *hetongkuan* was still due by the peasants at year's end (one-third of the village families were affected). In order to accomplish the higher level assigned task, the village was obliged to borrow from some rich individuals, with high annual interest rates up to 30–36 per cent. This situation is not unique in the county. In another township, 39 out of 41 villages were indebted for a sum totalling 4.376 million *yuan* in 1996, or more than 110,000 *yuan* per village (12 of them had a debt over 200,000 *yuan*).

Financial Difficulties of the County

Funding their expenses is therefore a big headache for the local administrations and a major source of the peasant burden. The situation is not very different at the level of the county where financial difficulties are the more pressing, as it has a large grain-producing basis.

The agricultural nature of the county is well reflected in the composition of its financial resources. From 1987 to 1991, the agricultural tax contributed up to 21.7 per cent of the revenues whereas this proportion was only 3.9 per cent for the whole province of Hubei in the same period. The fiscal reform of 1994 in China further exacerbated the weight of agriculture in the county finance.[14] In 1995, the agricultural tax provided no less than 45 per cent of the county financial revenues, three times higher than it was in the province (13 per cent). By comparison, industrial and commercial taxes contributed only 28 per cent, far less than the amount from agriculture.

This dependence on agriculture brings often big problems because of the wide fluctuations in agricultural production that are due to the climate, and the variations of peasant incomes due to the market. In 1996, the county witnessed a great flooding, which resulted in a sharp decline of the agricultural tax, from 40 million *yuan* the previous year to 30 million, or a 25 per cent decline. This decrease was worsened by the fluctuations of the market with a fall of market price, at the end of the year, below the level of the quota price, affecting the peasants' income and their ability to pay the taxes (owing to the grain agencies' financial difficulties and their own surplus stocks, the national policy of guaranteed price for grain could not be implemented effectively).

As for the financial expenditure of the county, the major part is used for paying the salaries of the state cadres and other administrative expenses. In 1991, more than 80 per cent of the expenditure was of that kind (locally called *chifan caizheng*, the 'finances for the rice bowl'), leaving practically no significant resources, either for welfare expenses (only six per cent) or for funding the economic development of the county. Since then, the situation has not changed, which explains why the townships must bear most of the charges of public utilities, welfare and education.

Moreover, the county's finances are in the red. From 1990 to 1994, the county experienced four consecutive years of budgetary deficit. At the end of 1994, the deficit totalled 26 million *yuan*. Even to pay the salaries of its cadres, the county government was sometimes obliged to borrow from banks, to beg for money from higher levels of government, or simply divert some special fixed funds (assigned for specific other uses). As agriculture is the major contributor to the county's finances, the peasants should get corresponding returns from the government. But the real situation was just the reverse. As with most of the big grain-producing counties, this particular county in Hubei suffers from low per capita incomes and poor financial revenues, making impossible any help for the countryside and the villages.[15]

Under the present commercialization system and production policy, grain production has become a big burden for the county's finances and for the state grain enterprises. For example, the grain bureau of county had been in the red every year from 1982 to 1991, the losses stemming from the implementation of the national grain policies. Since then, the situation has further deteriorated, and, at the end of November 1996, the cumulated losses totalled 188 million *yuan*. These losses place the county government in an impossible position. On the one hand, it has the responsibility to develop the grain production; on the other hand, it must subsidize the losses of the state grain enterprises (losses increasing with the very increase of the grain production and deliveries). From 1982 to the end of 1991, the cumulated fund assigned for subsidizing the grain bureau was 130 million *yuan*, but only 16 million had been really used for that purpose. Along with the ever-increasing losses of the grain bureau, the burden for the county's finances becomes heavier. According to current policy, the county would have to give 17 million *yuan* as subsidies for the grain bureau, but not a cent is to be transferred as the county has not enough money even to pay its own cadres.

Decline of the Public Services

Among the various responsibilities of governments, the provision of the necessary public services to the people is at the core of their very *raison d'être*. The county government, like the central government, must cover all kinds of public functions, except national defence and diplomacy. It is particularly responsible for social welfare and for providing the infrastructure necessary for economic development. In theory, these functions should be carried out by means of the county finances. But in this poor agricultural county, as already explained, the financial revenues are used principally for the mere survival of the administrations, leaving few resources for public services and economic development.

The 1994 fiscal reform further weakened the local governments' financial capacity, but it provided them more autonomy, actually strengthening their motivation and ability for raising funds on their own. At the national level, in the early 1970s, the local share in revenues reached 85 per cent. By 1994, only 44 per cent of the budgetary revenues was retained by local governments. On the other hand, local shares in expenditures have steadily increased. In 1995, 71 per cent of total state expenditure was made by the local governments, as opposed to only 52 per cent in 1977. For the local government, this means that new avenues had to be found to finance this increased expenditure not covered by regular budgetary funds. Hence the levy of off-budget resources such as extrabudgetary revenues, self-raised funds, or diversion of other public funds [*Lu*, 1997: 125].

The case of our surveyed county is a very good illustration of this tendency and its consequences. As the regular budget could no longer satisfy the needs of public services, the government, mainly at the township level, took the measures of collecting *jizi* and *tanpai* from the peasants, these funds becoming the main source for the working of public services.

These are precisely the fields covered by the items funded by *jizi* and *tanpai* in the surveyed township: expenses of the No.1 High School, preventive medicine (for a special local disease), land reclamation, grain quota collection and so on (Table 1, category 4).

In the case of the township, the more revealing item of expenditure is the one devoted to education. With three-quarters of the five *tongchou* remitted to the township, education occupies an overwhelming place in the budget. Nonetheless, this public service is not well endowed and the problem is grave enough to require further examination.

For the county government as well as for the township one, public education is an important service. Even if the government is impotent in many other fields, it cannot escape its responsibilities concerning education for two reasons. First, the primary and junior middle school education is mandatory in China according to the law. Second, the teachers in the public schools are civil servants and must be paid accordingly by the state.

In this particular case, the salaries (including the bonuses) are therefore to be covered by the local finances. But these finances have simply not enough funds for that purpose. In 1996, the county counted 8,429 public teachers, the total corresponding payroll mounting up to 42.91 million *yuan* (on the basis of 5,090 *yuan* per teacher and per year). But the finances could provide only 27.31 million *yuan*, or 64 per cent of the total needs. If other school expenses are to be taken into consideration, that means that county finances could fund only half the needs of public education services. Even so, the education expenses had already a lion's share in the county budget, with 35.2 per cent for the period 1992–94. And, being in the red for years, the county finances were just unable to do more.

So the county was obliged to find other solutions to solve the problem of the lack of funds for education. The solution was the establishment of a system called the 'unified collection of education funds' (*jiaoyu jingfei tongchou*). This system enabled the collection of different levies (such as the No.1 High School item), the promotion of income-generating activities in the schools and the imposition of an 'education supplemental fee' in the five *tongchou*, all the resources created in this way being used through a unified management.

Despite all these measures, aggravating the peasant burden, the students must still pay very high school fees for the nine years of mandatory education: for example, in the surveyed township and village, no less than 250 *yuan* per semester and per pupil for primary school, 450 *yuan* for the junior middle school. Whereas public compulsory education is free of charge in Western countries (as it was in China during the collectivization period), the school system in the Chinese countryside is following a kind of privatization, at the expense of the peasants who must pay, directly and indirectly, a very high price for having their children educated. Despite the fact that Chinese peasants still give a lot of attention to educating their children, expecting thereby to raise their social status (particularly if they can leave the countryside and change their agricultural *hukou* – household registration system – still the dream for most of the peasants), the school fees and other expenses at school become a burden that many families cannot bear anymore. Our survey shows that the children get less education now than during the pre-reform period. Taking into consideration school expenditure and the lost opportunity of having their children working earlier outside, the majority of peasants just let their sons complete junior middle school and daughters the primary school.

As far as the village committee is concerned, it has no formal budget from the state, as the administrative village does not constitute a state administration level, and is managed by the 'people'. The only financial resources come from the three *tiliu*. This must be used for paying the salaries of the village cadres, the administrative expenses, the public welfare and the funding of economic development. The village must also cope with many other matters, such as education (primary school in each village), the dissemination of agricultural techniques, public health, the supply of drinkable water and electricity. In the surveyed village, the township-designated funds cannot even cover the salary of the cadres, so no money is left for public services. In these circumstances, the village either collects fees from the peasants, or lets things go. As we have already seen, when the village wanted to build a new school, the peasants had to pay. In the same way, when the village tried to install meters in each family for better control of the electricity uses and fees, it was of course up to the peasants to pay. For every public project, even the very small ones, implementation is just impossible without the peasants' payment.

Decentralization therefore strengthened the role and responsibility of local government in the domain of public services. Accordingly, it put more financial pressure on them. As public finances could not provide the necessary funds, the *jizi* and *tanpai*, these very sources of the peasant burden became the unwelcome but necessary means of coping with the new situation.

The Swelling of Government Staff

Generally speaking, we can say that the peasants' payments are closely related to the working and performance of the administration, and especially to the number of personnel of the government institutions. This linkage has two aspects. First, one part of the personnels' salaries and administrative fees is not covered by the government finances, but supported directly or indirectly by the peasants' contributions.[16] Second, different government institutions or agencies control certain economic resources and have the authority to use their power for imposing apportionment and fees on the peasants. Faced with the strong state apparatus, the peasants are situated in a weak position, owing to a lack of self-organization, so they cannot do anything but pay the sums required.

In the present analysis, we will not try to assess the performance of government institutions, or judge the real use of public funds (in fact, we have no direct evidence to make such a judgement). So we will just focus our analysis on the size of the staffs of the different government institutions, their related administrative expenses and their relationship to the peasants' payments.

Staff-swelling in local government is a rather common phenomenon in China. At the national level, some figures showing the inflation in the number of cadres employed by the state have already been published. In his major study Yang Dali [1996] indicates that the ratio of cadres to agricultural labourers had risen from 1.2 cadres for 1,000 workers in 1978 to 2.1 in 1984, and further up to 3.4 in 1989, in other words, a threefold increase in ten years!

The studied county has just followed a similar path. We can take the county's main institutions as examples. In 1979, there were 48 administrative units employing 1,157 persons. These figures increased respectively to 58 units and 1,864 persons in 1985, that is to say 69 per cent more personnel than in 1979 (16 times the level of 1950 and 2.8 times that of 1965). In 1991, these numbers rose further to 97 units and 2,132 persons, 14 per cent higher than in 1985. The increase was uneven depending on the institutions, so that the rate of growth of the staff was still higher for some of the government administrations. According to the information given by one person working in the government of the county, the number of personnel in the government institutions of the county was somewhere between 3,500 and 4,000 in 1996.

Normally the number of state cadres working in the administrations is governed by the quota system of the listed posts (*bianzhi*), but this quota is often exceeded. If we take the year 1991 as an example, the available data show that almost all of the 29 bureaux surveyed had staff in excess of the quota, excepting the Agricultural Bureau, for which the manpower was only equivalent to 70 per cent of its quota. The Light Industry Bureau had the highest rate of excess with 171 per cent. On average, the real numbers of staff employed were 52 per cent more than was authorized by the quota.

For the township level institutions, no detailed figures are available on the past tendencies of their staff. But we can assume that the situation and trends are similar to those observed at the county level. That means the overstaffing is more than 50 per cent. As for the village itself, it has also redundant personnel. According to the national Villagers' Autonomy Law, the state sets a three to seven cadres quota for an average village, but in our surveyed village, and also in surrounding villages, the actual figure of the cadres is between ten and twelve.

Now we can try to examine the impact of overstaffing on the peasants' payments. From Table 1, we can see that the township charged directly the village 27,814 *yuan* of fees as 'administrative fee of *xiangzhen*'. This item of *tanpai* is devoted to the salaries of the 'temporary employed persons' (overstaff). If we make a calculation for the whole township, we find that the sum of *tanpai* for this part was roughly equal to the sum provided by the state finance budget for the regular cadres' salaries. As regards the village level, we have strong evidence to assume that the village also adds about 50 per cent on top of its nominal administrative fee for paying the overstaff personnel (up to an additional amount of 13,255 *yuan*). Adding the two items means that for paying the salaries of the overstaff of both the township level and the village level's personnel, the peasants in the village had to contribute directly up to 41,069 *yuan*.

As far as overstaffing at the county level is concerned, the peasants pay indirectly. It is clear that the peasants do not pay directly as they do for the township and village. But the overstaffing of the county's offices consumes much of the county finances, leaving most of the government responsibilities (such as education, infrastructure construction and rural development) to be paid at lower levels by the peasants themselves. According to our own estimates, the village should pay in this way at least the same amount as the one it is providing for the township extra personnel (27,814 *yuan*). So if we take together the three levels (county, township and village) of local government, the villagers must pay 68,883 *yuan* for the overstaffing, that is to say 32 *yuan* per person, equivalent to two per cent of their previous year's net income, for that one reason.

CONCLUSION

The peasant payments are constituted of four parts: the agricultural tax and its supplements for the state; the five *tongchou* for the township; the three *tiliu* for the village; and different kinds of *jizi* and *tanpai* for the governmental institutions at different levels. From our surveyed village, the total payments accounted for 13–20 per cent of the peasants' previous year's net income. But, within this payment, the part of three *tiliu* and five *tongchou* represented only less than three per cent of this income. This part, the one considered officially as the peasant burden, constituted therefore only 20–25 per cent of the total charges actually paid.

The government is directly involved in the determination of the *hetongkuan*, the sum to be paid by the peasants. This final payment is the result of interaction, discussion, consultation and bargaining between the different governmental levels and their respective institutions. But in this process, the peasant participation is not even taken into consideration.

The collection of the *hetongkuan* is closely related to the collection of the quota of grain. Not surprisingly, considering the big difference between the administrative cost of the quota and the market price of grain, the peasants are quite reluctant to deliver the quota. The government is therefore obliged to intervene in the process, mobilizing its different institutions that cooperate for that purpose. These simple and direct administrative measures result in face-to-face confrontations, conflicts and sometimes violence between the peasants and the government's cadres. The way this peasant burden is collected has also negative effects on the agricultural economy. Farmers lack the necessary funds for production in the busy agricultural season, and one-third of surveyed families go into debt.

The peasant burden is the final result of the interaction of multiple factors. These factors include mainly: the low level of local economic development, the fiscal and financial difficulties of the county, the changes in scope and the decline of public services provided by the state and the collectives, and the staff-swelling of government institutions at different levels.

Of course, some countermeasures could, and should, be undertaken to solve the problem of the peasant burden and lessen the tensions between farmers and cadres. The government should establish new criteria to measure, monitor and evaluate the peasant burden. These criteria should take into account not only the township and village collected fees, but also, and much more important, the peasants' payments to the state and their contributions to the different government institutions and different projects. Those payments should be considered together in a global way, in order to reflect the all-round picture of peasant payments. The ongoing national tax-for-fees reform cannot limit itself to the means of distribution and methods of collection. It should tackle the core of the problem, which is the reduction of the whole peasant burden and cut the possible sources that currently aggravate the peasants' burden.

Furthermore, the most urgent measure should be to go on reforming the present administrative system: reducing the staff, improving work efficiency. In 1998, the central government promoted daring and radical reforms in that regard; this reform should be extended and be implemented at all levels of administration, provincial as well as county levels, township level and village level.

But, of course, the success of administrative reforms cannot be separated from the improvement of the economic environment, which alone can provide the resources necessary for the good working of public services. For relatively poor regions such as the one surveyed in Hubei, this economic progress will take time to take effect.

In practice, administrative reforms and economic improvements will not result in significant changes if the peasants cannot really control and supervise the local administrations and their cadres. The very efficiency of administration, the equitable distribution of economic benefits cannot be achieved without the participation of peasants who should be aware of and able to control the use of public funds, in a democratic and transparent manner. In other words, the solving of the peasant burden is closely linked to the realization of democracy at grassroots level.

NOTES

1. As regards the peasant burden, there does not exist a standard definition. Some people tend to include all the items affecting the peasants income: for example, Xie *et al.* [1999] includes even the 'price scissors' (price difference between the agricultural and industrial products) within the peasant burden, but without empirical research. Another point of view takes into consideration only the part of charges above what the government officially asked for. This article will clarify the real content of this 'burden', and compare it to the official definition given by Chinese authorities in their regulations.

2. For more information, see Lu [1997: 127]. According to a report published in the Hong Kong *South China Morning Post*, 9 Feb. 2000, 'in 1999, there were more than 2,000 cases of farmers staging riots and other violent demonstrations against rural authorities. The majority of these confrontations were caused by the excessive tax and corruption'.

3. As early as 1990, in February and September, the State Council issued an 'announcement' (*tongzhi*) and made a 'decision' (*jueding*) on the problem of the 'peasant burden'. See Ministry of Agriculture [1992: 142].

4. 'Regulation on Peasant Burden and Labour' (*nongming chengdan feiyong he laowu guanli tiaoli*). The regulation decided that the three *tiliu* and five *tongchou* that the peasants paid for the village and township levels could not exceed five per cent of the net income of the previous year. For the complete text, see Zhang and Li [1999: 76–83].

5. Ibid., pp.85–90.

6. To protect the anonymity of the surveyed localities, the names of the county and village will be omitted.

7. After the 1994 fiscal system reform bywhich the tax coverage is divided between the various levels of government, this part of the tax is kept by the county government. For more general information on sharing items of taxation between different levels of government and the consequences of fiscal reforms, see Oi [1999].

8. For a general discussion about the distribution issues in the countryside, see Ministry of Agriculture [1980: 382–3]. Detailed information is also given in Oi [1989: 16–29, 105–13]. Description from some Chinese communes can be found in Chen and Ridley [1969], in Burki [1969], and in Lefebvre [1979].

9. In 1990, 25 government departments issued the documents for charging fees from the peasants. These documents concern eight categories and 148 items of this kind of unofficial payment. See Ministry of Agriculture [1991: 140–41].

10. According to Li Xiangang [1995], in 1994, peasants paid on average 41 *yuan* per person for the three *tiliu* and five *tongchou*, which was equivalent to 4.9 per cent of the peasant income of the previous year and accounted for only 18.7 per cent of the peasants' total payments. In another farmers' survey in Zhejiang province, from 1995 to 1998, the distribution of the

different payments was as follows: the three *tiliu* and five *tongchou* accounted for 18–23 per cent of peasants' total payments, against 23–40 per cent for the agricultural tax, and 43–59 per cent for the various *jizi* and *tanpai*; see Chai *et al.* [1999: 42].

11. In China, the status of the village government is very different from that of higher levels of government. The village committee is an autonomous organization, whereas the latter ones are the state organs or institutions. Therefore, the treatment for cadres is also different. The cadres in the village are called 'popular cadres' (*minban ganbu*) who just receive their remuneration from the villagers' contribution without being covered by the state insurance. After the cadres leave their position in the village, they become again ordinary peasants. The cadres at township or higher levels are considered as 'state cadre' (*guojia ganbu*) who receive regular salaries, with bonuses and insurance. Their status is similar to that of civil servants in Western countries.

12. The best analysis of the grain quota system and its role during the collectivization period is to be found in Oi [1989].

13. Unfortunately, the villages without rural enterprises or badly managed ones are quite numerous in China. According to a survey, two-thirds of the villages had no collective rural enterprises, so no collective economy [*Qin*, 1998: 8]. In another national survey, the proportion of *kongkecun* villages (without collective property and financial resources) in 1995 was 24.7 per cent of the villages surveyed, of which 59.3 per cent related to the western regions of China. See Policy Research Section of Central Party [1997: 47–50].

14. The most important change brought by the 1994 fiscal system reform was to establish a new system for tax sharing (*fenshuizhi*) between central and the local government, with a new distribution of the different taxes. In general, the taxes can be classified into three categories: those devoted to central government, those devoted to local government, and those shared between central and local government. For more details about this sharing scheme, see Oi [1999: 217].

15. According to research, 8 out of 11 principal grain-producing provinces in China had a significant low revenue; see Xian [1997].

16. In China, the personnel working in the government institutions can be divided into two categories: those with a post (*bianzhi*) and those without a post (temporarily employed persons). This increase in staff can be partly attributed to the abuse of power of certain key cadres who put on the payroll friends or relatives; it can be also partly attributed to the changes in functions and working methods of the local government institutions. For example, when the harvest arrives and the payment of *hetongkuan* is due, the township mobilizes almost all its available staff, which seems then far from sufficient to achieve the required tasks. Normally, the budgeted finances can and must cover the salaries of the cadres with a post. But for the temporarily employed persons, the government must find other solutions to pay them. These solutions more than often take the forms of *jizi*, *tanpai*, fines, coming from the peasants' contribution.

REFERENCES

Burki, Shahid Javed, 1969, *A Study of Chinese Communes 1965*, Cambridge, MA: Harvard University Press.

Chai, Pongyi, Zhou Jiehong and Xie Jiaqi, 1999, 'The Empirical Studies on the Rationality of Peasant Burden', *Problems of Agricultural Economy*, No.12, pp.41–5.

Chen, C.S. and Charles Price Ridley, 1969, *Rural People's Communes in Lien-Chiang*, California: Hoover Institute Press.

Lefebvre, Alain, 1979, *Le district Guanghan au Sichuan: Matériaux pour l'etude de l'economie rurale chinoise*, Toulouse: Université de Toulouse le Mirail.

Li, Xiangang, 1995, 'Some Considerations on Agricultural Tax and Fee Collecting Reform', *Problems of Agricultural Economy*, No.7, pp.35–9.

Lu, Xiaobo, 1997, 'The Policies of Peasant Burden in Reform China', *The Journal of Peasant Studies*, Vol.25, No.1, pp.113–38.

Ministry of Agriculture, 1980, 1991, 1992, 1998, *China Agricultural Yearbook*, Beijing: China Agricultural Press.

Ministry of Agriculture, 1990, 'Survey on Peasant Burden', *Problems of Agricultural Economy*, No.2, pp.57–60.

Oi, Jean C., 1989, *State and Peasants in Contemporary China*, Berkeley, CA: University of California Press.

Oi, Jean C., 1999, *Rural China Takes Off: Institutional Foundations of Economic Reform*, Berkeley, CA: University of California Press.

Policy Research Section of Central Party, 1997, 'Economic Development and the Characteristics of Financial Income and Expenditures at Village Level', *China Rural Survey*, No.1, pp.47–50.

Qin, Hui, 1998, *Rural Enterprise Ownership Transformation in Zhejiang Province: A Case Study*, USC Seminar Series No.13, Hong Kong: The Chinese University of Hong Kong.

Sun, Meijun, 1998, 'The Current Situation of Peasant Burden and Its Sources', *Chinese Rural Economy*, No.4, pp.7–12.

Xian, Zhude, 1997, 'Adjusting the Price Relation and Increasing the Peasant Income', in *Study on China's Countryside, Agriculture and Peasants*, Beijing: China Statistical Publishing House (zhongguo tongji chubanshe).

Xie, Jiaqi, Zhou Jiehong and Chai Pongyi, 1999, 'Systematic Considerations about the Problem of Peasant Burden', *Problems of Agricultural Economy*, No.3, pp.42–4.

Yang, Dali, 1996, *Calamity and Reform in China: State, Rural Society and Institutional Change since the Great Leap Famine*, Stanford: Stanford University Press.

Zhang, Mingwei and Li Ling, 1999, *Zhongguo nongcun ganbu gongzuo shouce* (Handbook of cadres' work in rural China), Beijing: Commercial Affairs Publishing House (shangwu ying shu guan).

How Not to Industrialize:
Observations from a Village in Sichuan

JACOB EYFERTH

INTRODUCTION

Among the many success stories of post-Mao China, the rise of township and village enterprises (TVEs) stands out as the most spectacular. Throughout the 1980s and 1990s, the TVE sector grew at double-digit rates, bringing wealth and employment to millions of rural people. By 1995, rural enterprises employed 128 million people, produced one-third of China's gross national product, and provided one-third of China's exports [*Zhongguo Nongcun*, 1996: 329]. Entire regions were transformed from agricultural backwaters to urbanized industrial districts. The economic success of the sector produced a burgeoning literature, which largely focused on the most characteristic features of TVEs: the predominance of collective over private ownership and the close links between enterprises and the local state [*Byrd and Lin*, 1990; *Findlay* et al., 1994; *Oi*, 1992, 1999; *Walder*, 1998; *Wong*, 1988, 1991]. Since the late 1990s, however, Western observers have turned away from the sector; it sometimes seems as if TVEs provoke embarrassed silence rather than debate.

There are several reasons for this. First, the sector, already ailing in the mid-1990s, was badly battered by the Asian financial crisis and the ensuing economic slowdown. The extremely high growth rates of the early 1990s (65 per cent in 1993) had been sustained by pent-up consumer demand after decades of shortage; flagging demand in the late 1990s revealed huge overcapacities and other problems, such as low productivity, a tendency of firms to cluster in the same branches, and an isomorphous structure of small, cellular firms overly dependent on local patronage [*Gore*, 1999]. Second, the most characteristic and interesting feature of the TVEs – collective ownership – was disavowed and abandoned by the Chinese state.[1] Faced with increasing losses, the central government in 1998 launched a

Jacob Eyferth, Assistant Professor for Modern Chinese History at Simon Frazer University, Vancouver. The author wishes to thank Guo Xiaoming and Lei Xiaoming of the Sichuan Academy of Social Sciences for their help with the fieldwork.

restructuring drive in which local authorities at all levels were encouraged to 'sell, merge, turn into joint-stock companies, or declare bankrupt' (*mai, bing, gu, po*) all but the most profitable publicly owned enterprises. In practice, this amounted to a massive and hastily executed privatization campaign. Third, privatization has deprived the sector of much of its former identity and coherence. TVEs still appear as a rubric in statistics, but Chinese sources increasingly classify firms by size or legal form. Despite these changes, rural industries continue to shape the lives of millions in the countryside, in ways that owe much to the recent past. It would be naive to assume that China had now reverted to a 'normal' pattern of capitalist development, characterized by private ownership and a purely regulatory state. Many rural Chinese have lived through 20 years of rapid, state-led industrialization; for them, this experience represents industrial modernity. For better or worse, the developmental agenda that drove TVE expansion has taken root and continues to shape economic thought and action. TVEs, in short, are still with us and need to be studied.

This article looks back at TVE development in the years 1986 to 1998 in a single locality: Chenyan village in Muchang township, Jiajiang county, Sichuan province. It does not claim to be representative; rather, it offers a frog-in-the-well perspective on the why and how of rural industrial growth. Though my main focus is on TVEs, I also discuss handicraft papermaking, the traditional source of livelihood for most people in the village. The paper industry – small-scale, household-based, market-oriented, and operating outside the scope of the local state – provides an interesting contrast to Chenyan's TVEs.

OLD AND NEW INDUSTRIES IN JIAJIANG

Jiajiang county is located in Leshan city (Leshan *shi*, formerly Leshan district, *qu*), about 150 km south of Chengdu. With an average rural income of 2312 *yuan* per capita in 2000, Jiajiang is moderately well off but lags behind the counties immediately adjacent to Chengdu, not to mention China's coastal regions. Jiajiang's main claim to fame is its paper industry, documented since the mid-seventeenth century. Jiajiang paper is made from bamboo, one of the few plants that grow abundantly in the hilly western part of the county, where the industry is concentrated. During World War II, when the industry was at its peak, Jiajiang and a few other paper districts single-handedly supplied the wartime government in Chongqing with paper. At that time, an estimated 60,000 – one-third of the county's population – depended on the paper industry. After the socialist revolution of 1949, the industry was gradually reduced in size and eventually phased out. Part of the reason was that handicraft production was superseded by machines; but the main reason was that rural papermakers – now classified as 'peasants' – consumed rather than produced grain. Paper producers in Jiajiang had always relied on foodgrain from the markets, simply because land in the hills was so poor. With the nationalization of grain markets, papermakers became clients of the state grain bureau, a situation that came to be seen as anomalous and problematic. Throughout the 1950s, the state tried to reduce 'grain entitlement', but most people in the hills remained dependent on state grain.

During the Great Leap Forward (1957–59), grain supplies in the Jiajiang hills broke down. At the end of the ensuing famine, the hill townships had lost 24 per cent of their population – far more than the agricultural plains. The lesson state planners drew from the famine was that rural non-agricultural producers could not be adequately provisioned, and that they therefore had to become self-sufficient farmers. In the post-famine years, grain supplies in the Jiajiang hills were phased out, and papermakers were made to uproot their bamboo and plant corn on the steep slopes – which, once deprived of their protective bamboo cover, were soon eroded.

De-industrialization in the Jiajiang hills coincided with the growth of commune and brigade enterprises (*shedui qiye*, the precursors of the TVEs) in the rich and fertile plains around Jiajiang city. In the 1960–70s, agricultural productivity rose, while state grain extraction was held at a constant and comparatively modest level. Collectives in the plains, freed from the need to devote all their resources to grain cultivation, branched out into cash-cropping, sidelines and industry. Maoist autarky policies thus produced results that were at odds with the professed aim of reduced spatial inequality. Papermakers, who had developed their specialization in order to escape the limitations of a peripheral and resource-poor habitat, were 're-peasantized' at great costs to the environment and themselves. At the same time, people in the already advantaged fertile plains were allowed to take some of the county's best land out of grain cultivation and to engage in profitable industries and sidelines.

After the opening of grain and paper markets in the early 1980s, papermaking recovered. Jiajiang paper had been traded on the black market throughout the 1960–70s; when market controls were relaxed in the early 1980s, private traders began peddling their wares all over China, and the industry quickly recovered. Jiajiang natives now sell paper in all major cities of the PRC; through middlemen in Guangzhou and Hong Kong, they export paper to Japan and Southeast Asia. At the same time, the production structure in the paper districts underwent radical changes. The few surviving collective workshops were dismantled and their equipment distributed to the households. With the help of cheap loans from the Rural Credit Cooperative, household producers replaced the run-down collective equipment with modern machinery. Paper production is still largely manual, not because of conservatism or technical ineptitude, but because artists and calligraphers insist on handmade paper.

Today as in the past, paper workshops employ mainly household labour, with perhaps one or two long-term hired workers. The industry is small-scale and fragmented, with hundreds of household workshops dispersed in the hills. Since the industry is officially classified a 'rural household sideline' (nongcun jiating fuye), it is neither taxed nor registered; precise data on its size are therefore impossible to come by. One source [Anon., 1998: 4] estimates that 900 vats were active in 1997. With an average employment of four to five persons per vat, plus porters, traders, repairmen, steamer operators and people employed in supporting industries, total employment in that year must have been around or above 5,000, out of a rural working population of 160,000. Employment in rural industry (including papermaking) was around 10,000; in other words, half of Jiajiang's rural industrial workforce worked in the handicraft paper industry.

TVE industrialization dates back to the late 1970s, when communes and brigades in the plains built up the first enterprises, mostly in the food-processing sector. From there, they branched out into construction materials and chemistry. The pioneer was Huangtu township, which in the course of the 1980s built up glass, fertilizer, electronic components and chemical factories. Other townships followed in Huangtu's steps, investing in exactly the same branches. After a slowdown in 1989–91, industrial growth accelerated again with Deng Xiaoping's 1992 'Southern Tour'. County publications speak of the 'three big industries' of Jiajiang: building materials, ceramic tiles and machine-made paper [Anon., 1998: 1]. Insiders, however, spoke of 'the three failures' (sanci daomei): overinvestment in branches that promised quick success led to huge excess capacities. From 1994 to 1999, the county's TVE sector suffered six years of consecutive losses [JJNJ, 2000: 65]. Nonetheless, industrial expansion continued unabated, and by 2000, the flat and fertile plains around the county seat were littered with ceramic tile factories.

GROWTH WITHOUT DEMAND:
VILLAGE ENTERPRISES IN CHENYAN

Chenyan village, the focus of this article, is located in the hilly western part of Jiajiang. Among the 11 villages of Muchang township, only Chenyan owns collective enterprises. By 1998, the Chenyan village committee owned a saltpetre factory, an acetylene factory, a calcium carbonate factory and a 30 per cent share of a brick factory. None of the enterprises was contracted out: the acetylene and calcium carbonate factories were run by the village party secretary himself, the Xinghuo saltpetre factory by a manager who was appointed by the village committee. From 1983 to 1998, the village leadership devoted most of its energy to the expansion of the enterprises. Their success earned them praise and aroused the envy of village leaders in neighbouring communities, but most villagers derived little benefit from industrial expansion. By 1998, only the acetylene factory remained operational: the Xinghuo factory had closed down, and the calcium carbonate factory had never actually started production. Village debts totalled six million *yuan*, against nominal assets of 9.4 million. The general view in Chenyan was that the local Rural Credit Cooperative (RCC) would continue to bail it out, but that the debts would paralyze the village for years to come.

Hunting for a Project: The Xinghuo Factory

When the collective structure was dismantled in 1983, Chenyan was in danger of becoming an 'empty-shell village' (*kongke cun*) – a village without income, unable to pay its officials, finance the local school or provide benefits to its members. In 1985, the six-member village party cell began to search for a revenue-generating project (*xiangmu*). Given the large number of skilled papermakers in the village and the rising demand for paper, they naturally opted for a paper factory. Papermaking promised fast returns and needed little initial investment. Yuan Zhili,[2] a paper trader and member of the party cell, drew up the plans. Though not a papermaker, he knew enough about the trade to design a half-mechanized factory with a large pressure steamer, a mechanized pulp beater and three moulding vats. The six men offered all their personal property – houses, workshops, paper stocks and savings – as collateral for a 160,000 *yuan* loan from the Muchang RCC. Official regulations required a much higher collateral, but RCCs at that time were happy to find outlets for their money. Moreover, the director of the Muchang RCC, who was from Chenyan himself, lent them his support. The loan was granted, and the Xinghuo ('Spark') paper factory started producing in early 1987. In the next two years, ten more vats and a hot-air drying chamber were added.

In 1993, the Xinghuo factory gave up paper production and switched to saltpetre. The background of the change is unclear: Yuan Zhili maintains that the factory was sound, and that he abandoned paper production only under pressure from county and township authorities. Xinghuo produced expensive paper for calligraphers and artists – a profitable market, but one that permitted only gradual growth. At a time when yearly growth rates of 20 per cent were considered low, county officials pressured for a more aggressive approach. More importantly, the county tax office expected and indeed demanded high profits and tax revenues. Yuan claimed that Xinghuo was a handicraft workshop, which would have put it into a low tax category, and that it deserved tax breaks for processing agricultural inputs. The county tax office, by contrast, insisted that Xinghuo was a factory and should be taxed as such. The conflict came to a head in 1992, when tax officials produced evidence that Yuan had evaded taxes. Yuan admits that he had done so ('everybody did') but said that charges were trumped up to extort bribes and presents and to make him give up his cautious business strategy.

In Yuan's version of the story (which is contested by other villagers), he finally got tired of the tax office's harassment and gave in to their demands. The shift to saltpetre cost 600,000 *yuan*, borrowed, like the initial investment, from the Muchang RCC. Product change had the desired results: with a product tax of 30 per cent on turnover (rather than six per cent for paper) and a much higher turnover, Xinghuo began to produce high revenues. Initially, profits were also high, but the price for saltpetre collapsed in the following year. This could have been foreseen: lured by temporarily high prices, dozens of village factories entered the market at the same time as Xinghuo. According to Yuan, this was of little concern to the tax authorities, which were interested in revenue rather than long-term profit.[3] In 1996, Xinghuo could no longer pay its electricity bills; since then, it stood idle for most of the time.

The Acetylene Factory

The initial success of the Xinghuo factory encouraged village leaders to pursue further expansion. Few people in Chenyan had technical skills outside papermaking, and none knew how to develop and manage a large factory. The search was therefore for a ready-made project, complete with technical blueprints, permits and loans, and ideally with strong links to the state sector. After some unsuccessful scouting, the delegation learned that neighbouring Shazui village had been 'fishing' for a strawboard factory (*caoban chang*) but had failed because of internal conflicts. Chenyan's village head Chen Fucai immediately began to lobby the county authorities, and in early 1986 sent a delegation to Beijing and Liaoning province to purchase blueprints and equipment. When the delegation returned with a provisional contract for a large factory, some of the village leaders raised doubts about the capacity of Chenyan to handle such a project. Fucai, though not convinced himself, admonished them to close ranks and remain silent lest they lose support from the 'higher levels'. Having secured the consent of the county TVE office, Fucai travelled to Chengdu to negotiate with the provincial TVE bureau. Fortunately, the bureau's director was a Jiajiang man, who promised to arrange a loan for the project. This left the county government as the final hurdle. Since Fucai had provincial backing, county leaders could not directly refuse, but they remained sceptical; after all, if the factory failed, the county would have to pick up the bill. Without informing the village, they sent off their own fact-finding mission to Beijing and Liaoning.

In the meantime, Chen Fucai pressed ahead: 30 *mu* of bamboo land were levelled for the factory site, and a motor road was built to link the factory to the main road. This was a deliberate show of determination, designed to impress the county government. In late 1987, the county mission returned from Liaoning, reporting that a factory of the projected type and size was not feasible in Jiajiang. Chen Fucai realized that he would have to find a replacement for the project, or accept personal responsibility for the loss of money and labour incurred by the village. He pawned his property for one last trip, this time to Shanghai. A few hours before his departure, he received a phone call from a friend who told him about plans to build an acetylene factory somewhere in Leshan district. Fucai immediately cancelled his trip to Shanghai and set off to Leshan, then to the Provincial Economic Planning Committee (*sheng jiwei*) in Chengdu. He raced not only against time, but also against a delegation from Emei county that competed for the same project – if Fucai is to be believed, the two cars literally raced each other and arrived in Chengdu neck to neck. Thanks to his connections, Fucai was awarded the contract.

The planned investment for the acetylene factory was two million *yuan*. In September 1988, when the village was about to start construction, the central government announced strict austerity measures to cool down the overheated economy. Loans promised by the provincial TVE bureau were withdrawn; county guarantees also evaporated. Once again, Fucai lobbied the 'higher levels', and once again, luck was on his side. The provincial Poverty Alleviation Bureau had just granted a two million *yuan* loan to Jiajiang county, and Fucai secured more than one-third of the sum for his village – despite the fact that Chenyan was a moderately wealthy village by local standards and certainly not in need of poverty alleviation. With 750,000 *yuan* from the province, another 800,000 *yuan* from the Muchang RCC, 200,000 *yuan* from share sales and workers' security deposits (*fengxianqian*),[4] and 200,000 *yuan* direct investment from a factory in Leshan, the village now had 1.95 million at its deposal, only slightly less than projected.

The acetylene factory, Fucai explained, was a 'fixed point' (*dingdian*) project. This meant that it was included in the state plan, and that a large share of its output was contracted to state units. Such a project, Fucai said, could not fail; even if it made losses, the local authorities would bail it out. The factory was fully automated; nobody from the village was involved in or even understood production technology. For repairs and routine checkups, technicians were called over from the county seat. Chenyan provided 37 unskilled shopfloor staff who worked in two 12-hour shifts and 23 administrative staff and salesmen.

The factory started operating in December 1989. In the first year, sales were slow because of the central governments' austerity policies.[5] This led to a leadership crisis, in which Chen Fucai was ousted from his position as factory director and replaced by the village party secretary, who had spent much of the previous years abroad.[6] In 1992–95, a renewed building boom in rural Sichuan brought high profits to the factory. As in the case of Xinghuo, high demand caused an increase in the number of competitors, followed by oversupply and a collapse of prices. In 1998, the factory had debts of more than two million *yuan*.

The Calcium Carbonate Factory

In 1993, Chenyan obtained the go-ahead for a third project, a calcium carbonate ($CaCO_3$) factory. Calcium carbonate, or lime, is widely used in the building industry. It usually comes from quarries, but it can also be produced by mixing slaked lime ($Ca(OH)_2$) – a by-product of acetylene production – with carbon dioxide. The original idea was to vertically integrate calcium carbonate production with the acetylene factory, but for technical reasons, this never worked. This time, Chenyan received immediate support from banks and county authorities: the village's previous track record seemed to ensure success, and after Deng Xiaoping's Southern Tour, the credit taps were once again wide open. Fixed investment for the new project was four million *yuan*, twice the amount of the acetylene factory. Most of the loan came from the RCC; the acetylene factory, itself still heavily indebted, gave security.

During the first trial run in autumn 1995, it became apparent that the factory boiler did not generate sufficient steam. Rumour in the village had it that 'someone on our side took commissions' (*women zhefang de ren chi le huikou*), in other words, that the village leaders accepted substandard equipment in exchange for kickbacks, and that the village spent four million *yuan* on equipment worth less than three million. However, substandard equipment was not the only reason for the failure of the project. When the factory was completed, the market for lime, as for building materials in general, was saturated. Even with functioning equipment, it would have been difficult to compete with factories that got their limestone directly from quarries. After the failed trial run, the factory was never switched on again. It would have been possible to replace the boiler, but the village lacked the funds for new equipment. Some people suggested opening a karaoke bar in the factory office building. Similar bars – brothels in all but name – line a road that passes by the village, but to encourage prostitution right in the centre of the village, in a building owned by the village and adjacent to the village administration, was considered just one step too far.[7]

The Ceramic Tile Factory

The ceramic tile factory, of which Chenyan owned one-third, originated in Qingshan village, directly north of Chenyan. Qingshan, like Chenyan, has a tradition of handicraft production, in this case the production of bricks and tiles in small, coal-fired kilns. Thanks to the kilns, which have replaced agriculture as the main source of income, Qingshan was quite wealthy; what it lacked, however, were village factories. This was of no concern to villagers who were fully employed in their fields and kilns, but it was a problem for the village cadres. In 1996, monthly cadre income in Qingshan was around 80 *yuan*, against 200 *yuan* in Chenyan. Cadres complained that the collection of collective fees (*tiliu*) left them no time for actual community service. *Tiliu* fees in Muchang township were very low, but people resented paying fees to cadres whose seemed to do nothing but tax them. Understandably, cadres in Qingshan were demoralized and envied their colleagues in Chenyan.

Around 1990, the Qingshan village committee began drafting plans for a brick factory. The project was opposed by the township, which wanted to protect its own brick factory, but received backing from the county. Like Chenyan, Qingshan relied heavily on an administrative patron: the secretary of the Leshan City Political Consultative Conference, who hailed from the village. He counselled them to enlarge the project to a state-of-the-art ceramic tile factory, knowing from experience that only ambitious plans got county support. The village committee did so and promptly received the promise of a bank loan. It then began to raise money from the village; by 1995, it had sold 410 shares worth 1,000 *yuan* each, and the factory was half completed. The promised loan, however, never materialized. In November 1995, the committee lost hope and sold the half-completed factory to 'Chenyan' (in fact, to the acetylene factory, which in their eyes was the same). They received 180,000 *yuan*, less than one-half of their investment. Qingshan villagers claim that Chenyan bought their project with a loan from the township RCC – which previously had denied loans to Qingshan, on the grounds that the project was not feasible. In their view, Chenyan had been successful only because the RCC director channelled savings from the entire township into his home community. In fact, only one-third of the purchase sum came from the RCC; two-thirds came from a private investor. In 1996, Chenyan sold its share to this man who in turn sold it to a third party. By 1998, the factory was still unfinished.

WHO GAINED AND WHO LOST FROM TVE DEVELOPMENT?

Village leaders in Chenyan stressed that they built the factories for the benefit of the entire community, not for their own, private gain; TVEs, they hoped, would generate the funds needed to subsidize welfare and education, improve the local infrastructure, and provide employment for unskilled and disadvantaged villagers. How far were these expectations fulfilled?

The village enterprises contributed to village fiscal income in three different ways: (1) through a one per cent management fee (*guanlifei*) on gross income, which was divided between village and township (0.4 per cent for the village, 0.6 for the township); (2) the village, as the legal owner, had a claim to profits after taxes and expenses; (3) the village could demand irregular 'charges' and 'contributions' (*tanpai, zhanzhu*) from the factories. Officially, it could do so only after all other obligations were fulfilled, but loose accounting and supervision gave the village a *de facto* first claim. In 1994, direct village revenue from the 0.4 per cent management fee was around 15,000 *yuan*; in all other years, it was less. This was the only reliable source of revenue from the factories. The combined taxes and profits (*li-shui*) of Xinghuo and the acetylene factory amounted to 700,000 *yuan* – a much larger sum, but one that had to be shared with the township and the county. It is not clear how much of it was retained by the village; whatever was retained, however, was sunk into the new calcium carbonate factory and thus lost. *Ad hoc* contributions are in theory voluntary donations from the enterprises to the village, which do not appear in the books. Since the village party secretary and the manager of the acetylene factory were one and the same person, money could be transferred without consultation.

A newspaper article [*Leshan Ribao*, 1995] reports that the village TVEs financed the following expenses: support for three poor households (unspecified); subsidies to cadre salaries (unspecified); disaster relief for a villager whose house had collapsed (10,000 *yuan*); renovation of the village school (38,000); construction of a motor road and two bridges (100,000); renovation of a historical building (50,000). The relatively small recurrent expenses for cadre subsidies and welfare were probably covered by the enterprise management fee; all other expenses were irregular *tanpai* contributions. The main item on the list – 100,000 *yuan* for a road and bridges – came from the initial RCC loan, not from enterprise profits. Even if we include this sum, total expenses amount to no more than 0.5 per cent of the village gross value of industrial output (GVIO) for the years between 1988 and 1995. Of course, even small sums can be helpful, but the question remains whether the same objectives could not have been reached without plunging the village into debt.

A frequently cited reason for TVE development is that tax income from industry helps to lower the tax burdens of rural households. This was not the case in Chenyan, where agricultural taxes were already low, simply because landholdings were extremely small. Per capita agricultural tax was two to five *yuan* per year; village and township fees (*tiliu*) were just below 20 *yuan* per capita.[8] TVE expansion had no impact on taxation in the village. This leaves employment as the main potential benefit for the village. In 1994, Chenyan's workforce numbered 740 able-bodied adults, of which 130 worked in agriculture, 15 in construction, two in transportation, ten in small commerce, and 40 in service industries (including artisans other than papermakers). The remaining 543 were 'industrial personnel': factory workers and papermakers. At their peak, the village factories employed about 110 staff and workers, but only one-third of them (mainly staff) came from Chenyan. This leaves us with 50 villagers, at the very most, in factory employment; the remaining 493 worked in the paper workshops.

Factory jobs came in two sorts: backbreaking manual labour in the Xinghuo factory and clerical jobs in the clean, automated acetylene factory. Manual work at Xinghuo held little attraction for people in the village: it was as hard and dirty as papermaking and incomes were slightly lower. What is more, wages were often withheld for months.[9] Office jobs (and jobs as drivers, cooks or doormen) were coveted, but there were only about 30 of them, and years went by without vacancies. One of the arguments in favour of TVEs was that they would provide employment for unskilled workers. However, even unskilled workers could find better-paying jobs in the paper industry. The main beneficiaries of the factories were thus the 30 persons employed in clerical and managerial functions, as managers, accountants, sales agents, secretaries, etc. All of them are villagers, and many have been cadres under the collectives. Their wages are not high (factory directors earn 350 *yuan* a month, 50 more than workers) but they are paid with greater regularity; moreover, these jobs offer opportunity to earn money on the side.

On the negative side of the balance sheet, there is the debt of six million *yuan*. The general opinion in the village is that debt payment will never be enforced. Theoretically, debtors could sue the village, but a court-enforced auction of factory assets would bring in so little money that it is hardly worth the trouble. People also say that the Muchang RCC, as the main debtor, will continue to protect the village factories. However, even if debt payment is not enforced, the village is paralysed by its crippling debt. As one villager remarked, 'whoever will be the next party secretary will be in trouble' (*shei dang shuji shei daomei*).

A Bifurcated Village Economy

Economic activity in Chenyan falls into two distinct spheres: collective (*jiti*) and household-run (*jiating jingying*). Here as elsewhere in China, rural residents are classified as 'agricultural population' (*nongye renkou*), regardless of actual occupation. Papermaking is classified as a domestic sideline (*jiating fuye*), not an industry, and therefore neither taxed nor registered and only minimally supervised by the state.[10] This is despite the fact that some household workshops are, in fact, factories comparable in size to small TVEs. Since the return to household production, the paper industry has undergone a minor technological revolution. Mechanical pulp beaters, aggressive chemicals and steel-reinforced pressure steamers have reduced the production cycle from two or three months to about ten days. Most household workshops own only a diesel-powered pulp beater (the pressure steamers are owned and run by specialists who rent out their services to household producers), but since 1994, the first fully mechanized workshops have appeared. In Chenyan, mechanization was pioneered by Chen Fucai, the village head who had so energetically pursued the early 'projects' but lost his position in 1990. After years of unsuccessful experiments with private projects, ranging from household appliances to a chicken farm, Fucai returned to papermaking. His son, a worker in the county paper factory, built a continuous-belt paper machine from scrap metal; amazingly, it worked. Fucai's workshop was soon imitated by a Chenyan paper trader, and a third and much larger project is under way. Despite their size and complexity, these factories (for that is what in fact they are) are classified as household sidelines, not as businesses.

On the other side of the private–collective divide, there are the village factories. Though they would fail to impress visitors from Chengdu or Beijing, they look distinctly urban: they are housed in walled compounds; their gates are decorated with nameplates watched by doormen; workers wear white coats and caps, similar to those of urban employees. Bruun [1993] noted the importance of dress codes in the occupational hierarchy: white coats symbolize high status of clerical and managerial jobs, where one does not dirty one's clothes. The difference between clean, quasi-urban factory jobs and dirty manual labour is underlined by different terms for work: papermakers and farmers 'work' (*gan huo*) or 'toil' (*da gong*, used only for wage work); factory workers, like urban people, 'have a job' (*gongzuo*) or 'go to the office' (*shang ban*). In contrast to papermakers, who return to work immediately after gulping down their lunch, factory personnel eat good meals in their canteens and enjoy long breaks after lunch. This gives them opportunity to socialize with village leaders or play table tennis in the factory courtyard. The difference between TVE 'workers' and papermaking 'peasants' was brought home to me at an athletic competition in the township seat. Chenyan was represented by a truckload of young men and women – basketball players, runners, dancers, singers, and so on. Practically all of them were factory personnel. Youths from the paper workshops lack the leisure for such activities and are excluded from 'urban' forms of social intercourse.

A Bifurcated Village Administration

The most palpable contribution of the factories to village life is that they pay reasonable salaries to village officials, who co-function as factory directors, sales representatives, security officials, and so on. Compared to an 'empty-shell' village such as Qingshan, officials in Chenyan are well paid and motivated. The drawback is that village functionaries spend more time working for the enterprises and increasingly see themselves as factory employees, rather than officials. The village administration is housed in the acetylene factory, whose office space, canteen, guesthouse, and car park it shares. No attempt is made to keep village and factory functions apart; depending on the need of the moment, officials represent the village or the factory. Since the factory lies on the very margin of the village territory, the village committee decided to establish a second office in the Xinghuo factory, closer to the hills where most people live. The Xinghuo office is staffed by two persons – the village head and the director of the village women's federation, who are in charge of household registration, tax collection and birth control. Both complain about their work, which brings them into frequent conflict with other villagers; in fact, the village head has stopped attending to his work. The main office in the acetylene factory houses the party secretary, the accountant, the security officer and 15 to 20 staff. From time to time, villagers pass by to make phone calls or enquire about administrative matters, but by and large, work is oriented towards the outside world. Village officials now tend to see the household economy as outside their scope of activity. Some regret this and would like to see a return to a collective system, but most accept that households 'can no longer be controlled' (*guanbuliao*) and therefore has to be left alone. Papermaking, which still dictates the rhythm of life for most Chenyan villagers, remains untaxed, unregulated and unnoticed. Papermakers do not complain about their invisibility, which (in the short term, at least) they see as beneficial.

Statistical Distortions

Officials from the village to the county level describe papermaking as a remnant of the past: worth preserving, perhaps, for folkloristic reasons, but economically irrelevant. Since household-owned paper workshops are not registered and output is no longer counted, such claims are difficult to check. Evidence from the village and the township, however, points to a systematic pattern of statistical distortion reminiscent of the Maoist period [*Cai*, 2000]. Township cadres, whose careers depend on their ability to meet mandated targets, systematically overreport growth in industrial output and household incomes. Village cadres have less of an incentive to exaggerate, but often find it impossible to resist pressure from above. The bias is cumulative, with each administrative level adding to the figures they receive. Let us look at how this worked in the case of Chenyan. According to the village accountant, the total output value of the village factories in 1994 was 3.7 million *yuan*. By rounding up this figure and adding three million *yuan* for the handicraft paper industry, he arrived at an industrial output value of seven million. A 1995 newspaper report quotes the figure of ten million and attributes all of it to the village factories; papermaking is no longer mentioned as a contributing factor [*Leshan Ribao*, 1995]. Township statistics more than doubled this already inflated figure, arriving at a GVIO of 18.8 million. In short, the output value of the factories quintupled from 3.7 to 18.8 million on the way from the village to the township; it is likely that it further increased in reports to the county.

Another distorting factor comes from the emphasis on output rather than profit. Maoist China, like other socialist economies, fetishized output growth at the expense of other indicators, and the same emphasis on brute volume continued to shape TVE growth in Jiajiang. Until 1994, turnover taxes accounted for the lion's share of fiscal revenue, so governments had a strong incentive to increase output volume even at the expense of profits; similarly, output growth, rather than profitability, is a core target in cadre assessments [*Edin*, this issue]. In Jiajiang, the emphasis on quantitative growth resulted in a preference for high-output, low-profit industries such as bricks or saltpetre. Papermaking and other low-output, high-value industries were neglected partly because they did not provide the kind of dramatic growth that officials wished to see. According to imperfect data, paper output grew by an annual seven per cent between 1990 and 1999 – respectable but a far cry from growth rates in TVEs. In contrast to TVEs, however, paper workshops produced reliable profits.

Although ignored by the local state, papermaking is still an important source of income and employment. In Muchang, where papermaking is most concentrated, 43 per cent of the rural workforce works in industry (which is practically synonymous with papermaking), compared to 6.5 per cent in the county as a whole, and 18 per cent in Huangtu, the most industrially advanced township. Papermaking, with an estimated employment of 5,000, provides one-half of the jobs in rural industry [*Anon.*, 1998]. Sixty-two per cent of gross rural household incomes in Muchang came from industry, against 33 per cent for the county as a whole [*Anon.*, 1995]. From the perspective of the rural population, then, papermaking is still important.

CONCLUSION

'Blind development' (*mangmu fazhan*) and a 'greed for size' (*tanda qiujin*) were common characteristics of TVE development in Sichuan. Guo Xiaoming [1996] found that TVEs in Sichuan were overly dependent on bank loans, clustered in a few sectors, technically backward, and did too little research on market demand. Instead of making use of cheap rural labour, they clustered in capital-intensive but low-tech branches that were out of line with their factor endowment. TVEs in the 1990s, in the view of some Chinese critics, had become 'small state-owned enterprises'.

Western scholars, too, pointed out problems inherent in rapid TVE growth. One early critic [*Wong*, 1991: 694] argued that distorted tax signals 'ensured that much of the investment [in TVEs] was wasted in duplicated and socially irrational projects', and that the convergence of interests between local governments and enterprises was 'good for growth, as shown by the willingness of local financial departments to support investment, working closely with enterprises in hammering out investment packages ... [but was] not conducive to efficiency' [711]. A recent article [*Gore*, 1999] argues forcefully that TVE development is shaped by the legacy of the Maoist past. Until the late 1990s, localities were assigned growth targets, leaders who failed to meet them were punished, target overfulfilment was rewarded. Budget constraints for TVEs were hard compared to those of state-owned enterprises [*Byrd and Gelb*, 1990; *Chen* et al., 1994] but softer than in private firms. Sjöberg and Zhang [1998] found that loss-making collective firms continued to have access to bank loans for a much longer time than did private enterprises; when they ran out of bank loans, they still had access to other sources of credit, such as delayed wage payments. Taxation, too, was soft, as local governments tolerated arrears by their own firms. Attempts to impose credit controls on TVEs were sabotaged by officials who controlled local lending; banks often saw themselves as developmental agencies whose main purpose it was to facilitate growth [*Oi*, 1999]. All this was in sharp contrast to the hard constraints under which papermakers (and other rural households) operated: if their workshops lost money, nobody bailed them out. All but a few well-connected villagers found it impossible to get loans, since banks and RCCs prefer to lend to TVEs. As one Qingshan villager put it, 'without money or power, you just can't get a loan' (*meiqian meiquan de, daibuliao kuan*).

POSTSCRIPT

In 1998, Jiajiang county embarked on a twofold restructuring drive: practically all remaining collective TVEs were privatized, and all energies were mobilized to expand Jiajiang's 'pillar industry', ceramic wall and floor tiles. Privatization was conducted campaign-style: the county government issued detailed guidelines (including quotas), which were then implemented by the 'lower levels'. Despite half-hearted injunctions against 'one size fits all' policies, the county clearly aimed at, and nearly achieved, 100 per cent privatization: by 2000, private enterprises accounted for 97 per cent of gross output value. Privatization did not mean that the state withdrew from the scene; rather, it changed its mode of operation [*Oi and Walder*, 1999; *Unger and Chan*, 1999]. Rather than mobilizing local resources, state officials now focus on providing a stable, low-cost environment that will attract investors. This includes, next to good infrastructure and 'relaxed policies', the promise of social stability. As Jiajiang's party secretary put it, 'stability is the precondition for the development of our specialized economy. The county's party and government have to do a good job in detecting and resolving social conflicts; disturbances affecting the masses have to be nipped in the bud' [*Li*, 1999: 139].

At the same time, the county mobilized all its resources to put Jiajiang on the map as the largest producer of ceramic tiles in western China. The industry has expanded at a tremendous rate; in 2000, 87 factories were operational and another 29 under construction. Production value is planned to increase sixfold until 2005; by 2010, the industry should account for 85 per cent of the county's total economy. Until 1998 at least, the county used local banks to steer development and to sustain rapid growth through six consecutive years of losses [*Anon.*, 1998]. Since then, it has relied on Mao-style exhortations,[11] zoning policies, regulatory powers and incentives to realize its vision of Jiajiang as 'the ceramic tile capital of western China'. It may be that this time county leaders got it right, and that ceramic tiles are indeed the ticket to prosperity. If not, the county as a whole will replicate the experience of Chenyan village, and end up heavily indebted.

NOTES

1. To be precise, the term usually translated as TVE (*xiangzhen qiye*) refers to all rural enterprises, whether owned by collectives, individuals or partnerships. Collective rural enterprises are more properly called *xiangcun qiye*, sometimes rendered as township-and-village-owned-enterprises (TVOEs). In everyday speech, however (at least in the areas I am familiar with), *xiangzhen qiye* is reserved for enterprises closely identified with the local state.
2. Names of individuals and villages have been altered.
3. The same observation is made by Oi [1999: 35–6, 171].
4. This practice is known as 'bringing in capital when one joins the factory' (*daizi ruchang*). In the Chenyan factories, workers were required to invest 1,000 *yuan* in shares, and to pay another 1,000 as security deposit.
5. Acetylene is used for welding in the construction industry, which is sensitive to economic downturns.
6. From 1983 to 1987, Chen Hongli toured the United States, demonstrating traditional

papermaking in exhibitions organized by the Chinese Association for Science and Technology.

7. Ruf (1998: 31, 45) reports a similar case from Qiaolou village, some 40 km from Chenyan. In this case, 'a young man with ties to a sworn brotherhood organization had coerced Qiaolou authorities into leasing him several rooms in the village office building for use as a restaurant and private karaoke club'.

8. Taxes elsewhere in Jiajiang were slightly higher. Huatou township, which is almost entirely agricultural, collects 26 *yuan* in *tiliu* charges, and 24 *yuan* agricultural tax. Even this is extremely low by rural standards of the 1990s.

9. Xinghuo pays piece-rate wages, which average around 300 *yuan* a month; additional benefits (health care, bonuses, New Year presents) amount to 200 *yuan* a year per worker. The acetylene factory pays an average monthly wage of 270 *yuan*, for far less demanding work. Average wages in the paper industry are above 300 *yuan*.

10. The paper trade, however, is taxed, and is a major source of revenue.

11. Officials and managers are exhorted to 'firmly grasp the Five Destroy and Five Establish', which include the 'destruction of the small peasant mentality of fearfulness, satisfaction with small progress, contentment with modest wealth' and the 'establishment of a new mentality of being wealthy and desiring more, doing great deeds, striving to break through, climbing new steps', and similar slogans.

REFERENCES

Anon., 1995, '1994 nian nongye shengchan, nongcun jingji qingkuang' (Agricultural production and rural economic conditions in Jiajiang county, 1994), Jiajiang (xeroxed manuscript).

Anon., 1998, 'Jiajiang zhiye shengchan jingying de diaocha baogao' (Survey report on production and management of the Jiajiang paper industry), *Diaocha yu xinxi*, Jiajiang: Zhongguo renmin yinhang, Jiajiang zhihang (xeroxed manuscript).

Bruun, Ole, 1993, *Business and Bureaucracy in a Chinese City: An Ethnography of Private Business Households in Contemporary China*, Berkeley, CA: Institute of East Asian Studies, University of California.

Byrd, William A. and Alan Gelb, 1990, 'Why Industrialize: The Incentives for Rural Community Governments', in Byrd and Lin (eds.) [1990].

Byrd, William A. and Lin Qingsong (eds.), 1990, *China's Rural Industry: Structure, Development, and Reform*, Oxford: Oxford University Press.

Cai, Yongshun, 2000, 'Between State and Peasant: Local Cadres and Statistical Reporting in Rural China', *The China Quarterly*, No.163 (Sept.), pp.783–805.

Chen, Chunlai, Christopher Findlay, Andrew Watson and Zhang Xiaohe, 1994, 'Rural Enterprise Growth in a Partially Reformed Economy', in Findlay *et al.* [1994].

Findlay, Christopher, Andrew Watson and Harry X. Wu, 1994, *Rural Enterprise in China*, New York: St Martin's Press.

Gore, Lance L.P., 1999, 'The Communist Legacy in Post-Mao Economic Growth', *The China Journal*, No.41 (Jan.), pp.25–54.

Guo, Xiaoming, 1996, 'Lüelun xinan sanshengde nongcun gongyehua fazhan' (Brief discussion of the industrial development of the three southwestern provinces), *Sichuan daxue xuebao (zhexue shekeban)*, No.4, pp.3–7.

JJNJ, Jiajiangxian difangzhi bianzou weiyuanhui, 1990–2000, *Jiajiangxian nianjian* (Yearbook of Jiajiang County), Jiajiang: Sichuansheng Jiajiangxian difangshi bangongshi.

Leshan Ribao, 1995, 'Zhixiang daitouren – ji sheng laomo Chen Hongli' (A leader of the paper county: Interviewing provincial labour model Chen Hongli), *Leshan Ribao*, 9 Oct. 1995, p.3.

Li, Liugen, 1999, 'Fazhan tese jingji, peizhi zhizhu chanye' (Develop an economy with special characteristics, cultivate the pillar industry), in Jiajiangxian difangzhi bianzou weiyuanhui, 1999, *Jiajiangxian nianjian* (Yearbook of Jiajiang County), Jiajiang: Sichuansheng Jiajiangxian difangshi bangongshi, pp.138–9.

Oi, Jean C., 1992, 'Fiscal Reform and the Economic Foundation of Local State Corporatism in

China', *World Politics*, No.45, pp.99–126.

Oi, Jean C., 1999, *Rural China Takes Off: Institutional Foundations of Economic Reform*, Berkeley, CA: University of California Press.

Oi, Jean C. and Andrew G. Walder (eds.), 1999, *Property Rights and Economic Reform in China*, Stanford: Stanford University Press.

Ruf, Gregory A., 1998, *Cadres and Kin: Making a Socialist Village in West China, 1921–1991*, Stanford: Stanford University Press.

Sjöberg, Örjan and Zhang Gang, 1998, 'Soft Budget Constraints in Chinese Rural Enterprises', in Flemming Christiansen and Zhang Junzuo (eds.), 1998, *Village Inc.: Chinese Rural Society in the 1990s*, Richmond: Curzon Press.

Unger, Jonathan and Anita Chan, 1999, 'Inheritors of the Boom: Private Enterprise and the Role of Local Government in a Rural South China Township', *The China Journal*, No.42 (July), pp.45–74.

Walder, Andrew G. (ed.), 1998, *Zouping in Transition: The Process of Reform in Rural North China*, Cambridge, MA: Harvard University Press.

Wong, Christine P., 1988, 'Interpreting Rural Industrial Growth in the Post-Mao Period', *Modern China*, Vol.14, No.1, pp.3–30.

Wong, Christine P., 1991, 'Central–Local Relations in an Era of Fiscal Decline: The Paradox of Fiscal Decentralization in Post-Mao China', *The China Quarterly*, No.128 (Dec.), pp.691–715.

Determinants of Income from Wages in Rural Wuxi and Baoding: A Survey of 22 Villages

EDUARD B. VERMEER

INTRODUCTION: THE NEED FOR ACCURATE RURAL WAGE AND INCOME DATA

During the collective period until the early 1980s, natural resource advantages and location were the main determinants of income differentials between Chinese villages. Cash income was obtained mainly from sales of vegetables from the private plot and minor farm products. Politicians stressed the human factor and particularly village leadership as a major factor in the development of the village economy. However, severe restrictions on the scope and size of village non-agricultural activities and very limited access to urban labour markets did not permit much differentiation of economic activities and off-farm income. Since the introduction of private farming and the booming development of both urban and rural economies, opportunities for off-farm income have increased tremendously. In this article, we will identify the main determinants of wage income in rural China on the basis of a 1998 survey of about 3,500 households in 11 villages in Wuxi municipality (eight of which are located in present Xishan municipality, three in the city) in Jiangsu province and another 11 in Baoding municipality (nine of which are in Qingyuan county, two in the city) in Hebei province.[1]

The following includes all reported wage earnings of individual rural residents, irrespective of the enterprise, sector or locality where they were earned. First, we consider their size and contribution to average household income. Second, we will isolate contributing factors to wage earnings, such as age, position in the household, household composition, gender, education, profession and place of work. Finally, we will examine in detail the wage earnings of Communist Party and Youth League members. These aspects will be considered at the individual, household, village or county level.

Eduard Vermeer, Senior Lecturer, Sinological Institute, Leiden University. Email: e.b.vermeer@ let.leidenuniv.nl.

Wages are to some extent related to non-wage income from agricultural undertakings and sidelines. In order to be able to attract rural labour, in theory off-farm jobs should offer higher wages than the expected income from farming. However, individual labourers may be attracted to off-farm employment for reasons other than monetary reward. Moreover, the forfeited net income from farm labour is not entirely predictable or constant, so labourers cannot make a perfectly rational choice. Farm households are restricted in their choice of employment because of legal or contractual obligations towards village government and the state (such as growing grain for their own consumption). Finally, labour markets are not free, but controlled to a considerable extent by township and village cadres and city governments. Nevertheless, the very high level of underemployment in agriculture in China makes it possible to allocate a substantial or main part of farm household labour to non-agricultural undertakings and wage employment.

'Off-farm income' is not limited to income from paid labour, but includes non-farm business. The 1997 First National Agricultural Census showed 24.4 per cent of rural main jobs to be unrelated to farming (industry 9 per cent, construction 3.7 per cent, retail, trade and catering 3.3 per cent, and transportation 1.6 per cent). Forty-two per cent of the 136.5 million non-farm jobs were urban. In the eastern region of China, rural non-farm employment was 33.5 per cent of total employment or twice the all-China average. This classification does not capture the economic and social contribution of secondary occupations.[2]

The two rural survey areas may represent the agricultural north and industrialized east of China. In Qingyuan, rural income is slightly below the national average, in spite of the area being only 100 miles away from Beijing. The main reasons are a lack of diversification in farming, and a relatively small number of off-farm labourers; both factors might be attributed to a lack of capital and industrial experience, and to the mutually reinforcing conservative attitudes of local political leaders and farmers. With an average of 0.4–0.7 hectares per farm, during much of the year there is not enough work in crop cultivation even for one labourer. Returns have become barely enough for subsistence. Any substantial increase in income has to come from animal husbandry, sidelines, or from off-farm employment.

In contrast, Wuxi/Xishan is rich. It has a long-standing tradition of commercial agriculture, silk cultivation, skilled labour and rural industries, and a favourable location. Since the 1970s, using their acquired skills and personal connections, local returnees from Shanghai set up new factories with machinery, financial support or subcontracting agreements from their previous Shanghai companies. In recent years, most farmland is tended by outside farmers or labourers, under the so-called two-field system; thus, most villagers have been freed from crop cultivation and find their primary work in diversified undertakings and factory jobs.

Several reasons may be put forward to explain the until recently rather low-income differentials *within* villages in China: the tradition of collective ownership of production means, and their rather equal distribution (and as for land, periodic redistribution) since 1984; the tradition of egalitarian income distribution on a mixed per capita and per labourer basis; the short period of post-collective individual savings and capital accumulation; and the rather equal number of children since the adoption of the two- or one-child policy. Other trends may have had an equalizing effect, but await confirmation from research: taxation and fees demanded by village governments and cadres weighing most heavily on the rich; allocation by village government of new off-farm employment to the young; the earnings by out-migrants, usually from the younger and poorer segments of the village labour force; and Chinese Communist Party policies supportive of the poorest households. Most likely, the effects differ between rich and poor regions. Local cadres have considerable influence on management and income from collective village assets and job allocation. But the egalitarian tradition is disappearing fast.

Official Chinese statistics do not provide household-based and individual-based wage earnings data like our 1998 survey. The State Statistical Bureau (SSB) publishes three types of rural wage data, none of which distinguishes between gender, age, education or other factors. First, it reports the total wage sum and the number of employees (based on the all-year average) of both collectively owned and private rural industries; from that, one cannot simply deduce an average wage per full-time employee because the wage sum includes non-wage expenditure such as pensions and social security payments. Moreover, many enterprises do not provide their employees with the opportunity to work the whole year. In 1998, we noted daily wages of about 10–15 *yuan* in Qingyuan and of about 25 *yuan* in Wuxi (one *yuan* equals US$ 0.12). Second, the SSB reports average rural per capita wage earnings, called 'labourers' remuneration', on the basis of its annual sample of 70,000 rural households who are asked to keep day-to-day accounts of their income and expenditure. According to this survey, in Hebei and Jiangsu provinces 1997 rural wage income averaged 762 *yuan* and 1,235 *yuan*, respectively, which was 33 and 38 per cent of total net income. [*State Statistical Bureau*, 1998: 347]. However, because of selection biases and limited sample size, the margin of error is considerable. Third, data are collected from over 20,000 rural so-called fixed observation households, almost 80 per cent of which have been in this sample since 1986. They show that in 1997 in the eastern Chinese provinces, 66.4 per cent and 12.3 per cent, respectively, of total household income came from household business and

wages earned outside [*Nongcun*, 2000]. The representativeness of this sample
has suffered from ageing, and its size is rather small. The three types of
surveys have rather different outcomes. In a recent article, a director of the
SSB indicated the impossibility of producing rural household income and
expenditure data according to the international standard for national economic
accounts and the data on rural household income and expenditure from
irregular activities as two main weaknesses of the present system [*Xu*, 1999].
There is a clear need for more reliable and extensive data about rural
individual and household wage earnings.

WAGE EARNINGS, BUSINESS AND OTHER RURAL INCOME SOURCES

Our survey showed average wage earnings of 13,033 *yuan* per household,
or 3,385 *yuan* per capita in Wuxi, and 3,792 *yuan* per household, or 943
yuan per capita in Qingyuan.[3] Four factors contributed to the difference: a
higher participation rate, a higher percentage of people of working age,
more working days per labourer, and higher wage rates. A fifth factor,
average household size, differed only slightly between the two regions (3.85
persons in Wuxi and 4.02 in Qingyuan), but more between villages (3.4–4.3
in Wuxi, 3.5–4.4 in Qingyuan).

Ninety-one per cent of the 1,118 Wuxi households earned wages as
compared to 62 per cent of the 2,003 Qingyuan households. Seventy per
cent of our Wuxi sample population was of working age (defined as 18 to
60), as against 61.5 per cent in Qingyuan. Percentages varied between 64 in
Xi'nan and 74–76 in Qianjin and Wutang, both belonging to Wuxi city and
subject to the one-child policy. In Qingyuan, only suburban Xueliuying and
Dazhuze had such high percentages, likewise because of a small number of
children. In other Qingyuan villages 28–36 per cent of the population was
below the age of 18, two-thirds more than in Wuxi.

Villagers in Wuxi working for wages outside the village worked 28 per
cent more days per labourer and earned 50 per cent higher daily wages than
those from Qingyuan.[4] That Wuxi wages were higher is shown in Tables 4
and 5; the most common non-farm category of workers (*gongren*), earned
58 per cent more in Wuxi than in Qingyuan (8,507 *yuan* as against 5,398
yuan), and in most other categories the difference was even larger. Wage
levels reported to us in both places pointed to a larger difference for daily
or short-term labour than for permanent jobs; in Qingyuan, daily wage
levels vary according to season, and are highest during the harvest. Fewer
households in Wuxi had members working outside the village, namely 44
per cent as against 54 per cent in Qingyuan, but Wuxi had more outside
workers *per household*, namely two as against 1.5 in Qingyuan. In general,

a higher participation rate and wage reflect greater employment opportunities and greater emancipation of women from work at home (see Table 6). However, in the village with the highest level of income, Taihu, over one-third of households (many of whom are entrepreneurs or independent fishermen) did not have wage income.

In Wuxi, seven out of 11 villages had household wage earnings below the 13,000-*yuan* average. Linong, which is entirely industrialized, stood out with almost 30,000 *yuan*, and suburban Qianjin with over 17,000 *yuan*. Managing directors may have difficulty in defining income as either from their own business or from wage. Wages averaged 55 per cent of total income, with large variations between villages. In Qingyuan, wage earnings differed even more between villages: over 11,000 *yuan* and 6,000 *yuan* of wages per household in urbanized Xueliuying and Dazhuze; 3,300–4,600 *yuan* in three other villages; and only 1,700–2,500 *yuan* in the other seven. This demonstrates the effects of urbanization and labour market barriers in rural China, and the unevenness of industrial and commercial development in Qingyuan.

Remunerated labour is only one source of rural income. In Tables 1 and 2, we have listed income from four categories. 'Wage' refers to income from remunerated labour. 'Business' corresponds to the Chinese term 'household business', mostly farming or other industry. 'Transfer income' consists of remittances by people working elsewhere, gifts from relatives and friends, insurance, relief funds, pensions and other social security payments, compensation for renting land, etc. 'Property income' may be interest on deposits, dividends, rents received, and other items; it is limited to monetary income, and additions to stock or capital gains are not included. The number of respondents was larger than that for the question about individual wages, and reported totals in Qingyuan were not always accurate. Moreover, net income from business is hard to define. Respondents were asked to report net earnings, but in China as elsewhere, there is no single accounting method to establish net business income. Often, depreciation is too low, some capital costs are not accounted for, added or lost value embedded in animal stock is disregarded, and input costs are overestimated. So figures are approximations only.

Wuxi

Business income yielded 37 per cent of the total household income of 23,588 *yuan*. Of that, crop growing only yielded nine per cent. Local governments in south Jiangsu have instituted the 'two-field system' (forbidden elsewhere) under which most land is rented out by the village collectively to 'big farmers' (*danonghu*), and most villagers take care only of the land needed for their own grain consumption. Moreover, they

TABLE 1

AVERAGE HOUSEHOLD EARNINGS FROM VARIOUS SOURCES IN
WUXI/XISHAN VILLAGES

Village	Wage income (yuan)	Business income (yuan)	Of which crops (yuan)	Transfer income (yuan)	>0 (n)	Property income (yuan)	Total income (yuan)	Wage % of income	House-hold size (p.)	n
1 Qianjin	17,279	6,511	1,584	1,305	34	1,764	26,860	64	3.84	114
2 Wutang	12,514	6,688	4,269	1,363	41	1,228	21,793	57	3.89	74
3 Ma'an	10,831	9,457	2,707	1,387	17	304	21,979	49	3.73	51
4 Zhuangqiao	13,609	2,026	1,334	795	26	681	17,110	80	4.03	94
5 Taihu	8,653	46,642	1,874	1,930	34	852	58,077	15	4.28	60
6 Caozhuang	9,087	12,202	3,212	2,468	85	48	23,805	38	4.15	113
7 Liugang	12,207	4,635	1,824	986	44	725	18,554	66	3.70	187
8 Yudong	9,810	7,034	2,612	672	25	46	17,562	56	3.85	126
9 Huasanfang	7,370	13,714	2,127	957	43	72	22,112	33	3.39	79
10 Linong	29,969	4,972	2,676	2,114	42	691	37,747	79	4.25	52
11 Xi'nan	15,753	3,376	1,405	1,020	159	78	20,227	78	3.60	167
Total	13,033	8,730	2,192	1,267	550	559	23,588	55	3.85	1,118

Data in this table and all other tables are from the 1997 WuBao survey, see endnote 1.

may sublet their plots to others. Income from crop growing is still important to the households of some villages, but in most it yields less than ten per cent of total household income. Taihu village (no. 5) stands out because of high income from fisheries, and Linong (no. 10) because of high managerial wages.

Transfer income. Half (550) of all households reported to have transfer income. In villages with a high response rate, such as villages nos. 11, 10 and 6, transferred incomes averaged 1,000–2,500 *yuan*. Underreporting may have been rather high for remittances from people living elsewhere and rather low for social security payments. Pensions were responsible for 47 per cent of all transfer incomes. Two hundred and twenty-seven households (20 per cent) reported income from pensions, averaging 2,953 *yuan*. Pensions are correlated with high wage income; in four out of the five villages with the lowest average wage income less than ten per cent of sampled households received any pension. This may be explained by the fact that some village governments have instituted pension schemes while others have not. Only 22 households received some kind of relief payments, of between 400 *yuan* and 4,200 *yuan*. Underreporting was most obvious for the category 'gifts received from relatives and friends in the village'. Only 82 households reported that they had received such gifts, to a total of 277,000 *yuan*. In contrast, over ten times as many (923 households) reported having donated such gifts, amounting to 1,307,000 *yuan*. Apparently, our respondents chose to record what they gave rather than what they received.

Property income. Only 25 per cent of all households reported to have had property income, averaging 2,250 *yuan*. The mean figure of 559 *yuan* for all households is an understatement. Local bank managers stated that the average household had 30,000–50,000 *yuan* in savings, yielding an annual interest of about 2,000 *yuan*. Some high incomes were derived from share dividends. Nine households reported 10,000–20,000 *yuan*, and another 22 households reported 5,000–10,000 *yuan* of income from capital assets. Per capita, our survey figures of transfer income and property income were 329 *yuan* and 145 *yuan*. The first is almost double the 1997 rural Shanghai figure of 171 *yuan*; the second is almost the same as the Shanghai figure of 144 *yuan* [*State Statistical Bureau*, 1998]. Our survey appears to show figures superior to official statistics for transfer income, but equally wanting with regard to property income.

Qingyuan

Results for transfer and property income and income were uneven. In two villages, ten per cent or more of income came from property income; in other villages almost nothing. Transfer income varied between one and seven per cent. The combined average of seven per cent was only slightly lower than in Wuxi. Labour remuneration was responsible for 28 per cent, with seven villages in a range from 16 to 23 per cent, or half the Wuxi figure.

TABLE 2

AVERAGE HOUSEHOLD EARNINGS FROM VARIOUS SOURCES IN
BAODING/QINGYUAN VILLAGES

Village	Wage income (*yuan*)	Business income (*yuan*)	Transfer income (*yuan*)	Property income (*yuan*)	Total income (*yuan*)	Wage % in income	House- hold size (p.)	n
1 Xueliuying	11,460	4,094	772	1,784	18,110	63	3.83	189
2 Dazhuze	6,383	13,033	373	2,922	22,711	22	3.50	216
3 Dongguzhuang	2,284	8,797	267	22	11,370	20	3.94	179
4 Heqiao	2,032	6,615	315	49	9,011	23	4.44	232
5 Dayangxijie	3,997	13,373	567	203	18,140	22	4.02	131
6 Liluohou	4,589	4,794	568	14	9,966	46	4.10	165
7 Gushang	1,976	10,412	130	7	12,525	16	4.12	300
8 Xiezhuangcun	1,961	7,709	780	7	10,458	19	3.76	226
9 Dongmeng	1,658	14,446	354	4	16,461	10	4.20	138
10 Nandengcun	2,503	8,854	346	33	11,737	21	4.24	156
11 Caijiaying	3,304	6,291	328	0	9,924	33	4.14	71
Total	3,792	8,951	428	510	13,681	28	4.02	2,003

The variation between villages in Qingyuan reflects different levels of economic development. Some villages had cooperative shareholding schemes, while others had not. We were not entirely successful in overcoming people's reluctance to disclose non-labour income, and response rates were low. The survey showed that average income from business was 2.4 times wage income, namely 8,951 *yuan* versus 3,792 *yuan*, and in seven villages over three times as high. Household business, mainly farming, still is the mainstay of the Qingyuan rural economy.

WAGE EARNINGS OF VARIOUS HOUSEHOLD MEMBERS

Qingyuan

On average, almost one member per household participated in wage labour. In suburban Xueliuying and Dazhuze over half of the household heads, three-quarters of adult children and about half of the spouses earned wages, totalling 1.5 to two members per household. In contrast, three villages had 0.2–0.4 wage earners per household only, with less than 20 per cent of their household heads participating, and few spouses and adult children. On average, 44 per cent of household heads had wage earnings, and in only two villages less than 20 per cent. In most villages, adult child participation rates were 25–50 per cent, and spouse participation rates between five and ten per cent only. Apparently, not only did off-farm wage employment opportunities differ greatly, but also the propensity of heads, spouses and children to work for wages. See Table 3.

TABLE 3

NUMBER OF HOUSEHOLD HEADS, ADULT CHILDREN AND MAIN WAGE
EARNERS BY POSITION IN HOUSEHOLD, BAODING/QINGYUAN
(wage earnings above 500 *yuan* only; wage-earning children aged 18 and above)

Village	Household heads	Adult children	*of which*: Wage earners				Per h.h.
			Head	Spouse	Child	Sum	
1 Xueliuying	193	239	105	99	189	393	2.0
2 Dazhuze	221	158	133	91	111	335	1.5
3 Dongguzhuang	177	115	62	8	39	109	0.6
4 Heqiao	231	152	79	13	47	139	0.6
5 Dayangxijie	133	86	55	21	45	121	0.9
6 Liluohou	167	106	113	17	48	178	1.1
7 Gushang	302	176	209	3	43	255	0.8
8 Xiezhuangcun	233	137	32	2	9	43	0.2
9 Dongmengzhuang	140	93	28	7	20	55	0.4
10 Nandengcun	158	92	69	6	37	112	0.7
11 Caijiaying	71	57	8	7	8	23	0.3
Total	2,026	1,411	893	276	629	1,788	0.9
Average participation rate			44%	14%	45%		

A truer picture of wage-earning household members emerges if one selects wage earnings between 3,000 *yuan* and 12,000 *yuan*, in order to show more or less full-time wages, leaving out both low and exceptionally high earnings. Mean wage earnings of different members then become strikingly similar, with a variation of only ten per cent (n=1,289; see Table 4). Surprisingly, on average household heads earned less than spouses, namely 4,188 *yuan* versus 4,381 *yuan*; their *median* earnings were 20 per cent lower however, as one-third earned less than 3,000 *yuan*. Closer analysis reveals two reasons. First, spouses engaging in wage labour lived mainly in Xueliuying and Dazhuze, where wage earnings were highest. Second, 80 out of 275 spouses were male, most working in industry, and *their* average wage earnings were 5,742 *yuan*, as against 3,823 *yuan* for female spouses. Being a male spouse was work-related. Absence from home and the farm made men less suitable than their wives to head the household.

Wuxi

In Wuxi, differences in wage earnings between household members were substantial. Household heads had 63 per cent more wages than spouses and 21 per cent more than adult children. Exclusion of earnings below 3,000 *yuan* and above 12,000 *yuan* reduced wage differentials between heads and spouses to 26 per cent, and with adult children to seven per cent.

Table 5 shows that in Wuxi gender was the main explanation for different average wage earnings of heads and spouses. Male heads and spouses earned almost twice as much as their female equivalents. Omitting highest and lowest wages hardly changes average earnings of the spouses (5,380–5,449 *yuan*); in contrast, it makes male heads' average wage earnings drop from 8,991 to 6,686 *yuan* and all other male earnings (irrespective of household position) drop likewise by a considerable margin. About 15 per cent of household heads and sons had wage earnings above

TABLE 4

AVERAGE WAGE EARNINGS BY POSITION IN HOUSEHOLD,
BAODING/QINGYUAN

	500 *yuan* and above			3,000–12,000 *yuan* only			
	Mean	Median	Index	n	Mean	Median	Index
Heads	4,188	3,600	101	585	5,058	5,000	102
Spouses	4,381	4,500	106	229	4,944	4,800	100
Children >17 years.	3,992	3,600	96	455	4,809	4,800	97
Grandchildren	4,406	—	106	13	5,177	5,000	105
Head's parents	4,375	—	105	3	5,000	6,000	101
All	4,147	4,000	100	1,289	4,947	4,800	100

TABLE 5
AVERAGE WAGE EARNINGS BY POSITION IN HOUSEHOLD, WUXI/XISHAN

	500 yuan and above				3,000–12,000 yuan			>12,000 yuan		
	n	Mean	Median	Index	n	Mean	Median	n	Mean	Median
Head	819	8,765	7,000	122	629	6,650	6,300	121	22,803	20,000
– male	777	8,991	7,000	125	605	6,686	6,500	119	22,934	20,000
– female	42	4,568	4,000	63	24	5,748	5,250	2	15,000	15,000
Spouse	646	5,380	4,830	75	503	5,449	5,000	23	22,826	18,000
– male	37	9,604	6,000	133	29	6,315	6,000	7	24,429	20,000
– female	609	5,123	4,500	71	474	5,396	5,000	16	22,125	15,000
Child*	702	7,221	6,000	100	578	6,367	6,000	57	22,375	15,000
– son	389	8,692	7,000	121	307	6,972	7,000	51	23,361	15,000
– daughter	311	5,393	5,000	75	269	5,683	5,000	6	14,000	14,000
Grandchild	12	5,592	5,250	78	10	6,400	5,750	0	—	—
Head's parent	47	6,278	4,200	87	28	5,554	4,860	3	38,333	35,000
– male	26	9,175	4,960	127	21	5,653	4,920	3	38,333	35,000
– female	21	2,690	1,800	37	7	5,257	4,500	0	—	—
Other	(not included)									
All	2,235	7,211	6,000	100	1,750	6,258	6,000	204	22,914	18,000

* the gender of two children is unknown

12,000 *yuan*, with considerable effect on average earnings. Within the 3,000–12,000 *yuan* wage earnings range, position in the household still had considerable influence, heads' wage earnings of 6,650 *yuan* being 20–22 per cent above spouses' and grandparents', but not much higher than adult children's earnings of 6,367 *yuan*.

Adult daughters earned five per cent more than mothers, but sons slightly less than fathers. Sons earned 60 per cent more than daughters, but the difference narrows to 20 per cent in the category earnings between 3,000 *yuan* and 12,000 *yuan*. Similar to Qingyuan, in Wuxi male spouses reported the highest wage earnings, averaging more than 9,600 *yuan*, followed by the household head's fathers. Household head's mothers earned least, which may have to do with responsibilities for the care of children and other chores, but also with a tradition whereby elderly women do not work outside the home. For incomes above 12,000 *yuan*, averages for heads, spouses and children are almost the same, but with a similar gender bias. The great differences in average wage income between household members in Wuxi suggest different propensities to work for wages, a division of labour in the household, and a flexible labour market, which rewards skills and experience but has a definite gender bias.

THE EFFECTS OF AGE AND GENDER ON WAGE EARNINGS

Western scholars such as Emily Honig and Gail Hershatter have pointed to the gap in wages earned respectively by men and women in China, and mainly blamed it on gender discrimination [*Honig and Hershatter*, 1988]. In state-owned urban industries, the wage gap between men and women workers (*gongren*) used to vary between 10 and 20 per cent, depending on age [*Chinese Women*, 1991]. However, most urban women work in the lowly paid service sector. Chinese studies are rare and often contradictory. For example, a study of a Shanghai village concluded that in 1990 'gender difference is no longer a factor that decides work income', but noted a clear trend of feminization of agricultural labour, with off-farm and higher jobs being taken by men [*Fei*, 1993]. Indeed, only one-third of the workforce in non-agricultural township and village enterprises in China (and Hebei) is female, though in developed areas the ratio has become more even.[5] Our sample in Table 6 shows 163 per cent more male than female wage earners in Qingyuan, and in Wuxi 25 per cent more.

Average wage earnings differ with age and gender. In Wuxi, 62 per cent of all people above 15 earned more than 500 *yuan* in wages, twice as many as in Qingyuan. The difference is most pronounced in the age group 41–50. Between 21 and 50 years of age, the percentage is rather constant at 74–79 per cent in Wuxi, but in Qingyuan it drops with age from 46 per cent among those aged 21–25 years, to 30 per cent of those aged 46–50 years. It shows the more recent industrial establishment and employment of a younger (and smaller) segment of the population in Qingyuan. Because of earlier adoption of anti-natalist policies and falling birth rates, Wuxi has a smaller young generation than Qingyuan. In both, below the age of 21 more women than men engage in wage labour. This has to do with the fact that girls leave school earlier. In 1997 14 per cent more rural boys than girls below the age of 18 were economically active in China.[6]

Under 40 years of age, Wuxi had about as many male as female wage earners. Around marriage and childbearing age the latter numbered somewhat less. Above 45, their number fell off; above 50, to one-half or one-third of the men. Elderly women stop or reduce working for wages for various reasons. They may have lost some of the dexterity and speed required by employers. The need to supplement family income becomes less. Once children become wage earners themselves, they give less help around the house. Elderly women (and men) may sacrifice their jobs (voluntarily or not) in order to make place for their children (the *dingti* system, forbidden since 1988, but still widely practised).

Average male earnings in Wuxi rose with age, to about 10,000 *yuan* for those aged between 26 and 55. There was a much less pronounced rise for women, whose average wage earnings peak in the age group 36–40; their average stays around 5,000 *yuan*, before dropping off after the age of 55. Except for people under 20, averages for males are consistently higher than those for females. Between 26 and 35 years, when women are most engaged in childrearing, they earn only half the wages that men earn. In the age bracket 36–40 years old, this rises to two-thirds, but at later ages it drops again to one-half or less.

In Qingyuan above the age of 25 three times as many men as women earned wages. After the age of 50, the ratio became five to one. Unlike Wuxi, all Qingyuan women above 65 years had stopped working for wages. In Qingyuan age and gender-based differences between wage earnings were rather small. Wages for men peaked between in the age group 41–45 years, and wages for women peaked in the age group 46–50 years, both ten years later than in Wuxi. See Table 6.

Limitation of our sample to wage earnings between 3,000 and 20,000 *yuan* reduces the effect of part-time wages and entrepreneurial salaries. If earnings below 3,000 *yuan* are excluded, in Wuxi overall male wage earnings averaged 9,451 *yuan*, 60 per cent more than the average female wage of 5,920 *yuan*. In Qingyuan the gender difference was only 25 per cent, namely 5,905 as against 4,702 *yuan*. If earnings above 20,000 *yuan* are excluded as well, in Wuxi the differential remains the same in the age category 40–50 (namely 7,750 vs. 4,810 *yuan*), and in Qingyuan it goes up slightly to 30 per cent (namely 5,606 and 4,374 *yuan*). The gender

TABLE 6

WAGE EARNERS IN DIFFERENT AGE GROUPS AND
AVERAGE EARNINGS BY AGE AND GENDER
(wages above 500 *yuan* only)

Age	Wuxi/Xishan					Baoding/Qingyuan				
	Wage earners (%)	M n	Mean wage (*yuan*)	F n	Mean wage (*yuan*)	Wage earners (%)	M n	Mean wage (*yuan*)	F n	Mean wage (*yuan*)
16–20	25	33	4,427	42	4,604	14	76	3,292	93	2,841
21–25	74	142	7,245	109	5,611	46	165	4,213	107	3,491
26–30	79	153	9,767	157	4,969	42	185	3,908	61	3,805
31–35	75	181	10,662	172	5,357	35	180	4,107	55	3,780
36–40	79	98	9,524	120	6,406	37	168	4,549	58	4,243
41–45	78	175	9,485	151	5,027	33	179	5,339	58	3,880
46–50	74	183	8,720	128	4,615	30	156	4,461	38	5,037
51–55	62	128	9,760	53	4,962	32	105	4,397	21	4,619
56–60	47	73	7,860	20	3,668	25	56	4,011	10	3,800
61–65	32	30	5,220	12	3,339	21	35	3,707	3	4,400
66–70	21	19	4,049	6	2,573	9	16	4,088	0	—
71–	14	18	7,520	13	1,707	3	7	3,200	0	—
Total	62	1,233	8,905	983	5,126	31	1,328	4,355	504	3,775

differential is much smaller in the category 20–24 years, namely 22 per cent both in Wuxi and in Qingyuan.

Overall, Qingyuan has more equal wage levels than Wuxi. In Qingyuan middle-aged male workers earned 28 per cent more than female workers did, but both earned only slightly more than the young. In Wuxi, middle-aged male and female workers earned 17 per cent more and 11 per cent less, respectively, than the young. Whether these differences reflect different productivity, gender or age bias or all three is hard to say. In any case, gender difference is most pronounced. The fact that the gender gap is smallest for young workers suggests that wage discrimination rises with age. Advances in equal education, greater labour demand, fewer children and changed social values have begun to reduce gender-based wage differences.

WAGE EARNINGS AND EDUCATION

Wage earnings reflect education and skills to some extent. The increase in middle and higher education since the 1980s has been a contributing factor to greater income differentials of urban residents [Li et al., 1998], but their effects on the rural population have not yet been studied. Skills are not measured easily; therefore our survey limited itself to formal education as reported by the interviewees. Of course, such self-definition produces a bias. Not all respondents indicated their educational status, and some that attended primary school may not have admitted their present functional illiteracy. Therefore, the resulting number of illiterates and semi-literates is very low, five per cent of the adult population in Wuxi and eight per cent in Qingyuan. This was slightly lower than the 1997 Agricultural Census count and much lower than provincial averages.[7] We expected participation in paid labour and wages to rise with educational level, and they did, but to a different degree in the two regions and for men and women. Almost all respondents interpreted our question about educational level to include not only graduates, but also those still in school and dropouts, so the answer 'junior high school' did not necessarily mean that a diploma had been obtained. In Tables 7 and 8 we used a lower age limit of 25 years in order to filter out those who still attended school or university and therefore had no wages.

In Qingyuan wage labour participation increased from 25 per cent of those with primary school education to over 40 per cent and 70 per cent, respectively, of those with middle school and tertiary education. Illiterate women and those with primary school hardly participated. As the educational level rises, the average male to female gap of 48:14 is reduced. Among primary school graduates five times as many men as women earned wages, after lower middle school still 2.5 times as many, but with higher middle school the difference was only 26 per cent. Actually, male higher middle school graduates had a *lower* participation rate than those from lower middle school, namely 48 against 56 per cent, possibly because those in search of a profession have been prone to leave the village for good. Wage earnings were hardly different for those with or without primary education, but rose by 30 per cent for lower middle school graduates and again by 11 per cent for higher middle school graduates. The average wage rise for men from lower middle to higher middle school graduates went from 4,783 *yuan* to 5,851 *yuan* (+22 per cent), but there was a *decline* for women from 4,317 *yuan* to 4,033 *yuan* (–7 per cent). Explanations might be sought in propensity to work, age, and the type of jobs available for rural residents.

TABLE 7

PARTICIPATION IN WAGE LABOUR AND AVERAGE WAGE EARNINGS BY LEVEL OF EDUCATION, BAODING/QINGYUAN
(25 years and above; annual wages above 500 *yuan* only)

	Population			*of whom* Wages >500 *yuan*			Average earnings		
	Total	Male (persons)	Female	Total	Male (%)	Female	Total	Male (*yuan*)	Female
Il/semi-literate	521	147	374	7	20	2	3,655	3,456	4,400
Primary school	1,772	863	908	25	42	8	3,605	3,589	3,691
Lower middle	1,972	1,109	863	41	56	22	4,674	4,783	4,317
Higher middle	325	189	136	43	48	38	5,193	5,851	4,033
Special secondary/ college/university	23	15	8	70	80	50	4,519	4,533	4,475
All	4,612	2,323	2,289	31	48	14	4,374	4,441	4,141

TABLE 8

PARTICIPATION IN WAGE LABOUR AND AVERAGE WAGE EARNINGS BY LEVEL OF EDUCATION, WUXI/XISHAN
(25 years and above, annual wages above 500 *yuan* only)

	Population			*of whom* Wages >500 *yuan*			Average earnings		
	Total	Male (persons)	Female	Total	Male (%)	Female	Total	Male (*yuan*)	Female
Il/semi-literate	244	39	205	17	26	16	3,395	5,000	2,893
Primary school	942	444	498	57	66	49	5,670	7,035	4,044
Lower middle	1,416	766	650	74	75	73	7,624	9,501	5,355
Higher middle	322	200	122	80	84	74	10,439	12,161	7,292
Special secondary	52	33	19	77	82	68	7,902	8,605	6,442
College/university	31	22	9	77	82	67	10,871	11,884	7,833
All	3,007	1,504	1,503	65	73	57	7,410	9,222	5,115

In Wuxi, the great demand for wage labour has pushed up participation rates of both men and women with little or no education. Primary education increases the chance of wage earnings above 500 *yuan* to 57 per cent (66 per cent for men and 49 per cent for women), and lower middle education to 74 per cent. Further education increases the chance to over 80 per cent for men, but not so for women; those with tertiary education score only 67 per cent. Relative to Qingyuan, the gender difference is limited; 73 per cent of men against 57 per cent of women have wage earnings. Wage levels rise rapidly with each level of education, by 67 per cent with primary school, by 34 per cent with lower middle school and by 37 per cent with higher middle school. College and university graduates earn about the same as higher middle school graduates. Unlike the Qingyuan situation the gender difference in average wage earnings is remarkably constant: 73 per cent for illiterates, 74 per cent for primary school, 77 per cent for lower middle school and 67 per cent for higher middle school. It drops to 34 per cent for technical secondary schools, but remains as high as 52 per cent for college and university graduates.

These findings are rather different from a 1993 social survey of ten representative counties as analysed by Parish *et al*. According to them, a high school education increased one's chances of getting non-farm work by 2.8 times, irrespective whether one lived in a high labour demand locale or not [*Parish* et al., 1995]. Our survey data show an improved chance (for wage earnings above 500 *yuan* or above 3,000 *yuan*) of 72 per cent or 109 per cent, respectively, in Qingyuan and by 40 per cent or 61 per cent, respectively, in Wuxi. All these chances are very sensitive to gender. Education does not have a uniform effect on employment rates or wages.

We have seen that age influences average wage earnings (Table 6), so the effect of education is measured best within age categories. From the (supposedly mostly full-time) labourers reporting wage earnings of 3,000 *yuan* and above, we selected two groups: those aged 25–34 years, about 90 per cent of whom have received a lower middle school education, and those aged over 45 years, about 50 per cent of whom have lower middle school education. The outcome in Table 9 reflects not only objective differences in education and scarcities between generations, but also subjective cultural traditions of remuneration.

In the age group 25–34 years, Wuxi men with lower middle education earn 40 per cent more and those with higher middle education 50 per cent more than men with primary school education only (10,558 and 11,231 *yuan* respectively as against 7,500 *yuan*). In Qingyuan, the differences are only half those of Wuxi. The difference between lower and higher middle education is small (six to seven per cent) both in Wuxi and Qingyuan. In the category above 45 years of age, the wage difference between men with

TABLE 9

AVERAGE WAGE EARNINGS IN TWO AGE GROUPS, BY EDUCATION
(wages of 3,000 *yuan* and above only)

	Age 25–34				Age above 45			
	Male n	Female n	Male (*yuan*)	Female (*yuan*)	Male n	Female n	Male (*yuan*)	Female (*yuan*)
Wuxi/Xishan								
Primary	25	27	7,500	5,120	187	95	7,914	5,147
Lower middle	225	198	10,558	7,500	201	73	9,822	6,414
Higher middle	52	30	11,231	7,393	40	3	11,892	10,500
Baoding/Qingyuan								
Primary	17	4	4,741	4,225	87	25	5,755	4,228
Lower middle	153	59	5,522	4,808	111	31	6,150	5,823
Higher middle	25	16	5,812	4,988	8	1	5,550	4,000

primary school and lower middle school education is considerably less, namely 25 per cent in Wuxi and seven per cent in Qingyuan. The difference between lower and higher middle school education is greater for senior men, namely 20 per cent as against six per cent for the younger age group. An explanation might be that in the younger Wuxi age group, full-time earners with only primary education have a limited earning capacity, while in the older age group the lack of continued education does not, or at least not as much, reflect lesser earning capacities. This seems particularly true for women.

Qingyuan higher middle school graduates in the older age group earned less than their less educated fellow villagers did; none earned more than 9,000 *yuan*. Statistically, it is not significant. One might speculate that in the past strong urban labour demand for the highly educated made the most capable higher middle school graduates leave the rural Qingyuan area, and that those who stayed behind had a lesser earning capacity.

WAGE EARNINGS IN DIFFERENT PROFESSIONS

Professions require different skills and have different scarcities, so their remuneration is never the same. Between societies and periods, differentials may vary widely, as they are culturally determined. We expected that Wuxi would show greater wage differences than Qingyuan, because it had developed more rapidly and shed more of the communist egalitarian tradition. However, in some professions a lower propensity to work for wages instead of setting up one's own business might be a complicating factor.

For some professions we had to follow specifically Chinese classifications. 'Individual labourers' (*getihu*) is the Chinese term for independent businessmen or producers who for reasons of size cannot register their business as an enterprise, so their income is classified as being from labour. In Wuxi, two-thirds of the *getihu* lived in villages 11, 6 or 7, and there were almost none in villages 3, 8 and 10, which suggests that registration policies and practices differed between villages. 'State cadres' (most of whom have a managerial function) are a particular communist Chinese category denoting those rural professionals who are on the state payroll. Finally, rural traders include those who do not trade at their own risk. The category 'workers' is the largest by far, and covers a wide range of jobs and skills.

Tables 10 and 11 show the average wage earnings of different professional groups. Because of taxation, the reporting bias may have been greatest among those who did not draw a fixed salary. Entrepreneurs had the highest earnings, followed by state cadres and traders. All three are male-dominated professions. Teachers, doctors and accountants are mostly female, and the first two professions are among the lowest paid. Technicians and managers earned about 75 per cent more than the category of 'workers' who averaged 6,509 *yuan*. In most professions men earned 40–60 per cent more than women. Combined with the fact that gender differentials were only 20–25 per cent among self-employed entrepreneurs and individual labourers, this suggests strong gender discrimination by employers.

The final columns of Table 10 show wages of more than 12,000 *yuan*, which were earned by 237 people or 13 per cent of all wage earners above 3,000 *yuan*. About one-third of the managers and accountants were in this category (one technician's earnings of 250,000 *yuan* pushed up their average wage; the next highest wage was 75,000 *yuan*). A comparison of average workers' wages between villages shows lows of 5,000 and 5,300 *yuan* in villages 9 and 4 (n = 143) and highs of 9,000 and 8,600 *yuan* (n = 115) in villages 10 and 5, a considerably greater difference than for the total average wage, which varied between 7,000 and 10,000 *yuan*. This is rather surprising, considering the economic level and developed transport and other infrastructure of Wuxi, and suggests an imperfect labour market with regional barriers.

In Qingyuan, there were few people in specialist professions, and in all professions average earnings were about one-third less than those in Wuxi. None of the interviewed identified themselves as entrepreneurs, and the ranking was rather different from the one in Wuxi. Among men, managers *and* 'workers' topped the list, but they earned just ten per cent more than other professions, and security personnel and individual labourers earned about 20 per cent less. Among women, accountants with wages of 6,000 *yuan* stood well above other professions, and accounting was the only profession in which women earned more than men did. Women, whether manager, technician or teacher, all earned about the same, about 4,500 *yuan*. They earned 20–30 per cent less than men did, except for the large group of 'individual labourers', where the difference was only seven per cent. As in Wuxi, for the self-employed there was less room for gender discrimination.

WAGE EARNINGS BY PLACE OF WORK

Incomes earned by people working outside the county were about 30 per cent higher for the Wuxi villagers than for Qingyuan. A 1995 study noted

TABLE 10

AVERAGE WAGE EARNINGS BY PROFESSION, WITH GENDER, WUXI/XISHAN
(wages of 3,000 *yuan* and above only)

Profession	Total n	Mean wage (*yuan*)	Male n	Mean wage (*yuan*)	Female n	Mean wage (*yuan*)	Wages >12,000 n	Mean (*yuan*)
Entrepreneurs	21	20,238	17	21,000	4	17,000	17	23,412
State cadres	11	16,136	9	17,444	2	10,250	9	17,667
Traders	54	14,037	51	14,529	3	5,667	21	25,048
Technicians	105	11,550	79	13,266	26	6,335	17	34,952
Managers	142	11,219	94	13,221	48	7,298	45	20,566
Accountants	58	9,523	20	12,729	38	7,836	15	15,867
Individual labourers	201	9,474	158	9,873	43	8,009	35	22,757
Security personnel	18	8,097	17	8,221	1	6,000	3	16,667
Teachers	33	7,709	8	8,175	25	7,560	0	—
Doctors	12	7,375	4	8,375	8	6,875	0	—
Workers	1,204	6,509	631	7,582	573	5,327	75	17,272

TABLE 11

AVERAGE WAGE EARNINGS BY PROFESSION, WITH GENDER,
BAODING/QINGYUAN
(wages of 3,000 *yuan* and above only)

	Male		Female	
	n	Mean (*yuan*)	n	Mean (*yuan*)
Entrepreneurs	0	—	0	—
Managers	29	6,176	6	4,466
Workers	478	6,019	308	4,467
Accountants	3	4,867	7	6,014
State cadres	4	5,625	1	5,000
technicians	46	5,680	6	4,466
Teachers	8	5,538	10	4,370
Doctors	3	5,500	4	4,650
Security personnel	9	4,733	1	3,600
Individual labourers	338	4,626	29	4,303
Traders	0	—	1	3,000

that households with migrant workers had lower average incomes than households without such workers had, both per capita and per labourer. In Hebei they were lower by 23 per cent and 29 per cent, respectively, and nationwide by one per cent and 14 per cent. However, the study could not offer a satisfactory explanation.[8] According to economic theory, which has been confirmed by some studies, the size of the urban–rural income gap is positively related to migration decisions.[9] Our data are not comparable. We asked for the number of days lived away from home, and whether the place of work was outside the county or not. Both in Baoding/Qingyuan and in Wuxi/Xishan, the labour distance was rather short, while most migration surveys focus on long-distance labour in or outside less developed provinces.

In Qingyuan wages were mostly earned within one's own village. In the higher wage category (full-time or almost full-time) the county capital was most important. The higher-earning jobs were in industry (231); commerce and catering came second (69), followed by agriculture, construction and services (35 to 38 each). Outside the county, construction and industry were main occupations. The township *xiang* was least important. Forty out of 55 women earning over 5,000 *yuan* worked in the county capital, ten in their own village and only two outside the county; in the county capital, their average wage of 7,630 *yuan* equalled that of men. One hundred and five people above the age of 17 had lived half a year or more outside Qingyuan and earned over 3,000 *yuan*. Most had earned between 4,000 and 7,000 *yuan*, and their wage earnings averaged 5,750 *yuan* (4,671 *yuan* for the 13 women). In Table 12 we use the lower limits of 500 and 5,000 *yuan* for both areas, even if the latter limit is rather high for Qingyuan.

For Wuxi, because of its importance we added the gender factor. Wuxi villagers were not very mobile, but their horizon had moved beyond the village to the township *xiang*. More people had paid jobs in the township

TABLE 12

AVERAGE WAGE EARNINGS, BY PLACE OF WORK

	Wuxi/Xishan								Baoding/Qingyuan			
	>500 *yuan*				>5,000 *yuan*				>500 *yuan*		>5,000 *yuan*	
	Total		Male only		Total		Male only		Total		Total	
	n	mean	n	mean	n	mean	n	mean	n	mean	n	mean
Village	732	7,114	362	9,127	394	10,211	256	11,342	1,019	3,624	163	7,400
Xiang	1,059	6,973	579	8,514	541	10,190	388	10,863	173	4,156	55	6,449
County	234	9,327	162	10,827	148	12,385	117	13,338	450	5,337	183	7,470
Outside	77	9,368	61	10,133	49	12,551	39	13,713	156	4,563	45	7,918

than in their own village. Only 15 per cent worked in the county capital or outside. Those who worked outside their township in Wuxi had about 30 per cent more wage earnings than those in the village or township had. For earnings above 5,000 *yuan* only, the difference was about 20 per cent. Many more men than women worked outside their township and particularly outside the county, which explains part of the higher average wage earnings there. For male wage earners only, the difference between working in one's village and outside the county was 11 per cent or 21 per cent, depending on the lower wage limit. Wage earnings in the county capital averaged 27 per cent and 23 per cent, respectively, more than those in the township. The fact that many female part-timers work in the village and township, depressed average wage earnings there. However, the difference almost disappeared for earnings above 5,000 *yuan*. One may conclude that men went to the county and beyond to earn a higher wage, but that the same did not hold for women. This conforms to the general Chinese pattern whereby long-distance migrants are mainly men.

WAGE EARNINGS BY POLITICAL AFFILIATION

There is a common view that rural Chinese Communist Party (CCP) members and their families have higher incomes than ordinary people do. Opinions differ as to why this is so. A common explanation is their leading position, which not only entitles them to a higher than average wage but also provides benefits in the form of employment or financial rewards to themselves and their family.[10] Here, the question of causality will be put aside, and our data will be used to isolate some factors besides political position, which help explain differences in wage earnings. The question about the relation between political affiliation and wage earnings will be answered at the individual level first.

Wuxi

Because of recruitment criteria, their outstanding position in the village community, and professional orientation, we expected CCP and Youth League members to earn significantly more than non-members. For the sake of comparison, however, one needs to make some adjustments. The average age of the CCP members in our sample was 49 years, considerably older than average. As we have seen above that age is positively related to wage income, we reduce this effect of age by limiting the sample in Table 13 to those above 29 years. Youth League members had an average age of 23, ranging from 14 to 44 years, and therefore we treat the young generation separately. We distinguish two subgroups of high earnings above 12,000 *yuan* and middle earnings between 3,000 and 12,000 *yuan*.

CCP and Youth League members earned 73 and 35 per cent, respectively, more wages on average than non-members did. Three factors were mainly responsible: gender composition (for CCP, not for Youth League), wage labour participation rates and the share in top income. First, 90 per cent of CCP members were male, and the overall male wage earnings average was 84 per cent higher than the female wage. Second, 81 per cent of the CCP and Youth League members earned more than 500 *yuan*, as against 60 per cent of non-members. Third, 23 per cent earned more than 12,000 *yuan* as against only five per cent of the non-members. Female CCP wage earners netted twice the female average. Male Youth League members reported the highest average earnings, of 12,353 *yuan*, but their female counterparts only earned about average.

The gender difference in wages was smallest (10–15 per cent) with CCP members and largest with Youth League members. The former may reflect the scarcity of women who qualified for the Communist Party in the past; in contrast, about as many women as men are members of the Youth League. Possibly, male Youth League members see their membership as a move into a profitable business career, while female Youth League members have chosen or been allocated less profitable careers such as education, healthcare and birth control.

Over 200 respondents did not declare their political affiliation, and the results for this group are remarkable. These men and women had a 28 and 42 per cent, respectively, higher than average wage. As is shown in Table 14, the difference is even more pronounced with young people. This suggests a positive relation between respondents' impatience with this question (and possibly the political system) and high income.

In the age category where the Youth League is represented, the strongest that is from 21 to 34, the highest wage earnings were enjoyed not by CCP or Youth League members, but by the young men and women who declined to respond to the question about political affiliation. Male CCP members earned 15 per cent more than non-members, a much smaller difference than in the age group above 30 years. Surprisingly, male Youth League members had ten per cent lower wage income than non-members, but female members 14 per cent more wage income. Apparently, the Youth League did not attract young men who earned well, but it did attract young women who did.

As for age categories, above the age of 55, wage-earning male CCP members had average wage earnings of slightly over 10,000 *yuan*, almost twice as much as non-members. In the age groups 21–40 and 41–55 their wage earnings averaged 12,873 *yuan* and 11,860 *yuan*, respectively, 38 and 34 per cent more. So the differential was greatest in the oldest age category

The higher educational level of the male CCP members also explains some of the different wage earnings. One-quarter had not attended lower middle school, as against 35 per cent of all others. Thirty-three per cent had attended higher middle school or university, as against 12 per cent of other people. If we include all wages, male CCP members with primary education only earned almost twice as much as non-members. The difference was still sizeable (34 per cent) for those with lower middle school education, while it was 18 per cent for higher middle school graduates.

TABLE 13

RURAL WUXI AVERAGE WAGE EARNINGS IN 1997, BY POLITICAL AFFILIATION
(30 years and above)

	Population	Average Wage Earnings in Three Groups (*yuan*)					
		>500 *yuan*		3,000–12,000 *yuan*		>12,000 *yuan*	
	n	n	Mean	n	Mean	n	Mean
CCP	144	118	11,843	75	7,067	39	22,042
– male	130	107	12,000	67	7,157	36	22,129
– female	14	11	10,318	8	6,313	3	21,000
Youth League	34	27	9,270	22	6,832	5	20,000
– male	18	15	12,353	10	8,530	5	20,000
– female	16	12	5,417	12	5,417	0	—
Non-CCP*	2,249	1,354	6,857	1,053	6,118	108	23,299
– male	1,068	732	8,619	583	6,746	97	23,580
– female	1,180	621	4,781	469	5,338	11	20,955
Not answered	211	152	10,014	117	7,120	24	28,062
– male	105	88	12,028	66	7,810	16	32,938
– female	106	64	7,259	51	6,097	8	18,313
Total*	2,638	1,651	7,543	1,367	6,279	176	23,585
– male	1,321	942	9,380	726	6,914	154	24,097
– female	1,316	708	5,102	540	5,426	22	20,000

*gender unclear in one case

TABLE 14

AVERAGE WAGE EARNINGS OF YOUNG PEOPLE BY POLITICAL AFFILIATION
AND GENDER, WUXI/XISHAN
(21 to 34 years old; earnings between 2,400 and 30,000 *yuan*)

	n	*yuan*	M	*yuan*	F	*yuan*
Youth League	103	6,968	58	7,573	45	6,188
Communist Party	14	9,354	13	9,612	1	6,000
Non-members	593	6,967	310	8,364	283	5,437
Non-respondents	61	9,187	32	11,009	29	7,176

Qingyuan

In Qingyuan, though average wage earnings of party members (aged 30 years and above) were higher than those of the others, the difference was only ten per cent (4,804 *yuan* as against 4,373 *yuan*), slightly greater for men than women. This was due to higher earnings in the middle and higher wage (see Table 15). The highest-earning CCP member received 13,000 *yuan* in wages, but 17 non-members averaged 25,000 *yuan*. Political affiliation had little effect on the wage difference between men and women, CCP member or not. However, no female CCP members earned more than 6,000 *yuan*. Unlike Wuxi, Qingyuan Youth League members did not do well in wages. None of the female Youth League members earned wages, and only four out of 15 male Youth League members.

In Qingyuan, the main difference that CCP membership made was not in the level of wages, but in the chance that any wages were earned. Of the CCP members aged 30 years and above, 42 per cent earned wages of 500 *yuan* and above, as against 30 per cent of the others. This was entirely due to a different female wage labour participation rate. For men, it was the same. One reason why party members earned more or higher wages than non-members is that they held more professional jobs. Party membership was over-represented among managers (16 out of 46), state cadres and accountants, and absent among the lowest-paid categories such as security personnel and doctors. Even so, most CCP members were in the broad categories of 'worker' and 'individual labourer'. Twice as many CCP members (16 per cent) had attended higher middle school, technical school

TABLE 15

AVERAGE WAGE EARNINGS BY POLITICAL AFFILIATION, BAODING/QINGYUAN
(30 years and above)

	Total pop.	Wage earners and earnings in four groups (*yuan*)					
		>500		2,000–6,000	6,000–10,000		>10,000
		(p.)	Mean wage	(p.)	(p.)	Mean wage	(p.)
CCP	223	94	4,804	61	19	8,432	1
– male	188	87	4,822	56	19	8,432	1
– female	35	7	4,576	5	0	—	0
Youth League	28	4	4,375	4	0	—	0
– male	15	4	4,375	4	0	—	0
– female	13	0	—	0	0	—	0
Others	3,826	1,108	4,373	819	113	7,889	17
– male	1,840	861	4,446	608	104	7,878	16
– female	1,986	247	4,117	211	9	8,022	1

or university. On average, CCP members earned a slightly higher wage than other villagers.

Finally, the demographic composition of CCP and YL households was favourable to higher income from wages or otherwise. CCP households had a high percentage of people in the labouring age of 18 to 60, in Qingyuan 68 per cent as against 61 per cent for the others. They were comparatively large, 4.39 persons in Qingyuan and 4.33 persons in Wuxi, as against 3.94 and 3.73 for other households. This may be attributed to their higher than average age. CCP members were subject to strict one-child policy requirements. Only 18 per cent (Qingyuan) and 16 per cent (Wuxi) of their household members were under 18, as against 29 and 21 per cent, respectively, of other households. This was partly offset by a higher percentage of people above 60 years of age (about 15 per cent as against 10–11 per cent for the others). In Youth League households the labourer: dependent ratio was about 15 per cent higher than average, because they had very few people over 60, and also (particularly in Wuxi) fewer children. The larger than average CCP and Youth League household size and their lower percentage of dependants drove up their average income *per household* by 24 per cent in Qingyuan and 18 per cent in Wuxi for the CCP, and in both places by 27–28 per cent for the Youth League. Of course, the larger than average household size means that *per capita* their income from wage earnings was correspondingly less.

SUMMARY AND CONCLUSION

Our 1998 survey of over 3,000 resident households with about 12,000 members in 22 villages in Wuxi/Xishan in the lower Yangtze River valley and Baoding/Qingyuan on the North China Plain has yielded rich data for rural income analysis. Official rural income surveys do not consider gender, position in the household, age, education or political affiliation. Yet decomposition along these lines provides a better understanding of the role of wage earnings in rural households in the rapidly changing Chinese economy. We found that average wage earnings per capita in the Wuxi villages were almost four times as high as in Baoding, which was indicative of their different levels of industrialization and income. Higher participation in wage labour explained one-third of this difference, different family composition another 12 per cent, and a higher wage level and more paid working days explain most of the remainder. The gender difference in wage labour participation was large in Qingyuan, but rather small in Wuxi, namely 163 per cent and 25 per cent, respectively more men than women. The reverse was true for the level of the wage. Between villages, differences were considerable, particularly so in less developed Qingyuan.

Wage income constituted 55 per cent of total household income in Wuxi, but only 28 per cent in Qingyuan. This percentage varied greatly, particularly between suburban and more remote villages. Transfer income and property income were underreported, respondents being hesitant to fully disclose their wealth. Both in Wuxi and Baoding, together they constituted less than ten per cent of total income.

In Qingyuan wage employment opportunities and the propensity to work for wages differed substantially between household members. Within each household, the highest wage earner was the male spouse, followed by the household head. In Wuxi, within the wage range of 3,000–12,000 *yuan* household heads earned one-quarter more than spouses but only seven per cent more than adult children, and sons earned 20 per cent more than daughters. These differences become much larger if one includes all earnings, because many women had part-time wages only, and men had the highest incomes. Wage-earning adult daughters earned slightly more than their mothers. Wage earnings rose with age to a fairly constant level for those aged between 26 and 55 years in Wuxi, and peaked at the age of 36–55 years for men in Qingyuan. Gender differences in wage earnings were much larger among the 40 to 50-year-olds than among the young. This suggests that gender discrimination is diminishing, which may be attributed to increased and more diverse labour demand, more equal education, fewer children to care for and changed social values. Overall, age and gender-based full-time wage differentials were much smaller in Qingyuan than in Wuxi.

Wage labour participation increased with education, from 25 per cent of primary school graduates to over 40 per cent of lower middle school graduates in Qingyuan, and their average earnings differed by over 30 per cent. In Wuxi, lower middle school education increased the chance of having wage earnings (above 500 *yuan*) from the primary school graduates' 57 per cent to 74 per cent. Middle school education did not have much effect on wage earnings of Qingyuan men, but quadrupled the participation rate in wage labour for women. In Wuxi, it pushed up the average wage level by over one-third. Education-based wage differences for 25 to 34 year-olds were twice or more as large as for those over 45. An explanation might be that, because the older generation had much less opportunity to obtain a high school education, their lack of formal education did not reflect a lesser ability and earning capacity.

Between professions, wage differentials were not very high, particularly in Qingyuan. Male-dominated professions such as entrepreneurs, state cadres and managers had the highest earnings and female professions such as doctors and teachers had low earnings. In most professions men earned about half as much as women, which is a clear indication of gender discrimination. Technicians and managers earned about 75 per cent more than common workers. These are net differences, because only the highest wage (above 800 *yuan* per month) paid income tax. People working at the county capital or outside earned 20–30 per cent more than those with local jobs in Wuxi, and (depending on the lower wage limit) from about the same to 15 per cent more in Qingyuan.

Communist Party members averaged 73 per cent higher wages than non-members in Wuxi and ten per cent more in Qingyuan (disregarding those under 30 years of age). Three factors were mainly responsible for the difference in Wuxi: male predominance (90 per cent of CCP members were male), a higher wage labour participation rate, and a greater share in top incomes. The higher than average educational level of CCP members was a positive factor, too. Because CCP households had significantly more members (4.3–4.4 persons as against 3.7 in Wuxi and 3.9 in Qingyuan), the contribution of wage earnings to per capita income of the household was somewhat less. Female CCP members earned almost as much as their male comrades did. In this age category, Wuxi Youth League members also earned significantly more than average, but in the category 21–34 years of age male Youth League members had lower, and female members higher earnings than average. The attractiveness of membership of the Youth League may have been greater for young professional women as they tended to work more in government-related sectors such as education and healthcare. Interestingly, respondents who did not answer the question about political affiliation noted the highest average income. Female Youth League members earned only about average. In Qingyuan, CCP membership raised the chance (again excluding those under 30) of having wage earnings by 12 per cent, entirely due to female members. In contrast with Wuxi, it hardly affected the average wage.

These demonstrated statistical correlations do not answer the question of causality. Wage earners, particularly cadres and those working in industry, are more likely to be recruited into the Communist Party than farmers are. But it has also been shown that CCP members use their relations with higher authorities and local networks to their own advantage. It seems political affiliation brought different advantages: in Wuxi a higher wage, and in Qingyuan more participation in wage labour.

Urban proximity, degree of industrialization, income level, alternative income sources, but also more subjective factors such as local political and cultural traditions determine the opportunity for wage earnings and the propensity to work for wages of rural households. Our study has shown that under different economic conditions individual attributes such as gender, age, position in the household, education, and membership of the Communist Party or Youth League have had a quite different impact on the chances of having wage earnings and the height of wage income. Analysis of rural wage income differentials should take such individual attributes into account as important determinants of wage labour decisions, and because socio-economic change has different effects on the income position of households and individuals.

NOTES

1. The villages were surveyed before in 1930, 1958 and 1987. Short descriptions of each are provided in *Zhongguo cunzhuang jingji* [*Wubao ketizu* (WuBao Research Group), 1999]. Households were a random sample of one-third of all resident households in each village. The survey was undertaken jointly by the CASS Institute of Economics and Leiden University (Shi Zhihong, Wu Li and the author) and generously funded by the Dutch Ministry of Education.

2. Calculated from National Agricultural Census Office of China [1998: 59–61, 24, 42–4].

3. We left out 15 households (nine in Wuxi, eight of which were in Taihu; and six in Baoding, four of which were in Dazhuze) who reported over 500,000 *yuan* of income, because of sample-size related distorting effects, and because some needed further checking. Our average labour remuneration was slightly lower than the 1997 Xishan rural average of 3,735 *yuan* per capita [*State Statistical Bureau*, 1998a: 430–31].

4. In Qingyuan, 1,092 households (out of 2,010) had a total of 1,593 persons working for wages outside the village; they put in a total of 350,326 labour days (averaging 220 days) and earned 6,216,525 *yuan*, or 18 *yuan* per day. In Wuxi, 977 members from 489 households (out of 1,122) worked a total of 275,211 labour days (averaging 282 days) outside, earning 7,348,214 *yuan* in wages, or 27 *yuan* per day.

5. In Jiangsu, Shanghai and Guangdong the female shares were 43, 50 and 53 per cent, respectively, in 1997. See *National Agricultural Census*, Office of China, 1998, 269.

6. Calculated from *National Agricultural Census* [Office of China, 1998: 10]. In the 1980s, 78 per cent of girls and 71 per cent of boys aged 15–19 had some kind of labour participation, see Ye [1987: 280].

7. The 1997 Agricultural Census recorded (semi-)illiteracy rates of 9.9 per cent in Qingyuan and 8.6 per cent in Xishan; junior and senior middle school rates were 36.6 per cent and 4.1 per cent in the former and 44.2 per cent and 8.7 per cent in the latter. Special secondary schools, colleges or universities had been attended by 0.3 per cent in Qingyuan and 2.8 per cent in Xishan (data supplied to author by SSB through FAO).

8. In six out of 18 provinces households with outside labourers had *higher* average incomes because of lower average wage income in their home provinces [*Li*, 1999].

9. Zhu [2002]. This study is based on a survey of mainly long-distance migrants from the interior province of Hubei. It is not clear whether the gap should best be measured in relative or absolute terms.

10. E.g. Cook [1998]. In a study of some villages in the same Zouping county Murdoch and Sicular [1998] suggested that the focus on membership is misplaced, as they found little income advantage for CCP members and their households. Holding a cadre position is much more relevant for the collection of *political* rents. Their income data show no difference between cadre and non-cadre households in 1990–91, and a 30 per cent difference in 1992–93, when more liberal policies were introduced again.

REFERENCES

Chinese Women Federation and Shaanxi Women Federation (eds.), 1991, *Zhongguo funü tongji ziliao, 1949–1989* (Statistics on Chinese women), Beijing: Zhongguo tongji chubanshe.

Cook, Sarah, 1998, 'Work, Wealth and Power in Agriculture: Do Political Connections Affect the Returns to Household Labor?', in Andrew G. Walder (ed.), *Zouping in Transition: The*

Process of Reform in Rural North China, Cambridge, MA and London: Harvard University Press, pp.157–83.

Fei, Juanhong, 1993, 'The Rural Reform of Our Country and the Gender Division of Labor', *Chinese Sociology and Anthropology*, Vol.31, No.2, pp.42–56 (originally in (Chengdu) *Shehui kexue yanjiu*, 1993, No.4).

Honig, E. and G. Hershatter, 1988, *Personal Voices: Chinese Women in the 1980s*, Stanford: Stanford University Press.

Li, Shi, 1999, 'Zhongguo nongcun laodongli liudong yu shouru zengchang he fenpei' (China's rural labour migration and the increase and distribution of income), *Zhongguo shehui kexue* (Social sciences in China), No.2, pp.16–33.

Li, Shi, Zhao Renwei and Zhang Ping, 1998, 'Zhongguo jingji chuanxing yu shouru fenpei biandong' (The transient form of China's economy and shifts in income distribution), *Jingji yanjiu* (Economic research), No.4, pp.42–51.

Murdoch, Jonathan and Terry Sicular, 1998, 'Politics, Growth and Inequality in Rural China: Does it Pay to Join the Party?', Development Discussion Paper No.640, Harvard University.

National Agricultural Census Office of China, 1998, *Abstract of the First National Agricultural Census in China*, Beijing: China Statistics Press.

Nongcun Guding Guanchadian Bangongshi, 2000, 'Woguo nongmin shouru quyu chayi fenxi' (Analysis of regional income differentials in our rural population), in Nongyebu Nongcun Jingji Yanjiu Zhongxin, *Zhongguo nongcun yanjiu baogao 1990–1998* (China rural research report), 3 vols., Beijing: Zhongguo caizheng jingji chubanshe.

Parish, William L., Zhe Xiaoye and Li Fang, 1995, 'Non-farm Work and Marketisation of the Chinese Countryside', *The China Quarterly*, No.143 (Sept.), pp.697–730.

State Statistical Bureau, 1998, *China Statistical Yearbook 1998*, Beijing: China Statistics Press.

State Statistical Bureau, 1998a, *1998-nian Jiangsu tongji nianjian*, Beijing: China Statistics Press.

Wubao ketizu (WuBao Research Group), 1999, *Zhongguo cunzhuang jingji: Wuxi, Baoding 22 cun diaocha baogao 1987–1998* (Chinese village economy: Report of a survey of 22 villages in Wuxi and Baoding 1987–1998), Beijing: Zhongguo caizheng jingji chubanshe.

Xu, Ronghua, 1999, 'Nongye tongji zhibiao tixi gaige chutao' (Enquiry into a reform of agricultural statistical indicators), *Zhongguo tongji* (Statistics of China), No.6, pp.12–14.

Ye, Zhonghai, 1987, *Nüxing rencaixue gailun* (Synopsis of female human resource management), Beijing: Beifang funü ertong chubanshe.

Zhu, Nong, 2002, 'The Impacts of Income Gaps on Migration Decisions in China', *China Economic Review*, Vol.13, Nos.2–3, pp.213–20.

The Wasteland Auction Policy in Northwest China: Solving Environmental Degradation and Rural Poverty?

PETER HO

According to the statistics, China had a total of 108 million ha of undeveloped land or wasteland in 1995. Of this figure, 35.4 million ha is suitable for agriculture and 63.0 million ha is suited for forestry purposes [*Zhang and Li*, 1997: 1413]. Wasteland includes a wide variety of land resources scattered over the whole nation. It varies from forested hills and mountains in the subtropical region of Yunnan province to the dry steppe and pockets of desert in the Inner Mongolia autonomous region. According to the definitions of the Chinese Ministry of Agriculture, this undeveloped land can be divided into wasteland, waste mountains, sandy waste and waste gullies (*huangdi, huangshan, huangtan* and *huanggou*). The term 'wasteland', however, is misleading as a great portion of this land is in use by peasants for animal grazing, small-scale forestry and the exploitation of forest by-products, such as Matsutake mushrooms, medicinal herbs and animals. The direct use of wasteland generally yields low economic returns, while its ecology is often fragile. For this reason, the Chinese state has for long sought means to develop wasteland either for purposes of rural poverty alleviation, soil and water conservation, and even defence.

In the 1980s, Lüliang prefecture in Shanxi province embarked on a new path to harness soil erosion on the barren mountains of the Loess Plateau by allocating use rights to individual farmers or joint households. Village regulations strictly prohibited reclamation of the erosion-prone, Loess soil for agricultural purposes, but the use rights to wasteland did allow for economic forestry (fruit and nut growing) and animal husbandry. By 1992, the Lüliang model had gained national fame and was proclaimed as the

Peter Ho, Assistant Professor in Environmental Policy, Environmental Policy Group, Wageningen University, Hollandseweg 1, 6706 KN, Wageningen, The Netherlands. Email: peter.ho@wur.nl. I am indebted to Jan-Michiel Otto, Ngo Tak-wing and Jim Harkness for their invaluable comments and suggestions on this article. For the purpose of privacy the names of some of the respondents quoted in this article have been changed. This research was funded by the Dutch Organization for Scientific Research (NWO).

'Four Wastelands Auction Policy' (*Sihuang paimai zhengce*, hereafter the Wastelands Policy). It soon spread to other provinces and autonomous regions, including the Ningxia Hui Muslim autonomous region (hereafter Ningxia) in northwest China.

In Ningxia the policy was hailed as a breakthrough in land management that would open up undeveloped natural resources, improve the ecological environment and increase farmers' income. Two years after the first wasteland contracts were sold to the highest bidding party, the auctions were suddenly halted because of large-scale soil erosion induced by agricultural reclamation. Despite the fact that the Wastelands Policy is still executed elsewhere in China, it has come to a complete standstill in Ningxia, a phenomenon for which the regional authorities are reluctant to give an adequate explanation. Many questions have remained unanswered: What were the origins of the policy? How was the policy executed? What problems were encountered during execution and how were they dealt with by the responsible authorities? And why did the Wastelands Policy come to a halt?[1]

To answer these questions, I will analyse the formulation and implementation of the Wastelands Policy in Ningxia.[2] The article starts by exploring the historical background of the Wastelands Policy, followed by a description of the auction procedures, the policy content, and the institutions and administrative layers involved in the drafting and implementation process. The analysis of state organs at the county and township level is based on the 'institution building model' designed by Milton Esman and further adapted to rural development studies by Jan-Michiel Otto. I have made particular use of Esman's 'institution variables': leadership, doctrine (the inherent mission and duties of an institution), programme (the policy that has to be implemented), resources (financial and personnel), and internal structure (management divisions and their interrelations) [*Esman*, 1972; *Esman*, 1991; and *Otto*, 1987]. The implementation process will be illustrated with two village case studies from Ningxia: the village 'where it all began' – Changcheng village in Pengyang county – and a village which to which the policy spread during a later stage – Guanting village in Guyuan county.

I will argue that the Wastelands Policy signals a dual break with the past. First, the formulation process of the Wastelands Policy is an example of the space opened up by the reforms, which allows the lower administrative levels (county and below) to initiate and shape policies generally considered sensitive or too innovative. Second, the policy entails great possible socio-economic changes because it removes the so-called rural–urban divide. The Wastelands Policy permits 'open auctions' in which not only farmers, but also cadres, urban entrepreneurs, and legal entities such as mass organizations and companies are allowed to participate and, more important, gain access to rural land.

The main political instrument that institutionalizes the rural–urban divide is the household registration system (*hukou*). Through this system rural–urban migration was strictly controlled. Those with a rural *hukou* were excluded from the urban job market, social welfare system and education, although over the years, government control on migration has relaxed [*Cheng and Selden*, 1994; *Selden*, 1998; *Potter*, 1983]. The rural–urban divide also ensures that the right to lease agricultural land is reserved for members of rural collectives. However, some policy-makers believe that wasteland can only be adequately developed through free market competition, which requires removing the divide in order to bring out the most capable and financially strong. On the other hand, I will also show that the Wastelands Policy bears traits of the way of policy-making and implementation that characterized the collective period (1956–78). Its manner of implementation could be described as 'commandist' or 'Dazhai fashion':[3] authoritarian, with great pressure exerted on state institutions to spread a policy model allegedly proved 'good'. As the policy is turned into orthodoxy, regional variation and voices of dissent are disregarded because of its high momentum.[4]

GEOGRAPHY OF THE RESEARCH SITES

This article is based on fieldwork conducted in Ningxia during the spring and summer of 1997. In addition to interviews, a quantitative survey of 90 farm households was carried out. The survey was done in four natural villages in two counties – Guyuan and Pengyang – in the south of Ningxia. Ningxia shares borders with Shaanxi province in the east, Inner Mongolia in the north and west, and Gansu province in the south (see Figure 1). Instead of being administered as a province, it was carved out as an autonomous region for the Hui Muslim minority in 1958.

Ningxia is situated in the central Asian steppe and desert region with a continental, temperate climate increasing in aridity from the south (subhumid) to the north (arid). In the north, it is enclosed by the Tengger (northwest) and Mu'us deserts (northeast). The total land area is 51,800 km² and the total population in 1993 was 4.95 million people, of which 1.64 million (33 per cent) were Hui Muslim Chinese.[5] The Hui are far descendants from Persian and Arab merchants that came to China during the heydays of the trade over the Silk Road in the Tang dynasty (AD 618–907). The Hui are a religious and ethnic minority that socio-economically lag behind the majority of the Han Chinese. This becomes clear from a brief look at the statistics: 64 per cent of the Hui live in the seven poorest

FIGURE 1

MAP

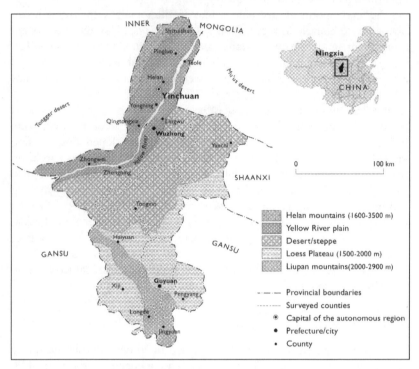

counties[6] in the autonomous region, in contrast to only 29 per cent of the Han Chinese. Furthermore, 60 per cent of the Hui, which includes 78 per cent of the women, are defined as illiterate, against 36 per cent of the Han, including 49 per cent female [*Ningxia Tongjiju*, 1994: 65; *Gao*, 1995: 57].

Guyuan and Pengyang counties are located in the highly erosion-prone Loess Plateau in the south of Ningxia, with mixed farming (agriculture and animal husbandry) as the main activity. The Loess Plateau covers seven provinces and autonomous regions: Shanxi, Inner Mongolia, Henan, Shaanxi, Ningxia, Gansu and Qinghai. The plateau is notorious for its soil erosion, as a popular adage goes: 'The Loess Plateau is the reason why the Yellow River is yellow: it's all soil'. The total area of the Loess Plateau is 626,800 km², of which 530,000 km² has been reported affected by erosion (and 430,000 km² seriously affected) [*Yang and Yu*, 1992: 1]. Guyuan is the poorer of the two counties and has been designated as a poverty region by the Ministry of Agriculture. The county has inadequate access to drinking water and a poorly developed infrastructure [*Guojia Tongjiju*, 1994;

Frances and Su, 1990]. Pengyang county was administered by Guyuan before 1988. In contrast to Guyuan, Pengyang is relatively wealthy. Farmers earn a considerable income through tobacco cultivation, which can yield an annual gross income of Rmb 1,500–2,000 per *mu*. In 1996, the cultivated area of tobacco in Pengyang was 11,000 *mu*.[7]

GENERAL AUCTION PROCEDURES

The initiative to formulate and implement the Wastelands Policy was originally the responsibility of local people's congresses (which are the local version of the National People's Congress or the national parliament). In response to a rapid proliferation of local wasteland auctions, the central government issued a notice in 1996 stating the general principles and purposes of the Four Wastelands Auction Policy [*Secretariat of the State Council*, 1997]. To date, it is the first and only proclaimed guideline by the central state. Within the Ministry of Agriculture, the Bureau of Law and Policy System Reform is charged with the coordination, monitoring and evaluation of the Wastelands Policy.

In spite of some regional differences in the lease period or the terms of the contract, the basic format of the Wastelands Policy is similar throughout China. In principle, the auctions follow the model set by Lüliang prefecture. In this section the auction procedures in Lüliang will be described and deviations from practices in Ningxia indicated.

In policy documents and writings on the auctions, it is repeatedly stressed that what is being sold are the use rights and *not* the ownership rights. The use rights are surface rights and do not pertain to subsoil use rights (such as mining rights). The term 'wasteland' is not defined ecologically and includes different land types, such as forested land, steppe and mountain pastures. As a result, the responsibility for wasteland management falls under different ministries and bureaux.

The use rights are sold in three ways: (1) open auction, in which people from outside the village can participate; (2) closed auction, held when farmers in the village show sufficient interest in buying wasteland leases and there is no need to invite outsiders; and (3) negotiated sales, if wasteland is of inferior quality, or the plot has already been contracted for afforestation purposes and the tenant wants to extend the contract.

The preparatory work for the auction starts with the establishment of a 'Four Wastelands Leading Team' consisting of leaders from relevant county sections. The leading team is responsible for the formation and training of a 'Four Wastelands Work Team', which comprises township cadres and village representatives chosen by the farmers. The Four Wastelands Work Team carries out the actual auction and preparations, such as a wasteland survey, a list of the plots to be auctioned, determination of land categories (soil fertility, relief, vegetation, and so forth) and the starting bidding price. The work team also decides on the method of payment.

Payment can be effected in the form of lump sum payments, instalments and even in the form of a mortgage with land use rights as collateral! (which is one of the few cases that rural land can actually be used as a collateral in China today). In reality, however, payment methods other than lump sum payments are rarely practised in China. In Ningxia, it is stipulated that the revenues of the auctions belong to the administrative village, but are administered by the Township Financial Office as a special afforestation fund. The administrative village can apply for afforestation and revegetation subsidies from the fund.[8] Approximately one month prior to the auction the work team provides information to the villagers about the auction and the wasteland plots.

To avoid a clash of interests, the 1997 Auction Law makes a distinction between the auctioning party, the commissioning party (selling party), and the buying party,[9] whereby the auctioning and commissioning parties are forbidden to buy under penalty of revocation of the right to auction, or confiscation of acquired goods and property.[10] The structure of the Four Wastelands Work Team, however, does not conform to the stipulations of the Auction Law. The commissioning party (the village committee) is simultaneously the auctioning party,[11] and worse, sometimes also the buying party. This can and, as we will see below, does give rise to monopolization and the abuse of power by village cadres.

The wasteland contract is signed between the tenant and the administrative village. The contract is issued in triplicate and notarized at the Township Rural Economic Station. Copies of the contract are held by the tenant, the administrative village, and the Rural Economic Station [*Hanstad and Li*, 1997: 558].

According to the prefectural stipulations, the contract should state:

1. Term of the lease (50 to 100 years);[12]
2. Rights of the tenant, including usufruct, transfer, mortgage, inheritance, and right to construction, such as fences, houses (forbidden in Ningxia), corrals, or other structures for wasteland development;
3. Duties of the tenant and lessor, in terms of afforestation and revegetation (in Lüliang 30 per cent of wasteland must be developed in three years). The lessor must supervise wasteland development and provide seeds, saplings, and technical support;
4. Restrictions on use: wasteland can only be used for forestry and animal husbandry, whereas agriculture is allowed only on slopes with a gradient below 25°;

5. Reward and penalty rules (in case of serious mismanagement, authorities can revoke the contract and re-auction the plot);
6. Description of the physical boundaries of the lease.

The fact that the Lüliang regulations – in line with article 14 of the Soil and Water Conservation Law – prohibit agricultural reclamation on slopes steeper than 25° does not imply that the cultivation of all land below this gradient is encouraged.[13]

More detailed regulations for wasteland use can be drafted by local authorities. To conserve the ecological benefits of certain lands, the following categories of wasteland cannot be auctioned in Ningxia: (1) arid wasteland with an annual precipitation lower than 200 mm; (2) forests or afforested areas; and (3) state and collective forests, livestock farms, and nature reserves [*Zhonggong Guyuan Diwei*, 1994b: 23].

In addition to the wasteland contract, the County Land Management Section is required to issue a land use permit. The daily supervision of duty fulfilment by the tenant, the handling of matters relating to the lease (transfer, inheritance, extension, revocation, etc.) and the mediation of land disputes arising from the auctions, rests with the village committee. Overall supervision and serious conflicts are dealt by the Township Rural Economic Station, the Township Forestry Management Station and the County Land Management Section.[14]

THE FOOLISH OLD MAN WHO REMOVED THE MOUNTAINS: ORIGINS OF THE POLICY

Already during the first years of the People's Republic, the Chinese government was concerned about soil degradation and rural poverty on the mountainous, erosion-prone Loess Plateau. Much effort has been made in constructing dykes and terraces to diminish the run-off of the soil. After the communist takeover, the new leaders viewed the 'development of the mountainous regions' with optimism and enthusiasm: China had ample labour resources and by deploying the masses, the barren and eroded mountains could be turned into lush, fertile fields and rural poverty overcome.

In the old revolutionary base areas (the Shaan-Gan-Ning border region and Jiangxi Soviet) the need to harness nature and build a new rural society was strongly felt, as development of these regions was also a tribute to the communist revolution. In line with Mao's speech at the Seventh National Congress of the Chinese Communist Party, the local authorities exhorted farmers to work in the spirit of Yugong, the foolish old man who, according to legend, attempted to remove the mountains [*Mao*, 1977]. In the struggle against the vicissitudes of nature, willpower was more important than anything else. It was believed that with the help of science man could and should dominate nature. In Mao's words: 'If people living in nature want to be free, they will have to use natural sciences to understand nature, to overcome nature and to change nature; only then will they obtain freedom from nature' [*Mao*, 1966: 44].

Chen Yonggui, the leader of Dazhai Production Brigade in Shanxi province, took great pains to propagate the transformation of nature through labour-intensive mass movements. During the Cultural Revolution (1966–76), the achievements of soil and water conservation in Chen's brigade would evolve into a nationwide campaign and spiritual model for all collectives in China: 'Learn from Dazhai' (*xuexi Dazhai*). Not only were the land management measures widely copied, but also the remuneration system (the so-called work-point system) based on labouring ability and the intangible criterion of 'political attitude'. The reasons for the failure of the Dazhai model lie in the extreme moral and social pressure exerted on collectives to adopt it. In the perspective of a model deemed 'good', regional variations were overlooked [*MacFarquhar and Fairbank*, 1991: 140, 524, 652–3].

Although the Dazhai work-point system was a fiasco, and the model was in later years exposed for its false claims on land improvement, it is uncertain what the overall effect of mass movements has been on agriculture [*MacFarquhar and Fairbank*, 1991: 517]. At the end of the Cultural Revolution, a shift occurred in the government's perception of the value of mass movements for natural resource management. The Dazhai model with its emphasis on collective action and responsibility was replaced by the principles of the Household Contract Responsibility System (hereafter Household Contract System). The initial successes of the economic reforms since 1978 (increasing grain production and a bumper harvest of over 400 million tons in 1984) legitimized the trend in rural policies towards a privatization of agriculture through land leases.

The Household Contract System was also applied to the management of wasteland. Long before the Wastelands Policy became official policy in the early 1990s, the idea of individual management of wasteland had already firmly taken root. In line with national policy, the provincial governments stipulated that use rights of wasteland could be vested in the natural village, the joint household or the individual farmer. The term of the lease was initially 15 years – corresponding to the stipulations in the 1984 Rural Work Document No.1 of the Chinese Communist Party. In the early 1990s, the party determined that the period of land leases (including wasteland) could be extended by 30 years on top of the original contract. In contrast to the Rangeland Law (but not the Forest Law), the transfer of wasteland use contracts was allowed. This fitted in with the trend of national land policies over the period 1984–87 that promoted the 'mobility of land' [*Cheng and Tsang*, 1996: 53–4; *Zizhiqu Dangwei*, 1985; *Wang*, 1994b: 4–5].

EVOLUTION OF THE WASTELANDS POLICY

As stated above, Lüliang prefecture in Shanxi province is the region where the first wasteland auctions were organized in the early 1980s. The initial results were not encouraging as the majority (a report mentioned 60–80 per cent) of the contracted wasteland was poorly managed or not managed at all. Problems arose from the lack of security in the contract period, the right of transfer and inheritance of contracts, as well as the legal basis for capital investments in wasteland development [*Wang*, 1994b: 5].

In addition, conservative forces in the prefectural party committee opposed the 'open auction' which allows the rural and non-rural populace to participate and thus gain access to rural land. The green light to the auctions in Lüliang was given after Deng Xiaoping's 'Southern Tour' in 1992 prompted a renewed nationwide emphasis on the need for further reforms [*Wang*, 1994a: 21]. In the same year, the Four Wastelands Auction Policy was formalized and auctions were organized throughout the prefecture. The Wastelands Policy gained national fame after the auctions of Lüliang were promoted through the media as a breakthrough in land policy. The auctions gradually evolved into a new model for rural development and soil conservation. The Wastelands Policy is not restricted to Shanxi province alone. Similar policies for the management of wasteland are implemented in widely different ecological locations such as Chifeng (Inner Mongolia), Huaihua (Hunan), and Hechi (Guangxi) and Yao'an (Yunnan) [*Zhang*, 1997: 49–52; *Huang*, 1996: 23–6].[15]

Over time the national government attempted to standardize the amalgam of variations in wasteland auctions. In 1996 the Secretariat of the State Council promulgated a notice on the control and development of wasteland resources [*Secretariat of the State Council*, 1997: 425–6]. The Notice is important on several counts. First, it offers legitimacy to the use of auctions to develop wasteland resources. There is a legal problem of definition involved in the term 'auction'. According to the 1997 Auction Law 'an auction is the manner of buying and selling whereby the rights to specific goods or property are transferred to the bidder of the highest price by means of open competition' (article 3). However, in most localities the use rights are not auctioned but bought by farmers through negotiated sales, while farmers have also been forced to buy land leases: practices not much different from the allocation of land leases in the Household Contract System. Li Sheng,[16] one of the most fervent advocates of the Wastelands Policy and simultaneously also its strongest critic, commented:

> The 'Four Wastelands' auction is actually not an auction, but a lease of the 'Four Wastelands' ... To call this lease an auction falls short of reality and causes confusion in the use of fundamental concepts, although it may appeal to the psychological needs of buyers [*Li*, 1995: 30].

Second, the Notice stresses that 'entrepreneurial work units, social and other organizations, or individuals may use various methods to manage and develop "Four Wastelands"' under the condition that 'villagers of the village itself enjoy priority'.[17] This stipulation is much contested. Its advocates assert that the best way to develop wasteland is to encourage competition among the most capable and financially strong. Others argue that competition will lead to further impoverishment of the rural poor.

Third, the Notice determines that wasteland can be used for 'agriculture if suited to agriculture, forestry if suited to forestry, fruit cultivation if suited to fruit cultivation ... and animal husbandry if suited to animal husbandry'. At the same time, it stipulates that agricultural reclamation is prohibited on slopes or hills steeper than 25°.

Fourth, guidelines are given for the wasteland contracts concerning: (a) the contract period (not longer than 50 years – in Lüliang 100 years); (b) the right to inherit, transfer and mortgage the contract; (c) the right to set up share-holding cooperatives supervised by the township government and with the permission of the county government. The contract procedures (number of copies, notarization, need for land use permit, and so forth) are less clearly spelled out.

Lastly, the legal definition of wasteland is addressed. At this point, there are two issues at stake: the difference between state and collective ownership of land and the ecological definition of wasteland, notably, the distinction between forest and rangeland. In Ningxia, wasteland comprises desert steppe and dry grassland, and it is seldom forested. But in provinces such as Guangxi and Yunnan, wasteland might also refer to (communal) forests. The Notice does not clarify what 'wasteland' denotes ecologically, but briefly stipulates that it is strictly forbidden to auction forest land as 'Four Wastelands'.

Concerning state and collective wasteland, both the 1984 Forest Law and the 1985 Rangeland Law define forest and rangeland to be state-owned, unless owned by the collective. Before decollectivization, collective landownership rights were laid down in party documents ('Sixty Articles'), but not in law. When the former collectives (commune, brigade and team) were dismantled and replaced by the township, administrative village and natural village, collective ownership rights to rangeland and forest were formalized in the 1982 Constitution, yet without specifying the nature of the 'collective'. Over time, the commune, brigade and team came to regard the forest and rangeland in their vicinity as their own, which led to ambiguity and controversy over state and collective property between state institutions *vis-à-vis* the collectives, and between collectives themselves.[18]

In order to avoid problems over state and collective property rights, the Notice states that wasteland should not be leased if the limits between state and collective wasteland are unclear or disputed. It adds that 'it is strictly forbidden to alter state-owned land into collectively owned land' [*Secretariat of the State Council*, 1997: 425–6]. Yet, as property rights to rangeland and forest are unclear it is unavoidable that collectives in some cases will auction use rights to land not legally their own, which is a transgression against article 6 of the Auction Law:

> The commissioning party must own or be able to take legal disciplinary action against the good or property for which a bid is made at the auction.[19]

The confusion about the legal definition of wasteland (forest versus rangeland, and collective versus state-owned land) translates into dual confusion about the duties over land tenure and management. On the one hand, the duties are confounded between the State Forestry Bureau (formerly Ministry of Forestry), the Ministry of Agriculture (and the subordinate Bureau of Animal Husbandry), and the Ministry for Land and Natural Resources (formerly State Land Administration). On the other hand, the issue of responsibilities remains unclear in regard to the aforementioned state institutions and the rural collectives (township, administrative village, natural village) that lay ownership claims to forest, rangeland or wasteland. We will see in the case studies the implications for the implementation of the Wastelands Policy.

CONVINCING THE LEADERS: CHANGCHENG VILLAGE

Village Description

Changcheng village ('Great Wall village') owes its name to some of the most ancient stretches of the Great Wall in its neighbourhood. These sections of the wall were constructed during the reign of Qin Shi Huangdi, China's first emperor (221–207 BC). Today not much more than some man-sized heaps of mud scattered in the fields remain,[20] but they do bestow the village with a halo of historical romanticism of which the farmers are proud.

The surrounding landscape of the village is typical of the Loess Plateau, high hills interspersed with gullies and chasms formed by erosion. The landscape has changed little since the time Andrew Findlay described it in the 1930s:

> Water erosion has carved out of a surface once level, strange gullies and ravines, weird pillars, great arches and tunnels, which make a journey into this area a memorable experience for the present-day traveller [*Findlay*, 1937: 57].

Changcheng administrative village[21] is located about 5 km away from its administrative centre, Chengyang township. Changcheng has 14 natural villages within its jurisdiction, with 611 households and a total population of 3,080 inhabitants. The population in the village is fully Han. The total area of agricultural land within the boundaries of the administrative village is 20,896 *mu*. The main agricultural crops are wheat, linseed, corn, millet and potato. A part of the fields is irrigated for the cultivation of tobacco. The major physical constraints are a lack of level land and harsh climate. Annual precipitation is 450–500 mm. Frequent droughts, hail, storms, frost, and occasional earthquakes ravage rural life [*Zhongguo Ziran Ziyuan Congshu Bianyi Weiyuanhui*, 1995].

Average net annual income per capita in 1995 was Rmb 786. Forestry has good development prospects in this region and has been stimulated by the local authorities. The most commonly planted tree species are Xinjiang poplar (*Populus alba var. pyramidalis*) and almond (*Prunus armeniaca*). The Xinjiang poplar is a fast-growing, drought-resistant tree, and its wood is suitable for paper pulp, building material and furniture. It has been planted with relative success in Pengyang since the early 1950s, although it is vulnerable to pests. The almond, too, is suited to semi-arid conditions and offers farmers a welcome extra source of income. The tree bears fruit after five years (which can be eaten fresh or dried) and the nuts can be processed into valuable almond oil or Chinese medicine. In 1996, the price for 1 kg apricots was Rmb 1–2, while the almonds went for Rmb 12.

Guided by the County Section of Forestry, the villagers have planted alfalfa (*Medicago sativa*), Siberian pea tree (*Caragana korshinskii*), and milk vetch (*Astragalus adsurgens*) as forage for livestock. Virtually every open space, shoulder or gully has been planted.[22] Despite the fact that sheep and goats are kept as a sideline activity and flocks are small (15–20 ruminants), the grazing of animals poses a serious threat to forestry. The farmers state that the customary practice of overlap grazing (*chuanmu*) makes tree planting a precarious undertaking, while fencing leads to land disputes.

The village is relatively well developed, with a good infrastructure and a daily bus service to the county seat. Marketing of agricultural produce is carried out in Pengyang, although the township market is also popular.

Changcheng has its own market every three days and it attracts farmers from far and wide. There are about ten shops, a small infirmary and a primary school. The village school is better equipped than other nearby schools where pupils are forced to write characters on the ground for lack of paper. An important centre for social gatherings is the temple that hosts festivals to which the village *qinqiang* opera group adds colour. That Changcheng is no ordinary village becomes obvious when looking at the many state awards and prizes, proudly hanging next to Mao's portrait in the village meeting hall. The most prominent and active figure in the village is the young party secretary, Li Yurong. Under his leadership, the village committee developed into a relatively efficient and effective institution, and recently moved to newly built offices.

A Tale of Village Assertiveness

The Wastelands Policy is confined to Guyuan Prefecture (in total six counties: Pengyang, Guyuan, Haiyuan, Xiji, Longde and Jingyuan).[23] The policy was initiated neither by the provincial nor by the prefectural authorities, but originated from Changcheng administrative village. In 1992, a small trial auction was held without the knowledge of the township. As the auction seemed successful, Li Yurong decided to put the entire wasteland area under the hammer and requested permission from the Chengyang township authorities. The township government feared getting its fingers burnt over an issue that directly pushed at the boundaries of the 'socialist market economy' and passed the plan to the County Forestry Section, which assisted Changcheng village with the organization and preparations for the auctions. The delicacy of the Wastelands Policy became obvious through a speech about it by the deputy prefect who stressed the need to eliminate 'leftist' thinking to develop the rural economy of Guyuan [*Zhonggong Guyuan Diwei Nonggongbu*, 1994: 196].

In the spring of 1993, the first full-fledged 'Four Wastelands Auction' of Changcheng village was held. The auction corresponded to those held in Lüliang. In a few months, the use rights to over 1 *mu* (1/15 ha) of wasteland had been sold. The County Section of Forestry planned to bring the auctions to the attention of Rui Cunzhang, the prefectural party secretary, through the *Guyuan Daily*, the newspaper most widely read in the prefecture.[24] At the time, a more liberalized atmosphere in China as a result of Deng's Southern Tour was already present. Moreover, the 'Four Wastelands Auction Policy' of Lüliang had by then gained full political justification. Rui ordered the powerful Agricultural Work Department of the Secretariat of the prefectural party committee to develop a policy framework for the auctions. This department is responsible for agricultural policy: it drafts local regulations, recommends and initiates changes in policy lines. It is also in charge of policy monitoring and evaluation, and is accountable to the Policy Research Office of the autonomous region party committee.

At the end of the year, the Changcheng village committee had earned Rmb 6,885 by selling use rights to 4,950 *mu* of wasteland. A total of 473 households (77 per cent of all households in the administrative village) had participated in the auction. The smallest area leased per household was 5 *mu*, whereas one farmer broke the village record with 120 *mu*. The minimum bid price had been set at Rmb 1 per *mu*, although some farmers claimed to have paid only Rmb 0.5 per *mu*. There was no maximum price level. The highest price was Rmb 50 per *mu* [*Changcheng Cunmin Weiyuanhui*, 1994; *Pengyang Xian Linyeju*, 1994]. The auctions were deemed a success and a political victory for the village authorities.[25]

On 18 March 1994, Rui Cunzhang spoke at a demonstration wasteland auction in Changcheng,[26] which marked the beginning of the campaign 'Learn from the "Four Wastelands" Auctions of Pengyang County' (*Xuexi Pengyang Xian 'Sihuang' paimai*). In spite of reservations about the movement's name, the tone of his speech was pragmatic and in no way reminiscent of past communist rhetoric of a 'learn-from-Dazhai' or any other 'learn-from' campaign. Several rules that Rui emphasized were subsequently incorporated in regulations proclaimed a few days later. It should be noted that he underlined the necessity of trial auctions before the formal implementation of the Wastelands Policy.

Of importance were his 'four no's', some of which – through an ironic twist of fate – did take place and led to the failure of the auctions. The 'four no's' were: (1) *no* egalitarian sales (dividing the wasteland into equal plots and selling the use rights to farmers at uniform prices); (2) *no* monopolization by clan heads; (3) *no* abuse of power by the cadres; and (4) *no* grain cultivation on wasteland. In order to appease the fear of the rural populace that the auctions were just another excuse by the government to extract money from the farmers, Rui stated explicitly that 'the reason why we auction "the Four Wastelands" is to step up the afforestation of waste mountains and not to earn a few more pennies' [*Zhonggong Guyuan Diwei*, 1994b: 3]. Two days after Rui's speech, the 'Four Wastelands Auction Policy' was officially proclaimed in the prefecture [*Zhonggong Guyuan Diwei*, 1994a: 2 and 6].

The Executing Agency: The County Section of Forestry

As the Agricultural Work Department charged the County Section of Forestry with the coordination of the auctions in Pengyang county, the majority of the members in the Four Wastelands Leading Team were from the Section of Forestry. As stated earlier, such a team conducts the surveying and mapping of the wasteland, provides free nursery stock, and supervises afforestation and planting activities. In practice, these tasks were carried out by subordinate units of the Section of Forestry.

The Section of Forestry seems an obvious choice for the wasteland auctions. First, in Guyuan the Section of Animal Husbandry assumes a great share of the duties in soil and water conservation. However, ecological differences have necessitated that the Section of Forestry is the responsible body in charge of soil and water conservation in Pengyang. The area of forested wasteland in Pengyang is larger because of higher precipitation (450–550 mm, compared with 350–450 mm in Guyuan).[27] For this reason, Pengyang is an important link in the 'Green Great Wall' – the shelterbelt covering China's northern provinces. A considerable portion of the prefectural funds is channelled to the Section of Forestry for afforestation.

Another factor why preference was given to the Section of Forestry instead of the Section of Animal Husbandry is the former's extensive network of township-based Forestry Management Stations. The staff of the Forestry Stations are backed up by a Forestry Police Force with equal rights as the regular police force (the rights to arrest and detain and to carry weapons). The stations are the instruments that allow the Section of Forestry to reach the dispersed rural settlements and maintain a close relationship with farmers. In contrast, the Section of Animal Husbandry operates from the county and only has an economic police force with insufficient powers.

The main activities of the Township Forestry Station are:

1. Afforestation, management and improvement of forests (including disease prevention and control, and pruning);
2. Support to farmers in fruit cultivation;
3. Supervision of grazing in forests and conflict resolution;
4. Stimulation of income-generating activities and organization of rural credits (for corn and tobacco cultivation).

The station is staffed by four people – all graduates of the forestry department of the middle agricultural school in Guyuan. The office is a shabby house at the township government compounds and is also the living quarters for one staff member and his young wife. The relatively low salary (Rmb 300 per month in 1996) is regarded as 'just enough', but the people at the Forestry Station seem well motivated.

When asked what the office still needs, one staff member replied, 'We most certainly lack a motorcycle.' Visits to the villages are done on foot. Every staff member visits about 20 to 30 households per day, covering a distance varying between 5 and 10 km. The members of the Forestry Station pay frequent visits to Changcheng village in order to keep in touch with any calls for assistance, land disputes, or other relevant news.

Hearing the Farmers: Results of the Auctions

The auctions in Changcheng were considered successful by the local authorities. But how were the auctions experienced by the farmers themselves? For a view from below, a small survey of 90 households (47 in Guyuan and 43 in Pengyang, including buyers and non-buyers) was carried out in 1996.[28] The survey, albeit not representative, was implemented to give a general idea of farmers' views of the Wastelands Policy. The experiences of farmers in Changcheng village are grouped around four categories: (1) the procedures and practice of the auctions; (2) the awareness of the policy aims and regulations; (3) the use of wasteland before and after the auctions; and (4) the appraisal of the policy.

1. Auction procedures and practice. The majority of respondents indicated that they had bought wasteland (81 per cent). About one-third of the farmers had bought less than 4 *mu* of land, while around 40 per cent had bought plots between 5 *mu* and 10 *mu*. Only one farmer had felt confident about buying a tract of wasteland larger than 20 *mu*. The chief limitation to wasteland development is the lack of labour capacity. Of the sample, 63 per cent indicated they wanted to buy more land, but lacked labour to work it. Approximately 12 per cent stated that their financial situation did not allow them to buy more land, and another 12 per cent mentioned that the village committee had imposed a limit on the land bought per household. The wasteland plots sold in Pengyang were not small and dispersed, but consisted of larger, consolidated plots in order to facilitate land management. In some cases, land consolidation occurred by reselling wasteland that had been auctioned before.

In Pengyang there is a rather even distribution among the various methods of price determination. Around 30 per cent of the farmers obtained wasteland in open sales with fixed prices posted prior to the selling. Another 30 per cent had negotiated with the village committee and bought land outside the auctions. The remaining 40 per cent acquired land through real auctions at which land was sold to the highest bidder (and two respondents said they did not know). There was no variation in the payment method. Despite the prefectural regulations, only lump sum payments were accepted by the village committee.

2. Awareness of the policy. The farmers in the region around Changcheng were well informed about the auctions. The Township Forestry Station and the village committee had made every effort to inform the farmers. Village meetings had been held, information about the wasteland plots had been posted, and forestry personnel had paid regular visits to prepare the auctions. The majority of farmers (93 per cent) heard about the auctions through the village committee. In addition, a body of county regulations had been proclaimed, and these provided the local interpretation of prefectural rules [*Pengyang Xian Renmin Zhengfu*, 1994a; *Pengyang Xian Renmin Zhengfu*, 1994b]. The proclamation of the 'Changcheng Village Forest Management Regulations' – similar to the county notices – was hung at a conspicuous place to serve as a reminder to the farmers.

The aims of the Wastelands Policy are soil and water conservation and poverty alleviation, while the authorities explicitly reassured farmers that auctions were *not* meant to generate revenues for the government. The farmers in Changcheng were aware of the first policy aim (70 per cent of the total sample), but the second aim was less known (44 per cent). When farmers were asked what rights they enjoyed, most knew that the contract does not grant ownership but use rights. It should be pointed out that farmers were unaware of the rights to transfer, inherit, usufruct and mortgage of wasteland (see Table 1). The rights to transfer and inheritance including those pertaining to wasteland are laid down in the 1993 Agriculture Law.[29] The only exception is the mortgage of land. However, according to the 1996 Notice on the Wastelands Policy 'those who buy use rights, have the right to inherit, transfer, mortgage and shareholding management' (article 6) [*Secretariat of the State Council*, 1997: 425–6].[30]

Farmers knew the restrictions imposed on the use of wasteland (prohibition of reclamation, road and house construction). But again, the rights they enjoy – land development and improvement by fencing, constructing corrals and rainwater reservoirs – are less known (see Table 2). If we look at the contract (standardized in the township) some things

TABLE 1

WHAT RIGHTS ARE INCLUDED IN THE WASTELAND CONTRACT?
(Pengyang sample; n = 43)

Type of right	Yes (%)	No (%)	Total (%)
Use right	88.4	11.6	100
Transfer of use right within village	14.0	86.0	100
Transfer of use right outside village	4.7	95.3	100
Inheritance right	30.2	69.8	100
Ownership right within village	11.6	88.4	100
Ownership right outside village	0.0	100.0	100
Usufruct	55.8	44.2	100
Mortgage right	2.3	97.7	100

Source: 1997 Survey by the author.

TABLE 2

WHAT ARE THE PROHIBITIONS TO THE USE OF WASTELAND?
(Pengyang sample, n = 43)

Type of prohibition	Yes (%)	No (%)	Total (%)
Agricultural reclamation	81.4	18.6	100
Cultivation of sorghum	69.8	30.2	100
Cultivation of millet	65.1	34.9	100
Cultivation of alfalfa	7.0	93.0	100
Afforestation	4.7	95.3	100
Fencing	37.2	62.8	100
Construction of corral	51.2	48.8	100
Construction of house	67.4	32.6	100
Construction of road	55.8	44.2	100
Construction of rainwater reservoir	25.6	74.4	100

Source: 1997 Survey by the author.

become clear. The contract does not mention the rights of transfer and inheritance, or the extension of the contract when expired. Reflecting the spirit of county rules, the contract specifies the duties and penalty rules related to the tenant rather than the tenant's rights (see Appendix A).

3. Wasteland use. Prior to the auctions, wasteland was mainly used as pasture, as indicated by 70 per cent of the respondents. After the auctions, wasteland was used for economic forestry purposes by 81 per cent of the farmers (90 per cent of whom planted almond) and sometimes for forage cultivation; 16 farm households managed one common almond orchard and each paid Rmb 2 to hire someone to guard an area of 40 mu against encroachment by sheep and goats.

4. Policy appraisal. The villagers of Changcheng were positive about the auctions. Of the sample, 67 per cent regarded the Wastelands Policy as 'quite successful' and 23 per cent as 'very successful'. The most frequently cited reason was the increase in income (70 per cent). However, it is unclear how the planting of almond, which takes five years to bear fruit, could yield returns within the three years that the auctions had taken place. There were also some disgruntled voices about the benefits of afforestation. One farmer said, 'The Wastelands Policy has succeeded, but we have seen no economic benefits yet. The trees grow slowly and there is the risk that exposure to the cold may cause them to freeze to death.' Another remarked, 'There really has not been much guidance on how we had to plant trees. Well, once a year someone from the Forestry Station comes by to check on us.' The issue of income generation arising from the Wastelands Policy remains a topic of future research.

There have been complaints about the party secretary. A farmer described the secretary's behaviour with the adage by the Song dynasty scholar Yu Wenbao, 'I really resent the fact that Li Yurong secured the best land for himself. Well, that is clearly a case of 'the tower closest to the water gets the moon' (*jin shui loutai xian de yue*).'[31] Regardless of whether the party secretary did get hold of the best tracts, he violated the law when – as a member of the village authorities – he participated in the auction. Article 22 of the Auction Law states that 'the auctioning party and its employees are not allowed to participate in the capacity of a competing party in auctioning activities organized by itself, nor to entrust others to compete on its behalf'.[32] The 1996 Notice on the Wastelands Policy does not exclude state officials from the auctions. But a senior official within the Ministry of Agriculture warned against the participation of cadres:

> It may seem rational that state and Party organs participate in the management of the 'Four Wastelands', but it can easily foster unhealthy tendencies ... We should prohibit the lease of the 'Four Wastelands' by cadres of state organs [*Li*, 1995: 30].

According to the Pengyang Section of Forestry, agricultural reclamation of wasteland did take place, notably in the poorer regions. Despite this, the prefectural authorities were satisfied with the results. The auctions were extended to other counties in the prefecture. However, in spring 1996 the Wastelands Policy was suddenly halted, less than two years after its promulgation. According to the Agricultural Work Department, over 50 per cent of wasteland in the prefecture was reclaimed for agriculture resulting in large-scale soil erosion. In the following sections, the background to the policy failure is provided through a case study of Guyuan county.

IMPOSING IMPLEMENTATION: GUANTING VILLAGE

Village Description

Nested in mountains that look like huge birthday cakes because of the terraced fields, Guanting village is conveniently located on the main road to Guyuan. It is an hour's bumpy ride from Guanting to the county seat (20 km northeast from Guyuan). Guanting administrative village[33] is concurrently the seat of the Guanting township government. One may wonder, but the name Guanting has nothing to do with a Qing dynasty (1644–1911) subprefecture. At the time when Mao's First Front Army marched into Guyuan in October 1935, Guanting had already developed into a walled market town, housing the public office of the township (whence its name 'Public Office').

Guanting administers 11 natural villages, a total of 398 farm households and 2,046 people. The population is predominantly Hui, with very few Han

Chinese (of 5,442 Hui in Guanting, four are Han Chinese). There is no significant ethnic tension, but the Han – condescendingly designated by the Hui as 'the old Han' (*lao hanren*) – are aware of their minority position. The agricultural crops grown are the same as in Chengyang. The main difference is the lack of irrigation, and thus, the impossibility of tobacco cultivation. The total cultivated area in Guanting village is 11,105 *mu*. Annual precipitation, which is lower than in Chengyang (around 450 mm per year), seems to make a critical difference for forestry. Afforestation has been attempted through repeated planting campaigns since the founding of the People's Republic, but the farmers state that the saplings face a sure death owing to the frequent droughts. Trees only grow in the vicinity of fields or close to cave dwellings, where small-scale irrigation is possible. The barren hills of Guyuan are in stark contrast with the green, forested mountains of Pengyang.

In 1995 the net average annual income was Rmb 312. Sheep and goat raising is more important in Guanting than in Changcheng. There are 1,115 sheep and 290 cashmere goats (1996), but farmers state that animal husbandry has been declining over the last ten years. The main reason cited is the increased reclamation of village pastures as a result of population pressure. Hills once in use as pastures have been turned into terraced – or worse, non-terraced – fields.

As Guanting is also the township seat, many state institutions are located in the village. The village hosts the granary, the supply and marketing cooperative, a credit cooperative, a veterinary station, and a forestry management station. In addition, there is a market, a primary school, an infirmary, a few groceries, and an antique shop that purchases jade seals, bronze buckles, Han-dynasty mirrors, and other art objects robbed from graves in the neighbourhood. Also important is the mosque, which serves a congregation (or *fang*) of believers from the 11 natural villages.

Guanting has frequently been the site of poverty alleviation projects. Poverty is aggravated by a poor infrastructure – although Guanting itself is relatively easy to reach, the other natural villages are remote and dispersed. In some cases, 10 to 15 isolated cave dwellings, scattered over a distance of several kilometres, may constitute one 'natural village'. This fragmented structure of villages in Guyuan inhibits contact with the farmers, a complaint often heard by the township cadres. Moreover, landslides cause major damage to the rural infrastructure.

Compared with the atmosphere of dynamism in Changcheng, Guanting exudes an air of apathy and indifference. The officials at the township are difficult to reach, cadres have been temporarily laid off and encouraged to become independent entrepreneurs.[34] Even the township head left the township for three years to set up a business. At the Forestry Station, the staff – unpaid for months – frequently while away the time by playing chess and poker. Cynical laughter was the response to the question of what their main tasks were. 'It does not matter what we do,' said an official, 'the trees we plant are eaten by the sheep and we have no money to carry out our tasks anyway.'

The Executing Agency: Who Is Responsible?

> The prefectural Agricultural Work Department is responsible for the Wastelands Policy. In each county a section is charged with policy implementation. For Pengyang this is the Section of Forestry. And in Guyuan ... I'm not sure which section would be responsible [official at Guyuan Section of Animal Husbandry].

On paper the Section of Animal Husbandry is charged with the auctions. But talks with officials in this institution and at the grassroots reveal there is no consensus about which state organ is responsible. Before turning to the details of the implementation or non-implementation of the Wastelands Policy, I will discuss this government body in terms of tasks and mission, resources and internal structure.

The prime responsibility of the Section of Animal Husbandry is the management and development of rangeland. In contrast to Pengyang where most wasteland is forest, wasteland in Guyuan is generally rangeland. Therefore, the Section of Animal Husbandry is the obvious institution for the Wastelands Policy. The institutional structure of the Section of Animal Husbandry is less extensive than that of the Section of Forestry. In the 1980s there were veterinary stations at the township level for livestock disease prevention and veterinary care. But over the past years, township personnel was laid off and stations contracted out to 'individual entrepreneurs' (in fact former state personnel). For effective rangeland management the Section of Animal Husbandry has to reach the grassroots level. At present, however, this agency operates from the county level.

There are 32 people at the county level – including 16 grassland (economic) police officers – responsible for 26 townships (compare this to the Section of Forestry that employs 36 people at the county level, not to mention the staff at the township). Despite provincial salary norms for state organs, the monthly income of personnel at the Section of Animal Husbandry is far lower (Rmb 210–220 in 1996) than that of their colleagues in the Section of Forestry (Rmb 300). The difference in salary is just one of many differences that separate these two institutions, promoting envy and competition among staff.

The regular duties of the Section of Animal Husbandry comprise:

1. The development and management of wasteland (revegetation and construction of forage bases);

2. Rangeland protection and increase of rangeland production (rodents and pest control, fire management, weeding of inedible plants and aerial sowing – halted owing to budgetary reasons);
3. Technical/veterinary extension and services;
4. The development and introduction of new forage varieties;
5. Law enforcement and conflict mediation (patrolling, control of illegal reclamation and grazing).

The period where it is least likely to encounter people in the county office is from April to July, when the staff has 'gone down to the countryside' (*xia xiang*) to patrol and investigate legal cases. These activities are impeded by the poor financial situation. The grassland police officers go to the township by bus or when there is money for gas, by car. The office has a 13-year-old, rusty Beijing Jeep. To reach farmers, grassland police often walk from the township to the villages.

The Section of Animal Husbandry had to carry out a comprehensive survey of wasteland resources in the county. For unknown reasons county funds were not committed to the Wastelands Policy, as a result of which no survey was done, nor was any support given to villages in setting up the auctions. It appears that the poorly equipped townships were fully saddled with the survey of wasteland and the organization of the auctions. Moreover, the implementation was hampered by a disagreement over the division of duties between the Section of Animal Husbandry and the Section of Forestry. These two institutions have clashed many times before over policies both deemed to be their responsibility. As noted earlier, the legal status of wasteland is unclear, and that leads to confusion over the tasks.

According to article 13 of the 1991 Executive Regulations of the Land Management Law, the development of state-owned wasteland must be approved by the (former) State Land Administration if the area is between 10,000 *mu* and 20,000 *mu*, and by the State Council if it exceeds 20,000 *mu*.[35] It was on this basis that a bureaucrat within the Ningxia State Land Administration asserted that the Wastelands Policy was illegal. He stated that:

> The State Land Administration alone has the authority to issue land use permits. The Pengyang Section of Forestry should not have approved of the auctions without our prior consent. The sections of forestry and animal husbandry believed they had authority, which created chaos.[36]

Why did the Section of Animal Husbandry and the Section of Forestry fight over responsibilities? One reason, of course, is the perception of their own mission. As remarked earlier, the greater part of wasteland in Guyuan is rangeland, not forested pasture. Therefore, the Section of Animal Husbandry felt it should be the agency to execute the Wastelands Policy. But this does not explain why the Section of Animal Husbandry was willing to implement a policy for which no funds had been committed. There are in fact several other relevant factors.

First, the auctions relieved the duties of the Section of Animal Husbandry. Each year the prefecture imposes revegetation quotas for the construction of artificial rangeland and forage bases. The Wastelands Policy shifted the duty for wasteland development from the local state to individual farm households. In 1996, the Section of Animal Husbandry revegetated 2,000 *mu* of wasteland. An additional 20,000 *mu* was planned for the future. However, one-third of this area had already been auctioned to farmers. In contrast to the policy guidelines, the Section of Animal Husbandry did not provide the farmers with free grass seeds. This institution, therefore, effectively allocated a substantial portion of its tasks to farmers without having to pay a penny.

Another reason for the involvement of the Section of Animal Husbandry in the Wastelands Policy was the high political priority attached to the latter. Disagreeing with the pragmatism of the party secretary, who called for trial auctions, control on reclamation, and the abuse of cadres, the deputy prefect declared in a speech:

> We demand that every county move quickly, and with great strides. One cannot deliberate first, try, and then execute … Of course, one will meet with problems during implementation, but we firmly believe that under the correct leadership of the prefecture and counties … a new breakthrough of the 'Four Wastelands' auctions can be realized.[37]

Failure of the Auctions

Reactions to the Wastelands Policy differed widely in Guanting. Similar to the Section of Animal Husbandry, the township authorities wanted to distinguish themselves with the auctions. In addition, it was financially attractive because revenues from the auctions would go to the township. Particularly for the poor townships, the lure of money provided a strong incentive.

Opposition, however, arose from the village leaders, who contested the auctions on two grounds: (a) privatization of wasteland would deprive herders from grazing grounds because most of it was used as common pasture; (b) the area of wasteland was insufficient to auction to the farmers. Either some would get large plots or everyone would obtain land too small for efficient management, a problem against which the prefectural party secretary had already warned. There was no fear of unfair competition from cadres and legal persons from outside the village. The prefecture had allowed open auctions, but the county restricted the auctions to the population of each village to avoid social unrest [*Zhonggong Guyuan Diwei*, 1994a: 3].

Despite the opposition, the county and township authorities exerted pressure to force the policy through. The policy rapidly gained momentum and in a year, over 40,000 *mu* of wasteland (one-third of the area planned for auction) had been sold. To evaluate the policy results, I will adopt the same categories as in the previous section on Pengyang: (1) auction procedures and practice; (2) awareness of the policy; (3) use of wasteland prior and after the auctions; and (4) appraisal of the policy.

1. Auction procedures and practice. A majority (87 per cent) of the households in the sample (n = 47) stated they had bought wasteland. Many farmers (70 per cent) wanted to buy more, but decided not to because of insufficient funds (39 per cent), a lack of labour capacity (27 per cent), intervention by the village committee (21 per cent), and a lack of suitable wasteland (13 per cent). For Guanting, the word 'auction' is misleading as the price was fixed by the township prior to the sale. In a few cases, the price was determined by negotiation. The average price was Rmb 4 per *mu*, with a maximum price of Rmb 6. A land ceiling of 5 *mu* of land was imposed on each household. As a result, wasteland was distributed evenly but plots were fragmented. An attempt was made to set up a communal wasteland management, but village leaders said that 'the undertaking failed as there was not enough non-disputed wasteland to sell'. Of the total sample, almost 50 per cent did not secure a consolidated tract, but got small and dispersed pieces of land.

2. Awareness of the policy. Like in Changcheng village, the overall majority (96 per cent) of respondents heard about the auctions through the village committee. The policy objectives were not well understood. Of the sample, one-quarter did not respond. Of the remaining three-quarters who did respond, 34 per cent said the auctions were meant for environmental protection, and 27 per cent for the increase in farmers' income. On the other hand, 15 per cent said the auctions helped the government to gain revenues, and 12 per cent ironically thought wasteland was sold to increase the acreage of agricultural land. Respondents were less aware of the rights and prohibitions than the Changcheng farmers; there was a remarkably high percentage of people who answered 'don't know' (21 per cent) (see Tables 3 and 4).

3. Wasteland use. Before the auctions, wasteland in Guyuan was virtually

TABLE 3

WHAT RIGHTS ARE INCLUDED IN THE WASTELAND CONTRACT?
(Guyuan sample; n = 47)

Type of right	Yes (%)	No (%)	Don't know (%)	Total (%)
Use right	66.0	12.7	21.3	100
Transfer of use right within village	17.0	61.7	21.3	100
Transfer of use right outside village	6.4	72.3	21.3	100
Inheritance right	23.4	55.3	21.3	100
Ownership right within village	4.2	74.5	21.3	100
Ownership right outside village	2.1	76.6	21.3	100
Usufruct	29.8	48.9	21.3	100
Mortgage right	2.1	76.6	21.3	100

Source: 1997 Survey by the author.

TABLE 4

WHAT ARE THE PROHIBITIONS TO THE USE OF WASTELAND?
(Guyuan sample, n = 47)

Type of prohibition	Yes (%)	No (%)	Don't know (%)	Total (%)
Agricultural reclamation	74.5	21.2	4.3	100
Cultivation of sorghum	55.3	40.4	4.3	100
Cultivation of millet	53.1	42.6	4.3	100
Cultivation of alfalfa	0.0	95.7	4.3	100
Afforestation	4.2	91.5	4.3	100
Fencing	8.5	87.2	4.3	100
Construction of corral	34.0	61.7	4.3	100
Construction of house	57.4	38.3	4.3	100
Construction of road	46.8	48.9	4.3	100
Construction of rainwater reservoir	19.1	76.6	4.3	100

Source: 1997 Survey by the author.

without exception used for herding, more than in Pengyang where forestry is another option. After the auctions, the wasteland was used for several purposes such as afforestation, pasture, the cultivation of forage and grass, and, unfortunately, grain cultivation. Large tracts of wasteland were reclaimed, despite the fact that the majority (74.5 per cent) of the farmers was aware that agricultural reclamation was forbidden (see Table 4). How can this contradiction be explained?

The Wastelands Policy stipulates that wasteland can be used for planting trees or grass (*zhong shu, zhong cao*). The government used the word 'grass' to refer to 'forage': alfalfa, milk vetch and pea tree. Of the respondents in Guanting, 46 per cent stated they used wasteland for planting grass (compared to 25 per cent in Changcheng). A crucial issue is *what* was planted. Of the respondents in Guyuan who planted 'grass', most of them (81 per cent) had in fact planted sorghum and millet. In comparison, of those who planted 'grass' in Changcheng, the majority (82 per cent) indicated they planted alfalfa. The contrast between the conception of 'grass' by Guanting and Changcheng villagers seems ludicrous. The following dialog with a Guanting farmer might illustrate this ironic misunderstanding of terms:

> 'Are farmers allowed to plant grain on wasteland?'
> 'No,' the farmer said.
> 'What do you plant at present?'
> 'Sorghum, millet and corn.'
> 'But isn't that grain?'
> No, it's grass, because we use the stalks as forage for our sheep and oxen.'

Other farmers answered in a similar fashion and claimed the government never clarified the meaning of 'planting grass'. As demonstrated above, the farmers of Guanting were badly informed about the auctions.

The contract, which ideally should have stipulated the rights and duties of the contractant and the administrative village, is nothing more than a farce. In contradiction with the 1996 Notice, no farmer signed or saw a contract. Moreover, the prefectural regulations stipulate that the contracts must be notarized and issued in triplicate (for the tenant, the lessor – the administrative village – and the Township Rural Economic Station). In practice, the contracts were held by the village leaders and the township. Despite the fact that *individual* farmers bought use rights, there were *common* copies for every five to ten households, labelled 'joint households' without their knowledge. In one case, a village of 25 households had only four contracts for all the farmers. The contract – a one-page, handwritten sheet of paper full of grammatical mistakes and unreadable characters – states nothing more than the price, the farmers' names of the 'joint household', the lease term, and the wasteland boundaries. The duties, explained in such detail in the Changcheng contracts, are merely described as 'planting trees and grass', not to mention the rights of the tenant (see Appendix B).

In addition to the factors above, there is another reason that caused the failure of the policy. Half of the respondents *were* aware that the cultivation of millet and sorghum was prohibited (see Table 4). Why did farmers decide to reclaim wasteland, while they knew it was prohibited? The probable answer is provided by the deputy director of the Agricultural Work Department:

The timing of the auctions in Guyuan County was most unfortunate. It coincided with a prolonged drought. Of course farmers illegally reclaimed the land they had gained. If we would not have auctioned the land, they might not have had enough to eat.

4. Policy appraisal. In Guyuan, the effects of illegal reclamation were not limited to soil erosion. Herding families complained that reclamation had destroyed the watering tracks for animals. Herders also witnessed a rapid decline in grazing grounds, which forced them to move to more remote pastures. Over the past years, land disputes between pastoralists and farmers intensified. Moreover, according to the township, the number of ruminants in Guanting decreased by more than 50 per cent compared with the period before the auctions. The destruction of the watering tracks has also led to greater isolation of villages and individual farm households. As villages often comprise not more than a few isolated cave dwellings, watering tracks are a crucial part of the rural infrastructure.

The overall experience of the wasteland auctions is negative. Of the total sample, only six per cent believed their income had increased, while 15 per cent felt that forage availability had improved. Many stated they faced increasing difficulties with the availability of suitable pasture (49 per cent). When asked what they thought of the auctions, 55 per cent said it had 'mostly failed', while 40 per cent felt it had 'completely failed'.

In spring 1996, the prefectural authorities reacted to the news of large-scale, illegal reclamation with an immediate halt to the auctions. The townships in Guyuan, where the situation had got most out of hand, were called upon to check illegal reclamation with heavy penalties. Special teams were established of township and village cadres. Each team was required to survey the wasteland, report the reclaimed area, and impose fines on those who had mismanaged wasteland. The fines varied from Rmb 50 to Rmb 200 per *mu* of reclaimed land [*Guanting Xiang Renmin Zhengfu*, 1996]. The revenues from the fines were supposed to go to an afforestation fund (the same fund for the profits from auctions) administered by the township. However, the fund was never established giving rise to the suspicion of rent-seeking.

The aggressive response by the government stirred up ill feelings among the rural populace. Farmers felt the authorities had once more forced their will upon them. One farmer commented, 'The Wastelands Policy was a failure for us because we are fined, time and again. But it was a success for the government because they get our money time and again. And I don't even know why we are fined.' Another stated, 'The government tells us to plant grass, but if we plant millet and sorghum we are fined! Can you understand that? From now on I won't plant anything, no grain, no trees, no grass.'

CONCLUDING REMARKS: THE COLLECTIVIST ROOTS OF CHINESE POLICY IMPLEMENTATION

In the introduction I put forward three theses on the Four Wastelands Auction Policy in Ningxia: (1) it is a symbol for the new space in China opened up by the reforms which allows the lower administrative levels (county and below) to initiate and shape policies generally considered sensitive or too innovative; (2) the policy entails great possible socio-economic changes because it removes the so-called rural–urban divide; (3) the manner of policy implementation bears the traits of the collectivist past when labour-intensive mass campaigns with scant regard for regional variations were considered the appropriate model for rural development.

In Ningxia the Wastelands Policy was initially not implemented in a top-down manner. As with the start of the Household Contract Responsibility System in Fengyang county (Anhui province) or the first wasteland auctions in Lüliang prefecture (Shanxi province), the policy originated from the grassroots level. The Wastelands Policy began in Changcheng village (Guyuan prefecture) in response to problems encountered in the management of hilly land. The village and township authorities displayed considerable countervailing power in initiating and shaping the Wastelands Policy. In China during the early 1990s, the use of auctions to transfer wasteland use and management rights to individual farmers still belonged to the danger zone of 'leftist thinking'. At the time, the pioneer in wasteland auctions – Lüliang prefecture – also met with considerable opposition from the Shanxi provincial authorities. Therefore, the policy was marked by deliberate scheming and lobbying by local authorities to push it through various administrative levels from the village to the level where decisions are taken: the prefectural party committee. In fact, the Guyuan party committee had been given a Hobson's choice as the auctions were completed in Changcheng village when a reporter brought the news into the open. The relative success of the early wasteland auctions granted them sufficient legitimacy for trials on a larger scale. In the end, what started as a local solution to soil erosion was turned into official policy.

The so-called open auction of the Wastelands Policy implies another break with the past. Under the current Household Contract Responsibility System the lease right to agricultural land is mostly restricted to rural residents (although this is stipulated neither in the 1993 Agriculture Law nor in the 1998 Land Management Law).[38] In contrast, the open auction implies the dismantling of the rural–urban divide, as it allows urban cadres, entrepreneurs and legal entities to participate in the auctions, and thus gain access to rural land.

The idea of open auction incited fierce debate among policy-makers and scholars. Its proponents believe that in a Darwinian process of live or perish, open competition will force the less educated and 'culturally backward' to innovate or leave the agricultural realm. The Deputy Head of the Ningxia Provincial Bureau of Animal Husbandry thinks the auctions are an excellent opportunity to stimulate the most active and capable of the rural and urban population to develop marginal lands. Yet, many others – not in the least some high officials within the Ministry of Agriculture – oppose this rationale. While they acknowledge the opportunities of the Wastelands Policy for soil and water conservation improvement, poverty alleviation and long-term economic development, they simultaneously stress the need to protect the rural poor. Although the State Council and the Guyuan prefectural party committee permitted open auction, it proved too sensitive in Ningxia and was subsequently banned by the county authorities.

In the course of economic development, an erosion of the rural–urban divide might be expected. In suburban areas or more developed coastal regions, such as the provinces of Zhejiang and Fujian, the rural–urban divide is less pronounced. In these regions, there are ample employment opportunities outside the agricultural realm, as a result of which farmers are less dependent on land. Under such conditions, the rural collectives are more eager to grant leases to hilly land to companies or urban entrepreneurs as they command greater financial and material resources and can operate on a larger scale. In Fujian province there was an instance in which a Taiwanese businessman obtained use rights to wasteland [*Yang*, 1999: 89–90].[39] However, for poverty-stricken areas such as Ningxia, with almost no rural industrialization and few alternative income sources, open auctions will surely prove socially disruptive. The choice by the counties for closed auctions and negotiated sales can therefore only be welcomed.

Eduard Vermeer once remarked that 'politics in China is still conducted in an overall campaign-style manner, rather than being geared to the specific needs of each separate economic sector, and that further decentralization and functional specialization of political and administrative powers are called for' [*Vermeer*, 1998: 165].[40] It is this commandist mode of implementation that ties the Four Wastelands Auction Policy to China's collectivist past.

The party secretary of Guyuan prefecture had not intended to launch another Dazhai mass movement when he urged 'Learn from the "Four Wastelands" Auctions in Pengyang'. Despite his attempts to identify the imminent dangers of rigid implementation whereby there is little room for local variation and to stress the necessity of trial auctions, the policy became another model turned orthodoxy. Once the policy was proclaimed, every state institution, county and township strove to implement the policy first, even when responsibilities were unclear and no funds had been committed to carry out basic duties such as wasteland surveys and guidance for the auctions. Furthermore, in order to be swift, authorities ignored farmers' opposition about the fragmentation of wasteland and loss of valuable common pasture through privatization.

Apart from the manner of implementation, the Four Wastelands Auction Policy can be improved in many ways. The most essential aspects concern the method of payment, the form of wasteland management, dissemination of information among the rural populace, the problem of monopolization by cadres and the village elite, and effective legal protection of the lessee. Particularly in poor regions, lump sum payments constitute a problem for farmers. The possibility of payment in instalments, mortgage and rural credit are essential instruments to enable the rural poor to compete on a more equal footing with the financially strong. Diversity in the form of management – individual households, joint households, share-holding cooperatives, or voluntary peasant associations – is necessary as the economic value of most wasteland is low and wasteland management would benefit from collective action. Through cooperation, farming families can pool together the financial and labour resources, while the greater economies of scale will allow for more efficient investments.[41] From the case studies it is clear that the dissemination of information among the rural populace is wanting. Many interviewed farmers were not aware of the policy goals or their specific rights and duties. The large-scale illegal agricultural reclamation after the auctions is partly a result of this.

The danger of monopolization by the village elite and cadres can be averted through better supervision of the auction practices – virtually absent in Guyuan prefecture as no budget had been committed to the policy, and responsibilities for the implementation were unclear. In fact, if the wastelands auctions were executed as auctions in the strictest sense, they should also conform to the 1997 Auction Law, which prohibits an overlap between the buying, commissioning and auctioning parties. The village authorities are then automatically excluded from executing as well as participating in the auction. In addition, the use of land ceilings per bidder can prove an effective means against the concentration of land in the hands of a few.

The success of the Four Wastelands Auction Policy in the future also hinges on effective legal protection of the lessee's economic interests. In Ningxia, the practice of issuing common contracts to five or ten households labelled 'joint households' without their knowledge, the lack of standardized contracts with clearly spelled-out rights and duties for lessor and lessee, and the absence of notarization are examples of cadres' weak grasp of legal issues. If the economic interests of lessees are not adequately safeguarded, they will be unwilling to bear the burden of long-term investments necessary for the development of marginal land. Related to this issue is land expropriation by the state.

The 1986 Land Management Law did not provide for an adequate valuation of wasteland to cover the investments for development. Wasteland development needs larger, long-term investments as returns are slower compared with agricultural land [*Hanstad and Li*, 1997: 571–2]. This problem has partly been overcome in the revised Land Management Law, which came into effect on 1 January 1999. It stipulates higher standards for monetary compensation of expropriated agricultural land. However, the rule that 'expropriated land will be compensated according to the original use of the expropriated land' (article 47) is problematic. If this implies 'that what is originally waste mountain and wasteland without economic profit will in principle not receive compensation' – as the legal interpretation by the Deputy Minister of Land Resources reads – the increase of the compensation standards would have been in vain.[42] As the revised Land Management Law has been proclaimed very recently it is still too early to assess its effects on the expropriation of wasteland.

A last problem, which touches on the interests of the lessee, is the unclear property rights structure of agricultural land and wasteland in particular (see also the section on the evolution of the Wastelands Policy). The issue is too extensive to be dealt with in detail here. At this point, it suffices to state that unless the ownership of wasteland is clarified and protected by law, many land disputes can be expected in the future when wasteland leases are transferred, mortgaged and sold. A senior official within the Ministry of Agriculture aptly identified the crux of the problem:

> In many cases land leases are issued by the administrative village, while the land belonged to the natural village in the past. It is like the ownership rights to land have been silently stolen from the natural village and vested in a level higher ... Yet, to date there are not many conflicts because farmers are not properly acquainted with the idea of 'property'. But problems are sure to arise in the future ... .[43]

Some of the policy recommendations mentioned above might not have been necessary if the Wastelands Policy had allowed for trial auctions and feedback from below. The real tragedy of the Wastelands Policy is that its initial strength – a local solution to locally perceived problems – was subsequently turned into orthodoxy and uniformly spread to dissimilar regions. This is what ultimately caused its failure.

APPENDIX A

CHANGCHENG ADMINISTRATIVE VILLAGE, CHENGYANG TOWNSHIP, PENGYANG COUNTY AFFORESTATION CONTRACT FOR 'FOUR WASTELANDS' SUITABLE FOR FOREST

In order to provide more incentives to farmers in the use and development of afforestation on the 'Four Wastelands' suitable for forest, this 'Afforestation Contract For "Four Wastelands" Suitable For Forest' has been specifically concluded according to the spirit of the Rural Meetings of the entire region and the consultations between Changcheng Village, Chengyang Township (hereafter Party A) and Villager [name], from [name] Team, Changcheng Village, Chengyang Township (hereafter Party B), to facilitate mutual compliance.

(I) Content, Area and Location of the Auction

Party A has auctioned the use rights to the 'Four Wastelands' suitable for forest for [area in *mu*] of land, to Party B for the use of afforestation (for the category of land, and boundaries refer to the table attached).

(II) Term of Use, and Term of Re-vegetation[44] and Rangeland Construction

The term of use is 50 years (with effect from the day the contract is signed), inheritance, transfer and rent are permitted, the term of re-vegetation and rangeland construction is one year (the end of 1994).

(III) Management of the 'Four Wastelands' Suitable for Forest

1. Party B has the right to use, management and usufruct of the 'Four Wastelands' suitable for forest.
2. The afforestation of the 'Four Wastelands' suitable for forest should adhere to the principle of 'suited to the soil, suited to trees', and should be implemented by engineering management, namely planning according to the engineering project; construction design according to the planning; supervision and approval according to the construction scheme.

(IV) Rights and Duties of Parties A and B

1. The 'Four Wastelands' use right bought by Party B is protected by law, no person has the right to change or infringe it.
2. Party A will provide Party B with saplings necessary for afforestation once.
3. At regular intervals, Party A will inspect and approve the entire plot, management and protection, and planting by Party B. If requirements have not been met, corresponding penalties will be imposed.
4. Party B has to use the 'Four Wastelands' suitable for forest for afforestation and it is not permitted to use it for other purposes.
5. Party B must fulfil its afforestation duties in time, and the survival rate[45] [of the saplings] has to be above 70 per cent.
6. Party B will carefully check the nursery stock provided by Party A. Nursery stock that is not up to the standard will be rejected, in which case Party A will be required to provide new nursery stock that meets the standards.
7. Party B has to plant and level the land according to the planning design and demands (standards are attached).

8. One can only proceed to fell the trees that have grown to full size after reporting to the Forestry Bureau.

(V) Rewards and Penalties

1. Rewards and awards will be given if the re-vegetation duties have been fulfilled in time and all quality requirements have been met.
2. Failure to fulfil the re-vegetation and afforestation duties on time will result in a levy of Rmb 10 per *mu* to compensate for the losses incurred as a result of the delay in planting duties. The portion that has not been afforested will be repossessed and auctioned again to households that are engaged in afforestation. The original auction fee will not be returned.
3. If the levelling of land does not meet the specified standards, a fine of Rmb 1 to Rmb 5 per *mu* will be imposed.
4. If the planting does not meet the standards a fine of Rmb 5 to Rmb 10 will be imposed.
5. If the survival rate of saplings does not meet the standards (except in the event of natural disasters), a fine of Rmb 10 to Rmb 20 per *mu* will be imposed. In addition, replanting is compulsory. A fine of Rmb 20 to Rmb 40 per *mu* will be imposed on those who do not replant.
6. Apart from levying a fee for the losses incurred by the delay in planting duties on those who reclaim and plant other agricultural crops on the 'Four Wastelands' suitable for forest, penalties will also be imposed on those who indiscriminately build houses, and those who cause soil erosion, as stipulated by the 'Soil and Water Conservation Measures'.
7. If Party A has not provided the nursery stock in time, thereby affecting the timely completion of the planting, then Party A must compensate the losses of Party B.

(VI) This contract is in duplicate, and both Parties A and B hold one copy each. [The contract] takes effect from the date of signing.

Party A: The Village Committee of Changcheng Village

Stamp [Village Committee of Changcheng Village, Chengyang Township, Pengyang County]

Party B: Farmer [name] of Team [name] of Changcheng Village

Stamp

Date

[APPENDIX]

Standards for land levelling and planting:

Stripping fields and counter-erosion on hills: These must be 1.2 to 2 m wide, with a distance of 4 m between the strips. Counter-erosion ditches with an angle of 15° must be constructed on the fields which have to be ploughed 30 cm deep. Both sides of the field must be level in order to prevent runoff. A small earth dyke has to be constructed at intervals of 5 m.

Fish ponds: These must be 80 x 80 cm, 50 cm deep, in the form of a winnowing fan, the layout in the form of the character *pin* [product], with 3 m in between the ponds, and 3 m in between the rows.
Planting: the roots must be shaken out and tightly packed [in the soil], the branches must be straight, the upper [part] must be open[46] and the lower [part] must be solid, the rows between the trees must be regular and well ordered, and the saplings must be planted in 10 cm of soil.

[TABLE]

Designation of the plot	Land category	Area	Boundaries

APPENDIX B

GUANTING ADMINISTRATIVE VILLAGE, GUANTING TOWNSHIP, GUYUAN COUNTY CONTRACT OF THE FOUR WASTELANDS AUCTION OF GUANTING TOWNSHIP[47]

In order to develop and use the Four Wastelands resources, to deal properly with the control of gullies, to improve the ecological environment, and [? 'to step up rangeland'] construction, the Four Wastelands Auction is executed – according to Party Document No.13/1994 issued by the County Party Committee, and [? 'the Guyuan Prefectural Party Committee'].

Party A: In the spirit of [?], [name] village has sold [amount of land] *mu* of wasteland, with a land price of [amount in Rmb] per *mu* (in total [amount in Rmb]) to [name], for the development and use of the land for planting trees and grass. During the period of use, both parties are not allowed to end the contract without legitimate reasons.

Party B: [name] has come to an agreement with the village to buy from Party A [amount] *mu* – in the east bounded by [place], in the south bounded by [place], in the west bounded by [place], and in the north bounded by [place] – to plant trees and grass. This takes effect from the date on which the contract is signed. The period of use is [number of] years. During the period of land use, the user of the land is not allowed to change its utilization. Its use is protected by law, and no work unit or individual may infringe the said law.

Signature of the Representative of Party A
Stamp [Guanting Village Committee, Guanting Township, Guyuan County]

Signature of Party B
Stamp [Farmer]

Supervising Authority
Stamp [Guanting Township Government, Guyuan County]

Date

NOTES

1. Over the past few years, the field of policy studies on China in general and environmental policy in particular has increasingly become the focus of academic exploration. However, the rationale for policy formulation and the details of the implementation process frequently elude scientific analysis. See also Ross [1988]; Sinkule and Ortolano [1995]; Lotspeich and Chen [1997] and Edmonds [1998].
2. There is an inherent tension in the attempt to separate 'formulation' from 'implementation' during the analysis. I regard both as parts of an evolutionary process in which they alternate in response to perceived problems, similar to the description provided by Pressman and Wildavsky. The issue raised by David Lampton about the difficulty of assessing policy failure or success is less problematic in the case of the Wastelands Policy because there is no hidden agenda involved. See also Grindle [1980: 7–8]; Lampton [1987: 5–7]; Pressman and Wildavsky [1979: 177–94].
3. The main difference between the Dazhai model and the Four Wastelands Auction Policy is

the manner in which soil erosion is fought against, the former through the use of the masses and the latter by means of privatization.

4. For a similar case in the sphere of forestry, see Ross [1987].
5. The official statistics give a total surface of 66,400 km². But recent surveys have shown that the actual surface is much smaller. The Hui are the predominant ethnic minority in Ningxia; other minorities like the Mongols and Uyghur only account for 0.45 per cent of the population.
6. Tongxin, Guyuan, Haiyuan, Xiji, Longde, Jingyuan and Pengyang. The rural net annual income per capita has been taken as the indicator for poverty in the counties.
7. Figures provided by the Pengyang county Section of Forestry.
8. Article 19 of the prefectural regulations [*Zhonggong Guyuan Diwei*, 1994b].
9. The buying party is in fact further differentiated into the competing party and the buying party or the (legal) entity that buys the good against the highest bidding price.
10. See 1997 Auction Law [*Zhongguo Falü Nianjian Bianji Weiyuanhui*, 1997: 285–8].
11. It should also be noted that the Four Wastelands Work Team seldom meets the requirements of the auctioneer or auctioneering firm stipulated in articles 10 to 17 of the 1997 Auction Law. According to this law, the auctioneer must have had special training and two years of relevant experience. In addition, the auctioneer needs to be registered with a national or local auction association. See Auction Law [*Zhongguo Falü Nianjian Bianji Weiyuanhui*, 1997: 285–6].
12. Fieldwork findings in Lüliang prefecture indicate that the actual period of the leases varies between 30 and 60 years [*Hanstad and Li*, 1997: 557].
13. The 25° gradient is defined as a guideline. The Soil and Water Conservation Law stipulates that the norms, for the gradient of land on which agricultural reclamation is prohibited, should be determined by the County People's Congresses. In Ningxia reclamation on all wasteland is forbidden [*Guojia Jihua Weiyuanhui Guotudiqusi*, 1996: 156].
14. For a discussion of the auction procedures in Lüliang prefecture, see Hanstad and Li [1997: 548–54]; Ai [1995: 42–7]; Li *et al.* [1994: 27–9].
15. The procedures of the auctions in Yao'an county, Yunnan are described in Zheng [1999].
16. Li Sheng is a senior official within the Bureau of Law and Policy System Reform of the Ministry of Agriculture, which is responsible for the national coordination of the Wastelands Policy.
17. In practice this means that outside buyers can only acquire use rights to wasteland if there are no interested parties within the village.
18. For a discussion of this problem, see also Ho [2000a: 227–50, and 2001].
19. See Auction Law [*Zhongguo Falü Nianjian Bianji Weiyuanhui*, 1997: 285].
20. In addition to the Qin Great Wall, parts from other dynasties can also be found, including the Tang, Song and Ming.
21. All the data for Changcheng village and Chengyang township apply to 1996, unless indicated otherwise.
22. In Chengyang there is 12,000 *mu* of forage base area.
23. In 1996, a few experimental auctions were also launched in Yinnan prefecture, but there has been no follow-up to these auctions as far as I know.
24. For the central policy level, Murray Scott Tanner notes the same 'adept use of publications and other mass media' in order to push a new policy proposal through the bureaucracy [*Tanner*, 1996: 50].
25. This is the story as narrated by the village Party Secretary and the village leader of Zhaoling. It has been confirmed by officials of the Township Forestry Management Station and the County Section of Forestry.
26. Before the speech in March, Rui had already approved of the auctions at the Rural Work Meeting in January 1994. In his words: '[We] have to step up the integral management of the gullies ... and boldly auction wasteland, waste mountains, waste gullies and waste riverbeds' [*Zhonggong Guyuan Diqu Weiyuanhui Bangongshi*, 1994: 6].
27. See also Ningxia Nongye Kancha Shejiyuan [1988].
28. Both samples contain approximately the same percentage of cadres: 11–12 per cent. The Pengyang sample comprises higher educated farmers (only 9 per cent with no education, against 19 per cent in Guyuan; and 32 per cent with a senior middle school certificate –

gaozhong – against 12 per cent in Guyuan).

29. See Agriculture Law, articles 12–15 [*Nongye Zhengce Tigai Faguisi*, 1994: 6–12].
30. In the 'Suggestions Concerning the "Reform of the South" and the Speeding up of Economic Development' issued by the prefectural Party Committee in August 1994, the right to mortgage land was explicitly put forward as a privilege for the poor regions. See Zhonggong Guyuan Diwei Nonggongbu [1994: 13].
31. On the other hand, some villagers defended the criticism by saying that the ones in office are always easy to blame. 'Isn't it true that the birds that stretch out their neck are the first ones to be shot?' remarked an elderly farmer (*qiang da chu tou niao*).
32. See Auction Law [*Zhongguo Falü Nianjian Bianji Weiyuanhui*, 1997: 286].
33. All the data for Guanting (village and township) apply to 1996, unless indicated otherwise.
34. Under the *fenliu* system, cadres may apply to be discharged from office to engage in entrepreneurial activities. By paying the equivalent of two months' salary per year, the cadres' original positions as well as the terms of employment will remain unchanged for a period of two years in order to allow them to set up their own enterprise. This is different from the *xiagang* system under which cadres are released from office permanently. See Zhonggong Guyuan Diwei Nonggongbu [1994: 19].
35. Executive Regulations of the Land Management Law (*tudi guanlifa shishi tiaoli*), in Guojia Jihua Weiyuanhui Guotudiqusi [1996: 93–4].
36. In Yao'an county (Yunnan province), where experimental wasteland auctions have been held, strife over the eventual division of responsibilities between state organs also led to the obstruction of the Wastelands Policy [Jim Harkness, oral communication, 1998].
37. In Yunnan the Wastelands Policy was executed overnight, uniformly and with scant regard for local variations after the provincial governor had called upon authorities to organize auctions. He commented afterwards that his call had been meant as a suggestion and not an order because experiments still had to be carried out [Jim Harkness, oral communication, 1998].
38. The revised 1998 Land Management Law is the first law that distinguishes between land lease by work units and people *within* and *outside* the collective economic organization (article 15). However, there are no specifications regarding the household registration of the lessee. See Li [1998: 79].
39. Note that in the English translation of page 90 of this article the term 'use right' has been wrongly translated as 'ownership right'. Through recent fieldwork in Zhejiang and Inner Mongolia, I encountered several cases in which private companies or individuals with an urban registration obtained leases to wasteland.
40. Murray Scott Tanner also notes the use of orthodox models in policy implementation in present-day China. See Tanner [1996: 56].
41. For a discussion of the common property aspects of rangeland management in Ningxia, see Ho [2000b: 385–412].
42. The revised Land Management Law stipulates that the expropriated tenant receives compensation based on six to ten times (formerly, three to six) the average production value of the land calculated over the last three years (article 47). See Fang [1998: 216–17].
43. Li Sheng, oral communication, 1999.
44. The term *zaolin* is translated as 'afforestation', while *lühua* has been translated as 'vegetate'. The term *zaizhi* has been rendered as 'planting'.
45. The term here is *shenghuolü* which is less demanding than *baocunlü*.
46. I have rendered *xu* (void, empty) as 'open', referring to the necessity of open space for the tree top to develop freely.
47. Handwritten copy; conjectures concerning unreadable sections indicated with '?'.

REFERENCES

Ai, Yunhang, 1995, 'Jiakuai "sihuang" ziyuan kaifa de zhongyao tujing' (Speed up the important means to develop 'four wastelands' resources), *Zhongguo nongcun jingji* (Rural economy of China), No.11, pp.42–7.

Changcheng Cunmin Weiyuanhui (ed.), 1994, *Changchengcun yilin 'sihuangdi' paimai zhili qingkuang jianjie* (A short introduction to the control and auction of 'four wastelands' suitable for forestry of Changcheng village), 28 Sept.

Cheng, Tiejun and Mark Selden, 1994, 'The Origins and Social Consequences of China's Hukou System', *The China Quarterly*, No.139 (Sept.), pp.644–69.

Cheng, Yuk-shing and Tsang Shu-ki, 1996, 'Agricultural Land Reform in a Mixed System: The Chinese Experience of 1984–1994', *China Information*, Vol.10, Nos.3–4, pp.53–4.

Edmonds, Richard Louis (ed.), 1998, 'Special Issue: China's Environment', *The China Quarterly*, No.156 (Dec.).

Esman, Milton J., 1972, 'The Elements of Institution Building', in Joseph W. Eaton (ed.), *Institution Building and Development: From Concepts to Application*, London: Sage Publications.

Esman, Milton J., 1991, *Management Dimensions of Development: Perspectives and Strategies*, Connecticut: Kumarian Press.

Fang, Weilian, 1998, *Zhonghua renmin gongheguo tudi guanlifa shiyong jianghua* (A discussion on the use of the land management law of the People's Republic of China), Beijing: Zhongguo minzhu fazhi chubanshe.

Findlay, Andrew G., 1937, 'Men and Matters in the Land of the Yellow Earth', *Journal of the North China Branch of the Royal Asiatic Society*, Vol.68, p.57.

Frances, Jeanne and Su Runyu, 1990, *Baseline Study Report: Improving the Status of Rural Women through Income-Generating Activities*, CPR/89/P03, UNDP.

Gao, Guiying, 1995, 'Yisilanjiao yu Ningxia funü wenti' (The issue of women in Ningxia and Islam), *Huizu yanjiu* (Research on the Hui), No.2, p.57

Grindle, Merilee S. (ed.), 1980, *Politics and Policy Implementation in the Third World*, Princeton: Princeton University Press.

Guanting Xiang Renmin Zhengfu, 1996, *Guanyu zhizhi, zhili luan kai huangshan gongzuo de anpai yijian* (Suggestions for the arrangement of work concerning the prevention and control of the indiscriminate reclamation of barren mountains), Government Document No.1996/24.

Guojia Jihua Weiyuanhui Guotudiqusi (ed.), 1996, *Zhonghua renmin gongheguo guotu fagui huibian: 1988–1996* (Compilation of regulations on state land of the People's Republic of China: 1988–1996), Beijing: Zhongguo jihua chubanshe.

Guojia Tongjiju (ed.), 1994, *Zhongguo tongji nianjian 1994* (China statistical yearbook 1994), Beijing: Zhongguo tongji chubanshe.

Hanstad, Tim and Li Ping, 1997, 'Land Reform in the People's Republic of China: Auctioning Rights to Wasteland', *Loyola of Los Angeles: International and Comparative Law Journal*, Vol.19, No.3, p.558.

Ho, Peter, 2000a, 'The Clash over State and Collective Property: The Making of the Rangeland Law', *The China Quarterly*, No.161 (March), pp.227–50.

Ho, Peter, 2000b, 'China's Rangelands under Stress: A Comparative Study of Pasture Commons in the Ningxia Hui Autonomous Region', *Development and Change*, Vol.31, No.2, pp.385–42.

Ho, Peter, 2001, 'Who Owns China's Land? Policies, Property Rights and Deliberate Institutional Ambiguity', *The China Quarterly*, No.166 (June), pp.387–414.

Huang, Xiangmou, 1996, 'Shenhua shanqu nongcun gaige de yige xin luzi: Hechi diqu paimai "wuhuang" shiyongquan de diaocha' (A new road for the deepening of the rural reforms: Research of the auction of the 'five wastelands' in Hechi prefecture), *Guangxi minzu yanjiu* (Guangxi ethnic studies), No.1, pp.23–6.

Lampton, David M. (ed.), 1987, *Policy Implementation in Post-Mao China*, Berkeley, CA: University of California Press.

Li, Sheng, 1995, '"Sihuang" shiyongquan paimai zhong de falü wenti' (Legal issues of the auction of use rights of the 'four wastelands'), *Nongye jingji wenti* (Problems of agricultural economy), No.4, p.30.

Li, Yongmin, Bai Zhiquan and Li Shiling, 1994, 'Lüliang diqu aimai "sihuang" de zuofa yu xiaoguo' (Methods and results of the 'four wastelands' auctions in Lüliang prefecture), *Zhongguo nongcun wenti* (Rural economy of China), No.5.

Li, Yuan (ed.), 1998, *Zhonghua renmin gongheguo tudi guanlifa shiyi* (An interpretation of the land management law of the People's Republic of China), Beijing: Falü chubanshe.

Lotspeich, Richard and Chen Aimin, 1997, 'Environmental Protection in the People's Republic of China', *Journal of Contemporary China*, Vol.6, No.14.

MacFarquhar, Roderick and John K. Fairbank (eds.), 1991, *Cambridge History of China, The People's Republic, Part 2: Revolutions within the Chinese Revolution 1966–1982*, Cambridge: Cambridge University Press.

Mao, Zedong, 1966, *Nongken* (Agricultural reclamation), No.6, p.44.

Mao, Zedong, 1977, 'The Foolish Old Man Who Removed the Mountains', 11 June 1945, reprinted in *Selected Works of Mao Tse-Tung*, Vol.3, Beijing: Foreign Languages Press.

Ningxia Nongye Kancha Shejiyuan (ed.), 1988, 'Ningxia zhibei quhuatu' (Regional planning map of vegetation in Ningxia), in *Ningxia zhibei* (The vegetation of Ningxia), Yinchuan: Ningxia renmin chubanshe.

Ningxia Tongjiju (ed.), 1994, *Ningxia tongji nianjian 1994* (Ningxia statistical yearbook 1994), Yinchuan: Ningxia renmin chubanshe, p.65.

Nongye Zhengce Tigai Faguisi (ed.), 1994, *Nongyefa quanshu* (A complete edition of agricultural laws). Beijing: Zhongguo nongye chubanshe, pp.6–12.

Otto, Jan-Michiel, 1987, *Aan de Voet van de Piramide: Overheidsinstellingen en Plattelandsontwikkeling in Egypte*, Leiden: DSWO Press.

Pengyang Xian Linyeju (ed.), 1994, *Changchengcun paimai yilin 'sihuangdi' shiyongquan de zuofa* (The methods of the auction of use rights to 'four wastelands' suitable for forestry by Changcheng village), 28 Jan.

Pengyang Xian Renmin Zhengfu, 1994a, *Guanyu yinfa 'yilin "sihuang" de paimai, chengbao, lühua shixing yijian' de tongzhi* (Concerning the distributed notice 'remarks on the implementation of the auction, contracting and afforestation of the "four wastelands"'), Government Document No.1994/8, 1 March.

Pengyang Xian Renmin Zhengfu, 1994b, *Guanyu yifa jiaqiang linmu guanli, zhizhi daofa huangshan de tonggao* (Proclamation concerning the strengthening of forest management according to the law and the prevention of illegal felling on waste mountains), 1 Aug.

Potter, Sulamith Heins, 1983, 'The Position of Peasants in Modern China's Social Order', *Modern China*, Vol.9, No.4, pp.465–99.

Pressman, Jeffrey L. and Aaron Wildavsky, 1979, *Implementation: How Great Expectations in Washington Are Dashed in Oakland*, 2nd edn., Berkeley, CA: University of California Press.

Ross, Lester, 1987, 'Obligatory Tree-Planting: The Role of Campaigns in Post-Mao China', in Lampton (ed.) [1987].

Ross, Lester, 1988, *Environmental Policy in China*, Bloomington: Indiana University Press.

Secretariat of the State Council, 1997, 'Zhili kaifa nongcun "sihuang" ziyuan jin yi bu jiaqiang shuitu baochi gongzuo de tongzhi' (Notice on the control and development of the rural 'four wastelands' resources and the intensified strengthening of soil and water conservation), in Zhongguo Falü Nianjian Bianji Weiyuanhui [1997].

Selden, Mark, 1998, 'Household, Cooperative, and State in the Remaking of China's Countryside', in Eduard B. Vermeer, Frank N. Pieke and Chong Woei Lien (eds.), *Cooperative and Collective in China's Rural Development: Between State and Private Interests*, New York: M.E. Sharpe.

Sinkule, B.J. and Leonard Ortolano, 1995, *Implementing Environmental Policy in China*, Westport: Praeger Publications.

Tanner, Murray Scott, 1996, 'How a Bill Becomes a Law in China: Stages and Processes in Lawmaking', in Stanley B. Lubman (ed.), *China's Legal Reforms*, Oxford: Oxford University Press.

Vermeer, Eduard B., 1998, 'Decollectivization and Functional Change in Irrigation Management in China', in Eduard B. Vermeer, Frank N. Pieke and Chong Woei Lien (eds.), *Cooperative and Collective in China's Rural Development: Between State and Private Interests*, New York: M.E. Sharpe.

Wang, Wenxue, 1994a, 'Paimai "sihuang" zhishan zhifu – Shanxi sheng pinkun shanqu paimai "sihuang" shiyongquan de shijian yu sikao' (Auctioning 'four wastelands': Harness the mountains, extend wealth – reflections and practice on the auction of use rights to the 'four wastelands' in the poor mountainous area of Shanxi province), *Nongye jingji wenti*

(Problems of agricultural economy), No.8, p.21.

Wang, Xiyu, 1994b, 'Huangshan kaifa zhili zhong de zhidu, zhengce he nonghu xingwei – Shanxi sheng Lüliang diqu paimai "sihuangdi" ge'an yanjiu' (System, policy and behaviour of rural households within the control and development of barren mountains – a case study of the auction of 'four wastelands' in Lüliang prefecture in Shanxi province), *Zhongguo nongcun jingji* (Rural economy of China), No.11.

Yang, Hongkui, 1999, 'Contract Dispute of Taiwanese Hou Ren Shou Accusing Liu Yi of Transferring Contract Management Rights over Hilly Lands Owned by the Countryside Collective Economic Organization', *China Law*, Vol.18, No.1, pp.89–90.

Yang, Wenzhi and Yu Cunzu (eds.), 1992, *Huangtu Gaoyuan Quyu Zhili yu Pingjia* (Evaluation and control of the Loess Plateau Region), Beijing: Kexue chubanshe.

Zhang, Shuchen, 1997, 'Guanyu "sihuang" paimai de diaocha yu sikao' (Research and reflections about the auction of the 'four wastelands'), *Jingji, shehui* (Economy, society), No.2, pp.49–52.

Zhang, Xiaohua and Li Yu (eds.), 1997, *Zhongguo tudi guanli shiwu quanshu* (A practical encyclopaedia of land administration in China), Beijing: Zhongguo dadi chubanshe.

Zheng, Baohua, 1999, 'Security of Use Rights for Forest Land: A Case Study of the Compensated Transfer of Use Rights over Collective Wasteland in Yao'an County, Yunnan Province', unpublished report prepared for a Ford Foundation project, Beijing.

Zhonggong Guyuan Diqu Weiyuanhui Bangongshi (ed.), 1994, *Guyuan diqu nongcun gongzuo huiyi cailiao huibian* (Proceedings of the rural work meeting of Guyuan prefecture), Jan.

Zhonggong Guyuan Diwei Nonggongbu, 1994, *Nanbu fangkai wenjian xuanbian* (A selection of documents on the opening up of the south). Restricted circulation.

Zhonggong Guyuan Diwei (ed.), 1994a, *Guanyu yinfa diwei shuji Rui Cunzhang, xingshu fuzhuanyuan Tai Weimin zai paimai 'sihuangdi' xianchang huiyi shang jianghua de tongzhi* (Notice of the speech delivered at the occasion of the auction of the 'four wastelands' by prefectural party secretary Rui Cunzhang and deputy prefect Tai Weimin), Party Document No.1994/28, p.3.

Zhonggong Guyuan Diwei, 1994b, *Zhonggong Guyuan diwei, Guyuan xingzheng gongshu guanyu paimai 'Sihuangdi' shiyongquan ruogan zhengce guiding* (Some policy regulations concerning the auction of use rights to the 'four wastelands' – the Guyuan Communist Party Committee and the Administrative Office), Party Document No.1994/20.

Zhongguo Falü Nianjian Bianji Weiyuanhui (ed.), 1997, *Zhongguo falü nianjian 1997* (China legal yearbook 1997), Beijing: Zhongguo falü nianjianshe, pp.285–8.

Zhongguo Ziran Ziyuan Congshu Bianyi Weiyuanhui (ed.), 1995, *Zhongguo ziran ziyuan congshu: Ningxia juan* (Encyclopaedia of China's natural resources: Ningxia volume), Beijing: Zhongguo huanjing kexue chubanshe.

Zizhiqu Dangwei, 1985, 'Guanqie zhixing zhonggong zhongyang (1985) 1 hao wenjian de shixiang zhengce guiding' (Ten policy regulations concerning the implementation of document no.1 (1985) of the Communist Party and central government), reprint *Ningxia Daily*, 5 April 1985.

Ningxia's Third Road to Rural Development: Resettlement Schemes as a Last Means to Poverty Reduction?

RITA MERKLE

There are very critical voices in the People's Republic of China (hereafter PRC) about the outcomes of development policies since China started its market-oriented reforms in 1978. In a recently published book the economists Wang Shaoguang and Hu Angang explore the issue of regional disparities and the role of the state in the development process (using a political–economic approach based on a provincial-level analysis). They conclude that 'First World and Third World coexist within China' and that regional disparities in both relative and absolute terms had grown to alarming levels by 1994.[1] They state that this disparity is worse than in many other Third World countries, and explain the 'uneven regional growth centres on two variables: the government's willingness to direct the flow of production factors on behalf of less developed regions, and its capacity to do so' [*Wang and Hu*, 1999: 13–14, 67, 129]. In other words, a convergence is only likely to occur if the state is willing and able to help the poorer regions. Although aware of the declining extractive capacity of the central government – owing to fiscal decentralization – they propose, as the general guideline for a regional policy, a balanced development between efficiency and equity and between market mechanisms and government intervention [*ibid.*: 16].

The Chinese government is well aware of the problem and seems willing to mitigate the tensions described above. Since 1994, it has changed the nation's development strategy fundamentally.[2]

When the rate of improvement in poverty reduction slowed down in 1993, the Chinese government initiated a poverty reduction plan aiming at

Rita Merkle, PhD student at the Free University of Berlin, Geosciences, Centre for Development Studies. Email: ritamerkle@wanadoo.fr. A word of thanks is due to Professor Wang Yiming and Ren Xuerong for their assistance in China and to Peter Ho, Jakob Eyferth, Thomas Kampen, Karl Eric Longstreth and Francisco Léon for their valuable comments on an earlier draft. Financial support of the Deutscher Akademischer Austauschdienst (DAAD) for the field research is gratefully acknowledged.

lifting the remaining 80 million rural poor out of poverty within seven years, the so-called National 8-7 Poverty Reduction Plan (1994–2000) – the '8' stands for *ba yi* (80 million) denoting the target group, the '7' stands for the time span of the project. In the plan three main goals are made explicit:

> Socialism will abolish poverty. In order to solve the rural poverty problem further, narrow the gap between eastern and western parts of the country, and attain the goal of common prosperity, the State Council decided to concentrate manpower, material and financial resources, and to mobilize forces from all walks of life between 1994 and 2000 in an effort to solve the subsistence problem of 80 million needy people in rural areas throughout the country within seven years. This is a daunting battle against a difficult problem [*GFKLXB*, 1996: 1].[3]

Obviously, the Chinese government saw itself far from having reached the ideologically motivated goal to establish socio-economic parity, meaning actual equity in the distribution of wealth between regions and between rich and poor. In trying to win that battle and to stress their willingness to mitigate tensions caused by growing regional disparities and worsening terms of trade for poor areas and poor people, the PRC states that the implementation of the Ninth Five Year Plan, which promotes an even development strategy, should be combined with the implementation of the National 8-7 Poverty Reduction Plan [*GFKLXB*, 1996: 46]. The important question is whether China – with the help of this new development strategy – will be able to win the battle or whether regional disparities as well as income disparities between rich and poor will even increase and eventually lead to the disintegration of the nation, a potential danger as experiences elsewhere show.[4]

In this article, I will focus on China's poverty reduction policy and assess one special means of alleviating poverty – government-directed resettlement projects – from the perspective of policy effectiveness and economic efficiency.

Given China's huge size and its diversity in natural environment it is very difficult to carry out an inclusive study. The article will focus on a localized resettlement project in Ningxia Hui autonomous region (hereafter Ningxia), but further research is suggested as there is hardly any understanding of resettlement projects in relation to poverty reduction in China.[5] The issue is of great interest because resettlement projects will become an essential part of the PRC's poverty reduction efforts in the future. At the Working Conference on Fighting Poverty, which took place in early June 1999 in Beijing, initiated by the Central Committee of the Chinese Communist Party and the State Council, the goal of lifting the remaining 80 million rural poor out of poverty within seven years was re-examined. Among the 42 million rural people who were still living in poverty in 1998, 20 million should be helped out of their miserable situation by the end of the year 2000. In a speech at that conference, Vice-Prime Minister Wen Jiabao stated that there will be two types of impoverished rural people left: first, disabled and people in need of social protection (this means people who are dependent on family support and social welfare) and second, 'those people who live in areas with an extremely adverse natural environment, especially in remote mountainous areas and some of the national minority regions, where lack of basic productive and living conditions is common. Some of the people living there have to be moved out and resettled.'[6]

A closer look at Ningxia, where resettlement schemes for the rural poor had already started in 1983, can therefore offer the opportunity to reassess the main approach to poverty reduction of the Chinese government after the year 2000.[7] Were the government-directed resettlement projects of the 1980s in Ningxia a success or a failure? Could the target group be reached and helped out of poverty sustainably?

To answer these questions, cross-county resettlement projects will be investigated. The projects move rural poor from the poverty-stricken area in the south of Ningxia to newly reclaimed irrigated areas in the middle and northern part of the region. In section one, the article begins with a brief introduction of the geographical setting and the natural environment of Ningxia and discusses the pattern of regional development as background information for the main topic of the article. Section two then provides some insights into identifying poor people in China in general and in Ningxia in particular. The comparison will shed light on the highly constructed nature of poverty indices in China and reveal that there exist in fact three methods for the calculation of poverty rates. Section three gives a description of the general guidelines of the 'Three West' development fund programme initiated by the central government in 1983 to reduce poverty in the designated region. These guidelines demarcated the framework for local governments that were then in charge of the implementation of specific poverty reduction projects. One of Ningxia's measures was to resettle rural poor in order to improve their living conditions sustainably. It was for this purpose that the 'suspended village projects' were designed. The approach, described in section four, was based on voluntary participation. The provincial government's efforts to gain the necessary social acceptance from the target group will be demonstrated. It will be argued that the general administrative organization allowed loopholes for county governments to assert their own interests. In section five the main characteristics and some outcomes of Ningxia's resettlement projects will be examined taking

Dazhanchang village as an example. In the inter-county resettlement project formidable obstacles had to be surmounted simultaneously, and in the course of which the local governments involved performed poorly. As we will see in section six, the case of Dazhanchang is representative for most of the other resettlement sites. After more than a decade's development only two of the settlements, which are situated near urban centres, performed well. In the last section, I will summarize the main points and arguments of the article and point out some implications for policy-making.

This analysis is mainly based on Chinese written material including government reports, books and articles. One article that was surprisingly critical draws on the case of Dazhanchang village. For that reason Dazhanchang is chosen as a case study. It can provide a more differentiated picture about the outcomes of the intervention than a study based only on generally very positive descriptions. The critical article is in a collection of papers presenting the results of a group of studies, which explored the prospects for a newly planned transmigration area. The experiences in Dazhanchang were reviewed for that purpose because the environmental conditions in Dazhanchang before the reclamation of the steppe were similar to this newly planned area. Empirical field research, which covered a total of 104 households with 600 persons, was conducted in 1997 in three administrative villages of Dazhanchang and the findings were compared with the objectives of early project plans.

A few issues arose in connection with my analysis. First, as noted by Binswanger and Kinsey [1993: 1478], there is no generally accepted methodological approach or theoretical basis for the analysis of resettlement schemes. Seeking to evaluate individual characteristics of resettlement, Binswanger and Kinsley distinguish two broad groups of interrelated variables: one contains the implementation characteristics of resettlement, the other the outcomes. For the most part, I will draw on the specific characteristics reviewed by Binswanger and Kinsey and use them as an analytical framework upon which the particularities in Ningxia's resettlement schemes will be examined. However, data constraints impose limitations on the use of some of their suggested characteristics. For example, the research material available never provides any detailed information on aspects such as the costs per beneficiary household, the modality of supply of basic production services (extension, marketing, transport, etc.), asset accumulation and savings, or the social cohesion at the settlement site. Moreover, existing data often differ significantly and do not even allow the dimension of the scheme to be assessed. This problem will become very clear in the discussion below.

NINGXIA'S NATURAL ENVIRONMENT AND PATTERNS OF
REGIONAL DEVELOPMENT

Ningxia is located in the lower part of the upper reaches of the Yellow River and covers an area of 51,800km², or about 0.69 per cent of China's total area. It is part of the central Asian steppe and desert region with a continental, temperate climate, which is characterized by low precipitation concentrated in the period from June to September. It has increasing aridity from the south (subhumid) to the north (arid), great temperature differences between the seasons, strong solar radiation and strong winds. (For further details see also the article of Peter Ho in this volume.)

Ningxia faces the typical problems of arid zones such as soil erosion, desertification and salinization. In the southern Loess Plateau, more than 80 per cent of the arable land is affected by soil erosion [Guo, 1998: 78]. In the Yellow River flood plains and the basins of the northern part of the region, where the Yellow River cuts through and which has been the main agricultural area of the region since Qin and Han Dynasties, about 40 per cent of the irrigated land suffers from salinization and decreasing fertility, and about one-third of the area is affected by desertification [Zhang et al., 1994: 248–9]. According to historical records and surveys, which exist for a period of over 700 years, natural disasters occur with a frequency of three in ten years [Qin, 1999: 61].

These developments are partly explained by the increasing population pressure. Ningxia had a total population of 5,289,000 people in 1997, a figure that has increased continuously since the foundation of the PRC in 1949. And as a consequence, the arable land per capita has dramatically decreased (see Table 1).

In 1949, Ningxia already had a population density of 21 persons per square kilometre. It has increased slightly to 23 in 1956, when the period of collectivism (1956–78) started.[8] After the Reform and Open-door policy began in the late 1970s, the population density grew to an alarming number. Ningxia's carrying capacity is far beyond the recommended standard of the United Nations of seven persons per square kilometre for arid zones and 20 persons for semi-arid zones.

A closer look will reveal that the conditions in the region itself vary considerably. In the following discussion, I will differentiate between the 'Yellow River Irrigated Region' (yin huang guanqu) and the 'Southern Mountains Region' (nanbu shanqu).[9] The distinction follows the Collection of Statistical Material about Ningxia's Rural Areas 1949–1997 [NNTZH 1949–1997], which is the most comprehensive statistical material about rural development in Ningxia to date. The focus will be on the development of the rural areas, first because poverty is mainly concentrated in the rural

TABLE 1

POPULATION DENSITY AND ARABLE LAND PER CAPITA IN NINGXIA

	Total population	Persons/ km²[f]	Arable land (mu)*	Arable land per capita[f] (mu/capita)	Rural population[e]
1949	1,197,500[a]	23	9,713,000[a]	8.1	1,073,109
1956	1,345,500[a]	26	13,455,000[a]	7.8	—
1979	2,149,000[a]	41	13,467,000[a]	3.7	—
1985	4,146,200[b]	80	11,927,000[e]	2.88	3,169,109
1990	4,656,800[c]	90	11,938,000[e]	2.56	3,427,129
1995	5,123,800[c]	99	12,108,000[e]	2.36	3,640,316
1997	5,289,000[d]	102	19,062,000[e]**	3.60	3,717,968

Source: Data marked (a) from Wang [1994: 297]; data marked (b) from Zhang *et al.* [1994: 259]; data marked (c) from Ningxia Statistical Bureau [*NSB*, 1996: 85]; data marked (d) from State Statistical Bureau [*SSB*, 1998: 42]; data marked (e) from *NNTZH 1949–1997* [7, 15] and data marked (f) is based on author's calculation.

Notes: * For this table the Chinese unit of *mu* for measuring areas will be retained, because normally this unit is used in Chinese statistics, calculations and economic plans. One *mu* equals about 1/15 hectare of land.

** There is no explanation for this surprising increase in arable land. It's only mentioned that the figure for this year is based on a detailed survey. For a good description of the 'tricky' statistical category of 'arable land', see Ho [1999: 72].

areas of southern Ningxia and second, because the official Chinese view perceives poverty as a primarily rural phenomenon. This point will be discussed in more detail in the next section.

Although 73.4 per cent of the total arable land under cultivation is found in the Southern Mountains Region, it lags far behind the Yellow River Irrigated Region in agricultural development. The production system in the south is based on dryland agriculture with low crop yield – in nine years out of ten, the harvest is very poor [*Chen*, 1995: 514] – and extensive, sedentary livestock farming. A total of 81.2 per cent of all irrigated land can be found in the Yellow River Irrigated Region where 74.9 per cent of Ningxia's total grain output is produced [*NNTZH 1949–1997*, 1998: 3, 33]. This uneven production pattern is also reflected in the income distribution. Bearing in mind that Ningxia, in terms of rural net income per capita, in a national comparison always ranked in the lowest quarter nationally – it even ranked third lowest in 1995 with 998.75 Renminbi (hereafter Rmb) after Shaanxi with 962.89 Rmb and Gansu with 880.34 Rmb[10] – it can be suspected that the rural population in the Southern Mountains Region is relatively poor. In fact, the rural net income per capita in that region is only fraction of what a person in a rural area in the northern part of Ningxia earns.

TABLE 2

RURAL NET INCOME PER CAPITA IN NINGXIA (IN RMB)

	1979	1985	1990	1995	1997
Southern Mountains Region (I)	64.04	199.65	362.50	599.62	896.67
Northern Irrigated Region (II)	149.88	418.95	804.92	1,529.81	2,349.08
Relation between (I) and (II) taking (I) as 1	1 : 2.34	1 : 2.10	1 : 2.22	1 : 2.55	1 : 2.62

Source: NNTZH 1949–1997 [98–9].

Two things are striking: first, remarkable income disparities among the rural population in Ningxia exist, and those disparities are widening. Intraprovincial development in Ningxia is highly uneven. Disparities reduced in the 1980s, but rose again dramatically in the 1990s. In 1997, the average rural net income per capita in the Southern Mountains Region was only 58 per cent of the province's average (1,545.08 Rmb), and only 43 per cent of the nation's average (2,090.10 Rmb).[11] What Wang and Hu found out for the provincial level – widening income disparities – is also true for the intraprovincial development in Ningxia. Second, in 1995 it was hardly above the official poverty line at that time of 500 Rmb.

SOME REMARKS ABOUT THE IDENTIFICATION OF POOR PEOPLE IN CHINA

The measurement and the definition of poverty is a fundamental issue in understanding poverty alleviation policies. In 1986, the Chinese government for the first time defined a poverty line. Zhu et al. [1997: 12] note that there were manifold policy considerations involved in the process of defining the official poverty line. For example, different income levels were chosen for identifying the poor counties in areas where minority ethnic groups concentrate and in the former revolutionary base areas.

The Chinese anti-poverty policy takes an approach of regional targeting, and by 1994, 592 counties had been designated as poverty-stricken counties where the average annual rural net income per capita is under 500 Rmb, calculated at the price level of 1990.[12] More than three-quarters of those counties are located in central and western China. In Ningxia, eight counties are designated as poverty-stricken counties, which are identical with the eight counties comprising the Southern Mountains Region: Yanchi and Tongxin and the six counties of Guyuan prefecture – Guyuan, Haiyuan, Xiji, Longde, Jingyuan, Pengyang (see Map 1). This approach to poverty reduction – spatially organized to targeted localities – was new in China's history and is used both in carrying out public work programmes and in implementing credit programmes. Prior to that time the main approach was to provide relief goods and grants to disaster-stricken people through the assistance system.[13]

However, as Kang [1995: 40] has pointed out, excluded in 1993 from China's official statistics were some 12 million urban poor. If one would use the standard set by the World Bank for defining poverty – 1 US$ per capita per day in real purchasing price parities – 29.4 per cent of China's total population would have been considered poor in 1993. The Chinese official poverty line is based on a 0.6 US$ per capita per day (in real purchasing price parities) calculation and therefore, taking the World Bank standard as reference, the use of the term 'poverty' in present China really means absolute poverty.

One is struck by the way the official poverty rate is calculated, namely the (rural) poor living in the designated poverty-stricken counties as percentage of the total rural population in the PRC. Why not use a percentage of the rural population in these counties or of the total population of China? A critical look at statistics about poverty rates is imperative.

In the case of Ningxia, this caution proves to be appropriate. We will see that there actually exist three reasonable ways of measuring the rate of poverty.

Wang and Hu [1999: 116] write 'that in 1993, the highest poverty rate was found in Ningxia (28.5 percent).' In the Action Plan of Ningxia for the China Agenda for the 21st Century the same rate is given [*Ningxia Huizu Zizhiqu Jihua Weiyuanhui and Kexue Jishu Weiyuanhui*, 1999: 31]. However, Ningxia's local poverty reduction plan for the years 1994 until 2000 states that 70 per cent of the rural population in the Southern Mountains Region in 1993 was still living beneath the standard for basic necessities (which is identical with the then used poverty line).[14] How is this possible, especially since in both cases the estimated number of people languishing in poverty is identical (523,000 people)? In the first case, the poverty rate was calculated by taking the rural poor as a percentage of the total population of Ningxia in 1993; in the second case it was calculated as a percentage of the total rural population of the Southern Mountains Region. This way of calculating the poverty rate differs, as we have seen above, from the national standard. Calculating it as a percentage of the total rural population of the province, the result would be 39 per cent.

For the year 1997, the poverty rate given in the Action Plan of Ningxia for the China Agenda for the 21st Century is a supposedly low 10 per cent. And again, we can find a different number in *NNTZH 1949–1997*, namely 24.8 per cent. The method for calculating the poverty rate corresponds to that in 1993, in the first case as a percentage of the total population of Ningxia, in the second case as a percentage of the total rural population of the poverty-stricken counties only. Calculating it as a percentage of the total rural population of Ningxia, the result would be 14.1 per cent.

The discussion has shown that the poverty line as well as the poverty rate are highly constructed indices, which reflect the different interests and intentions of those constructing and using them. It shows how politicized the issue of poverty has become. Although statistical data is growing in number, limitations to it are still enormous. The German economist Carsten Herrmann-Pillath [1995: xliv] has noted: 'Difficulties in dealing with the material are to such a degree that a pessimist could easily take the view to better avoid any judgement which is based on statistics. For an economist this would of course be equal to giving up on dealing with the issue totally. Therefore a certain optimism is a duty.'

PRIORITY TREATMENT FOR CHINA'S POVERTY CROWN AND THE THIRD ROAD IN THE WEST

The Southern Mountains Region has been known as one of China's most poverty-stricken areas for a long time, and it is sometimes referred to as 'China's poverty crown' (*Zhongguo pinkun zhi guan*) [*Guo*, 1998: 36]. Even taking into account that Chinese statistics have to be read sceptically when we recall that the poverty rate for the country as a whole was estimated to be 5.4 per cent in 1997, then for Ningxia the 14.1 per cent is enormous.[15] But now, at this point, the suggested optimism by Herrmann-Pillath seems to be appropriate. In 1978, Ningxia still had an estimated official poverty rate of 70 per cent.[16] The decline is impressive. In less than 20 years the poverty rate has been reduced by more than 50 per cent. How was that possible?

The success is to a great extent explained by the enormous effort the central government has put into this region. The Southern Mountains Region, also known as 'Xihaigu Region',[17] became part of the 'Three West' ('Sanxi') development fund programme, which started in 1983 and was scheduled for ten years (in a first phase). The scheme was based on a regional poverty reduction strategy with the poor regions of Dingxi and Hexi in Gansu province and Xihaigu of Ningxia as target areas.

As we have seen above, this approach to poverty alleviation through regional development was new in China, and it was only in 1986 that the Chinese government adopted this anti-poverty scheme nationwide. It was also the first time that a project approach was taken. Ningxia received about 336 million Rmb from the fund between 1983 and 1992 – about 30 million Rmb per year – and realized 304 projects with that money.[18]

The strategic principle of the 'Three West' programme was: 'Where water is available, the road of water-using measures should be taken, where there is not any water available, the road of fully taking advantage of the dryland should be taken, and where neither the first nor the second road are accessible, another road has to be found' (*you shuilu zou shuilu, mei shuilu zou hanlu, shui han lu bu tong ling zhaochu lu*) [*Chen*, 1996: 12]. This third road of rural development, defined below, represented the last means of easing the poverty strains in those regions. To put it in other words, the 'poverty crown' of China endured severe poverty a long time before the macro policies adjusted to it.

The measures taken for this third road were twofold: first, government-directed resettlement projects, and second, the export of human capital to more developed coastal areas. The literature reveals almost nothing about this second measure – except some plan figures – and a more systematic enquiry would be needed in order to be able to evaluate it. Therefore, in the following, only the first activity will be closely examined. With the implementation of the 'Three West' programme, first resettlement projects started. In the meantime, the programme has reached its second ten-year phase, new methods are taken on the third road and the new projects are adjusted to the new framework of the National 8-7 Poverty Reduction Plan. However, the focus in this article will be on those projects that were implemented in the first ten-year phase (1983–92), as the outcomes are more readily assessed than those of new projects (which are still in the implementation stage).

NINGXIA'S RESETTLEMENT PROJECTS IN THE 1980S –
'SUSPENDED VILLAGES'

The central government formulated the very general strategic principle of the 'Three West' construction programme, but the local governments were charged with the implementation. Ningxia's Commission of Agricultural Construction formulated its own principle for the third road to poverty reduction: 'The rivers should be of help to the mountains, mountains and rivers do help each other' (*yi chuan ji shan, shan chuan gong ji*) [*Wang*, 1994: 246]. What does that mean? *Diaozhuang* were the solution. Literally *diaozhuang* means 'suspended villages' and they have a long history in Ningxia. Since Ningxia belongs to the arid and semi-arid zone, intensive agriculture was – and of course still is – only possible on irrigated land concentrated in the plains of the Yellow River. In fields that could not be reached by irrigation, farmers practised rain-fed agriculture. In order to make full use of the valuable land, a member of the family temporarily – during the peak agricultural seasons (planting and harvesting) – moved to a little simple dwelling far away from their farms. These dwellings were called 'suspended villages' [*Chen*, 1996: 147]. The term was then used by the Ningxia government after 1983 to denote newly constructed villages in the Northern Irrigated Region used to resettle poor people from the eight poverty-stricken counties in the south.

In the early 1980s, there was a tremendous hesitancy about resettlement. First, people still had the large-scale non-voluntary settlement programmes of the past in mind, like the migration of educated urban youth to the countryside and mountainous areas during the Cultural Revolution or the transfer of about 97,000 people in 1959/60 from the densely populated Zhejiang province to Ningxia. Most of those resettled people have moved back to their native place [ibid.: 148]. Moreover, the environment of the new settlement areas was not at all attractive to the farmers from the poor counties. The main reason for their poor standard of living was exactly as in Ningxia, an adverse environment. It is understandable that they did not want to move to a semi-desert environment, which is not suitable for agriculture. However, by diverting water of the Yellow River and the construction of irrigation facilities, the government planned to change this land into cultivable land and develop suspended villages.

By giving the unpopular measure of resettling people the name 'suspended village project', the provincial government avoided the negative connotation of a non-voluntary migration process. Moreover, the new 'suspended village' model followed traditional practices of extensive agriculture. The settlers were allowed to keep their 'old' home, and land use rights, for some time after having moved to the settler villages. And they were free to leave the suspended village if they could not get adapted to it. After a period of three years they finally had to decide to give up one of the two places and settle down in the other. The organized resettlement of rural people by the government was now through a voluntary approach as compared to the imposed approach of the first three decades of the PRC.

To date, there exist officially 21 suspended villages.[19] Different information is circulating about the number of people who settled in the new villages. According to more recent statistics, around 250,000 people migrated to a new settlement.[20] Concerning the new land that was opened up, figures are also highly varying and range, to give just an example, between 30,670 ha and 38,530 ha until the end of the first phase in 1992 and between 27,530 ha and 34,670 ha until 1997.[21] This shows that there is actually little we can say about the physical scale of the project and further study is urgently needed on the extent of the suspended villages.

In terms of the spatial form of migration, two broad types can be differentiated: resettlement within the county boundaries and resettlement where county boundaries are crossed. I will call the first type intra-county migration and the second type inter-county migration. Guo differentiates further: he mentions a 'Putting flowers into a vase' (cha hua)-style

TABLE 3
'SUSPENDED VILLAGES': NUMBER OF VILLAGES AND NUMBER OF SETTLERS

	Intra-county migration	Inter-county migration	Inter-county 'cha-hua'-style migration	Inter-county migration as an East–West cooperation project
Number of villages	6	9 (already finished) 3 (in construction)	3	1
Number of settlers	56.334	90.061 ~120.000	7.300	6.000

Source: Guo [1998: 142–4].

migration, which actually is an inter-county migration whereby the poor are moved to already existing villages in the Yellow River Irrigated Region and one project which represents an inter-county migration but is financed through cooperation between the eastern coast and the west region.

The average distance between the place of origin and the target area is about 25–50 km for intra-county migrations and 250–600 km for inter-county migrations.[22] Map 1 shows the inter-county migrations. A listing of the names of all the suspended villages that belong to the inter-county group is not provided in any of the consulted literature.[23] However, more significant for the current study than exact names is the administrative organization of the projects. In the literature, it is always stressed that resettlement within the county boundaries does not pose major problems in terms of administrative organization and the adaptation of the targeted people to the new, yet already familiar environment. As a consequence, it is stated, within two years food security can be assured.[24] Comparably difficult to effect is the cross-county-boundary migration, which implies that people have to adjust to a new environment; this involves major administrative challenges.

The fundamental question of household registration has to be solved after the three initial years and the two local governments in charge – the county governments of the place of origin and the place of destination of the settlers – have to find an agreement on the status of the settlers. Introduced in 1958, the system of household registration drastically restricted the mobility of the population by dividing the residents into two categories – rural population and urban population. The system allowed a clear distinction between the countryside and urban areas so that in fact two relatively independent systems were created whereby different public services were related to the respective registration status.[25] The current household registration system is less restrictive than it was even 15 years

MAP 1

SUSPENDED VILLAGES – MIGRATION IN NINGXIA

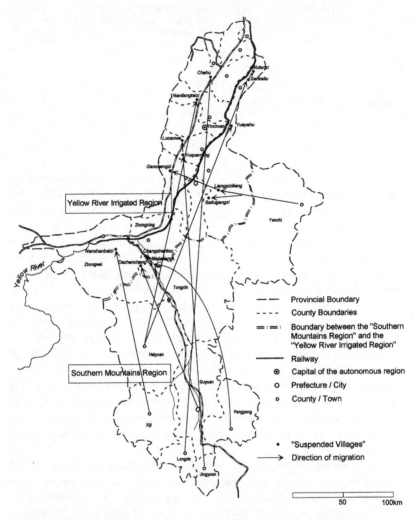

Cartography by Rita Merkle (Design based on Wang Yiming 1994, pp.186 and 248).

ago. People who move to another place where they are not registered will be unable to enjoy the public services related to the household registration. It is essential for poor people who move to another administrative unit to have the necessary assistance such as food or production subsidies from the government where they now live (at least in the first few years after having settled down). These obstacles had to be overcome in the inter-county migration projects in Ningxia.

To gain the necessary acceptance of the rural poor to migrate to a distant unfamiliar place, the Ningxia government used the suspended village approach, allowing the settlers to keep their land use rights for three years after having moved to the suspended village and allowing them to hold a preliminary residential registration for this period. Institutions on two administrative levels are responsible for the organization and management of a project. The Ningxia provincial government made many general tasks explicit in a notice on the administrative organization of the suspended villages resettlement scheme:[26] on the provincial level, the Commission of Agricultural Construction is entrusted with functions such as the formulation of policies for the projects, the coordination between various government departments involved in the project, and the responsibility for the planning arrangements or the management of the fund. County (and township) governments are the specific organizing institutions for the resettlement process. As a first step they have to apply to the provincial government for a suspended village project. When the provincial government accepts the plan, the officials at the county level are then responsible for further procedures. Provided that the migrants are transferred to a different county, the administrative organization and management is split up between the two county governments concerned in the resettlement project. The county of origin takes the main responsibilities during the 'period of construction' (*kaifa jianshe shiqi*) such as confirming the number of registered poverty-stricken households, the choice of the target place, the planning of an integrated development plan, publicizing relevant policies for the settlement (preferential policies, etc.), choosing and organizing the poor to move to the target place, providing the necessary means for production as well as financial aid to the settlers in the target place for the time when they only have a preliminary household registration, dispatching personnel to assist settlers and transferring their duties after the construction period to the government of the target county. The suspended village remains under the administrative control of the source county until the transfer to the target county. The tasks of the county governments where the suspended villages are established mainly consist of assisting in land requisition, establishing grassroots organizations, giving technical assistance and mediating in disputes between new settlers and residents of the target county.

The notice indicates that the counties of origin were heavily overloaded with tasks. Moreover, the local governments in the impoverished areas are relatively short of budget revenues. The notice also remains very vague about the time span of the 'construction period'. Although projects had a definite time span, implicitly or explicitly, infinite lengths of time were adopted for the 'construction period', so that there is a certain danger that it is never 'finished' and that the administrative duties are returned to the target county only after a very long period of time, if ever.

To obtain a clearer idea of how the policies were actually realized and what the outcomes were, we will now look at the case of Dazhanchang township.

CHARACTERISTICS AND PERFORMANCE – THE CASE OF 'DAZHANCHANG SUSPENDED VILLAGE'

Dazhanchang is located in Zhongning county (at the border to Zhongwei county) in the steppe and desert region of the tablelands and the hills of mid-Ningxia (see Map 1). It covers an area of 58.6 km². Construction already began in 1983 and it was the first suspended village that had been built up [*Qin*, 1995: 121–2]. The plan was to move 28,000–30,000 poor people from Guyuan county to Dazhanchang by the end of 1989, the intended completion of the project [*Zhang*, 1998: 54].

Scheme Organization and Administration

In 1998, Dazhanchang consisted of 18 administrative villages and 83 natural villages and obtained the administrative status of a township. However, even ten years after the completion of the project, the 'construction period' seems unfinished. It still belongs to the administration of Guyuan county and is therefore also statistically recorded in the Guyuan county statistics [*GXNB*, 1999: 2].

On the county level, a sub-branch of the provincial Commission of Agricultural Construction is entrusted with the organization and the management of the project. It created specific institutions responsible for specific tasks: the 'Command Post of the Dazhanchang Suspended Village Construction Project' (*Dazhanchang diaozhuang jianshe gongcheng zhihuibu*) located in Dazhanchang and established after negotiations with the Zhongning county government is responsible for the coordination of the project measures in Dazhanchang; the 'Leading Group of the Resettlement Work' (*yimin banqian gongzuo lingdao xiaozu*) with various offices located in the Guyuan county capital and directed by a deputy county head, is responsible for the organization of the resettlement work in the county of origin; the county council and party officials are to act as advisers to the project, visit the settlers and hold working conferences in Dazhanchang twice a year; and finally, for each township that sent settlers, deputy township heads coordinate resettlement tasks [*Li*, 1993: 178–9]. This bureaucracy does not seem to work very well and specific duties do not seem to be clearly defined. As implicitly admitted by the then vice-chairman of Ningxia, Li Chengyu, in a speech made at the Working Conference on the Agricultural Construction of the Suspended Village Settlements in June 1991, the coordination between the two counties in charge of the resettlement is very bad and the duties are not demarcated clearly.[27]

Nevertheless, the administering authorities are involved in every aspect of resettlement and show an excessive paternalism that expresses itself, as we will see below, in excessive constraints on settlers' decisions.

Modalities of Land Acquisition and Size of Holdings

In China, the state is the owner of land and leases land use rights to the farmers.[28] Therefore land acquisition presents no major problem. As mentioned above, settlers retained their land use rights in their native village for another three years after having moved to the suspended village. In the resettlement area, each settler was allotted another 2 *mu* of arable land with land use rights for 50 years. Egalitarianism was the leading principle guiding land distribution, which was employed very inflexibly. Everyone was allotted exactly 2 *mu* of land.

Settlers who did not want to stay in the suspended village had to give back their land use rights and their preliminary household registration. Explicitly, beneficiaries were strictly forbidden to sell their land use rights and their residence permit [*Li*, 1993: 106–7]. In practice however, as Zhang mentions, many of the poor settlers who were moved to Dazhanchang from Guyuan county left – reasons are not given – and sold their land use rights. An informal land market has developed where the price per *mu* had reached 1,000–2,000 Rmb in 1997, a few years ago the price still was 300–500 Rmb per *mu* [*Zhang*, 1998: 55]. It would be interesting to find out where those new settlers come from, what profession they have and how they use the informally acquired land. Further research is necessary. However, this finding points to a substantial problem in the land tenure system used for resettlement projects in Ningxia. It suggests that the management system for land use rights and the household registration system in the suspended village project are characterized by ineffectiveness.

Settler Selection and Practice

Extreme poverty and willingness to move were the main criteria for the selection of the settlers. Also, at least two people in the household should have been able to work. The head of the household was expected to be in good health, with a certain educational background, able to do farm work and between 18 and 45 years old [*Li*, 1993: 106, 110]. No further skills were required. The county organizations were expected to propagandize the policies related to the resettlement process and review and ratify settlement applications. Li notes: 'At the beginning of the resettlement process, people were very reluctant to move, ... now more people want to move' [*ibid.*: 177]. For the poor the main motivation to move was new land where they could attain their basic needs. It was a strategy for survival.[29]

Although Dazhanchang was planned as a suspended village of Guyuan county, Zhang learns in his survey that people living in Dazhanchang not only moved in from Guyuan county, but also from seven other provinces of the PRC. Most of them, however, came from 14 townships of Guyuan county. From the 12,500 settlers in 1996, about 10,000 were from Guyuan county and had moved to Dazhanchang at different periods. The survey reveals that 15.4 per cent of the 104 interviewed households moved to Dazhanchang between 1983 and 1985, 29.8 per cent moved between 1986 and 1989 and 54.8 per cent moved since the beginning of the 1990s. But, according to a report of the Command Post of the Dazhanchang Suspended Village Construction Project, 12,528 people were moved to the suspended village by 1989.[30] This figure is identical with the number of settlers who lived there in 1996. Combining the two figures, Zhang comes to the conclusion that a large number of the targeted poor returned to their place of origin and did not settle down in Dazhanchang.

This implies that the efforts the government made in organized resettlement were more or less in vain: the target group was not resettled permanently. The dropout rate was enormous and tight administrative control over the settlers could not be retained. Spontaneous settlement occurred on a great scale after 1989, the official completion of the project. There are many reasons for this failure; some of them will be discussed in the following sections.

Public and Private Costs

If all public and private costs are factored in then the full costs of the settlement project can be estimated to be very high, especially when a whole new economic and social system is required. According to the State Council Poverty Alleviation Bureau, the average cost to get a person out of poverty is 1,500 Rmb.[31] In a review of ten worldwide resettlement projects aided by the World Bank, the average cost per family in a resettlement scheme was more than $5,000 in 1974.[32]

Allowing for inflation, only a fraction of this average was invested for the Dazhanchang suspended village project.

The sources of the funds are manifold: In 1998, the biggest share came from the 'Three West' fund representing 62.8 per cent; funds such as the

TABLE 4

GOVERNMENT INVESTMENTS IN DAZHANCHANG

	In 1990[a]	In 1996[b]	In 1998[c]
Total population (in persons)	12,528	12,500	17,947
Realized investment until the completion of the project in 1989 (in Rmb)	—	7,894,500	—
Realized investment until present (in Rmb)	8,480,000	12,000,000	12,650,000
Total investments per capita (in Rmb)	677	960	714

Source: Data marked (a) from Li [1993: 173–9]; data marked (b) from Zhang [1998: 41–74]; data marked (c) from GXNB [1999].

'Development Fund for Underdeveloped Regions' or the 'Cooperative Organization Fund' contributed 25.5 per cent of the investments; 6.7 per cent came from food-for-work programmes and only the remaining 5.0 per cent of investments were provided by the Guyuan county government [*GXNB*, 1999: 7].

From Table 5, it can be seen that the government resources were mainly allocated in water works and the reclamation of the steppe land. These two activities were conducted as food-for-work programmes at the beginning of the settlement process.

Most of the funds were provided to the counties and the settlers without any obligation to pay them back. The beneficiaries were only expected to take over some of the project costs. Although the state subsidized the construction of houses and the moving expenses, the settlers had to take over the bigger share of those costs. In the case of Guyuan county, the local government gave only 66 Rmb for the expenses of relocation, the settlers themselves had to invest another 129 Rmb. In terms of the costs after arrival at Dazhanchang such as costs for seed or farm implements, the government provided 224 Rmb, whereas the settler expenses amounted for 985 Rmb [*Chen*, 1996: 153].

However, an exact cost comparison between the public and private investments is difficult to draw because it is not at all clear for example how much a settler household had to pay for its living expenses in the first few years after arrival or how much they had to invest in technology that became necessary for the new farming system based on irrigation (as opposed to rain-fed farming). There are no data available about the total costs on the side of the beneficiaries. It is not possible to come to any conclusions about

TABLE 5

ALLOCATION OF GOVERNMENT RESOURCES IN THE CONSTRUCTION
OF DAZHANCHANG

	Water works and land reclamation	Trans-migration subsidies to settlers	Social services (education, heathcare, technical training	Construc-tion of a shelter-belt	Develop-ment of animal husbandry	Infra-structure develop-ment
In Rmb	5,540,000	890,000	490,000	445,000	115,000	1,000,000
As per-centage of realized investments	65.3	10.5	5.8	5.3	1.4	11.7

Source: Li [1993: 173–4].

the maximum private investment share in the project that would be bearable for the asset-poor target group. When we recall the high dropout rate, one could come to the conclusion that many of the targeted settlers were disappointed with the state's insufficient financial support.

Supply of Services

In fact, even if the settlers tried to keep alive the spirit of self-reliance, as the government promoted it, this was hardly possible without assuming some debt. Although they did not have to take out credit for the purchase of land, they had to fund for example seasonal inputs into farming. However, these economically disadvantaged groups normally could not get access to the formal banking sector and the institutional credit net, so that they were forced to borrow money on the black market from money dealers with monthly interest rates between seven and ten per cent.[33]

Although the slogan for the implementation was 'opening up on one hand, construction on the other hand' (*yibian kaifa, yibian jianshe*), irrigation works and the reclamation of steppe land became the key focus and other important measures were put last. Especially in the sectors such as public education, electricity or roads, the development lagged far behind and the public sector demonstrated poor performance. Schools were constructed only some time after the settlers came, and so the children could not attend classes in the first two years. According to Zhang, the number of schools is still insufficient today. In terms of public health, the conditions in the new settlement are now worse than before. About 30 per cent of the settler population still does not have access to clean drinking water, but has to use unpurified water from the Yellow River. There are only two doctors in

Dazhanchang with only rudimentary medical equipment [*Zhang*, 1998: 59, 68]. Access to electricity is only possible in 16 out of the 18 administrative villages and roads are in very bad condition [*GXNB*, 1999: 6–7].

In terms of technical assistance, the farmers were unfamiliar with the natural environment and urgently needed guidance for suitable cultivation methods. Instead, an analysis of the investments made in all the suspended village projects conducted between 1983 and 1989 shows that only 0.9 per cent of all public investments went to training programmes for settlers [*Wang*, 1994: 253]. This was, as we have seen above, among the responsibilities of the target county.

Environmental Impacts

Resettlement in Ningxia was based on irrigation whereby major limitations of the environment had to be circumvented.

A major stumbling block in the future development of Dazhanchang will be the availability of water. According to the plans, Dazhanchang should get 2.7m³ of water per second or 540m³ of water per *mu* of cultivated land. Summer crops, like soybeans, corn or wheat, have to be watered ten times over a period of 100 days, winter crops only once or twice. Each time, 100m³ of water per *mu* is used, which is over 1,000m³ of water per *mu* of cultivated land per year. Therefore, a reasonable ratio of summer to winter crops can reduce the need for water. The planned 540m³ of water per *mu* of cultivated land was calculated to be sufficient for the suggested cropping pattern: 50 per cent summer crops, 30 per cent winter crops, 10 per cent grassland and 10 per cent root vegetables.[34] However, the current rate of water use is twice as much as was planned, so that water shortage is a common phenomenon nowadays. Summer crops have been increasingly cultivated in the past few years because farmers can get better prices for summer crops on the market than for winter crops. The share of winter crops in cultivation has declined to a mere 10 per cent. At this point, it has to be stressed that the mistakes are not only explained by the rent-seeking attitude of the farmers alone. It seems that they were also advised to grow more corn. Growing corn under plastic foil was promoted by the government as a measure that ensures high yield results (460 kg per *mu* on average) [*Liu*, 1997: 163].

Sand in the irrigation channels and the very high evaporation (with more than 1,500 mm per year [*Zhang* et al., 1994: 247]) has worsened the water supply problem. As a result, the price for water has more than doubled since 1984 (from 0.24 Rmb per m³ to 0.573 Rmb). As a consequence, disputes about water arose among the population [*Zhang*, 1998: 64].

A very generous use of water also had a severe impact on the quality of the soil. With an adequate, yet very cost-intensive technique, irrigation farming in an arid region could be managed without harm to the quality of the soil. However, in Dazhanchang, the bad water management has led to the salinization of the soil.

According to Zhang, beetles are the biggest problem in Dazhanchang at present because they severely damage the shelterbelt of the suspended village. They live by eating tree leaves and crops until the trees are dead. Apparently a solution to that problem has not been found. Rats are also a plague. Zhang estimates that there exist about 100,000 rats in Dazhanchang, or about eight to ten rats per capita. Calculating that every rat eats 5 kg of grain per year, this would create an economic loss of 500,000 kg of grain in one year [ibid.: 61, 63].

The environmental deterioration in the settlement is severe and the findings are rather disquieting for the future development of the area.

Population Growth

Ecological problems will become even more severe in the future if the demographic growth can not be controlled. In Zhang's survey, the 104 households had 600 members when they settled in Dazhanchang, or 5.77 persons per household. One hundred and three children were born into those families between their time of arrival in Dazhanchang – on average 6.9 years – and 1997. With this growth rate of 1.8 per cent per year – which is 0.3 per cent higher than in the source place and 0.4 per cent higher than the province's average – the population will have doubled within 39 years [ibid.: 65–6]. The high population growth is partly due to the age of the settlers, who are on average younger than in the source places. In addition, the population policy of Ningxia allows the rural Hui population to have three children as opposed to the Han with only two [Liu 1997: 163]. In the Southern Mountains Region, the percentage of Hui population is 47.59 per cent, but 60.59 per cent of the settlers were Hui [Chen, 1995: 517].

The high population growth in the suspended villages has developed to a severe problem. In some of the suspended villages the ratio of arable land per capita is already under the planned 2 *mu* and food security problems have already emerged [Chen, 1996: 157].

Yield and Income Levels

On the other hand, the economic development gives a rather positive picture. In reports on the overall economic progress in Dazhanchang measured in yield production and per capita income levels a great increase over the time can be ascertained for both indicators. Table 3 summarizes the data for Dazhanchang as provided in the quoted literature.

However, if we scrutinize the data for grain production per capita by dividing the total grain production by the total population, we would end up

TABLE 6

BASIC FACTS AND FIGURES FOR DAZHANCHANG

	In 1990[a]	In 1996[b]	In 1998[b]
Total population (in persons)	12,528	12,500	17,947
Newly developed irrigated area (in *mu*)	42,000	50,000	42,000
Total grain production per year (in tons)	2,510	10,623	13,340
Grain production per capita per year (in kg)	267	882	930
Rural net income per capita (in Rmb)	235	733	1.183

Source: Data marked (a) from Li [1993:173–9]; data marked (b) from Zhang [1998: 41–74]; data marked (c) from GXNB [1999].

with different numbers for the grain production per capita (200 kg in 1990, 850 kg in 1996 and 743 kg in 1998). The accuracy of the data is in doubt. In fact, Zhang writes in his paper that the figure for grain production per capita that he found out during field investigation (882 kg) differs greatly from that which had been reported to upper levels of the administration by county level officials, namely 702.5 kg [*Zhang*, 1998: 54]. However, instead of indulging in speculations about the reasons behind these inconsistencies, the data at least permits us to make some general statements.

We see that not only the rural net income per capita is above the poverty line, but also, in terms of food security, the norm of 300 kg grain per capita is also exceeded. This allows farmers to sell some grain on the market. The overall economic development can considered to be positive. According to Zhang, 90 per cent of the population has been relieved from poverty – used in China in its economic sense – and 10 per cent even reached a level of relative wealth; and 82.4 per cent of the interviewed persons feel that their lives had improved [*ibid.*: 44].

Yet the reality behind those figures is more complex. In the remarks about the measurement and the definition of poverty we realized that poverty is a highly politicized issue. This finding is confirmed in the case of Dazhanchang. In 1990, Li writes, there were 12,528 people living in Dazhanchang, 9,516 of whom had already officially settled down and given up their old home in the Southern Mountains Region (land use rights and household registration). If one continues to read, Li mentions that the figure for the grain production per capita per year is calculated on the basis of those people who have already settled down (9,516 persons) and not on the actual total population of Dazhanchang [*Li*, 1993: 175–6]. This has several implications: first, this means that, taking the total population as a base, the resulting figure would be much lower, namely 203 kg of grain per capita per year. Second, if we assume that this calculation method is also used for the calculation of the rural net income per capita, then the resulting figure would also be much lower, namely 179 Rmb per capita. Third, figures for the newly irrigated land provided for 1990 and 1998 are similar, and those for the total investments per capita do not differ very much for the two years (see Table 4 and Table 6); thus there is some fundamental doubt on how the figures for 1996 and 1998 were constructed.

Although the development was rather positive, the finding sheds a somewhat different light on the success of the poverty reduction efforts made in Dazhanchang. The project seems to be not as successful as the officials at local level pretend.

EXPERIENCES IN OTHER INTER-COUNTY SUSPENDED VILLAGES

To a great extent, the trend in the performance of Dazhanchang can be considered to be representative for the other inter-county suspended village projects in general: the overwhelming majority of the settlers feel that their living and production situation has improved greatly, government investments spent per settler were approximately the same and the government performance in the organization of the resettlement and the management of the suspended villages is rather poor.[35]

However, it seems that by the end of the year 1999 the performance in the two suspended villages of Chahu and Lucaowa is much better than in the other inter-county resettlement villages. The site selection played an important role in their development.

Whereas in the other suspended villages agricultural production was the core objective of resettlement, in Chahu, the development of a diversified economical structure was the goal. Chahu is located in the northern part of Ningxia, near Shizhuishan city, which is one of Ningxia's three major industrial production areas.[36] The industry takes advantage of the economically important mineral resources concentrated in this area such as coal, quartzite and gypsum. There is a transportation network: the Baotou–Yinchuan–Lanzhou railway, one of the main lines of northern China, passes by Shizhuishan. Chahu seems to be the only suspended village where the industrial sector plays an important role. Wang stresses that since 1988 more than 40 small enterprises of different ownership (collective, state owned, private) were established, and even products for the international market were produced [*Wang*, 1994: 253].

Lucaowa is another example of a positive development. Originally planned as a mainly agricultural dominated suspended village, it has since blossomed into a more diversified economy with a small industrial and a small service sector [*ibid.*: 253]. Lucaowa is located near Yinchuan, the capital of Ningxia.

In 1996, the Zhongning–Guyuan–Baoji railway opened a line connecting Ningxia directly with Xi'an. This will certainly contribute to the future development of the Southern Mountains Region.

SUMMARY AND CONCLUSION

The starting point for our analysis was to ask whether the resettlement projects conducted in Ningxia during the 1980s could be evaluated in order to be able to assess the nation's main approach to poverty reduction for the future.

The article has demonstrated that a simple answer to that question is not possible. From the perspective of the settlers, the vast majority of the people who live in the suspended villages see a definite improvement in their living and production conditions. This subjective perception finds confirmation in the statistics about the economic developments. But, first, those settlers do not necessarily correspond to the people who were chosen by the government to move from the Southern Mountains Region to the suspended villages. Spontaneous settlement occurred on a large scale after the completion of the projects. And second, these statistics do not reflect the economic loss owing to mismanagement and ecological problems. If we look at the economic performance from the perspective of ecological economy the project sustainability of most of the projects is questionable. In places where the population is totally dependent on agriculture land degradation is already obvious. In addition, the resource base becomes increasingly scarce owing to a high population growth. The Ningxia government should either change its population policy or calculate the population growth in the design of resettlement schemes and reduce the number for settlers. In addition, the objective of a mainly agricultural resettlement scheme should be changed. The evidence shows that in the long run the suspended villages with a diverse economic structure and located near cities perform better. The population (and employment) pressure is not solely on agricultural land anymore, but on a larger array of resources and then the same space can bear a higher population pressure. This had been the general experience in China during rural reforms when part of the agricultural sector workers were transferred to rural industries, thus reducing the population and employment pressure on land and increasing labour productivity and rural income. Site selection is therefore one of the critical points in the success of a resettlement scheme.

The government performance has to be judged as very poor. The scheme was designed on the premise that 100 per cent of the target group would be successful. As Binswanger and Kinsey [1993: 1490] found out, such outcomes never materialize. In Ningxia, planners and decision-makers have realized that the dropout rate was rather high, and they have tried to learn from the experiences of the suspended villages. They saw the reasons for the high dropout in a wrong assumption in the project design concerning the criteria for settler selection. In the plans for a follow-up transmigration project – the '1236 project' (*one* million people should be helped out of poverty, *two* million *mu* of land (which will be irrigated with the water from the Yellow River) should be reclaimed, the central government will invest *three* billion Rmb and the project will be finished after *six* years) – not only the absolute poor are targeted therefore, but also households with more assets. As an optimal relationship, 60 per cent of the settler households should be the poor, 30 per cent should be 'better off' and 10 per cent should be well-equipped households [*Jing and Yao*, 1998: 286]. It is anticipated that the latter two groups will act as drivers for the development, which is of particular relevance at the beginning of the settlement process. A strong positive correlation has been seen between the high dropout rate and the capital assets of the households, which again is considered to be positively correlated with the level of education. But again, the assumption is that all of the settlers will be successful and stay in the resettlement area, which, according to Binswanger and Kinsey, has never happened in the projects they reviewed. The Chinese (or Ningxia) government should therefore better design their resettlement schemes with the flexibility to anticipate that some settlers will always leave. In addition, a briefing for would-be settlers as part of the formal selection procedure could prevent unrealistic expectations about how long it would take for them to reach a certain level of living conditions.

The aim of voluntary participation mainly determined the land use rights system adopted in Ningxia for the suspended villages projects. At the same time it was a solution that was within the national legal framework of the land tenure system. The ownership of the land is still with the collective, only the reform of land use rights was adapted to local needs. Settlers had the opportunity to keep land use rights at their native place for three years after they had moved to the new home. Although the rights were clear, an informal land market emerged and settlers sold their leased rights. The lessons learned for the '1236 project' were that settlers now have to register in the new settlement within the first year after arrival. This reflects the strong desire of the government to retain tight administrative control over the settlers. Binswanger and Kinsey [1993: 1480] however show that restrictions on rental and sales can rarely be enforced and prohibitions are almost uniformly damaging. The Ningxia government should therefore deliberately design resettlement schemes and react more flexibly to former bad experiences, for example in allowing the settlers to sell parts of the leased land use rights. This again could have positive side effects such as a more appropriate size of land holdings adjusted to the family labour force, the capital available to settler families and agricultural skills. To date, the land distribution practice in Ningxia reflects the dilemma in which, according to Chen and Davis [1998: 134], land reform in China since the mid-1980s has been caught: 'where social equality or equity considerations predominate, economic efficiency has been held back'.

The case of Dazhanchang has shown that environmental deterioration is severe. Although water problems have already emerged, farmers obviously do not relate them to the cropping pattern. Instead of just making regulations and rules, the state should intensify its efforts to provide the settlers with the technical assistance and knowledge necessary for irrigation farming systems. At this point, the local government in charge, namely the target county, showed a very poor engagement. If existing problems are not taken seriously the findings are rather disquieting for the future development.[37]

Administrative ineffectiveness is the main error of the suspended village projects. The coordination between the two responsible counties has been very bad. Although the projects had a finite time span, the inter-county suspended villages still belong to the administration of the source counties of the settlers. It seems that either the source county has a certain interest in keeping the suspended village or the target county is not willing to take over the administrative tasks and other related responsibilities. The provincial government does not seem to be inclined to intercede. If we look at some statistics, a great deal of evidence points to the conclusion that the counties in the poverty-stricken Southern Mountains Region do have an economic interest in keeping their suspended villages. In the case of Chahu, the gross value output (hereafter GVO) in 1990 represented 20 per cent of the GVO of Longde county or in the case of Lucaowa, the suspended village produced one-sixth of the total grain production of Jingyuan county in 1990.[38] These are the two suspended villages that performed relatively better than the others. But even if the other suspended villages do not perform as well as these two, they do contribute significantly to the budget of the source county [*Chen*, 1996: 60]. And this again might be a reason for the provincial government not to intervene.

The discussion about income and production indices showed that the issue of poverty is also highly politicized in the lower government levels, and political interests are very important. Why do the poor county governments of the Southern Mountains Region provide a better picture of the performance of their suspended villages than is actually the case? This could be due to the fact that a consistent system for evaluating and monitoring does not exist. But it might also be explained by the lack of financial resources of the county governments in the impoverished areas.

They have a low domestic tax base, so that the subsidies they can get from the provincial government for poverty alleviation could fill holes in the local budget, and the better they perform in their suspended villages, the higher the chances of getting more subsidies. One could ask why there is a problem of consistency in the calculation method of the poverty rate as is evidently the case in provincial level government documents. At this point, any explanation would not represent more than a vague speculation.

All in all, we can state that resettlement projects are very difficult to manage in order to become sustainable and that they are a very cost-intensive attempt to reduce poverty. After more than a decade's development, the outcomes of the resettlement projects in Ningxia are mixed. If the central government tries to implement resettlement projects in the future as a last means to reach the poor, and eventually the intended goal of common prosperity, it should learn from the mistakes made in Ningxia. A realistic and detailed cost analysis should be made in advance considering also the private investment share and it should be transparent to all the people involved in the project. Resettlement projects should be deliberately designed and flexibly implemented. Resettlement schemes in China hinge very much upon the issues of household registration and land use rights. If the local governments involved in an inter-county (or inter-provincial) resettlement project cannot solve the problems of permanent residence registration and land tenure, the overall project sustainability is in doubt and the attempt will be little more than a costly but futile solution to poverty reduction.

NOTES

Abbreviations in the notes:
GFKLXB = Guowuyuan fupin kaifa lingdao xiaozu bangongshi
GXNB   = Guyuan xian nongjian ban
NGZB   = Ningxia guotu zhengzhi bangongshi
NNTZH = Ningxia nongcun tongji ziliao huibian
NSB   = Ningxia Statistical Bureau
RMRB   = Renmin Ribao
SSB   = State Statistical Bureau

1. However, the World Bank states: 'China's reduction in poverty became increasingly clear … perhaps the most spectacular poverty reduction in the history of the world' [*World Bank*, 1999: 5]. According to Chinese official numbers, more than 200 million people have been lifted out of poverty in the past 20 years. In 1978 about 250 million people lived in absolute poverty, in 1998 there were only 42 million people still languishing in absolute poverty. Thus, the poverty incidence among rural people apparently decreased from 30.7 per cent to 4.6 per cent. See Lu and Xue [1997: 144] and Wen [1999: 2].
2. During the 1980s a trickle-down development strategy giving preferential treatment to the coastal region predominated, but in the Ninth Five Year Plan (1996–2000) the priority has shifted to the central and western regions. By 1995, in a proposal in the Ninth Five Year Plan (1996–2000), the Chinese government frankly pointed out that the distribution of wealth was

increasingly uneven and that the anticipated trickle-down effect on the central and the western regions did not occur: 'we promoted a few regions to develop faster and become rich first and supported the process that those, who took off first should entail the others and help them ... Yet, due to several reasons, regional disparities have widened.' See N.N. in RMRB, 5 Oct. 1995, p.2. With eastern and western regions two of the three macro-economic regions as they were pointed out in the 7th Five Year Plan are denoted. The third region was the central region.

3. There is also an English translation of the document provided. In fact, it is a collection of documents that also includes the 'Decision of the CPC Central Committee and the State Council on Solving the Problem of Providing Adequate Food and Clothing to Poverty-Stricken People in Rural Areas on an Early Stage' (pp.31–8 in Chinese, pp.39–54 in English) published 23 Oct. 1996; a speech given by President Jiang Zemin – 'Mobilize the Entire Party and the Entire Society to Strive for the Accomplishment of the 8-7 Poverty Reduction Plan' (pp.55–65 in Chinese, pp.66–82 in English) and another speech, given by Premier Li Peng – 'Intensity Efforts for Poverty Reduction and Resolve the Problem of Feeding and Clothing the Poor as Soon as Possible' (pp.83–92 in Chinese, pp.93–110 in English), which were both given at the Conference on Poverty Reduction and Development on 23 Sept. 1996.

4. The 1993 Human Development Report of the UNDP pointed out that widening regional disparities can threaten the unity and stability of a nation. One year later, in their 1994 report, China was listed as one of the countries where regional gaps had become excessively large. China 'will need to take care that existing regional disparities do not widen further'. Cited in Wang and Hu [1999: 10–11].

5. There has been some writing on involuntary resettlement projects in China, but only in relation to the construction of dams in hydropower projects. See Cernea [1998: 32] and Eriksen [1998: 121–44]. Eriksen uses five pairs of projects in five countries, including China, with each pair containing the two types of resettlement projects under comparison (involuntary resettlement programmes and voluntary settlement programmes). For the case of China, the analysis of the voluntary resettlement project is very unsatisfactory and basically not discussed in the article. In the Appendix some characteristics are described in the form of tables.

6. The speech is given in full in the *Peoples Daily*. See Wen Jiabao in RMRB, 22 July 1999, pp.2–3.

7. Guangxi Miao autonomous region is the other province where resettlement projects started already a few years ago in 1993. For some basic facts see Liu [1997: 159].

8. I will use this periodization according to Ho [1999: 52].

9. The *yin huang guanqu* is also sometimes referred to as *beibu guanqu* (Northern Irrigated Region).

10. In 1985 it ranked fifth lowest, in 1990 eighth lowest, in 1994 third lowest, and in 1997 again eighth lowest. See SSB [1998: Tables 10–16].

11. See *NNTZH 1949–97* [1998: 99] and SSB [1998: Tables 10–13]. It should be mentioned here that there is also a big income gap in terms of rural incomes versus incomes of urban people in Ningxia. The urban average net income in Ningxia in 1995 was 3,027 Rmb. See NSB [1996: 70, Tables 1–7].

12. See Liu [1997: 137]. For an excellent discussion of the various problems in defining the first poverty line in 1985, see Zhu and Jiang [1996: 9–10] and for the redefinition of the official poverty line by provincial governments, see Zhu et al. [1997: 12]. The authors give the example of Yunnan province where the poverty line was set at 300 Rmb only in 1996.

13. In addition to these centrally designated poverty-stricken counties, provincial governments have identified another 368 counties as poverty-stricken counties on the basis of standards that were set by them and were meant to reflect the particularities in the provinces' development.

14. The plan is cited in Chen [1996: 298].

15. See Ningxia Huizu Zizhiqu Jihua Weiyuanhui and Kexue Jishu Weiyuanhui [1999: 29], Guo [1998: 36–7] and Chen [1996: 65].

16. This number is given in those materials that say that the poverty rate for Ningxia in 1997 was ten per cent.

17. 'Xihaigu' is an abbreviation of the counties of Xiji, Haiyuan and Guyuan, but the other five counties of the Southern Mountains Region are also included in the name.

18. See Xu [1994: 63]. Project activities ranged from digging groundwater wells and terracing hills, to education, the development of industrial zones in townships and the improvement of the marketing structure. For a detailed listing of the main 12 categories of projects with information presented in tables (for the years from 1983 until 1992) see Chen [1996: 41–55].

19. See *NNTZH 1949–97* [1998: 10]. However numbers in the literature do vary between 21 and 23, in the more official literature however, the number is always 21, see Guo [1998: 145]; Qin [1999: 60]. For 22 see NGZB [1997: 1]. For 23 see Nongjianwei [1999: 144]. In other literature, which is based on older statistics, the common number given is 15 for the 'suspended villages' constructed in the years between 1983 and 1992. See Li [1993: 395]; Chen [1996: 13].

20. See the above-cited literature. Chen [1996: 14] for example notes that 143,000 people were moved until the end of 1992. Against that, Wang [1994, 250] notes that 209,000 people were settled until the end of 1992.

21. See Chen [1996: 141], Wang [1994: 249], *NNTZH 1949–97* [10] and Qin [1999: 60].

22. See Qin [1999: 62] and Qin [1990: 28].

23. To the first group of inter-county migration villages belong definitely Dazhanchang, Majialiang, Lucaowa, Chahu, Yueyahu, Liangpitaizi and Nanliangtaizi. To the 'Putting flowers into a vase'-style migration belong the villages of Nanshantaizi, Changshantou and Wutanzi. About the other mapped villages, no material has yet been found at the time of writing. See Chen [1996: 37] and Li [1993: 135].

24. See Chen [1996], Li [1993] and Wang [1994: 249].

25. See Cheng and Selden [1994: 644–99] as well as He [1997: 77–81].

26. The notice is cited in Li [1993: 105–9].

27. The speech is cited in Li [1993: 85–6].

28. For an excellent description of China's land tenure system since the mid-1980s and new models of land tenure see Chen and Davis [1998: 123–37].

29. In a survey conducted by the Ningxia Academy of Social Sciences – in which the year is not mentioned – 2,653 settlers were interviewed and asked for their motivation to move; 59.3 per cent answered that they simply saw it as a means for survival (*zhao shenghuo chulu*). For the results of the survey see Chen [1996: 149, Tables 2, 5, 6].

30. The report is cited in Zhang [1998: 54–5].

31. Cited in Liu [1997: 164].

32. Cited in Stevens and Jabara [1988: 172].

33. See Zhang [1998: 70]. Local money lenders have a long history in China going back until the third century BC. This tradition even continued after the PRC was established in 1949, but only relatives and friends were provided with money. However, after reforms started in the late 1970s, money lenders had a revival and play an important role in the still very restricted credit market. Depending on the pace of development and the grade of competition, usurious monthly interest rates have to be paid on the non-state credit market and can vary from around 10 per cent in Zhejiang and in Anhui to 50 per cent in the northeastern provinces up to 70 per cent in Shenzhen. See Hu and Zhu [1997: 26–52].

34. The numbers are given in Zhang [1998: 63–4].

35. The government investments per capita for all the suspended villages, this means also the ones that belong to the category of intra-county migration, was 960 Rmb. See Chen [1996: 60]. For further literature see for example Chen [1995], Chen [1996: 141–59], Guo [1998], Li [1993], Qin [1999], Wang [1994: 245–54].

36. The other two areas where industry is concentrated are the cities of Yinchuan and Qingtongxia. In 1994, approximately 40 per cent of the total industrial output of Ningxia was produced in Yinchuan city, 27 per cent in Shizhuishan city and 16 per cent in Qingtongxia. See NSB [1995: 167, 171 and 335].

37. From a fieldtrip conducted to the '1236 project' area in September 1999, it can be assumed that the decision-makers have not taken the problem seriously enough. First settlers in the newly developed area do not have the necessary financial assistance to buy coal for cooking and therefore collect shrub from the surrounding steppe land to make fire.

38. See Li [1993: 137, 143]. In a personal interview with Prof. Chen Zhongxiang from Ningxia University in September 1999 I was told that 85 per cent of the budget of Longde county come from taxes of its suspended village Chahu in Pingluo county.

REFERENCES

Binswanger, Hans P. and Bill H. Kinsey, 1993, 'Characteristics and Performance of Resettlement Programs: A Review', *World Development*, Vol.21, No.9, pp.1477–94.

Cernea, Michael, 1998, 'Why Economic Analysis Is Essential to Resettlement: A Sociologist's View', in Michael Cernea (ed.), *The Economics of Involuntary Resettlement: Questions and Challenges*, Washington, DC: The World Bank, pp.5–49.

Chen, Fu and John Davis, 1998, 'Land Reform in Rural China Since the Mid-1980s', *Land Reform*, Vol.2, pp.123–37.

Chen, Wenjun (ed.), 1996, *Zouchu pinkun – Xihaigu fan pinkun nongye jianshe yanjiu* (Leaving poverty – research on anti-poverty rural construction Xihaigu), Yinchuan: Ningxia renmin chubanshe.

Chen, Zhongxiang, 1995, 'Ningxia fupin gongcheng yu yin huang guanqu kaifa zhong de diao zhuang yimin' (Poverty reduction projects in Ningxia and the suspended village migration within the development of irrigated land by diverting water of the Yellow River), *Dili xuebao (Acta Geographica Sinica)*, Vol.50, No.6, pp.514–19.

Cheng, Tiejun and Mark Selden, 1994, 'The Origins and Social Consequences of China's Hukou System', *China Quarterly*, No.139 (Sept.), pp.644–69.

Eriksen, John H., 1998, 'Comparing the Economic Planning for Voluntary and Involuntary Resettlement', in Michael Cernea (ed.), *The Economics of Involuntary Resettlement: Questions and Challenges*, Washington, DC: The World Bank, pp.83–146.

GFKLXB (Guowuyuan Fupin Kaifa Lingdao Xiaozu Bangongshi) (The State Council Leading Group Office of Poverty Alleviation and Development) (ed.), 1996, *Guojia ba qi fupin gongjian jihua (1994–2000)* (National 8-7 Poverty Reduction Plan (1994–2000), Beijing: internal document.

Guo, Zhanyuan, 1998, *Lun shiji gongjian. Ningxia xi hai gu fan pinkun shijian yu sikao* (Discussion on the strongholds of the century. The experience of Xihaigu in Ningxia on attacking poverty and some thoughts about it), Ningxia: Ningxia renmin chubanshe.

GXNB (Guyuan Xian Nongjian Ban) (Guyuan County Bureau for Agricultural Construction), 1999, *Guyuan xian diao zhuang jianshe qingkuang huibao* (Report on the situation of the construction of suspended village in Guyuan county), Guyuan: internal document.

He, Tieguang, 1997, 'Causes and Consequences of Insistence on the Dual Household Registration System', *Inside China Mainland*, Vol.19, No.4, pp.77–81.

Herrmann-Pillath, Carsten (ed.), 1995, *Wirtschaftliche Entwicklung in Chinas Provinzen, 1978–1992*, Baden-Baden: Nomos.

Ho, Peter, 1999, *Rangeland Policy, Pastoralism and Poverty in China's Northwest: Ningxia Province in the Twentieth Century*, Leiden: Leiden University, Faculty of Arts, Leiden University.

Hu, Haiming and Zhu Delin, 1997, *Zhongguo de hueiheise jinrong. Shichang fengyun he lixing sikao* (China's grey and black financial market. The market's unstable situation and rational considerations), Shanghai: Lixin huiji chubanshe.

Jing, Mingsen and Yao Jiasheng, 1998, '"1236"gongcheng Hongsipu guanqu nongye yimin gongcheng de kechixu fazhan' (The sustainable development of the agricultural migration project to the irrigated area of Hongsipu within the '1236' project), in Sun, Shiwen *et al.*, *Ningxia shishi kezhixu fazhan zhanlüe yanjiu* (Studies on Ningxia's implementation of the sustainable development strategy), Ningxia: Ningxia renmin chubanshe, pp.274–92.

Kang, Shaoguang, 1995, *Zhongguo pinkun yu fan pinkun lilun* (Theory about poverty and poverty reduction in China), Guangxi: Nanning: Guangxi renmin chubanshe.

Li, Zhong (ed.), 1993, *San xi yimin lu* (Records on the 'three west' migration), Lanzhou: Gansu renmin chubanshe.

Liu, Hui, 1997, 'Zhuyao pinkun qu tuo pin zhengce yu jingji fazhan' (Main poverty reduction policies for the poor regions and their economic development), in Lu and Xue [1997: 135–65].

Lu, Dadao and Xue Fengxuan (eds.), 1997, *Zhongguo quyu fazhan baogao 1997* (Report on the regional development in the PRC 1997), Beijing: Shangwu yinshuguan.

NGZB (Ningxia Guotu Zhengzhi Bangongshi) (Ningxia Bureau for Territorial Management), 1997, 'Ningxia yimin diao zhuang ji fupin kaifaqu diaocha baogao zhi er' (Field report on Ningxia's suspended village migration and the construction of development zones for poverty reduction in Ningxia), in NGZB, *Ningxia fupin kaifaqu jianshe yanjiu* (Research on the construction of development zone for poverty reduction in Ningxia), Ningxia, Oct. 1997, Annex, pp.1–12.

Ningxia Huizu Zizhiqu Jihua Weiyuanhui and Kexue Jishu Weiyuanhui (Ningxia Hui Autonomous Region Planning Commission and Commission for Science and Technology)(ed.), 1999, *'Zhongguo 21 shiji yicheng'* – *Ningxia xingdong jihua* ('China agenda for the twenty-first century' – action plan of Ningxia), March 1999.

N.N., 1986, 'Zhonghua renmin gongheguo guomin jingji he shehui fazhan di qi ge wu nian jihua 1986–1990' (The Seventh Five Year Plan for the economic and social development of the PRC 1986–1990), *Renmin Ribao* (*Peoples Daily*), 15 April 1986, pp.1–4.

NSB (Ningxia Statistical Bureau) (ed.), 1995, *Ningxia tongji nianjian 1995* (Ningxia statistical yearbook 1995), Zhongguo tongji chubanshe.

NSB (ed.), 1996, *Ningxia tongji nianjian 1996* (Ningxia statistical yearbook 1996), Zhongguo tongji chubanshe, Beijing

Qin, Jun, 1995, *Fupin xihaigu* (Poverty reduction in Xihaigu), Xi'an: Xibei daxue chubanshe.

Qin, Junping, 1990, 'Ningxia nongcun kaifa yimin tedian ji qi qishi' (Characteristics of Ningxia's rural organized migration and some enlightening remarks on it), *Ningxia shehui kexue*, Vol.39, No.2, pp.27–33.

Qin, Junping, 1999, 'Nongcun diao zhuang yimin jizhi shulun' (Commentary on the mechanism of rural suspended village migration), *Ningxia daxue xuebao*, Vol.21, No.2, pp.60–64.

SSB (State Statistical Bureau) (ed.), 1998, *Zhongguo tongji nianjian* 1998 (China statistical yearbook 1998), Beijing: Zhongguo tongji chubanshe.

Stevens, Robert D. and Cathy L. Jabara, 1988, *Agricultural Development Principles: Economic Theory and Empirical Evidence*, Baltimore: The John Hopkins University Press.

Wang, Shaoguang and Hu Angang, 1999, *The Political Economy of Uneven Development: The Case of China*, Armonk: M.E. Sharpe.

Wang, Yiming, 1994, *Bu fada diqu guotu kaifa zhengzhi yanjiu* (Territorial development and management studies in underdeveloped regions), Yinchuan: Ningxia renmin chubanshe.

Wen, Jiabao, 1999,'Jianding xinxin, jiada lidu, quebao ruqi shixian fupin gongjian mubiao' (Persevere the confidence, increase the strength and make sure to achieve the aim of poverty reduction on time), *Renmin Ribao* (*Peoples Daily*), 22 July 1999, pp.2, 3.

World Bank, 1999, *World Development Report 2000/1. Attacking Poverty. Approach and Outlines, September 2, 1999*, at http://www.worldbank.org/poverty/wdrpoverty/appr999.htm.

Xu, Fen, 1994, 'Ningxia "san xi" zijin de touxiang yu guanli' (The use and management of the investments of the 'three west' fund in Ningxia), *Ningxia shehui kexue*, Vol.63, No.2, pp.61–7.

Zhang, Pingqing, Liu Hui and Zhao Peidong, 1994, 'Ningxia zizhiqu shengtai pohuai jingji sunshi fenxi' (An analysis of the economical loss due to the destruction of the ecology), in Jin Jianming (ed.), *Lüse de weiji: Zhongguo dianxing shengtai qu shengtai pohuai xianzhuang ji qi huifu yanjiu wenji* (The green danger: Collection of research papers on the condition of the ecological destruction in China's typical ecological regions and their recovery), Ningxia, pp.246–60.

Zhang, Tongji, 1998, 'Dazhanchang yimin diao zhuang huanjing yu fazhan wenti kaocha baogao' (Field investigation report on some problems of the environment and development in the *diaozhuang* of Dazhanchang), in Ningxia fupin yang huang guangai yiqi gongcheng keti zu (Study group on the first project phase of the Ningxia poverty reduction project through the development of irrigated land by bumping Yellow River water upward), *Ningxia fupin yang huang guangai gongcheng yiqi gongcheng. Lunwen* (First project phase of the Ningxia poverty reduction project through the development of irrigated land by bumping Yellow River water upward. Collection of papers), Ningxia, pp.41–74.

Zhu, Ling and Jiang Zhongyi, 1996, *Public Works and Poverty Alleviation in Rural China*, Commack, NY: Nova Science.

Zhu, Ling, Jiang Zhongyi and Joachim von Braun, 1997, *Credit Systems for the Rural Poor in China*, Commack, NY: Nova Science.

Zizhiqu Nangjianwei (Autonomous Region Commission for Agricultural Construction), 1999, 'Ningxia fupin kaifa gongzuo de diaocha' (Survey on Ningxia's Work in Poverty Reduction), in Ningxia Qu Dangwei Zhengce Yanjiushi (Policy Research Bureau of the Ningxia Party Committee), *Juece zhi ji – 1997–1998 quan qu yonxin diaocha baogao xuanbian* (Foundations of Policy Decision – Selected Compilation of Outstanding Investigation Reports from all over the Region in 1997 and 1998, Ningxia), internal document, pp.138–154

Zizhiqu Tonjiju, Jiwei, Nangjianwei, Nongyeting, Linyeting, Xumuju (Autonomous Region Statistical Bureau, Planning Commission, Agricultural Construction Commission, Agricultural Department, Forestry Department and Animal Husbandry Bureau), 1998, *NNTZH (Ningxia nongcun tongji ziliao huibian) 1949–97* (Collection of statistical material on Ningxia's rural areas 1949–1997), internal document.

A Comparative Study of Projection Models on China's Food Economy

XIAOYONG ZHANG

INTRODUCTION

Food security has always been the top priority on the Chinese government's agenda for historical and political reasons. However, China's food vulnerability and insecurity did not catch the world's attention, not even during the most severe famine in human history, which took about 30 million Chinese lives in the late 1950s [*Lin*, 1990: 1229]. Only since the mid-1970s, when the Chinese economy gradually opened up and more information became available to outsiders, have researchers and politicians paid attention to the food situation of the most populous country in the world. Owing to the rapid economic development during the last two decades, the consumption pattern in particular has changed dramatically. Consumers are moving away from a cereal-based diet towards highly valued livestock products. The rising food demand and sheer market size in China have brought great concerns among researchers and politicians about world food availability. China's development poses serious questions to the world, like 'Can China feed itself?' or 'Will China starve the world?'. This is an obvious question since the world food market is tiny when compared with China's demand. Any change in China's food trade policy may challenge the stability of global food markets. In response, the Chinese government asserts that China will not starve the world and can feed itself in the future. The United Nations Food and Agriculture Organization (FAO), in revised calculations in 2001, estimated that China had 362 million metric tons of wheat, corn, rice and other cereal grains, while at the same time, the United States Department of Agriculture (USDA) also quadrupled

Xiaoyong Zhang, Agricultural Economics Research Institute (LEI), Wageningen University and Research Centre, The Netherlands. Email: x.y.zhang@lei.dlo.nl. The research reflected in this article was conducted as part of a much larger, joint project 'China's Food Economy in the Early 21st Century and the Implications for EU Countries' financed by the Dutch Ministry of Agriculture, Nature and Fisheries. The author appreciates valuable comments from Jikun Huang, Paul Veenendaal, Frank van Tongeren, Jaap Post, Claude Aubert, Eduard Veermeer and Jacob Eyferth.

its estimation of China's wheat reserve. Researchers are trying to project the Chinese food economy and its implications for world trade. Several dozens of alternative projections on this topic have been made during the last two decades. Given the complexity of projecting China's food economy, a large variance of results exists. The aim of this article is to review the most influential projection models by comparing their research methodology and projection results in order to provide insights into their differences and to suggest improvements for further research.

The article is organized as follows. Several influential projection models are briefly introduced in section two. The third section is devoted to the methodological differences, including model structures, major assumptions, alternative scenarios and parameters used. In the fourth section, the projection results concerning China's food supply, demand and trade are compared. The similarity and difference of the comparison are summarized in section five. At the end, general discussions and some suggestions for future research are presented.

DEFINITION AND SCOPE

There is a large body of literature available on China's food security during the last two decades. Brown's *Who Will Feed China?* [*Brown,* 1995] functioned as a wake-up call and ignited the intensive debate over China's food supply and demand. Based on a series of assumptions and on the development experience of Japan, South Korea and Taiwan, Brown projected a massive shortfall in China's grain production. A summary of different projections on China's food security can be found in Fan and Agcaoili-Sombilla [1997] and Huang and Rozelle [1998]. Major projections on China's food security include Chinese Academy of Agricultural Sciences [1985], Carter and Zhong [1991], Garnaut and Ma [1992], Simpson *et al.* [1994], Brown [1995], OECF [1995], Huang *et al.* [1999], ERS [different versions, started in 1994], OECD [1995], FAO [1995], Rosegrant *et al.* [1995], Nyberg [1997], etc. Some projections were not systematically modelled, or their structure and major assumptions are not explicitly reported, while some studies are outdated. Therefore, it is not appropriate to compare them all here. Instead, we choose several most influential and up-to-date projectors for a detailed comparison in our study. These are the CCAP model of the Chinese Academy of Agricultural Sciences, the IFPRI model, the OECF model, the USDA model and two World Bank models.

Of course, different projectors have their own hidden assumptions and intellectual constraints. The CCAP is the only Chinese research institute among the others. Its assumptions and projections are firmly built upon Chinese government policy, particularly its long-term strategic planning.

Grain supply–demand projection is not the only objective in the OECF study. It also intends to examine policy options and to propose agricultural development policies for future assistance. Therefore, detailed projections at individual provincial level are needed and applied. The projection of USDA intends to provide detailed foreign supply, use and trade projections that support the baseline outlook for US agriculture and trade. IFPRI and World Bank are projecting world food demand and supply at the beginning of the twenty-first century when the world faces a series of problems, such as population growth, increasing food demand and environmental deterioration. The main objective here is to develop an international consensus about future demand and supply in the world food market. In their projections, China is not the only country focused on, but an important one. Definitions and scope of each model are explained in the following paragraphs.

CCAP Model

The China's Agricultural Policy Simulation and Projection Model (CAPSiM) was developed at the Centre for Chinese Agricultural Policy (CCAP), Chinese Academy of Agricultural Sciences. A description of the latest version of the CCAP model can be found in Huang *et al.* [1999], Huang and Chen [1999]. It is a partial equilibrium model that has been constantly updated and improved by CCAP staff. The latest version of this model explicitly accounts for those economic and market developments in China that are crucial elements for a transitional economy. The model covers a wide range of agricultural products (12 crops plus seven livestock products) and can be used for long-term projections until 2020. The demand functions are modelled separately for rural and urban areas. The database is mainly fed with primary data, or with secondary data supplemented with field surveys.

IFPRI Model

The International Model for Policy Analysis of Agricultural Commodities and Trade (IMPACT) was developed at the International Food Policy Research Institute (IFPRI). It is a partial equilibrium model with focus on the agricultural sector. The model has a global coverage of 35 countries and regions, including 17 commodities ranging from groups of crops, livestock products to processed products. Its database is mainly taken from FAO's AGROSTAT. In IMPACT, each country or region has a specified structure with domestic supply, demand and price determination, and these submodels are linked through trade. The model has been continuously modified and extended by IFPRI staff. The IMPACT model's documentation and its projection results are presented in IFPRI 2020 vision discussion paper 5 [*Rosegrant* et al., 1995].

OECF Model

The OECF model is the outcome of joint research between the Overseas Economic Cooperation Fund (OECF) in Japan and the Ministry of Agriculture (MOA) in China. Results are published in an OECF discussion paper entitled 'Prospects for Grain Supply–Demand Balance and Agricultural Development Policy in China' [*OECF*, 1995]. The main objectives of this research are to estimate grain supply–demand balance by crop and by province (region) until 2010, and to identify exporting, self-sufficient and importing regions by crop, in addition to other agricultural developments. The projection is based on single equations to assess production and consumption of major crops (rice, wheat, maize, soybeans and others) for the period 1994–2010. The database mainly comes from the designated rural observation points, collected by the Research Centre for Rural Economy, Ministry of Agriculture in China.

USDA Model

The Economic Research Service (ERS) of the US Department of Agriculture developed a model named 'Country Projections and Policy Analysis' (CPPA). What we focus on here is the China component in the CPPA model [*ERS*, 1994 and 1997, and Colby, et al., 1997]. This partial equilibrium model can be used to project supply, demand, trade and prices for 34 major agricultural commodities, such as grains, feeds, oilseed, horticultural products, livestock, sugar, tobacco, coffee and so on. The production for individual crops is projected for six regions in China named northeast, north, east, northwest, central and south, and the data are aggregated at the provincial level, while demand is separately modelled for rural and urban consumers. The China CPPA model can be used to generate 5–30 years' projections up to 2020 and it can be operated independently, with exogenous world prices, or alternatively be linked with ERS's modelling system.

Mitchell Model

The Mitchell model, also called 'World Grains Model', was developed at the World Bank in the early 1980s and has been revised and updated several times. This final version can be seen in Mitchell *et al.* [1997]. It is a partial-equilibrium, net trade model and has been used in projecting grain prices, production, consumption, trade and stocks. It is global in scope with the 15 largest economies modelled individually and the remaining countries grouped into nine regions. It covers wheat, rice, and coarse grains (maize, oats, barley, sorghum, rye, millet, and mixed grains). Individual models are estimated for each commodity and economy or region, with price linkages between commodities. The latest version projects for 1990–2010. The database mainly comes from the USDA while some other exogenous variables such as population and GDP are taken from UN or World Bank sources.

Nyberg Model

A more up-to-date projection of China's food economy from the World Bank was carried out by Nyberg *et al.*, in 1997. It was the latest instalment in a series of World Bank studies and reports on China's food security options in 2020. Nyberg published the main research results as part of the China 2020 Series entitled 'At China's Table' [*World Bank*, 1997]. In fact, two approaches were used to assess developments on the production side. First, an economic model, which is the main instrument of the Global Trade Analysis Project (GTAP), was modified to evaluate separately several agricultural subsectors. In addition to the economic model, a physical constraint model was developed to evaluate the impacts of various water options on domestic grain supplies. The GTAP model is a computable general equilibrium model for global trade analysis [*Hertel*, 1997]. The current version (version 4) of the GTAP database covers 50 commodity groupings and 45 regions. In this application, in order to focus on the agricultural sector and keep the model within computational limits, it was aggregated to ten regions and 15 commodities of which five are primary agricultural goods. Another feature about GTAP is that an extended version is available for taking global climate change into account. This is done in conjunction with a geographic information system, called Future Agricultural Resource Model (FARM). More details can be found in Darwin *et al.* [1994].

The scope of the six models is summarized in Table 1, which includes the projection period, geographic and commodity coverage, and data sources. All projection periods start in the 1990s and end at the beginning of the twenty-first century. The main argument is that China will become a middle-income country and its food demand will stabilize around 2020. The IFPRI and the two World Bank models yield projections at the global level, while others have a single-country focus. The OECF is modelled at 30 provincial level for both supply and demand, and the USDA model projects the supply for six regions in China. For the demand side, both CCAP and USDA separately assess rural and urban demands. The CCAP model selects 12 crops (rice, wheat, maize, sweet potato, potato, other coarse grain, soybean, cotton, oil crop, sugar crop, vegetable, and other crops), and seven livestock and aquatic commodities. Commodities covered by IFPRI's IMPACT model include eight crops (wheat, indica rice, standard rice, japonica rice, maize, other coarse grains, soybeans, roots and tubers), six livestock products (beef, pigmeat, poultry, sheepmeat, fluid milk, eggs) and three processed products (manufactured milk, meals, oil). The OECF model

TABLE 1

THE SCOPE OF SELECTED PROJECTION MODELS ON CHINA'S FOOD ECONOMY

Projectors	Projection period	Geographic coverage	Commodity coverage	Database
CCAP	1998–2020	China (demand separated for rural and urban areas)	12 crops, 7 livestock and aquatic products	CCAP
IFPRI	1990–2020	Global (35 countries /regions)	17 commodities	FAO/IFPRI
OECF	1994–2010	China at provincial level (30)	4 crops (rice, wheat, maize, soybeans and others)	MOA
USDA	1993–2020	China with six regions (demand separated for rural and urban areas)	34 agricultural commodities	USDA
Mitchell *et al.*	1990–2010	Global (15 countries and 9 regions)	Wheat, rice and coarse grain	USDA, World Bank
Nyberg *et al.*	1992–2020	Global (10 regions)	15 commodities (7 agricultural subsectors)	GTAP

covers rice, wheat, maize and soybeans while the Mitchell model also contains wheat, rice and coarse grain. The USDA model covers a wide range of 34 agricultural products/groups. In addition to the major grains, it includes seven livestock products (beef and veal, lamb and mutton, pork, fish, poultry, eggs, and fluid milk) and several oils and meals. The Nyberg model covers 15 commodity groupings of which seven agricultural commodities are included: rice, wheat, coarse grain, non-grain crops, livestock, meat and milk, and other food products.

In addition to the model scope, Table 2 summarizes model specification, demand function restrictions, parameter sources and price endogeneity. Except for the OECF models, all other projection models are market equilibrium models, either of the partial or of the general equilibrium type. Partial equilibrium models treat a collection of selected sectors (here referring to agriculture) as a subsystem of the complete economy. Though external effects from the world or the rest of economy can be incorporated as exogenous variables in these models, the selected sectors themselves do not influence the outside world. The general equilibrium formulation allows models to capture the intersectoral competition for resources and the importance of overall resource constraints for sectoral developments. Four

TABLE 2

MODEL CHARACTERIZATION

Projectors	Model specification	Restrictions imposed on demand functions	Parameter sources	Price endogeneity
CCAP	Partial equilibrium model	Adding-up, homogeneity and symmetry imposed	Econometrically estimated	Domestic market price
IFPRI	Partial equilibrium model	Not applicable	Synthetic	World market prices
OECF	Single equation	Not applicable	Synthetic	Not applicable
USDA	Partial equilibrium model	Adding-up, homogeneity and symmetry imposed	Econometrically estimated	Domestic market prices
Mitchell et al.	Partial equilibrium model	Adding-up, homogeneity and symmetry imposed	Econometrically estimated	World market prices
Nyberg et al.	General equilibrium model	Homogeneity and adding-up restriction, constant different of elasticities	Synthetic	World market prices

out of six (CCAP, IFPRI, USDA, Mitchell) are partial equilibrium models while Nyberg *et al.* is a general equilibrium model, and the OECF is a system of single equations without economic content.

The most important model parameters are income elasticities and price elasticities. These are of crucial importance in assessing direct food consumption since small changes in these parameters could lead to substantial differences in the final projection results given China's large population base. Ideally, these parameters should be econometrically estimated. However, given the complexity of market equilibrium models and the lack of data available, most of the projection studies follow a synthetic approach by taking elasticities from other sources and adjusting them consistently. Economic theory tells that different restrictions should be imposed on demand functions, like the adding-up restriction and the homogeneity restriction. An adding-up restriction means that total expenditure must exhaust disposable income. Imposing the homogeneity restriction implies that consumers do not have money illusion. That is, if all prices and income change in the same proportion, the volumes demanded remain unchanged (because the real value of consumers' income and the relative prices of the goods remain unaltered).

CCAP's partial equilibrium model considers all cross-price impacts for both demand and supply equations. Using the framework of the Almost Ideal Demand System (AIDS), demand parameters are estimated from the State Statistical Bureau's (SSB) household survey data supplemented with data from field surveys, with the imposition of theoretical constraints. Expenditure elasticities are also estimated so that they may vary according to income level. In projections prices can be determined endogenously or exogenously. The IFPRI model does not impose theoretical restrictions on its demand functions since its parameters are synthesized from other sources. Prices are endogenous in the model. World prices are determined at marketing-clearing levels, which is when world imports equal world exports. Domestic prices are derived from world market prices, using market margins and producer/consumer subsidies. The OECF uses a single formula to forecast supply and demand separately by individual provinces. Four values of elasticity are obtained from the past trend of average national income elasticity and are then allocated to each province according to the consumption level of the province.

The parameters used in the USDA projection are derived from Cobb-Douglas functions. A complete demand system approach is hampered owing to limited data availability. A special technique is developed to calculate cross-price elasticities by providing own-price and income elasticities and a weighting scheme based on base period expenditure shares. Similar to the CCAP model, a consumer demand system is simultaneously estimated by using the AIDS framework in the Mitchell model. A series of parameters (price elasticity, income elasticity) is derived from the estimation. In the Nyberg approach, the model also specifies a complete demand system, the constant difference of elasticities (CDE) function, which allows expenditure share of food to vary with income.

In all general equilibrium models, prices are determined endogenously by the model while assumptions can be formulated on some exogenous variables, such as population, GDP, factor endowments, technology growth, etc. The USDA also defines several prices for the China submodel. All trade prices are derived from world prices at a major world market. Chinese border prices are defined in Chinese *yuan* taking account of transportation costs from the major world market to a Chinese port. Trade prices are defined as prices of import/export goods moving between the border and the Chinese market, including all trade barriers, taxes or subsidies. Producer prices are defined as the weighted average of government policy (procurement) prices and free market prices. In the Mitchell model, endogenous variables include world crop prices, production, harvested area, crop yields, net trade and opening stocks while exogenous variables are population, GDP, the exchange rate and the consumer price index. The model reaches equilibrium at the level of world prices, which reflect zero global net imports.

PROJECTION COMPARISON

Model Structure

The CCAP model has a clear conceptual framework. As presented in Figure 1, this partial equilibrium model includes domestic production, demand, trade and market clearing submodels. In addition to traditional prediction determinants such as income and population, the CCAP includes also structural change elements to capture the rapid transformation toward industrialization in China. Demand equations are projected separately for rural and urban regions and explicitly account for urbanization and market development, while supply equations include producers' response to agricultural investment and environmental stress.

FIGURE 1
THE FRAMEWORK OF THE CCAP MODEL

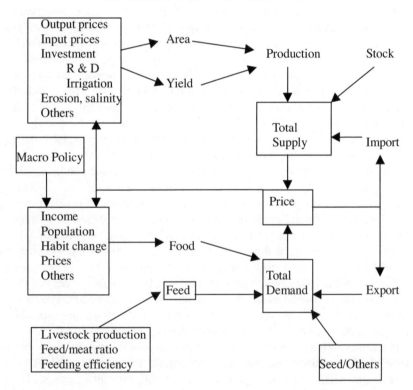

In the CCAP model, crop production is estimated as the product of crop area and yield. Crop areas are specified as functions of farmers' input/output prices, and area changes owing to climate and other shocks. Yields are determined by technology level, irrigation level, erosion trend, salinity trend, and so on. Total demand can be subdivided into direct food consumption, feed demand and other uses including seed, industrial use and waste. Food consumption is estimated separately for rural and urban consumers and determined by consumer price, per capita income in rural and urban areas, food market developments and population. Total feed grain demand is a function of livestock production, efficiency of grain in feeding livestock and the feed:meat ratio. Livestock production is responsive to price changes and other exogenous variables. World price projections are generated by the IFPRI model.

Similar to the CCAP model, IFPRI's IMPACT model estimates domestic production as the product of yield and crop area. Harvested area is derived from crop prices, competing crops' price and growth trends in harvested areas, while yield responds to output prices, input prices and a trend factor for technological improvement. Livestock production is modelled similar to crop production except for the yield per head only reflecting the expected technology development.

Total demand is the sum of direct food consumption, feed usage and other industrial use. Food consumption is specified as a function of consumer prices, per capita income and total population. Feed demand is estimated from the changes in livestock production, feed ratios and feed crop prices. Other uses are simply calculated as a ratio of the previous year's demand, based on food and feed demand changes. The China submodel is linked with other 34 country and regional submodels through trade. Although the IMPACT model mainly focuses on the agricultural sector, it incorporates non-agricultural sectors through the use of intersectoral growth multipliers. More details can be found in Rosegrant et al. [1995].

In the OECF model, grain supply by crop and by province is projected as the product of cropping area and yield per unit of land. It is assumed that the cropping area of crops that showed an increasing trend in the last ten years (1984–93) will level off and stabilize at current level, while those that showed a tendency of decreasing in the last ten years will continue to decrease at the same rate. The yield per unit of land is assumed to continue to increase at the same rate as shown in the last ten years, but a maximum yield is imposed for each crop.

Total grain demand is the sum of food demand, seed use and loss. Food demand includes all consumption by type of usage (food, feed and food processing). The quantity of seed used per unit of land is assumed to stay at base level while the loss is set at five per cent of production.

FIGURE 2
THE FRAMEWORK OF THE IFPRI MODEL

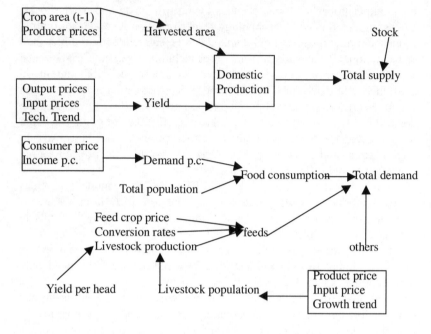

FIGURE 3
THE FRAMEWORK OF THE OECF MODEL

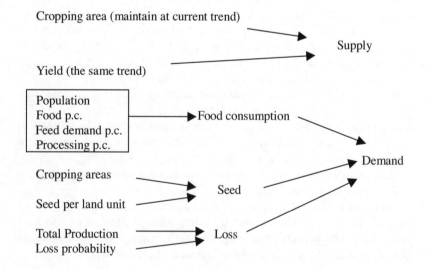

FIGURE 4

THE FRAMEWORK OF THE USDA MODEL

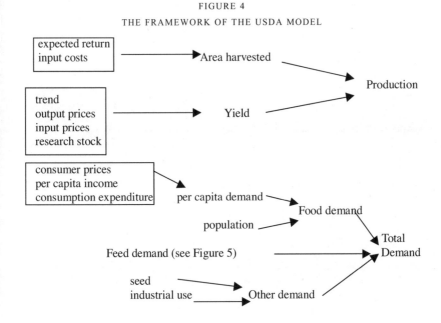

The USDA model endogenizes cropping area as follows. Farmers are assumed to allocate their land to those crops for which they expect to get the highest net returns per hectare and these returns will depend on expected prices and yields. The yield depends on trend, output/input prices and research stocks. The trend is used to capture technology improvement over time, such as the adoption of high yield seeds and better growing practices. Changes in the stock of research and irrigated areas also affect yield. Production is defined as the product of area harvested and yield.

Total demand consists of food, feed and other demand. Total food demand is projected separately for rural and urban consumers, and arrived at as the product of per capita demand and projected population for the two groups. Per capita demand is derived from consumer prices, income and consumption expenditure. Since the calculation for feed demand is fairly complex, it is presented separately in Figure 5. Total feed grain demand is the product of the grain–feed conversion rate and the production of animal products that use feed, the latter being derived from total production of animal products and the share of production from fed animals. This share reflects production that occurs using modern feed technology. After adjustments for the degree of commercialization and multiplication by energy and protein conversion ratios, aggregated energy and protein needs are then distributed among grains and oilseed meals.

FIGURE 5

THE FEED–LIVESTOCK PROJECTION FRAMEWORK IN THE USDA MODEL

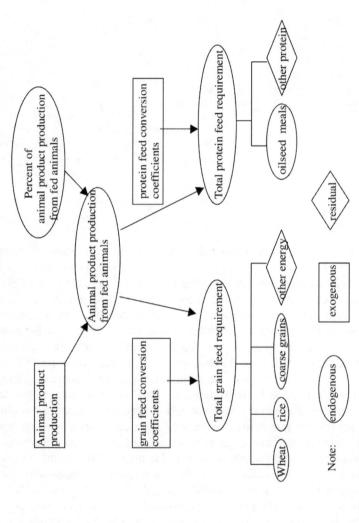

Note:

endogenous

exogenous

residual

Source: Taken from ERS [1997].

FIGURE 6
THE NYBERG MODEL

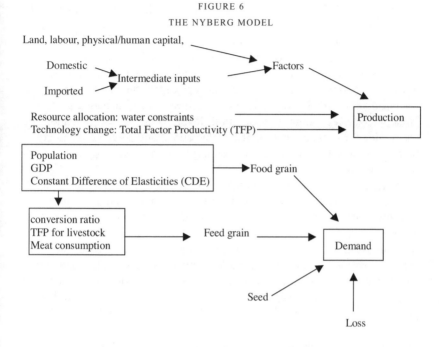

Agricultural production growth in the Nyberg model is driven by investment and total factor productivity (TFP) growth. The main factors included are available arable land, skilled and unskilled labour and physical and human capital. The technology trend in this model is captured by TFP growth, which is measuring the changes in output relative to the changes in input. One per cent of TFP growth rate is assumed for China's crop production, while two per cent of TFP is entered for livestock subsectors. This assumption is based on existing studies showing relatively low TFP growth rates for agriculture [*Lin*, 1992: 35] and declining public investment in agricultural research. Given the water scarcity in China, particularly in the northern corn- and wheat-growing regions, a natural resource model is developed to reflect water constraints. By taking into account the irrigated crop area, current water consumption, irrigated cropping pattern, etc., the model estimates the percentage of total sown irrigated area for each crop in nine water regions and their output. In the supply function, water constraint is incorporated in the projection model through their influence on yield. Three scenarios are developed by considering three yield growth rates under different water availability assumptions: (1) continuously increasing at one per cent level; (2) at one per cent level until 2010 then slowing down at 0.5

per cent level; (3) at one per cent until 2000 then reduced to 0.5 per cent level.

Total demand consists of food grain, feed grain, seed and five per cent of production loss. In food grain demand estimation, the CDE demand functions are adopted, which allows the budget share to vary with income. For high economic growth countries, such as China, the income elasticities for basic staple foods are expected to be low or even negative given the already relatively high consumption levels. On the other hand, the elasticities for products with higher value added and services are likely to be considerably higher and can not be kept constant over a period of high income growth.

Mitchell *et al.*'s World Grain Model for China is presented in Figure 7. Total production is calculated as the product of harvested area and yield. Harvested area is determined by a two-stage process. First, total cropland for wheat, rice and coarse grains is estimated from the weighted per hectare revenue based on world prices in the last year, total grain closing stocks in the last year and a time trend to capture unknown factors. Harvested areas for each commodity are then derived from the total cropland, lagged crop revenues and a trend. The yield is estimated as a function of trend, lagged price ratio of the crop and fertilizer and the percentage of total area planted under high yield varieties for the commodity. The time trend is used to measure seed improvements over time. The lagged ratio of world crop price to world fertilizer price is used to measure the incentives for farmers to use fertilizer. High yielding varieties (HYVs) are included to account for the shift towards higher yield curves. Total consumption is calculated as the sum of total production, net imports and stock changes. Net imports are assumed to be a function of real per capita income, real import price, and relevant demand shifters, induced by food aid, balance of payments constraints, etc. The level of closing stock is based on domestic consumption in the previous year and real price of the commodity.

Major Assumptions

The projection results heavily depend on the accuracy of all sorts of assumptions. Unrealistic assumptions could produce absurd forecasts. Tables 3 and 4 summarize the assumptions made for supply and demand in all six models. In the projections of the CCAP, IFPRI, USDA and Mitchell models, both cropping areas and yields are endogenous variables. They are determined by a series of variables, such as prices, technology, etc. In the OECF model, cropping areas are assumed to develop differently for crops with increasing and decreasing trend over the last ten years. Given the reduction trend of cultivated agricultural land, the Nyberg model assumes that China will maintain its current cropping land base. The newly

FIGURE 7

FRAMEWORK OF THE MITCHELL MODEL

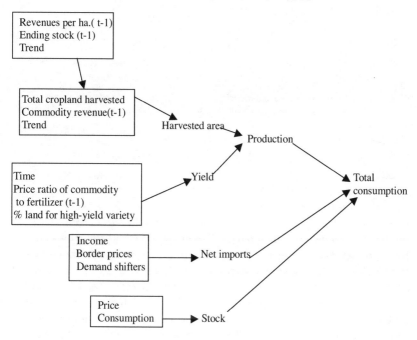

promulgated Land Management Law will strictly enforce measures to prevent the loss of agricultural land to commercial/industrial uses. The grain yields will grow at rates of 0.5–1 per cent per year, based on investment in agricultural research to maintain TFP growth and to expand the area under irrigation.

Major demand side assumptions are about population and economic development (either income growth or GDP). These are the most important determinants of total consumption (both direct and indirect) in China. Following United Nations' demographic predictions, annual population growth in the CCAP model is assumed to be 1.1 per cent during 1996–2000 and 0.88 per cent for the following five years. Considering the income growth rates over the last decade and the trends in their development, it is predicted that per capita income growth in the urban sector will slow down to 4.5 per cent per year, and that the rural sector will begin to pull out of its recession, per capita income growing at four per cent per year. The data source used for population projections in the IFPRI model is also the United Nations projection of 1993, in which the world population is expected to

TABLE 3

MAJOR BASELINE ASSUMPTIONS FOR THE SUPPLY SIDE

Projectors	Cropping area	Yield
CCAP	Endogenous variable	Endogenous variable
IFPRI	Endogenous variable	Endogenous variable
OECF	Crops with increasing trend will stop and those with decreasing trend will continue	Increasing at the same rate, but a maximum value is set
USDA	Endogenous variable	Endogenous variable
Mitchell *et al.*	Endogenous variable	Endogenous variable
Nyberg *et al.*	Maintain the existing cultivated land base	0.5% to 1% growth annually

grow at 1.4 per cent per annum to 2020 and the growth rate in China will be lower, one per cent. The economic growth rates are taken from the World Bank's World Development Reports, which assume that China's GDP growth rate will stabilize at a lower level of six per cent after nearly ten per cent growth over the last several years. The population projection in the OECF model is based on China's population census conducted in 1990 with certain adjustments over time. The average annual growth rate of per capita gross rural domestic production (GRDP) is assumed to stay the same as in the last ten years (1984 to 1993).

Strong economic growth is assumed for China in the USDA model, over eight per cent for the period 2001–2005. Population growth is forecast to slow down to less than one per cent. The GDP assumption for China in the Mitchell model is 8.4 per cent, quite a high level, while the growth rate of the Chinese population is projected to drop, based on United Nations' population projections of 1991. The Nyberg model distinguishes two projection periods, ranging from 1992 to 2005 and from 1992 to 2020. The choice for the period ending in 2005 is made because it is the end of the implementation period of the Uruguay Round. Following a literature review and adjusting income elasticities, it is assumed in the Nyberg model that there is a seven per cent annual GDP growth between 1995 and 2020. Population growth is predicted at 0.89 per cent per annum for 1992 to 2005 and 0.76 per cent for 1992 to 2020 based on the GTAP database.

Main Scenarios

Baseline assumptions reflect projectors' best assessments of future developments. However, projectors may also use alternative choices to

TABLE 4

MAJOR BASELINE ASSUMPTIONS FOR THE DEMAND SIDE

Projectors	Population growth rate	Economic development
CCAP	1.11% in 1996–2000 0.88% in 2001–2005	4% per capita income growth in rural sector 4.5% in urban sector
IFPRI	1% growth rate until 2020	6% GDP growth rate until 2020
OECF	1.45% in 1995–2000 1.245% in 2000–2005 1.19% in 2005–2010	Per capita GRDP will remain the same growth rate as the past
USDA	0.9% in 1996–2000 0.7% in 2001–2005	9.1% GDP growth rate in 1996–2000 8.4% in 2001–2005
Mitchell *et al.*	1.3% in 1990–2000 0.7% in 2000–2010	8.4% GDP growth rate in 1990–2010
Nyberg *et al.*	0.76% in 1992–2020	Average annual GDP growth at 7% in 1995–2020

TABLE 5

ALTERNATIVE SCENARIOS IMPOSED

Projectors	Alternative scenarios
CCAP	Free trade Productivity enhancement growth
IFPRI	Low population growth Low investment, slow growth High investment, rapid growth Trade liberalization
OECF	No scenarios imposed
USDA	No scenarios imposed
Mitchell *et al.*	Rapid population growth Higher GDP growth Double petroleum prices
Nyberg *et al.*	WTO accession Grain import 5% of domestic consumption TFP growth high or low

answer 'what if' questions to supplement the baseline prediction. Technically, any exogenous variable can be changed from baseline level to establish a new scenario. Depending on projectors' interests and focus, alternative scenarios could help to deepen the understanding of China's food economy. The results are particularly interesting for policy-makers because of the range of alternatives provided. A list of scenarios appearing in projectors' documents is presented in Table 5.

The two most important scenarios are presented in CCAP's latest projection version: free trade and productivity enhancement growth. Although China is not yet a WTO member after 13 years of negotiations, it is assumed that China will continue liberalizing its agricultural sector and reduce tariff levels, export subsidies and trade barriers until zero tariffs apply by the year 2005. Under the productivity growth assumption, it is assumed that annual investment in agricultural research and development will rise from four per cent baseline to six per cent. Several alternative scenarios are also formulated in the IFPRI model to explore the sensitivity of the model if fundamental assumptions are changing: a lower population growth, a significant reduction of international donor and public investment, a 20 per cent increase investment in research, a 25 per cent increase of non-agricultural income growth in developing countries, and finally a full removal of protection policies, trade subsidies and taxes.

In the Mitchell model, several scenarios are considered to simulate variations from the baseline. These include much more rapid population growth, faster GDP growth (ten per cent) and a doubling of the petroleum price in real terms over the period 1993–94 with a subsequent decline to the baseline level for the next four years. The rising petroleum price will affect crop yield through higher nitrogen fertilizer prices since petroleum is a major input in chemical nitrogen fertilizer production. In the Nyberg model, six scenarios are considered, which can be summarized as three major alternatives. The first one is China's accession to WTO membership; the second is that China's grain import level will be fixed at five per cent of its domestic consumption; and the last one is about productivity, simulating the consequences of a high TFP growth rate at 1.5 per cent annually and a low one at 0.5 per cent. Neither the OECF nor the USDA models simulate alternative scenarios.

Parameters Used

Several parameters can be used in projecting China's food economy, such as income elasticities, price elasticities, budget shares in the demand system, feed conversion rates, etc. These parameters are crucial elements in both food and feed grain predictions since small changes in these parameters may lead to significant differences in final projection results.

Table 6 lists income elasticities of demand for different commodities. As can be seen, the table is incomplete since the elasticities of the Mitchell model are not reported in their book in spite of the claims that these have been estimated.

The parameters used in the IFPRI model are taken from various sources. The income and price elasticities for developing countries are based on estimates from the ERS, USDA. The income demand parameters are aggregated for each country given the income level and urban and rural population ratios over the projection period. The income elasticities for cereals range from –0.4 (for maize) to 0.26 (for high quality rice), and for meats from 0.2 to 0.9. More details cannot be found in their report. In the OECF model, owing to the lack of consumption data by province and by usage, four levels of income elasticities are calculated from national consumption data and then assigned to each province according to per capita consumption levels. Income elasticities for food grain are assumed to be negative and those for feed grain and processing are supposed to be positive. The model also limits variability of income elasticities to a pre-selected range. Income elasticities may never fall short of the lowest value recorded in 1987–92 and their absolute value may never exceed 1.0.

More complete data on income elasticities and own-price elasticities are only available in the CCAP model and the USDA model. As presented in Table 7, both models estimate these elasticities separately for rural and urban areas in order to capture the differences in consumer behaviour between rural and urban households. The CCAP estimates the demand parameters from the SSB household survey data, supplemented by own field surveys. The parameters in the USDA model have been estimated on the basis of SSB data, with income elasticities adjusted for long-term projection purposes. These estimates show very low income and price responsiveness for staple foods; in the USDA model income elasticities for

TABLE 6

ESTIMATES OF INCOME ELASTICITY OF DEMAND

Commodity	IFPRI	OECF	Mitchell	Nyberg
Rice	–0.4 to 0.26	Range from	Cannot	–0.05
Wheat		–0.272 to 0.00	be found	0.07
Coarse grains				–0.18
Meat	0.2 to 0.9	0.252 to 1.00 for feed and 0.39 to 1.00 for processing		0.62
Source	Synthetic	Calculated	Estimated	Synthetic

TABLE 7

ESTIMATES OF INCOME AND OWN-PRICE ELASTICITIES IN
USDA AND CCAP MODELS

Commodity	Urban income		Rural income		Urban own price		Rural own price	
	USDA	CCAP	USDA	CCAP	USDA	CCAP	USDA	CCAP
Rice	−0.10	0.025	0.05	0.2	−0.30	−0.20	−0.20	−0.29
Wheat	−0.05	0.10	0.20	0.2	−0.30	−0.25	−0.12	−0.28
Coarse grains	−0.14	—	−0.10	—	−0.30	—	−0.05	—
Maize	—	−0.20	—	−0.12	—	−0.28	—	−0.25
Sweet potato	—	−0.1	—	−0.35	—	−0.25	—	−0.25
Potato	—	0.1	—	0.05	—	−0.20	—	−0.25
Other coarse grain	—	−0.2	—	−0.15	—	−0.28	—	−0.25
Soybeans	−0.10	0.1	0.05	0.15	−0.50	−0.25	−0.45	−0.30
Sugar	0.46	0.55	0.90	0.8	−1.05	−0.60	−1.25	−0.60
Pork	0.50	0.60	0.80	0.65	−0.96	−0.52	−0.65	−0.54
Beef & veal	1.75	0.75	1.80	0.85	−1.70	−0.77	−1.40	−0.76
Lamb & mutton	1.75	0.75	1.80	0.85	−1.75	−0.81	−1.33	−0.80
Poultry	0.99	0.75	1.10	0.85	−1.16	−0.69	−0.80	−0.76
Eggs	0.31	0.5	0.52	0.51	−0.80	−0.58	−0.55	−0.76
Milk	—	1.25	—	1.45	—	−0.86	—	−0.91
Fish	0.93	0.85	0.93	1.05	−0.96	−0.67	−0.75	−0.67
Edible vegetable oil	0.51	0.55	0.70	0.65	−0.85	−0.71	−0.80	−0.71
Fruits	0.76	1.17	0.90	1.0	−1.10	−0.65	−0.75	−0.78
Vegetables	0.45	0.38	0.70	0.35	−0.49	−0.62	−0.60	−0.55
Other food	0.35	1.10	0.70	1.12	−0.70	−0.44	−0.39	−0.61
Non-food	—	1.29	—	2.35	—	−0.86	—	−1.04

Source: the ERS and the CCAP.

all staple foods are even negative. Both models show relatively high income and price responsiveness for livestock products, edible oils fruits and vegetables. Particularly, both income and price elasticities for beef and lamb are close to 2 in the USDA estimation results. The CCAP also estimates high income elasticities for dairy and fruit products.

Once again, these parameters confirm that meats and other products with higher value added will be key factors in China's future food economy. Relatively small changes in income growth will significantly affect demand for these commodities and subsequently lead to large changes in demand when projected for 1.2 billion people.

Another important set of parameters used in the projection models consists of the feed:meat ratios, which are used to calculate the feed grain required for meat production. Unfortunately, in most cases, the feed-to-meat conversion rates are not empirically derived, but are based on approximations and assessments. Table 8 presents the conversion rates between products and their grain required. With the improvement of feed efficiency, the conversion rates are assumed to decrease gradually. In the table, high values refer to the base year of 1995, and low values to the year 2020. The CCAP conversion rates are based on Chinese literature, foreign studies focusing on China's feed and economy, and CCAP's field surveys in

TABLE 8

FEED CONVERSION RATES FOR DIFFERENT COMMODITIES

Products	CCAP	IFPRI	OECF	USDA	Mitchell	Nyberg
Pork	3.1–4.0	Not	4.5	3.484	Not	3.1
Beef, mutton	0.86–1.5	available	4.5	0.4	included	0.5
Poultry	1.18–2.2		2.7	2.092		2.0
Eggs	0.94–2.2		2.7	2.784		
Milk	0.5–0.7		0.32	0.5		0.5
Aquatic	0.6–0.7		0.80	0.35		
Alcohol			1.12			

the provinces Sichuan, Shandong and Jilin. Changes in feed conversion rates (assuming improvement in feeding efficiency) over time are based on expert interviews.

Feed demand ratios and elasticities in the IFPRI model have been derived from unpublished documentation about FAO's World Food Model dated 1986. The conversion rates used in the OECF model have been assessed from information of MOA's rural observation points throughout 30 provinces and of MOA's Animal Husbandry and Veterinary Department. For the Nyberg model feed consumption has been assessed separately for poultry, pork and other red meat on the assumption that technology will improve feed conversion rates by 2020. Comparing all these rates, pork turns out to require most feed, while beef has a much higher conversion rate in the OECF model than in the other ones.

PROJECTION RESULTS

Projected grain production, consumption and net imports under the baseline scenario are presented in Table 9. It is important to point out the differences in grain definitions. In China, grain statistically includes rice, wheat, maize, soybeans, other cereals, potatoes and sweet potatoes. Five kilograms of potatoes or sweet potatoes are converted to one kilogram of grain. The CCAP includes rice, wheat, maize, soybean, sweet potato, potato and other grains (mainly millet, sorghum and barley) in its grain projection. The IFPRI covers wheat, rice, maize, other coarse grains, soybeans, roots and tubers. In the OECF, grain is used as the general term for rice, wheat, maize and soybeans. The USDA, Mitchell and Nyberg all include wheat, rice and coarse grains (maize, Barley, Sorghum, etc.) in their grain projections and do not include soybeans and tuber crops.

The baseline projection of the CCAP model shows that total grain production will increase from 432 MMT in 2000 to 464 MMT at an annual

TABLE 9

PROJECTED GRAIN PRODUCTION, CONSUMPTION AND NET IMPORTS IN CHINA
(Metric Million Tons)

Years	CCAP	IFPRI	OECF	USDA	Mitchell	Nyberg
Production						
2000	432		483	387	411	
2002	442			397		
2004	456			412		
2005	464		503	419	445	493
2010			511		482	
2020		707				662
2030						
Consumption						
2000	446		507	400	422	
2002	460			418		
2004	468			436		
2005	484		572	445	460	516
2010			648		503	
2020		739				731
2030						
Net Import						
2000	14.8		23.8	8.2	11.3	
2002	17.9			9.9		
2004	19.6			12.0		
2005	19.8		69.1	13.8	15.6	23.0
2010			136.0		21.6	
2020		32.0				69.0

growth rate of 1.44 per cent, while grain consumption will increase at the faster pace of 1.6 per cent per annum. Therefore, a net import of 20 MMT grain is required in 2005, which still keeps grain self-sufficiency at a level of 95 per cent. The IFPRI forecasts that China will import 32 MMT of grain by 2020, 22 MMT of which will be net cereals import. Wheat imports will continue to increase and some export of rice, mostly japonica, is also forecast. Maize will shift from an export to an import position. The OECF projection results show a very high grain demand, which leads to a 136 MMT of net import. Further analysis with the OECF model at the regional level shows that the number of grain 'importing' provinces will increase from 12 in 1993 to 22 in 2010. The largest grain shortages are expected in the Yangtze delta region, the middle- and upper-reaches of the Yangtze, and the south coast regions.

The USDA projections are close to the ones by CCAP. They show net grain imports of around 10 MMT in the early twenty-first century. Wheat will be the major shortage commodity and the import volume is predicted to more than double during 1996–2005. Coarse grain exports will decline, largely owing to strong internal demand for maize as animal feed. The Mitchell model does not directly present volume results, but instead gives grain production growth rates per annum during the projection periods. It is projected that production will grow at a rate of 1.6 per cent per annum during the whole period, while consumption is expected to grow 2.4 per cent per annum in 1990–2000 and 1.8 per cent in 2000–2010. Using Mitchell's baseline data for 1990, it is easy to calculate total grain production, consumption and net trade for each projection year. As listed in Table 9, total production will be at the 482 MMT level with a net import of 21.6 MMT in 2010. Meanwhile, China's per capita grain consumption will rise from 298 kg in 1990 to 371 kg in 2010, surpassing Japan's present consumption level of 331 kg. The baseline projection of the Nyberg model results in a production total for rice, wheat and coarse grains of 493 MMT and net imports of 23 MMT, which leads to a per capita total grain consumption of 397 kg in 2005. The long-term projection to 2020 yields 662 MMT of total grain production and 69 MMT of net imports while per capita total consumption will reach 509 kg. Further analysis shows that an increasing share of grain production will be used as feed. Feed use will exceed half of total grain requirements by 2020.

In addition to projections of grain production, consumption and trade, some models generate detailed results on animal production and consumption as well. Table 10 shows the results for several animal products predicted by the CCAP, IFPRI and USDA. These are presented as equations in the table, indicating 'production minus consumption equals net trade'.

Given the concerns about the reliability of animal production and consumption data, The CCAP uses a data set that differs from published SSB data. Certain corrections are made to adjust for overreporting of livestock production and underreporting of household consumption. The projection results show that China will be a net exporter for the entire projection period for pork, beef and mutton, although the amount of exports is only a small percentage of total domestic production. The only animal products that have to be imported are poultry and dairy, while eggs and fish are at full self-sufficient level. IFPRI projects that China's total meat demand will grow in excess of three per cent per year. Much of this growth is due to solid per capita income growth and slow population growth. Per capita meat demand will more than double by 2020, up to 52 kg per head. This will leave China as a big importer of both beef and pork, and a small exporter of poultry. Beef production and consumption is not available in the USDA documentation since China is not a big country in terms of beef trade. However, it is predicted that China will continue to be a large pork exporter to the world market, among the US, Canada, the EU and Taiwan,

TABLE 10

PROJECTED PRODUCTION, CONSUMPTION AND NET TRADE FOR ANIMAL
PRODUCTS IN CHINA
(1,000 Tons)

Products	CCAP (2005)	IFPRI (2020)	USDA (2005)
Beef	27,703 – 27,462 = 241	3752 – 4056 = –304	
Pork	3,015 – 2,998 = 17	60595 – 60966 = –371	47971 – 4715 = 256
Mutton	1,746 – 1745 = 0.5	2,446 – 2426 = 20	
Poultry	7,595 – 7885 = –290	9,476 – 9300 = 176	19,348 – 19,997 = –649
Eggs	14,848 – 14,817 = 31	20,133 – 20050 = 63	
Milks	9,364 – 9,697 = –333		
Fish	15,081 – 14909 = 172		

although internal pork consumption in China is expected to increase at 3.5 per cent annually during the projection period. In the poultry market, it is predicted that China will continue to be both a major importer and exporter. Much of the import will be low-cost parts instead of whole birds. Given its continuing economic growth, total poultry consumption will surpass total production, which leaves China as a net poultry importing country during the whole projection period.

DIFFERENCE AND SIMILARITY OF THE PROJECTION MODELS

By comparing the above research methodology and their projection results, we found several similarities and differences as summarized in Table 11.

In terms of model structure, five out of six models are market equilibrium models. No time series projection model is applied here. In all models except for the Mitchell model, domestic production is calculated as the product of cropping area and yield, and total demand is the sum of food demand, feed demand and other uses, including processing and losses. All projection results show that China will have to import grains from the world markets under similar assumptions on (high) GDP and (low) population growth rates.

Several major differences can be identified across the models. First of all, model specification and variable definitions differ between the models. For example, four out of six cropping areas are endogenous variables, while two models fix areas at a stable cropping base. Feed-to-meat conversion ratios and income/price elasticities differ between the models. Although all models project a net grain import for China, the required amounts vary considerably, ranging from several MMT to up to 200 MMT. Projection results for animal products show even more variation, as some commodities are identified as export products in one model while they show up as major imports in others.

TABLE 11
DIFFERENCES AND SIMILARITIES OF THE PROJECTIONS

Comparison	Similarity	Difference
Model structure	Market equilibrium model; Production is the product of cropping area and yield; demand consists of food, feed and others	Model specification and variable definition
Baseline assumptions	Population will increase at a slow rate, high GDP growth rate	Land assumptions
Parameters used		Conversion rate, elasticities estimation
Projection result	Net import in grain projection results	Grain projection, animal products projection

GENERAL DISCUSSION

Validity of the Model Projections

Since most of the model projections were carried out in the early 1990s, the realized figures in the late 1990s offered an opportunity to test their quality. Table 12 presents actual data for grain production, GDP growth, population growth and arable land changes for the last decade. As shown in Table 12, realized grain production in China in the late 1990s was around 500 MMT, exceeding all projections. The real growth rate of the Chinese population in the late 1990s is a little under one per cent. This number is quite close to the baseline assumptions made by all most all projectors for population growth.

The time of model construction also affects the quality of assumptions. Later projectors had the advantage that they could adjust their major assumptions, particularly for cultivated land areas and GDP growth rates. Cultivated land areas in China decreased sharply in the beginning of the 1980s, at a speed of more than 1.5 million hectares in 1984 and 1985 (see Appendix 1). However, the central government soon curbed this trend of decline. Cultivated land areas not only stopped falling in the late 1990s, but made a substantial leap forward after the data correction from the 1997 First National Agricultural Census. After the adjustment, China's cultivated land was 130 million hectares in 1996, which was an increase of more than 40 per cent over previous years. It is certain that the massive land loss in the early 1980s affected OECF's land assumption, while the later Nyberg model assumed that the Chinese government would prevent further land losses, as

TABLE 12

ACTUAL FIGURES OF GRAIN PRODUCTION, GDP GROWTH, POPULATION
GROWTH, AND CULTIVATED LAND IN CHINA FOR SELECTED YEARS

Years	Grain production	Cultivated land	GDP growth rate	Population growth rate
	(MMT)	(1,000 ha)	(%)	(%)
1988	394	95,720	11.3	1.57
1990	446	95,672	3.8	1.43
1992	442	95,425	14.2	1.16
1996	504	130,039	9.6	1.04
1997	494	—	8.8	1.01
1998	512	—	7.8	0.96

Source: SSB [1999 and 2000].

it indeed did. This also applies to GDP assumptions. GDP growth rates in China were slowing down to seven per cent in the late 1990s, while in the 1980s China grew at an average of 8.9 per cent per annum. This led to optimistic GDP growth assumptions in the early models, like the Mitchell model, which assumed 8.4 per cent per annum in China for two decades. Later assumptions, like in the Nyberg and CCAP models, put GDP growth rates at about seven per cent, much closer to actual figures.

Concerns about Livestock Production and Consumption Data

There is wide concern about the reliability of Chinese meat production and consumption data. SSB data showed that 1996 red meat output reached 59.15 million tons in China, representing a per capita availability of 48 kg. But in the same period, consumption data from cross-sectional surveys – also conducted by the SSB – arrived at a total red meat consumption of only 18.5 million tons, with 12.9 kg per capita for rural and 20.4 kg for urban consumption. The gap between meat production and consumption was confirmed by the First National Census carried out in January 1997. The census showed that China's total meat production was around 51 million tons, 20 per cent less than reported previously.

It is now widely accepted that China's meat production was overreported and consumption was underreported. The main reason for the overreporting is that production data comes from a bottom-up reporting mechanism that induces local governments to exaggerate their economic performance. The underestimation of consumption data does not appear to be deliberate but stems from several technical biases. First, the household sample survey does not include outdoor consumption in canteens and restaurants, which accounts for an increasing share of meat consumption. Second, the consumption of millions of rural migrants working in the cities is not included in the rural sample. Finally, marketing losses and exports should also be taken into account.

Meat production and consumption data are the major variables in the projections. The above-mentioned biases of course affect projection quality. First, the estimated own-price demand elasticities will be too small; second, meat supply elasticities will be too high and feed conversion ratios too low. This does not imply that no data are available: the sectional consumption sample data are relatively reliable and can be used for further analysis, if corrected for eating-out consumption, rural migration and marketing losses. The Chinese government has acknowledged the problem and adjusted meat production data downwards based on the result of the 1997 Agricultural Census.

Importance of Livestock Projection

Despite its importance for China's food economy, the projection of the livestock industry is relatively neglected. Given its increasing importance for total grain demand, the livestock industry deserves much more attention. Owing to economic development and changing dietary habits, consumers' demand for high valued livestock products will rise continuously. In a case study of a rural area in China, Ye and Taylor [1995] reveal that the relative contribution of grains to calorie and protein intake declines at higher incomes, while food-expenditure elasticity of animal protein intake is high, implying a switch to more expensive protein sources as food expenditure rises. The average level of caloric intake from animal products has substantially increased in China during the last three decades (see Appendix 2). Expected grain deficiencies in China will mainly be caused by feed demand. In 1994, animal feed accounted for 23 per cent of total grain supply [*Huang* et al., 1999: 749]. The above projection results from the Nyberg model also show that feed grain demand will exceed half of total grain consumption within two decades. However, none of the above projections carefully modelled the livestock industry (for example through a cost function or production function analysis). Some models do not include the livestock industry at all, while others included it in a relatively simple way. Future projections could be improved at least in two aspects: accurate conversion rates and structure changes.

The conversion rates indicate the amount of feed grain needed to produce one unit of meat. The conversion rates used in the model projections vary considerably. Table 13 presents an example to illustrate the sensitivity of outcomes for the ratios used in the Nyberg and OECF models. The second column assesses incremental meat consumption in 2020 based on the Nyberg model. The feed grain conversion ratios used in both the Nyberg and the OECF model are chosen for comparison. The incremental

TABLE 13

THE SENSITIVITY OF DIFFERENT FEED CONVERSION RATIOS

Meat	Total meat increment (MMT)	Nyberg ratio	OECF ratio	Nyberg feed grain increment (MMT)	OECF feed grain increment (MMT)
Pork	30.8	3.1	4.5	95.6	138.6
Other red meat	9.5	0.5	4.5	4.7	42.8
Poultry	7.1	2.0	2.7	14.2	19.2
Milk	9.1	0.5	0.3	4.5	2.9
Total	56.5			119.0	203.5

feed grain requirements are the products of incremental meat consumption multiplied by these ratios. In the Nyberg model, the incremental feed grain demand is 119 MMT while in the OECF model it is 203.5 MMT, a much higher figure.

Generally speaking, the grain-to-meat conversion rates in China are higher than in developed countries and thus reflect less efficient feeding practices. All models except for the CCAP use single conversion rates to derive feed demand over a long period, without considering technological improvements in feeding. More dynamic, empirically better-founded conversion rates are needed in order to improve projection performance here.

In addition to conversion ratios, it is also important to account for structural changes in the livestock industry. Traditionally, Chinese livestock subsists on green fodder and kitchen waste. Until now, pork consumption accounts for 67 per cent of the meat consumption in China, followed by poultry (20 per cent) and beef (8 per cent) [*Zhang*, 1999: 361]. Eighty per cent of pigs are raised by individual farming households who engage in livestock raising as a secondary activity. Backyard pig production requires small amounts of grain, but animals have to be kept for 12–14 months before they can be marketed. However, increasing demand for meat has stimulated pig production. More farmers are operating at a larger scale and becoming specialized in pig production. Large commercial livestock companies also find their markets in China.

These commercial firms, reaching high feeding efficiencies, require more grain-intensive production modes and are a potential threat for backyard pig production. This new development will change the structure of the livestock industry and feed demand from two angles. First, backyard household production might decline while intensive commercial production might soar, which requires increasing amounts of feed grain. On the other hand, the new technology applied in commercial companies will improve feed efficiency and lead to lower feed-to-meat conversion ratios. In future research, structural changes in commercial, specialized and backyard livestock production and technological improvements in feeding practices should be taken into account and analysed in more detail.

Additional Research Directions

Future research on projecting China's food economy could be strengthened if the above-mentioned points are taken into account, such as data corrections and a more adequate representation of the livestock industry. In addition to these, two additional aspects also require attention. The first issue concerns the budget shares. Most models keep budget shares constant, but given the rapid increase of disposable income in China, it is not reasonable to assume that consumers' budget shares will remain unchanged over long periods. Future projections could improve on this score by allowing for more flexible budget shares. The other issue is the impact of massive migration between rural and urban areas. Only the CCAP model includes urbanization as an exogenous factor. However, the impacts of migration on both grain supply and demand deserve wider attention and full integration in projection models.

APPENDIX 1

AREA CHANGES OF CULTIVATED LAND IN CHINA (1,000 HA)

Year	Year-end cultivated land	Reduced cultivated land	Increased cultivated	Net reduction in cultivated land
1982	98,606.0	863.0		
1983	98,359.6	768.0	521.6	246.4
1984	97,853.7	1,582.9	1,077.0	505.9
1985	96,846.3	1,597.9	590.5	1,007.4
1986	96,229.9	1,108.3	491.9	616.4
1987	95,888.7	817.5	476.3	341.2
1988	95,721.8	644.7	477.8	166.9
1989	95,656.0	517.5	451.7	65.8
1990	95,672.9	467.4	484.3	+16.9
1995	94,973.9	621.0	686.7	+67.2
1996	130,039.0	—	—	+35,096

Source: MOA [1999]; SSB [2000].

APPENDIX 2
NUTRITIONAL INTAKES OF DAILY FOOD IN CHINA

Year	Energy (Kcal) Total	Protein (gram) Including animal products	Fat (gram) Total	Including animal products	Total	Including animal products
1970	2032	115	48.7	5.7	22.6	9.8
1980	2332	174	55.2	7.5	32.0	15.4
1990	2679	302	65.5	14.0	49.7	26.3
1992	2727	345	67.4	15.9	51.9	30.1
1995	2763	464	72.2	23.5	67.3	39.4
1997	2897	510	77.6	26.7	70.8	42.9

Source: Food Balance Sheet Report, at http://apps.fao.org, last updated 1 June 2000.

REFERENCES

Brown, L.R., 1995, *Who Will Feed China? Wake up Call for a Small Planet*, New York: W.W. Norton.

Carter, C. and F.N. Zhong, 1991, 'China's Past and Future Role in the Grain Trade', *Economic Development and Cultural Change*, 39 (July), pp.791–814.

Colby, W.H., M. Giordano and K. Hjort, 1997, 'The ERS China CPPA Model: Documentation', Washington D.C.: ERS, USDA.

Chinese Academy of Agricultural Sciences, 1985, 'Integrated Research Report on the Development of Grain and Cash Crops', Beijing: Research Group of Grain Economy.

Darwin, R., M. Tsigas, J. Lewandrowski and A. Raneses, 1994, 'Shifting Users for National Resources in a Changing Climate', *World Resource Review*, Vol.6, No.4, pp.559–69.

ERS, 1994, 'The Country Projections and Policy Analysis Model Builder: An Overview of Its Uses and Features', Washington D.C.: ERS/USDA.

ERS, 1997, 'International Agricultural Baseline Projections to 2005', Agricultural Economic Report No.750, Washington D.C.: ERS/USDA.

FAO, 1995, 'Global and Regional Food Demand and Supply Prospects', in Nurul Islam (ed.), *Population and Food in the Early Twenty-First Century*, Washington, DC: IFPRI.

Fan, S. and M. Agcaoili-Sombilla, 1997, 'Why Projections on China's Future Food Supply and Demand Differ', *The Australian Journal of Agricultural and Resource Economics*, Vol.41, No.2, pp.169–90.

Garnaut, R. and G. Ma, 1992, 'Grain in China', Canberra: East Asia Analytical Unit, Department of Foreign Affairs and Trade.

Hertel, T.W. (ed.), 1997, *Global Trade Analysis: Modeling and Applications*, Cambridge: Cambridge University Press.

Huang, J.K. and S. Rozelle, 1998, *China's Grain Economy to the Twenty-First Century*, Beijing: China Agriculture Press.

Huang, J.K., S. Rozelle and M.W. Rosegrant, 1999, 'China's Food Economy to the Twenty-First Century: Supply, Demand, and Trade', *Economic Development and Cultural Change*, Vol.47, No.4.

Huang, J.K. and C.L. Chen, 1999, 'Effects of Trade Liberalization on Agriculture in China: Commodity Aspects', Working Paper series, No.43, Bogor: CGPRT Centre.

Lin, J.Y., 1990, 'Collectivization and China's Agricultural Crisis in 1959–1961', *Journal of Political Economy*, Vol.98, No.6.

Lin, J.Y., 1992, 'Rural Reforms and Agricultural Growth in China', *American Economic Review*, Vol.82, pp.34–51.

Mitchell, D., M. Ingco and R.C. Duncan, 1997, *The World Food Outlook*, Cambridge: Cambridge

University Press.

MOA (Ministry of Agriculture), 1999, 'China's Agricultural Development Report', Beijing: China Agricultural Publishing House.

Nyberg, A., 1997, 'China Long-Term Food Security', World Bank Report No.16469-CHA, Washington D.C.: The World Bank.

OECD, 1995, 'The Chinese Grain and Oilseed Sectors: Major Change Underway', Paris: OECD.

OECF, 1995, 'Prospects for Grain Supply–Demand Balance and Agricultural Development Policy in China', Discussion Paper No.6, Tokyo: OECF.

Rosegrant, M.W., M. Agcaoili-Sombilla and N.D. Perez, 1995, 'Global Food Projections to 2020: Implications for Investment', 2020 Vision Discussion Paper 5, Washington D.C.: International Food Policy Research Institute.

Simpson, J.R., X. Cheng and A. Miyazaki, 1994, 'China's Livestock and Related Agriculture: Projection to 2025', Wallingford: CAB International.

SSB, 1999, *China Statistical Yearbook*, Beijing: China Statistics Press.

SSB, 2000, *China Statistical Yearbook*, Beijing: China Statistics Press.

World Bank, 1997, *At China's Table*, China 2020 Series, Washington D.C.: World Bank.

Ye, X. and J.E. Taylor, 1995, 'The Impact of Income Growth on Farm Household Nutrient Intake: A Case Study of Prosperous Rural Area in Northern China', *Economics Development and Cultural Change*, Vol.43, No.4.

Zhang, C.G., 1999, 'The Current Situation of Animal Husbandry in China and Its Development Project in the 21st Century', in *Annual Report on Economic and Technological Development in Agriculture. Institute of Agricultural Economics*, Beijing: Chinese Academy of Agricultural Sciences.

Social Welfare in Rural China

JUTTA HEBEL

INTRODUCTION

Rapid diversification in China's rural economy, the comeback of family farming and an increasing importance in the role of markets, as well as the restructuring of political institutions, created not only new opportunities but also new risks and vulnerability for the rural population. Therefore, social welfare affairs remain one of the basic problems in rural China. There have always been fundamental differences between the lives of rural and urban people, and the state primarily concerned itself with the urban dwellers and workers in the public sector. Universal work participation and residence were the key social inclusion and welfare entitlement factors. Rural regions experienced special welfare arrangements, mainly based on collective work, the distribution of local resources and self-help within the families. The state has never been directly involved in rural welfare affairs carried out by the communes and brigades and only intervened in residual relief work. The recent transformation in China's rural areas changed the former modes of work inclusion and participation in collective welfare provision.

The principal aim of all development efforts should be the enhancement of the welfare of the population. Development begins with a reduction in poverty, vulnerability and precarious living conditions. According to the understanding of the Chinese, the socialist system abolished exploitation and, by creating employment, reduced extreme poverty, served the human needs and thus contributed to social welfare. Market socialism intended to open up new economic opportunities and private activities in order to raise the overall standard of living. An unpredictable improvement in living conditions took place in both rural and urban areas, although accompanied by increasing regional disparities and growing social inequality. Welfare is also the aim of private household activities. Actors, appropriate institutions and resources are necessary for it to become reality.

In this article, the main focus is social welfare in rural China. The article uses the term 'social welfare' in a broad sense, which includes income and

Jutta Hebel, Researcher, Institute of Rural Development, Goettingen University. Email: jhebel@gwdg.de.

value generation (in cash and in kind, derived from various economic activities, subsistence and home production), services in kind (granted by household family members, relatives, neighbours, self-help organizations, communal organizations), transfers of payments and benefits (from different sources, such as the family, social security, enterprises) and state subsidies (collective benefits, such as education, health) or investments (infrastructure).[1] The state, economy, communal organizations, self-help groups, social networks and families are the main institutions within this arrangement. In this article, the process of accomplishment will be called '(social) welfare production' [*Zapf*, 1984; *Kaufmann*, 1994; *Andreß*, 1999; *Cook and White*, 1998]. Households and families are its locus and they use both individual and external resources, namely economic, human and social capital. Changes in the former mode of social inclusion and participation in rural China confront households and families with a new institutional setting that has altered the relations to the state, the market and several intermediate organizations. Households have to cope with these conditions to strive for a better life.

Social security – as used in this article – refers to the variety of schemes and measures that provide a safety net and help in cases of destitution. It includes social insurance in China during the past 40 years, targeted at urban public workers and employees, and presently in the process of change from a system of free distribution to one of cost sharing [*Hebel*, 1997]. Social insurance is provided not only by the state but can also be a marketable good, and in China an insurance market is already emerging.

This article does not present new empirical facts and data. Its objective is to present some ideas for the analysis of social welfare in rural China by offering a multilevel approach, which combines the level of institutions, where welfare arrangements are determined, with the household level, where welfare production takes place. The approach is drawn from the debate on welfare and poverty in both industrialized as well as developing countries, and its purpose is to enrich the welfare discussion on rural China. The following section briefly summarizes some approaches found in the debate on social welfare in China, while the subsequent section displays the theoretical elements of the model. I will continue by using this framework to ask whether it provides insights into social welfare in rural China and to suggest some new research issues focusing on welfare. The article is based on a review of secondary literature and primary data sources.

APPROACHES TO SOCIAL WELFARE IN RURAL CHINA

Social welfare, social security and poverty are issues addressed in various research approaches to rural China, each with a specific perspective. It is possible to distinguish three different approaches focusing more or less explicitly on social welfare: I will term them in my brief summary the 'security approach', the 'rural developmental approach' and the 'family approach'.

The Security Approach

Issues concerning social security in China's rural and urban areas have recently been addressed under the heading of an 'East Asian Welfare Model' [*White and Goodman*, 1998]. Case studies in different East Asian countries seem to reveal that their welfare systems have a number of key elements in common. China shares some of these key elements, although with distinctive features, ensuing not from its culture, but rather from its historical, structural and political (socialist) heritage [*White*, 1998: 194; *Wong*, 1998: 157].[2] The East Asian Welfare Model may be interpreted as a new welfare model, distinct from the three political 'Economies of the Welfare State' analysed by Esping-Andersen [1990]. The core of this model is its 'state-sponsored development' character, which avoids 'unproductive' welfare expenditures and concentrates on economic development ('developmental welfare system') [*White and Goodman*, 1998: 15], in other words, a mainly 'growth-led' policy [*Drèze and Sen*, 1991].

Besides this broader concept of welfare, the mainstream of social security research consists of studies on the social security system in rural and urban China [among others: *Ahmad and Hussain*, 1991; *Krieg and Schädler*, 1994, 1995; *Selden and You*, 1997; *Croll*, 1999; *Wong*, 1995, 1998]. Croll [1999: 696] describes the diversity of welfare arrangements as 'multi-level, multi-channel and multi-means approaches to welfare provisioning'.The Chinese system of social security consists of two main schemes: on the one hand, a means-tested system of social assistance for people in need who are not able-bodied and lack sufficient income or a family to support them (*shehui fuwu*); and, in addition, social and disaster relief for rural people as the core of social assistance (*shehui jiuji*; *shehui jiuzhu*). On the other hand, there is a social insurance system (*shehui baoxian*) in urban China, which provides cash income in the following cases: old age, unemployment, disability and illness. This is the heart of urban social security, covering the employees of government agencies, SOEs and larger COEs.[3] As already mentioned, it is presently being reorganized, as the *danwei* fade away [*Selden and You*, 1997; *Hebel*, 1997]. The Chinese terminology underlines the duality of the social security system.

During the 30 years prior to economic reform, welfare in China's rural areas basically relied on people's inclusion in the system of collective work in agriculture or rural industry and on equal participation in the distribution of local resources. The distribution of collective welfare, such as food subsidies, health services, education facilities (mostly *minban*, that is, run by and for local communities) and housing assistance surpassed individual cash benefits. Stable membership in the communes guaranteed this share in local resources even beyond active labour participation. The level of public support was low and did not supersede the role of the family in welfare production. Nevertheless, it contributed to raising the quality of life in rural regions; for example, rural health services improved overall health by means of prevention programmes, mass campaigns and provision of affordable basic medical care. The rural health system consisted of a three-tier service programme: health stations in almost all villages staffed by barefoot doctors; health centres in townships; and hospitals in each county, funded by governments, communes and users. Since the 1980s, the reform led to disparities within the health sector and between the poor and better-off counties and people. On the one hand, decentralization and privatization of health services released the system from bureaucratic control, but, on the other hand, stripped it of its public financing. Services are now primarily financed by patients, and they lack a regulatory frame for medical treatment and medicine. The costs of consultation and medical and in-patient treatment have increased, and poor people cannot afford the services they require [*Yu* et al., 1998]. It is widely agreed that the relatively equal access to healthcare that existed before the reform has been eroded by decentralization and deregulation and inequality increased at the regional and household levels [*Bloom and Wilkes*, 1997].

Most contributors to the welfare debate trace the picture of the state's retreat by means of decentralization policies and decollectivization and of the re-emergence of family households, not only in economic but also in welfare matters. They emphasize the fact that today's welfare production in Chinese rural areas is mainly based on the family. Detailed information is available on the existing systems of social security in general, as well as on the health sector, the underlying principles and rationales and on the reform objectives. Yet, we need more empirical information on the functioning of the system at the household level and on its role in welfare production and its contribution to well-being.[4]

The Rural Development Approach

Studies on rural society in China contribute to the welfare debate by focusing on changes in economic structure (for example agriculture, sideline and off-farm production, rural industry, cash sales and commerce) and ownership (land entitlement, industrial ownership) and on their impact on rural households and labour (for example labour redundancy, migration). Rapid industrialization and urbanization are central features in the recent rural development. Changes are so quick and intensive that urbanization of 'rural' areas is taken for granted 'throughout most of the country' [*Guldin*, 1997: 265]. This conclusion may not be consensual, but the radical economic and institutional changes are not contested, and they alter the conditions of welfare production. Yet, some regions, counties and villages are left behind.

There are several recent studies on rural households and their survival strategies under the conditions of economic and political reforms, including research on poverty [among others: *Cook and White*, 1998; *Croll*, 1999; *Khan and Riskin*, 2001]. Peasant households may respond to economic and institutional changes by remaining at the level of subsistence production, or engaging predominantly in cash-crop production and various non-agricultural activities. The placement of household members in non-agricultural activities includes migration (varying distances, permanent or temporary) [*Qian*, 1996]. Regional conditions are extremely diverse, not only between regions such as the Pearl River delta [*Johnson*, 1993], Sichuan [*Pennarz*, 1998] and north China [*Selden*, 1993], normally labelled as more or less developed, but also between villages located within short distances of each other. Welfare production at the household level stems from a mix of agricultural and industrial activities and is supplemented by rural out-migration [*Croll and Huang*, 1997].[5] Both physical conditions (for example quality and quantity of arable land, infrastructure, market distance, rural industry) and institutional conditions (collective organization, property rights, local elite, kinsmen outside the village, lineage dominance in the village) are decisive for the rural setting and household strategies. For example, Johnson demonstrates how overseas family ties contribute to economic development in the Pearl River delta. Kinsmen have become sources of investment and entrepreneurial skill, and the dominant feature of these villages are lineages as 'property-holding corporations that socially integrate groups of households whose male heads trace their descent to an apical ancestor' [*Johnson*, 1993: 131].

Therefore, agricultural, non-agricultural and institutional reforms restructure the rural regions and are of particular interest in regard to welfare issues. One issue is property rights. In the controversial debate over property rights, some argue that the clarification of property rights of village and township government was an incentive to local income control and the basis for rapid growth; others argue, contrary to the official position, that a process of privatization has taken place and has been at the origin of growth. A third position argues that members of the local elite are all tied together by kinship or friendship and, therefore, it is not important who officially owns the assets, but rather who has the control. As Lin and Chen [1999: 169] put it, 'one visible trend is the convergence of the corporate elite leaders and local family networks', displayed in their Daqiuzhuang study.

This institutional setting is of fundamental importance to villages and households as it defines particularistic participation criteria in employment and welfare shares.

Another aspect of transformation is the remaking of collective rural organizations into a civil administration responsible for counties, townships and villages. Heberer and Taubmann [1998] describe the transformation as long-lasting process of trial and error, rather than a switch from a planned to a market economy. Political and administrative changes shape the responsibilities between different levels of the administration, the relationship between cadres and the rural population and the structure of local society. The speeding up of economic growth became the central focus of all activities. Therefore, when talking about the 'state', it is necessary to go further into the details of local political institutions.

The rural developmental approach stresses the institutional setting of welfare arrangements, including central policy and government decisions and regulations, global influences and local conditions, all carried out and modified by local actors to include their own interests.

The Family Approach

The family approach includes perspectives on demographic development and on changes in family structures. Demographic studies emphasize the rapid transition of China's family and kinship structures and the ageing of the population, owing to the one-child-family policy and the interaction of mortality and fertility. One result of family development is the decrease in family size and a reduced number of lateral kin [*Selden*, 1993]. The overwhelming part of the rural population lives in small household families consisting of four or five members. Parents live longer, and there are fewer siblings to share the responsibility of care [*Lin*, 1995: 133]. The question arises as to whether care for elderly people and welfare in general can be borne by the family [*Lin*, 1995: 145]. Outlooks diverge: some authors maintain that an extended family can accommodate a much higher level of labour power division than a nuclear family; thus, a reduction in family size would lower the welfare production potential of the families. Others stress the lower dependency rates and, as a consequence, an increase in living standards.

In addition to demographic studies, the status of elderly people is a frequently addressed issue. On the one hand, it is argued that the position of older people has been upgraded by the changes in land entitlement under the Production Responsibility System. Their presence increases family landholdings, and their share in dealing with the burden of daily life – taking care of children and preparing dishes – is an important contribution to family welfare [*Huang and Odend'hal*, 1998: 106–7]. On the other hand, new employment, wage labour and income generation opportunities remove control of household incomes from the older generation. This is interpreted as a decrease in the status of the elderly.

Another group of studies focuses on the status of women. Women normally have an inferior status within the Chinese kinship system, and changes in their status are a subject of discussion. Education and female literacy prove to have important influences on rural women's decision-making power, the division of labour within the household and exposure to broader society, as has been shown in a Yunnan study. Nevertheless, the findings are mixed: family values and patrilineal and patrilocal joint household structures still limit women's autonomy and power, and the preference given to sons combined with women's declining fertility continues to affect their status [Li and Lavely, 1998].

Women became the principal source of farm labour, a factor that is said to have strengthened their position in the family according to findings of the Shandong Field Research Project [Huang and Odend'hal, 1998: 107]. A 'feminization' trend in agriculture has been reported, and even if this may not be a large-scale trend, it could be detrimental to women's status [Mallee, 1998: 227]. Others argue that the increasing participation of women in wage labour and even in migration – one of the main opportunities for women to enter the off-farm labour force, as stated by Rozelle et al. [1999: 368] – contributes to household earnings and improves the status of women. The growing demand for an industrial workforce increased opportunities for female employment outside the household, and external earnings contribute to the overall household incomes. Empirical findings from a Guangdong study seem to prove that the low status of women in the family influences their low status on the market: 'Market wage signals may serve to reinforce, rather than to ameliorate, sex-based differences that arise within the household' [Hare, 1999: 1012].

The multifaceted rural reform in China restored the peasant household as the basic unit in economic activities and led to changes in kinship structures, household size and composition, economic activities and labour arrangements within the family, and status of family members. Although general statements on the nature of these changes are problematic, kinship and family relations are deeply embedded in the local setting and have to be considered when analysing social welfare in rural regions. The concept of family as a nuclear co-resident kin group is too narrow. Findings on rural household strategies reveal great elasticity in coping with the new economic and social conditions. Survey results of a north China study [Selden, 1993: 164] suggest that the rural transformation produced major changes in family size and marital strategies and led to postponed conceptions. On the one hand, there is an increase in small nuclear families; on the other, a growth of stem and extended families that engage in entrepreneurial activities. Chances to invigorate family ties, to take advantage of an extended family, to allocate household labour among a variety of new opportunities and even to control the local economy and politics are unevenly distributed. These findings do not appear to be limited to southern China with its strong lineage connections. Households respond creatively to the local context and use the flexibility of kinship structures to buffer the impact of change and formulate strategies to maximize their well-being.

The three different approaches largely agree that the transformation of the countryside combines the return to the household as the basic economic unit and to family farming with the withdrawal of the state and collective institutions from their prior social obligations. Yet, changes in the institutional setting did not create a vacuum. Rural development opened up access to markets, various sidelines, and other non-agricultural activities, enhanced industrial employment, allowed or tolerated migration, and thus widened the economic opportunities available to families. The household family is overwhelmingly nuclear and small in size, but this does not provide sufficient information on the functional net of relatives in welfare production. Lineage and clan structures experience a revival. The obligation to support members and to provide for the elderly, the sick and the handicapped lies mainly in the hands of families. Increasing vulnerability is expected from population policies that strive to lower reproduction rates.

The state is involved in the local setting by way of family planning, agricultural policy, price and tax policies, and the regulation of land tenure, to name but a few of its pertinent policies. Between the conflicting principles of equity and equality, the Chinese state seems to stand for more inequality and less redistributive justice. It is expected that economic growth will further improve rural living conditions. Though poverty-stricken counties and disaster victims are eligible for relief, the creation of a social security system in rural areas is not yet on its way and even in the cities its development lags far behind the pace of economic reform.[6]

In order to assess the consequences of economic reform on welfare in rural China, research has to be broadened in several ways. On the one hand, we need a theoretical reconstruction of the institutional set that defines the conditions of welfare production; on the other, the process of welfare production has to be modelled, including changing needs and contingencies. Drawing upon existing studies of rural China, I would like to sketch a multilevel model that combines a set of welfare institutions with the analysis of the welfare production of rural households.

A MULTILEVEL MODEL

Welfare theories are concerned with the institutional instrumentation of welfare provision and social security schemes, the conditions that underpin their emergence and the impact on people's well-being. The role of the state is of particular interest in the welfare debate and in cross-national studies on welfare arrangements. One approach discerns two different strategies in the state's contribution to social welfare: a 'growth-led' and a 'support-led' development strategy [*Drèze and Sen*, 1991: 22 *ff.*]. In the case of Chinese development strategies, a shift in favour of economic growth and the promotion of a strategy of 'growth mediated security' is maintained [*White and Goodman*, 1998]. Yet, the welfare contribution of the Chinese state during the period of collective agriculture has often been overestimated.[7] The present withdrawal of state support affects primarily the relatively privileged urbanites, the public workers and employees, as state-owned and (big) collective enterprises reduce their comprehensive net of social security (such as permanent employment, housing and other subsidies, medical care and education, retirement payments). The rural population never experienced direct benefits or state support in welfare matters. Even before recent market economic reforms started, the role of the government in rural areas was residual and confined to disaster and famine relief. The notion of a general switch from a supporting state to a growth and market-oriented strategy obscures the particular welfare instrumentation in Chinese rural areas.

Another approach underlines the pluralism of contributors to welfare [*Evers and Olk*, 1996] and sees individual measures as part of a 'welfare mix' [*Kaufmann*, 1994; *Andreß*, 1999]. The state is not the exclusive provider of welfare, social security and insurance. Welfare production is embedded in the economic and political organization of the society, the family and other social networks. State, market, intermediate organizations and families form the institutional setting of welfare production. Each particular welfare mix is the outcome of politically and culturally valued assumptions regarding individual and collective responsibilities in welfare production and stems from the history of national institutions. In addition to that, there are large variations in the state's connections to the economy (for example socialist dominance, regulations by law, liberal independence) and to private households (in matters of distribution and reproduction). Rapid decollectivization in rural China brought about a rupture in the institutional setting, in collective responsibilities and in state activities. Changes in welfare production have to be analysed in the context of various contributors acting within the new mix of policies, opportunities and risks.

This brings me to five general assumptions. First, *welfare* analysis has to be broadened from a narrow focus on social security or insurance schemes, which are only one aspect of welfare production. Second, the state is just one contributor to welfare resources, and welfare production is embedded in a rather complex setting of conditions and rationales. This is not a zero-sum-relation in the sense that whenever the state (or the local commune and collective) withdraws from its obligations, the family assumes them. Only if both the institutional context and the family are defined in very formal ways might relations appear unambiguous. Third, in order to be produced, welfare needs actors, namely household and/or family members. Defining the family and household is not as easy as it seems at first glance, as the household family forms an intersection between kin and functional relations as well as domestic co-residence. Most studies consider the rural household to be the basic unit of welfare production, which copes with a set of favourable and detrimental conditions. Household strategies have to be reconstructed using a multilevel model, rather than only individual (micro) or structural (macro) factors. We need to know the conditions for actions and must include contingencies in the concept of action. Fourth, family and household members share the work and results of their activities, yet equal distribution of the results is the exception rather than the rule. The distribution of nutrition and other goods within the households may not correspond to individual needs, as those granted to the women and children are kept at minimal levels. Fifth, well-being should not be confused with a certain *standard of living* or a *level of income*. As has been underlined by Sen [1985], there are fundamental differences between the standard of living and well-being. *Well-being* is a matter of the quality of life and not confined to a certain level of income. Income may be an important resource and a meaningful precondition for well-being, but it is not (at least for most people) an aim in itself. Therefore, using the term 'well-being' in this article means that changes in the institutional setting of rural China and in welfare production should not be confined to problems of income generation. The subject goes beyond the scope of this article, but dimensions of well-being such as the enhancement of opportunities and personal decision-making or the reduction of political and social control should be kept in mind as aspects of well-being.[8] There are several widely accepted premises within the welfare discussion from which I want to draw for my argumentation.

Welfare is derived from different institutions ('welfare-mix' or 'welfare pluralism').[9] This is true even in industrialized countries with their highly developed social security systems. Despite considerable state provisions, families in industrialized countries are still a main provider of welfare. Resource transfer and help between the generations is widespread and considered normal.[10] This basic supposition is also valid in the case of developing countries such as China. It is also agreed that a particular mix reflects traditional values, welfare culture, governance functions and politics. There can be no doubt that during the reform China redefined its particular composition of welfare pluralism.

Well-being cannot be measured exclusively on the basis of the provision of income, material goods and services. Well-being and welfare do not depend on monetary income alone. Besides household incomes, a wide range of goods and services such as public goods, education, health institutions and the infrastructure contribute to well-being. Income poverty does not necessarily signify a poor standard of living or the absence of well-being. If basic resources are provided at almost no cost (as was the case in the Chinese urban *danwei*), a low income level does not signify absence of welfare. To refer again to Sen [1985], well-being does not depend only on the provision of material resources ('having'), but it also depends on psychological and social acceptance ('loving'; 'being') and inclusion. Although, this has to be kept in mind, economic reforms changed the role of income in China.

Resources are a precondition but not a guarantee for welfare and well-being. Well-being and welfare are the result of various factors and activities, and depend on people's capability to make use of resources. A given structure of opportunities does not necessarily guarantee welfare; people have to act (not only react); to perceive opportunities and make use of them. The economic reforms strengthened the role of individual and household decision-making but also led to the emergence of new types of vulnerability. In sum, the linkage between opportunity structures and people's capabilities and actions is of theoretical and practical importance for welfare in rural China. Social conditions influence, but do not determine human action. People make decisions (such as whether to seek employment or not) and act in a situation of incomplete information; people in similar situations perceive them differently and cope with problems in different ways. Thus, welfare production is a matter of conditions and actions, based on individual needs that need to be converted into claims and actions. Different theoretical frames analyse the interconnectedness of institutions providing welfare (macro level) with household activities producing welfare (meso level) and individual needs and motives (micro level). Theories of welfare pluralism and welfare production – such as social capital, rational choice or stress theory, which are all applied in welfare studies – tend to bridge the macro and micro level.

The Welfare Institutions

Each of the four welfare institutions shown in Figure 1 plays a role in defining welfare and in its relation to households. They differ with respect to their goals, basic logic and resources, entitlements and necessary activities. Although in the process of welfare production they may compensate for each other, their particular values diverge and they each have advantages and limits of their own.

The *state* (in its function as a producer of welfare) is present at diverse levels (central, provincial, county, local level) and in various administrative organizations. People's basic living conditions are directly determined by the state's provision of public goods, redistribution of incomes, provision of employment and social security measures. Governance functions and policies shape the welfare arrangement. Among the state's various governance functions are the regulation of production and reproduction (such as infrastructure, law, communication, tax and redistribution, public goods, industrial relations), domestic and international agricultural and industrial policies, policies of land entitlement, property rights, purchase and price policies, and, not to be forgotten, population policy.

FIGURE 1

WELFARE INSTITUTIONS[11]

Institution	State	Intermediate organizations	Kinship	Market
	Institutional structure: central, provincial, local authorities	Cooperation and self-help groups; local communal organizations; neighbourhood; NGOs	Lineage; kinship and extended family; relatives; nuclear family	Labour market; commodity market; capital market
Central value	Equality	Solidarity	Reciprocity	Freedom of choice
Mode of participation; entitlement	Legal entitlement; convention	Need; co-optation; residence	Ascription	Ability to pay; ability to work
Commitment	Civil rights; local residence	Voluntary nature; residence; social relations; membership; civic virtue	Personal duty	Work; rent
Resources services;	Payments; benefits; subsidies (collective or individual)	Mutual help; goods; (formal or informal) credits; services in kind	Care; services in kind; support; (informal) credits; gifts	Goods; payments
Medium of exchange	Law	Social relations; esteem	Trust; respect	Money

The state contributes to welfare with a wide range of policies in all these different fields and may establish a particular social security sector and introduce various insurance schemes (such as for old age, health). Although the welfare sector and/or a refined social insurance system are important, they are only one element in the welfare instrumentation.

The state actively incorporates the population by various means (education, labour, nation building, civil rights) and establishes entitlements to resources. Members of the nation are, by law or convention, entitled to state resources and enjoy rights as local dwellers and/or citizens (land entitlement, social welfare provision). Universal equality in conformity with the law is highly valued, but it may lead to the neglect of vulnerable groups and minorities. It may even be detrimental to individual efforts in welfare production and create (political) dependency. Regarding the rural–urban divide, the Chinese political pattern of entitlement and distribution did not conform to the universal norm of equality among its citizens.

The state does not provide welfare exclusively. The *economy* is the second important source of welfare. Employment and income generation, provision of goods and services (including a private insurance market and welfare resources) and employer-based welfare (such as life tenure, security schemes) are the main characteristics. Economic activities intend to create wealth by way of growth in output of goods and services and national income. They aim at satisfying wants and needs when the means available for the satisfaction of these wants and needs are scarce. Scarce means must thus be allocated between alternative uses ('choices') under specific conditions of value exchange. These include, among others, the supply of labour for income, of capital and investments for returns, or of money for goods and insurance. An ideal market exchange of equivalents is not linked to any social precondition.[12] Money is the most important medium, and the ability to pay is the criterion for participation in exchange and the satisfaction of needs ('claims').

Not all economic activities are market related and generate money income. In a subsistence economy, food, clothing, shelter and goods are consumed by the people who produce them. An informal sector of mostly urban services and petty production contributes to income generation. People working in the informal sector are excluded from formal rights and security. The economy in developing countries is strongly determined by the subsistence sector and informal production and distribution.

Welfare is also provided by *intermediate organizations*. The community is a major welfare institution and its key value is solidarity. It consists of formal and informal institutions and networks such as the neighbourhood, self-help groups, and more formal organizations like (in China) the local Women's Associations. Self-help groups include initiatives in saving and credit organizations, in migration networks as well as in mutual agricultural help and social services.

Local residence and/or organizational membership and/or need are the basis of participation. Support or esteem are not provided by virtue of formal entitlements, but rely on need or co-optation. The nuclear or extended *family*, *kinship* and *lineage* form very important welfare institutions. Kinship is bounded, but should not be reified as it is very flexible with respect to individuals. Distant members of a lineage may turn out to be of great value in the building of networks. Kin lines do not determine the claim system, they are just a potential.

Kin relationships express commitments and constraints that are embedded in long-term reciprocity or social exchange. The support and transfer of goods are carried out on the basis of mutual trust and in view of returns in an indefinite future. Exchange is not measured in value equivalents. Kin relations do not function as a system of formal claims, although the law enforces the support of (grand)parents by their offspring and vice versa. Reciprocal exchange between the generations is rooted in a value system that enforces gratitude and obligation on the part of the younger generation towards its elders.

All these institutions are welfare providers and a basis of resources. They are mutually exclusive in their logic, but they can complement each other in welfare production and constitute the network of external resources of private households. The availability of different resources is fundamental for welfare production. Welfare does not depend on shares in each of the four claim systems as there may be functional equivalents. Security in old age does not necessarily need a state-based old age pension scheme if the market offers compensation (private insurance market), or families are able to finance old age and take care of the elderly.

Welfare production takes place in the household, and it uses not only resources ensuing from its multilayered network but also personal ones. Therefore, the relationship between the four claim systems is important. A high exposure to risks, namely, 'vulnerability' can be expected when losses in one claim system are not compensated by others (for example the loss of the ability to carry out physical labour and, at the same time, the lack of compensation through a family and communal or state support).

Different welfare arrangements display more or less intensive state activity, emphasize particular policies and are due to historical pathways. They reflect concepts of collective and individual responsibilities in welfare production. In addition to the outlined institutional setting, welfare production within rural households has to be reconstructed as an action that implies decision-making and takes into account personal resources and needs. A household or a person has to decide whether or not to seek employment, to engage in some economic activity, to migrate in search of work, to invest capital or to buy security on the insurance market.

Needs and Claims

Private households and each of their members have a variety of needs. As has been mentioned, needs are not confined to material aspects of life (income, goods, services) but also include psychological and social aspects. Figure 2 displays the three central dimensions of needs. There is a discussion as to whether there is a hierarchy of physiological, psychological and social needs. Needs underlie social change, particularly in times of rapid transformation. The increase in communication media or in migration may induce comparisons with the standard of living of other (mostly urban) people. Resulting changes in the value system and in the average living standard (increased spreading of consumer goods) influence people's needs.

As all households and families comprise individuals, their human needs may compete. Not all needs are, or can be, converted into claims. The process of conversion takes place within social contexts and by means of interaction in which not all family members have equal opportunities to make their choices. In many cases we find a hierarchy of decision-making responsibilities with certain key areas of decision-making assigned to men as the heads of households and other areas to women. To analyse this process of conversion and choice made within families requires a theoretical frame (for example interaction, stratification theories, empowerment approaches), which cannot be outlined here. But speaking of households or families as 'actors' obscures the fact that they are not single actors with homogeneous interests.

Needs and resources do not necessarily match, and not all felt needs can be transposed into claims. There might be a fundamental gap between available resources and felt needs, resulting in discontent, absolute or relative deprivation or poverty and even social exclusion. Needs and claims in industrialized and developing countries differ widely. In industrialized countries, although poverty persists, relative deprivation prevails, whereas in developing countries it is often physiological needs (nutrition, shelter, health) that remain unfulfilled.

Welfare Production in Private Households

Figure 2 relates four different welfare institutions with the structure of needs and claims of households and individuals. Welfare production is a process in which private households strive to achieve well-being for their members[13] with respect to claims, making use of individual and external resources. The given institutional setting is a condition for action, but there is no deterministic relation between the institutional setting and household activities. Actors are free to make decisions in view of the structure of opportunities, chances that are perceived and can be seized and risks to be avoided. Choice and decision-making implies the possibility of alternatives. Yet insufficient resources and a lack of the means necessary for meeting one's basic needs may rule out the ability to make a meaningful choice. This perspective is related to the capability approach, which emphasizes freedom of action and decision-making by individuals as well as the constraints confronted by vulnerable groups and the denial of choice.

The logic of household activities, decision-making and actions by individuals (agency) has to be explained with respect to the institutional structure. The social sciences offer various non-deterministic approaches to action analysis. I will only point out two different approaches, which might bridge the macro-level of the institutional setting and the micro-level of households and their members.

First, studies on decision-making by households regarding migration conceptualize a macro- and micro-level and insert a third meso- or relational level [*Faist*, 1995]. The meso-level stresses the fact that decision-making takes place in social units rather than being carried out by isolated individuals, and decisions balance resources and claims with respect to various ends. As Faist [1995: 24] puts it: 'The basic assumption ... is that the resources of individuals are related to structural opportunities via social networks that constitute distinct sets of intermediate structure available to decision makers ... Fundamentally, structural constraints and opportunities and micro- and meso-level resources determine to a large part what kind of options people have ...'.

The relational level can be analysed by using the notion of 'social capital' in order to define the capacity of individuals to command scarce resources by virtue of membership in social networks. In this perspective, the above-mentioned kinship networks and the intermediate organizations link the individual and structural levels.

Second, recent studies on welfare and poverty use the concepts of 'careers', 'trajectories', or 'coping', particularly when focusing on the dynamics of poverty. Coping theories are derived from research on action under stress [*Andreß*, 1999; *Ludwig*, 1996]. I will not go into the details of this discussion and would only like to draw attention to the fact that these terms were coined by the authors to refer to the work (welfare production) carried out by members of collectives (families) in order to reach a common goal (for example to overcome poverty, to cope with illness), taking contingencies and control into account. The concept of 'socio-economic coping' intends to grasp the complex process of (inter)action with respect to different status careers, and thus to connect action with the social structure.

FIGURE 2

WELFARE PRODUCTION IN PRIVATE HOUSEHOLDS[14]

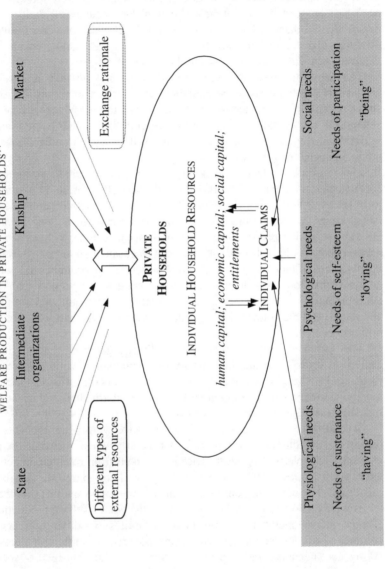

The basic concept of this probabilistic model is that a given situation does not determine careers and reduce people to a state in which they passively endure their unemployment or poverty. On the contrary, in objectively similar situations people develop different strategies to face their problems. Therefore, if poverty research defines an unfortunate situation only as the end of a descending career it might miss the point, as the situation can also be a transient period and the beginning of various careers. Of course, the coping strategies employed by households are not necessarily successful: some households will find a pathway to success, others will not overcome their difficulties, and yet others will only have provisional results. Among the various welfare institutions, intermediary organizations and kinship networks are of particular value, all the more so since social capital is overwhelmingly associated with these institutions.[15]

To sum up, social welfare and the process of welfare production have to be sociologically reconstructed at macro-, meso- and micro-levels. The concept of welfare pluralism may contribute to an analysis by stressing the various welfare institutions, each with its own rationale and resources. Welfare has to be produced, normally at the household level, and its aim is the satisfaction of individual material, psychological and social needs (well-being). Different approaches, such as the concept of social capital or coping theories, conceptualize agency and the process of decision-making relating to the macro- and the micro-level. The proposed multilevel frame will be used in the subsequent section of this article to generate some research questions on welfare in rural China.

ISSUES OF SOCIAL WELFARE IN RURAL CHINA

In the following section I wish to apply the above-mentioned frame and highlight some issues for further analysis of social welfare in rural China. In particular, I will first address the relationship between the different welfare institutions and households as units of welfare production, and second, the problem of agency in the welfare production of households in situations of poverty and vulnerability, drawing on the concept of social-economic coping.

The Relationship between Welfare Institutions and Households

One key research issue relates to the concept of welfare pluralism and its relevance for rural welfare in China. A focus on welfare pluralism would help us go beyond two widely held assumptions: that China switched from a state-led to a growth-led model of development and from a state-supported to a family-supported welfare system. The empirical reality in rural China is by far more complicated and heterogeneous. The concept of welfare pluralism would combine the three different approaches – the security, rural developmental and family approach – reviewed at the beginning of this article. Intermediate organizations and self-help groups have to be added as a fourth perspective. These different approaches and the wealth of empirical findings on rural areas underpin the relationship between the welfare institutions and their specific character in rural welfare production. The new mix of welfare institutions changed the fundamental logic and the resources available for people's production and reproduction activities. It altered the mode of social inclusion in work and participation.

One broad issue is the so-called retreat of the state from rural areas and the increase in economic opportunities and risks for households. Decentralization and deregulation led to an increase in local power, changed property rights and increased individual economic activities. The role of the state has changed, but its various functions continue to shape local conditions. It obviously would not suffice for research to reduce the function and activities of the state to its role in the welfare sector.

The state reaches down to the village and household levels with various policies such as land, agriculture, tax and price, labour and family policies, to name but a few. It more or less controls the supply and prices of certain strategic inputs such as fertilizer, seed distribution and irrigation. State purchasing and price policies (compulsory sales quotas on grain, cotton and other crops at state-set prices) determine the terms of trade between agriculture and industry, agricultural production and rural living conditions. As the complete policy mix is a prerequisite for local welfare, it could be a useful focus point for welfare research. In the past, politically imposed terms of trade have been detrimental to Chinese rural regions. Today, some policies improve economic conditions and provide room for new household strategies; other policy components hamper household activities.

Guaranteed access to land is one of the key elements of welfare production in rural China [*Ahmad and Hussain*, 1991: 253]. This is a key factor, although economic opportunities vary widely with local conditions and do not rule out poverty. Nevertheless, access to land is an exceptional condition when comparing China to other developing countries. Land use rights are leased to households on specified conditions and village officials retain the authority to redistribute the land. The Rural Economic Research Centre stated in 1991 that the lack of inputs and know-how and insufficient seeds, chemical fertilizer and pesticides were among the most important problems faced by rural households. Only the more entrepreneurial households were able to overcome some of these problems in specialized organizations, mutual-aid groups or partnerships, as was reported by Pieke in his Raoyang county study [*Pieke*, 1998]. In other words, welfare production depends on the whole range of resources provided by the four institutions.

Political and administrative decentralization strengthened the local authorities. Studies on the restructuring of institutions in China's rural sections are numerous and may be very useful for the welfare debate. Selden [1998: 20] points to three types of organizations in 'The Remaking of China's Countryside': (1) the township and village enterprises (TVEs); (2) small-scale mutual aid and cooperation as a type of self-organization at the level of production; and (3) a wide range of voluntary associations and cooperative commercial, service and technical support (Specialized Production Technology Associations, SPTA). The latter constitute an intermediate sphere between state, market and families/lineages. Members in the intermediate sphere of self-organization in new, specialized cooperatives are mostly drawn from the entrepreneurial and specialized households and are the best educated [Selden, 1998: 35]. Welfare is closely tied to local enterprise growth; yet the pattern of rural welfare provisioning is 'cellular' as noted by Croll [1999: 691]. Various studies on rural development report that local village authorities, townships and counties, CCP officials, TVE managers and entrepreneurs in collective or private economic undertakings form the new rural elite.

The debate on TVE property rights is an interesting contribution to welfare issues. TVE ownership is multilayered, involving state, township and village and/or private capital.[16] They play a leading role in rural industrialization and contribute to rural non-farm employment. They contribute to local welfare not only by providing employment in rural industries (wages), but by distributing dividends to local residents (who do or do not work in the TVE), by financing agricultural and industrial projects and by contributing to public welfare (education, health institutions, the infrastructure). Foreign capital infusion by kin-related investors underline the particular character of the TVE economy. Croll points out several new welfare trends and the role of local governments and the establishment of non-profit organizations (NGOs).[17]

Family policy is another crucial issue of state policy in rural regions. On the one hand, the state-dictated fertility reduction policy strongly affects the rural households by decreasing the number of members in the nuclear families and by reducing lateral kin with their care-giving potential. On the other hand, households experience a low dependency ratio (47.8 per cent in 1997 [HDR, 1999: 198]) which contributes to an increase in per capita income and living standards. As a number of family studies have shown, people rely increasingly on relatives in their economic activities. Extended families and lineage connections have become important in economic development [Walder, 1998] and can be decisive in welfare. In many cases, rural elites are closely linked to each other by kinship connections, as in the Fengjia village study in Shandong [Huang and Odend'hal, 1998]. They represent the particular 'welfare mix' to which private households are exposed. Households and individuals have more or less access to, or are excluded (as non-kin, non-locals, migrants), from the resources provided by the local setting.[18]

This brings me to the point that transformations in the opportunity structure and its inherent logic altered the mix of welfare institutions. As market opportunities increased, a shift took place to more direct value exchange (labour for income, money for goods). This process is frequently labelled 'marketization' and is said to have replaced the former collective and state distribution economy. However, this conclusion might be contested in two ways. First, there does not seem to be a clear-cut difference between the state's redistribution functions and the economic activities of the TVE. As Selden [1998: 24] puts it: 'The redistributive economy did not, however, simply disappear to be replaced by the unfettered autonomy of household and market.' Second, the rural economy is deeply infused by kinship relations and favours local and/or kin workers. This intermediate sector embodies 'elements of the redistributive economy in the provision of benefits to residents of their communities who further gain by access to secure jobs' [Selden, 1998: 31]. The distribution logic of rural industry and commerce (as a claim system) is based on kinship and/or local residency, and it functions – at least partially – on principles of (long-term) reciprocity and/or solidarity. Migrant workers and non-locals hardly benefit as they are excluded from local welfare and confined to the hard and insecure jobs. The new particularistic rules of distribution and inclusion are of special interest for the welfare debate.

To summarize, social welfare in rural China is best understood through the concept of welfare pluralism. The withdrawal of the state does not automatically mean an additional burden for the family as the institutional setting may compensate for losses. Although most co-residential units are composed of nuclear families, the revival of lineages and kinship relations changed the economic and political context in which they operate. Intermediate organizations play an increasing role, for example in providing access to credits. The four welfare institutions (see Figure 1) have their particular central values, modes of participation, and resources, but empirical findings from rural China display their interrelatedness. Values attributed to the market (freedom) or the state (equality) are often mingled with particularistic values of solidarity and reciprocity, in cases where the local representatives of the state (cadres) are at the same time economic entrepreneurs and kin members.

Agency, Poverty and Vulnerability

People act within given conditions. External resources (economic activities, credit, help from family members, transfers, CCP membership, kin-relations) and restrictions (scarcity of land, missing inputs, insufficient infrastructure, age, state of the family biography, size of family, age of children, political background) have to be perceived and evaluated ('appraised') with respect to individual and/or collective needs, values and preferences. Internal resources – such as education, experience, status, gender and age – influence how the situation is addressed and what type of (re)action and coping strategy will be produced. Therefore, an interesting issue in research on rural welfare is the analysis of household strategies in their changing institutional setting.

Since the 1980s, case studies in villages and households have been feasible and carried out in different rural regions. China is of course too diverse for a single village to be representative for the entire country, but case studies that focus on the households provide us with more detailed knowledge of household strategies in the production of welfare. This type of research will help us to understand how people act without being socio-economically and/or culturally deterministic.[19] Wilkes *et al.* [1997] proved the usefulness of this type of conceptual framework by presenting findings of a follow-up study on rural households in coping with severe illness and high medical fees. Households' responses were based on their resources, their consideration of available options, and their expected opportunity costs. A wide range of resources – labour, productive assets, stores of values, claims on other households, including kin, neighbours and friends, claims on local community organizations and claims on government – was used in a variety of strategies, which enabled households to overcome their adverse situation without damaging losses.[20] The very poor households were less able to cope.

This concept might allow for a better definition of vulnerable groups within the rural society. The focus on welfare pluralism and welfare production might suggest that poverty is no longer a crucial issue in rural China. On the contrary, the persistence of rural poverty (and emerging urban poverty with increasing layoffs from SOEs) is a well-recognized problem, addressed in the 1980s and 1990s by the Chinese government's poor area policies. China uses a particular concept of poverty and measures poverty on the basis of counties. The basic idea of this poverty concept is regional scarcity of natural resources, infrastructures, etc. in the Chinese hinterland. Poverty-stricken counties are targeted for special poverty alleviation programmes ('poor county concept').

It is open to question whether this regional concept has ever been appropriate for poverty analysis in China. Today, inter-regional disparities have been joined by intra-regional social stratification. In 1990, less than one-half of China's poor actually lived in designated poor counties [*Cook and White*, 1998: 12]. New types of risk (unemployment, redundancy, etc.)

have emerged and created vulnerability and poverty among individuals and households. Economic growth does not automatically lead to a reduction of vulnerability and poverty persists. Poverty is a real phenomenon in rural China, and people affected lack well-being in different respects.[21]

Income poverty is a widely used measure but, as mentioned above, income reflects only partially the living standard of people, particularly in rural areas. The more refined Human Poverty Index in developing countries (HPI-1) tries to assess basic living conditions [*HDR*, 1999]. In China 7.9 per cent of the total population do not survive to age 40; there is 17.1 per cent adult illiteracy; 33 per cent of the population are without access to safe water (1990–97), an unknown number lack access to health services (1981–92) and 76 per cent to sanitation (1990–97); 16 per cent of the children under age five are underweight (1990–97) [*HDR*, 1999: 147]. The index reports national averages; disaggregated for rural and urban areas, it would undoubtedly show much greater deprivation in rural areas. As to the Human Development Index (HDI), disparities exist not only between rural and urban areas, but also between regions (counties) and gender.

I do not want to go into a more detailed discussion on particular income and poverty indices.[22] In the assessment of well-being, a shift has been proposed from 'commodity or utility based frames' (possession of a commodity, utility it provides) to 'capability or functional frames' (what a person/household actually succeeds in doing with the commodities) [*Saith and Harriss-White*, 1999: 466]. Two ways to assess well-being (and poverty) in rural China can be suggested: first, we need better composite indicators of relevant 'functions' for health ('being healthy'), nutrition ('being nourished'), education ('being educated'), and others. This allows a better understanding of deprivation, for example in the context of gender inequalities. Second, I suggest the above-mentioned analytical framework and a focus on households and household members. Households seem to be a much better unit of measurement than counties or regions, although this is based on the questionable assumption of equal resource sharing between members of the households. The lack of access to core resources within and outside the household (economic, human and social capital) increases vulnerability and exposes rural people to a wide variety of risks. An institutional setting in which lack of access to the resources of one institution (state – market – intermediate organization – family) cannot be compensated for by access to the resources of another intensifies vulnerability and poverty.

CONCLUSION

Welfare in rural China is the outcome of a wide range of institutions, which contribute with their particular resources to people's livelihood. This institutional setting is best understood through the notion of 'welfare pluralism'. Rural households are no mere victims of unfavourable circumstances but actively respond to the situations in which they find themselves. Successful coping with anticipated fluctuations and unanticipated shocks depends on a variety of household resources and claims. A short-term and a long-term perspective on results is necessary ('sustainability'), as short-term responses (selling animals or crops) may solve a critical situation but rule out future incomes.

The debate on welfare in rural China has to address questions on how to empower and reduce the vulnerability of certain groups, households and families, women and the elderly. This includes direct welfare provision for those particularly vulnerable groups and/or impoverished people who are not in a position to achieve self-help in their local setting. The concept of welfare has a deep impact on matters of distribution and social inclusion of the population. During several decades, China had been upholding a rural–urban divide, with its exclusive and privileged enterprise-based system of welfare provision to urban workers. Now it faces a diverse and multifaceted system based on local residence, kinship and entrepreneurial activities. Growing vulnerability (owing to factors such as market imperfections, crises, globalization, WTO) may add new tensions and threaten social stability.

NOTES

1. Linda Wong [1998: 9–10] emphasizes that the Chinese term 'social security' (*shehui baozhang*) refers to an inclusive concept that covers all types of social arrangements for care and support. She cites Lu Mouhua's authoritative definition, which reflects the government's thinking. Lu subsumes 'social welfare' and 'social relief' under 'social security'. Wong states that in the West, the equivalent term would be 'social welfare'. 'Social security' is primarily identified with income maintenance, 'social welfare' incorporates social services in kind and transfers (payments, benefits).
2. Wong [1998: 157] states that the unique character of the Chinese welfare system stems from its 'bifurcation into two modes – one broad, one narrow – and differential entitlements for the rural masses and urbanites …'.
3. (SOE) state owned enterprises, (COE) collective owned enterprises.
4. There are pivotal research studies on the health sector such as the three county study in Donglan (Guangxi), Shibing (Guizhou) and Xunyi (Shaanxi) in 1994 [*Wilkes* et al., 1997, *Yu* et al., 1998].
5. Croll and Huang [1997: 146] propose to 'further investigate the relations between migration, agriculture and non agriculture and between migrant, household and village within the varying clusters of national and economic conditions that make up rural China'.
6. Nobody can expect China to build up a comprehensive social security system in urban and rural areas within a short time. The industrialized countries had 100 years in which to establish a state-based social security system, which is presently questioned because of diminishing public finances (a fact well recognized by Chinese observers!), and there is an intensive and never-ending discussion on the state's role in redistribution. It is a political debate on the rationale of the welfare state and the method of social inclusion.

7. Yao [2000: 447–8], states that the official figure of 270 million rural poor in 1978 was far too low.
8. The *hukou* system limited people's regional mobility and is now of less importance, family policy has been loosened but still constrains people's decision-making power.
9. 'Welfare mix' is the welfare situation of individuals as a result of resources and services of various public and private as well as formal and informal welfare institutions [*Andreß*, 1999: 18].
10. As far as we know from empirical research on old age in Germany, the overwhelming majority of elderly people remain in their private dwellings (95 per cent) and live within a short distance of at least one of their children.
11. Original idea for the table in Evers and Olk [1996: 23].
12. This ideal conception of economic exchange is contested by economists [*Granovetter*, 1985] and development sociologists [*Elwert*, 1985].
13. Well-being is not identical with a certain standard of living. 'The value of the living standard lies in the living, and not in the possession of commodities' [*Sen*, 1985: 25].
14. Original idea for the graph in Andreß [1999: 17].
15. Rotating savings and credit associations ('ROSCA') are a possible example [*Tsai*, 2000].
16. Selden [1998: 27] points out regional differences in ownership: a significant part of TVEs in southern Jiangsu is state owned, Guangdong has an 'eclectic mix of ownership forms, with a growing portion of private Chinese and foreign capital often linked with local government investment', and in northern Jiangsu and Wenzhou (Zhejiang), nearly all enterprises are family or jointly owned.
17. (1) Separation of social welfare from its previous enterprise base; (2) decentralization of welfare provisioning so that local governments became key actors; (3) establishment of non-profit organizations (NGOs) to fill gaps in vital welfare functions; (4) strengthening of the informal community and family self-provisioning [*Croll*, 1999: 694–6].
18. 'Making sense of the TVE phenomenon requires refining and recasting concepts of ownership and management in order to capture the range and complexity of the social relations linking individuals, communities, multiple layers of the state and corporate capital in the realms of labor, land, income, subsistence and much more than can ever be captured by formal title' [*Selden*, 1998: 29].
19. I admit that the research design will be rather complicated, and the empirical realization will face many problems. Croll and Huang [1997] describe the situation in their eight-village investigation as clusters made up of natural, economic and political conditions and with varying combinations between agriculture, non-agriculture and migration. In each cluster, emphasis is given to one or two of the economic activities, various action patterns corresponding to the local conditions.
20. 'Resources outside the household, particularly those accessed through informal social networks, were important sources of financial and labour support' [*Wilkes* et al., 1997: 23].
21. The measurement of overall poverty depends entirely on the concept, its operationalization and the definition of poverty lines. Therefore, estimates on poverty in rural China vary widely. The State Statistical Bureau estimated 65 million rural poor in 1995, using the annual per capita income of 500 *yuan*. The World Bank cites the national poverty line (1989–94) with 11.0 per cent poor among the total population. By contrast, when using the internationally comparable purchasing power parity measure (1985-PPP $1 a day) the World Bank estimated 29.4 per cent of the population living in poverty (urban and rural population, 1989–94) [*HDR*, 1999: 147].
22. In developed societies, great emphasis is given to elaborate a living standard index, reflecting the relative position or deprivation with respect to the nationally accepted standard.

REFERENCES

Ahmad, Ehtisham and Athar Hussain, 1991, 'Social Security in China: A Historical Perspective', in Ethisham Ahmad, Jean Drèze, John Hills and Amartya Sen (eds.), *Social Security in Developing Countries*, Oxford: Clarendon Press, pp.247–304.

Andreß, Hans-Jürgen, with Eckhard Burkatzki, Gero Lipsmeier, Kurt Salentin, Katja Schulte and Wolfgang Strengmann-Kuhn, 1999, *Leben in Armut: Analysen der Verhaltensweisen armer Haushalte mit Umfragedaten*, Opladen: Westdeutscher Verlag.

Bloom, Gerald and Andreas Wilkes (eds.), 1997, *Health in Transition: Reforming China's Rural Health Services*, IDS Bulletin, Vol.28, No.1, Brighton, Sussex: Institute of Development Studies.

Cook, Sarah and Gordon White, 1998, 'The Changing Pattern of Poverty in China: Issues for Research and Policy', IDS Working Paper No.69, Brighton, Sussex: Institute of Development Studies.

Croll, Elisabeth J., 1999, 'Social Welfare Reform: Trends and Tensions', *The China Quarterly*, No.159 (Sept.), pp.684–99.

Croll, Elisabeth J. and Huang Ping, 1997, 'Migration For and Against Agriculture in Eight Chinese Villages', *The China Quarterly*, No.149 (March), pp.128–46.

Drèze, Jean and Amartya Sen, 1991, 'Public Action for Social Security: Foundations and Strategy', in Ehtisham Ahmad, Jean Drèze, John Hills and Amartya Sen (eds.), *Social Security in Developing Countries*, Oxford: Clarendon Press, pp.1–40.

Elwert, Georg, 1985, 'Märkte, Käuflichkeit und Moralökonomie', in *Soziologie und gesellschaftliche Entwicklung*, Verhandlungen des 22. Deutschen Soziologentages in Dortmund 1984, Frankfurt/Main, New York: Campus Verlag, pp.509–19.

Esping-Andersen, Gösta, 1990, *The Three Worlds of Welfare Capitalism*, Princeton, NJ: Princeton University Press.

Evers, Adalbert and Thomas Olk, 1996, 'Wohlfahrtspluralismus – Analytische und normativ-politische Dimensionen eines Leitbegriffs', in Adalbert Evers and Thomas Olk (eds.), *Wohlfahrtspluralismus: Vom Wohlfahrtsstaat zur Wohlfahrtsgesellschaft*, Opladen: Westdeutscher Verlag, pp.9–60.

Faist, Thomas, 1995, 'Sociological Theories of International South to North Migration: The Missing Meso-Link', Centre for Social Policy Research, University of Bremen, ZeS Arbeitspapier, No.17.

Granovetter, Mark, 1985, 'Economic Action and Social Structure: The Problem of Embeddedness', *American Journal of Sociology*, No.91, pp.481–510.

Guldin, Gregory Eliyhu (ed.), 1997, *Farewell to Peasant China: Rural Urbanization and Social Change in the Late Twentieth Century*, Armonk, NY and London: M.E. Sharpe.

Hare, Denise, 1999, 'Women's Economic Status in Rural China: Household Contributions to Male–Female Disparities in the Wage-Labor Market', *World Development*, Vol.27, No.6, pp.1011–29.

HDR, 1999, *Human Development Report 1999*, New York: Human Development Report Office, United Nations Development Programme.

Hebel, Jutta, 1997, 'Chinesische Staatsbetriebe zwischen Plan und Markt: Von der 'danwei' zum Wirtschaftsunternehmen', Mitteilungen des Instituts für Asienkunde, No.277, Hamburg.

Heberer, Thomas and Wolfgang Taubmann, 1998, *Chinas ländliche Gesellschaft im Umbruch: Urbanisierung und sozio-ökonomischer Wandel auf dem Lande*, Opladen: Westdeutscher Verlag.

Huang, Shu-min and Stewart Odend'hal, 1998, 'Fengjia: A Village in Transition', in Walder (ed.) [1998: 86–114].

Johnson, Graham E., 1993, 'Family Strategies and Economic Transformation in Rural China: Some Evidence from the Pearl River Delta', in Deborah Davis and Stevan Harrell (eds.), *Chinese Families in the Post-Mao Era*, Berkeley, Los Angeles and London: University of California Press, pp.103–36.

Kaufmann, Franz-Xaver, 1994, 'Staat und Wohlfahrtsproduktion', in Hans-Ulrich Derlien, Uta Gerhardt and F.U. Scharpf (eds.), *Systemrationalität und Partialinteresse*, Festschrift für Renate Mayntz, Baden-Baden: Nomos Verlagsgesellschaft, pp.357–80.

Khan, Azizur Rahman and Carl Riskin, 2001. *Inequality and Poverty in China in the Period of Globalization. New Evidence on Trend and Pattern*. New York et al.: Oxford University Press.

Krieg, Renate and Monika Schädler (eds.), 1994, 'Social Security in the People's Republic of China', Mitteilungen des Instituts für Asienkunde, No.231, Hamburg.

Krieg, Renate and Monika Schädler, 1995, 'Soziale Sicherheit im China der neunziger Jahre', Mitteilungen des Instituts für Asienkunde, No.245, Hamburg.

Li, Jiang Hong and William Lavely, 1998, 'Determinants of Women's Status in Rural China', paper originally presented at the annual meeting of Population Association of America, 9–11 May 1996, New Orleans.

Lin, Jiang, 1995, 'Changing Kinship Structure and its Implications for Old Age Support in Urban and Rural China', Population Studies, No.49, pp.127–45.

Lin, Nan and Chen Chih-Jou Jay, 1999, 'Local Elites as Officials and Owners: Shareholding and Property Rights in Daqiuzhuang', in Jean C. Oi and Andrew Walder (eds.), Property Rights and Economic Reform in China, Stanford: Stanford University Press, pp.145–70.

Ludwig, Monika, 1996, Armutskarrieren: Zwischen Abstieg und Aufstieg im Sozialstaat, Opladen: Westdeutscher Verlag.

Mallee, Hein, 1998, 'Rural Labour Mobility in China', in Flemming Christiansen and Zhang Junzuo (eds.), Village Inc.: Chinese Rural Society in the 1990s, Richmond: Curzon Press, pp.212–29.

Pennarz, Johanna, 1998, 'Adaptive Land-Use Strategies of Sichuan Smallholders – Subsistence Production and Agricultural Intensification in a Land-Scarce Poverty Area of China', in Flemming Christiansen and Zhang Junzuo (eds.), Village Inc.: Chinese Rural Society in the 1990s, Richmond: Curzon Press, pp.159–76.

Pieke, Frank N., 1998, 'Networks, Groups, and the State in the Rural Economy of Raoyang County, Hebei Province', in Eduard B. Vermeer, Frank N. Pieke and Chong Woei Lien (eds.), Cooperative and Collective in China's Rural Development: Between State and Private Interests, Armonk, NY and London: M.E. Sharpe, pp.256–72.

Qian, Wenbao, 1996, Rural–Urban Migration and Its Impact on Economic Development in China, Aldershot, Brookfield, Hong Kong, Singapore, Sydney: Ashgate.

Rozelle, Scott, Li Guo, Shen Minggao, Amelia Hughart and John Giles, 1999, 'Leaving China's Farms: Survey Results of New Paths and Remaining Hurdles to Rural Migration', The China Quarterly, No.158 (June), pp.367–93.

Saith, Ruhi and Barbara Harriss-White, 1999, 'The Gender Sensitivity of Well-being Indicators', Development and Change, No.30, pp.465–97.

Selden, Mark, 1993, 'Family Strategies and Structures in Rural North China', in Deborah Davis and Stevan Harrell (eds.), Chinese Families in the Post-Mao Era, Berkeley, Los Angeles and London: University of California Press, pp.139–64.

Selden, Mark, 1998, 'Household, Cooperative, and State in the Remaking of China's Countryside', in Eduard B. Vermeer, Frank N. Pieke and Chong Woei Lien (eds.), Cooperative and Collective in China's Rural Development: Between State and Private Interests, Armonk, NY and London: M.E. Sharpe, pp.17–45.

Selden, Mark and You Laiyin, 1997, 'The Reform of Social Welfare in China', World Development, Vol.25, No.10, pp.1657–68.

Sen, Amartya, 1985, The Standard of Living, The Tanner Lectures, Clare Hall, Cambridge: Cambridge University Press.

Tsai, Kellee S., 2000, 'Banket Banking: Gender and Rotating Savings and Credit Associations in South China', The China Quarterly, No.61 (March), pp.142–70.

Walder, Andrew G. (ed.), 1998, Zouping in Transition: The Process of Reform in Rural North China, Cambridge, MA and London: Harvard University Press.

White, Gordon, 1998, 'Social Security Reforms in China: Towards an East Asian Model?' in Roger Goodman, Gordon White and Kwon Huck-ju (eds.), The East Asian Welfare Model: Welfare Orientalism and the State, London, New York: Routledge, pp.175–97.

White, Gordon and Roger Goodman, 1998, 'Welfare Orientalism and the Search for an East Asian Welfare Model', in Roger Goodman, Gordon White and Kwon Huck-ju (eds.), The East Asian Welfare Model: Welfare Orientalism and the State, London, New York: Routledge, pp.3–24.

Wilkes, Andreas, Yu Hao, Gerald Bloom and Gu Xingyuan, 1997, 'Coping with the Costs of Severe Illness in Rural China', IDS Working Paper No.58, Brighton.

Wong, Linda, 1995, 'Reforming Welfare and Relief – Socializing the State's Burden', in Linda

Wong and Stewart MacPherson (eds.), *Social Change and Social Policy in Contemporary China*, Aldershot, Hong Kong, Singapore, Sydney: Avebury, pp.50–69.

Wong, Linda, 1998, *Marginalization and Social Welfare in China*, London and New York: Routledge.

Yao, Shujie, 2000, 'Economic Development and Poverty in China over 20 Years', *Economic Development and Cultural Change*, Vol.48, No.3, pp.447–74.

Yu, Hao, Henry Lucas, Gu Xing Yuan and Shu Bao Gang, 1998, 'Financing Health Care in Poor Rural Counties in China: Experiences from a Township Based Co-operative Medical Scheme', IDS Working Paper No.66, Jan. 1998, Brighton, Sussex: Institute of Development Studies.

Zapf, Wolfgang, 1984, 'Welfare Production: Public vs. Private', *Social Indicators Research*, No.14, pp.263–74.

Gender Difference in Inheritance Rights: Observations from a Chinese Village

HEATHER XIAOQUAN ZHANG

INTRODUCTION

This article analyses intergenerational transfer of resources within households and village communities in Chinese rural society from both social policy and gender perspectives.[1] The process of intergenerational transfer of resources assumes varied forms. It can occur through market mechanisms, such as credit arrangements via either financial institutions or family and kinship networks. Government intervention in social welfare through its taxation as well as borrowing policies, and its spending on public good, such as education for the young and state pensions for the retired, represents another form of transfers between generations [*Ermisch*, 1989: 17–32; *Kessler*, 1989; *Lee and Miller*, 1994: 1027–63]. In addition, an important channel through which 'capital' flows from one generation to another is gifts, bequests and inheritance within the family [*Barro and Feldstein*, 1978; *Becker*, 1974: 1063–93; *Finch*, 1996: 120–34]. Despite its locus in the private domain and at the micro-level, the last vehicle has helped transfer as much resources between the generations as do public sector entitlements in industrial societies [*Mogey*, 1991: 47–66].

In spite of its recent inroads into Western social policy and welfare analysis, the phenomenon of intergenerational transfer of resources has received insufficient attention in studies on welfare provision in developing or transitional societies, despite the fact that the micro-socio-economic aspect of intergenerational relationships and its policy implications are very relevant there. On the other hand, feminist researches, inspired by Amartya Sen's model of 'cooperative conflicts' in household decision-making [*Sen*, 1990: 123–49], have attempted to open the black box of intra-household gender power relations, which are largely invisible in the predominant

Heather Xiaoquan Zhang, Lecturer, Department of Geography, Chester College, Parkgate Road, Chester CH1 4BJ, UK. Email: h.zhang@chester.ac.uk. I wish to thank Cecile Jackson, John Thoburn, Peter Ho and Jacob Eyferth for their helpful comments and suggestions on this article. However, I am solely responsible for the views expressed as well as any errors and omissions therein.

'unitary household' model.[2] What has been revealed in such studies is gender differentiation in household redistribution of resources as well as well-being outcomes manifested in such aspects as nutrition, education, life expectancy and sex ratios [*Harriss*, 1990: 351–424; *Saith and Harriss-White*, 1999: 465–97]. Combining the above two approaches in relation to the household, especially drawing on the insights provided by feminist analyses, this article intends to look at a special aspect of intra-household relations – the gendered intergenerational transfer of resources within the rural household and village society, and its welfare implications for women in the Chinese development context. Particular attention is paid to varied inheritance practices in different types of households and marriages (for example all-daughter households versus households with both daughters and sons; uxorilocal versus virilocal marriages). The article also examines the dynamics as well as continuity of the inheritance regime, and its interaction with the existing patriarchal structure on the one hand, and broader socio-economic changes on the other hand. In so doing, I hope both to contribute to feminist scholarship on intra-household gender relations and to bring a gender perspective to bear on the literature on intergenerational transfer of resources in order to serve as useful reference for decision-makers in their policy responses to the changing situations in rural families and communities.

The article is divided into six sections. Following this introduction, section two explains the methodology and sources of the research. It provides detailed accounts of the epistemological rationale of the qualitative methods adopted in this study, the interviewing and sampling criteria, as well as the selection and characteristics of the fieldwork location. Section three discusses gender differentiation in intergenerational transfer of resources in the form of inheritance in both national and local settings. It maps a tilting landscape where women's inheritance rights have been constantly negated by customs and norms. In the meantime, and more importantly, it presents a dynamic picture where agency is actively played out by women in their struggle against the patriarchal structure, questioning its legitimacy and contesting its gendered boundaries. The section especially pays attention to daughters' inheritance rights in all-daughter households, and the complex interactions between institutions, perceptions and practices on the one hand, and the more recent legislation on marriage, inheritance and women's rights on the other.

Section four analyses the linkages between the prevalent rural marital practice – virilocal marriage – and the customary exclusion of daughters from inheritance. Special attention is paid to women's inheritance rights in households with both daughters and sons, where intra-household competition over resources among the younger generation of opposite sexes exists. The section examines both the structural constraints and the more recent challenges to the patriarchal structure posed by broader socio-economic changes and women's increased access to waged employment and better education. This section also looks at the transfer and redistribution processes occurring in village communities, and examines how recent changes interacted with the existing structures have affected local policies, producing new gendered patterns of vulnerability and deprivation in respect of access to and control of resources. Counter-arguing against the cultural assumption that perceives a son as the sole, one-way supporter for elderly parents, section five looks at the direction of wealth flows from parents to sons prior to inheritance. In addition, it argues that apart from the inherent gender bias in the existing inheritance regime, the salient urban–rural division in terms of social provision serves as another structural barrier to fundamentally challenging the patriarchal and patrilineal inheritance system. The section discusses as well the declining role of the traditional tight-knit familial and kinship ties in providing security as a result of rapid industrialization, urbanization and the official family planning programme. The social policy issue concerning state responsibilities for establishing public social provision in the countryside, as well as the welfare implications of the current status for rural people in general, and women in particular are then examined. Finally section six draws tentative conclusions from the analysis of the earlier sections.

METHODOLOGY AND SOURCES

The research is based mainly on fieldwork conducted in a north China village in the summer of 1994. Broadly speaking, the fieldwork research strategy is informed and influenced by grounded theory developed by Glaser and Strauss [1967], who argued that concepts and theories in social sciences must be solidly 'grounded' in empirical reality represented by firsthand information and data gathered in fieldwork. In light of this understanding, they viewed the process of social research as inductive, where the social investigator starts his or her research with an open mind, and any theme, pattern or theory emerges and develops during the course of the study rather than being predetermined by hypotheses or existing theoretical frameworks.

The research method used in the study, accordingly, falls into the category of qualitative research. Adopting an observational, interactive and contextual approach, it is largely composed of in-depth interviews with village women. This approach is to enable the village women to represent themselves and to express their own understanding of the more recent legal, economic and social changes as well as their repercussions in the village. In this way, it is expected that rural women's experiences in terms of both the constraints imposed by the patriarchal structure on their lives and women's own agency role in questioning and contesting the existing arrangements will emerge from the interviews in all their complex reality. The selections of the people and the location for the fieldwork took into account the general accessibility of the women as social actors and their settings, the probability of their possession of the properties, processes and interactions most relevant to the present study, as well as available resources for the fieldwork.

The selection of the women informants followed the qualitative principle of non-probability sampling [*Denscombe*, 1998; *Erlandson* et al., 1993], where random or representative sampling of a large size was not given primary consideration, as my major concern was not with the generalizability of the research findings to a wider universe but with the exploration of the heterogeneous patterns and dynamic processes that took place in the village. My sampling method falls into the subcategory known as 'judgement or opportunistic sampling' [*Burgess*, 1984/1993: 55], where the informants were selected for interview in accordance with a set of criteria to meet my research needs, such as age, sex, occupation, marital status, education and household income levels, and in consideration of their availability and willingness to cooperate at the time.

The size of the interview sample is relatively small: 15 village women plus officials at village, township and county levels. The non-randomly selected small size, though non-representative by quantitative standards, is in keeping with the aims and parameters of the qualitative approach, particularly feminist methodology, which sets depth, details and insights into the intricacies of the gendered social reality and processes, as well as female experiences as its priorities [*Harding*, 1987; *Warren*, 1988]. It is worth noting as well that the size of the interview sample was not predetermined at the outset of the research. Rather, guided by the grounded theory, especially its concept of 'theoretical saturation' [*Glaser and Strauss*, 1967; *Marshall and Rossman*, 1989], and based on the qualitative understanding of social research as a process of discovering an unfolding reality, the study made the decision in the field: the sampling ceased when no fresh data were added to the already obtained information on the research categories and themes.

Face-to-face interviews with village women were conducted in repeated individual sessions lasting for three to four hours. These interviews were semi-structured, based on questionnaires and dominated by open-ended questions. Some group sessions took place with village officials. Interviews with other civil servants, such as women cadres, and officials at township and county levels were unstructured in situations resembling natural conversations. Unlike structured interviews with standardized schedules in terms of questions and answers, my interviews allowed the informants to describe events, give retrospections, relate processes and experiences, and express widely their perceptions and preferences on topics and issues that were significant to their lives and relevant to the research. The information and data gathered via such interviews also enabled me to assume a dynamic, historical perspective, linking the micro-aspects of women's experiences and intra-household power relations with meso- and macro-impact of legislation and policies. The 15 village women interviewed were chosen from different marital status categories (single, married, divorced, widowed), three age groups (25 and under, 26–45, 46 and above), and households at varied income levels (low, medium, high), as well as in different marital arrangements (virilocal, uxorilocal).

Dongdatun village in north China was selected as the location for interviewing rural women. It was a fairly big village with a population of more than 1,300 [*Lüzhuangzi Township Council*, 1992: 1]. The village was a brigade during the collectivization period from the late 1950s till the late 1970s. Nowadays, it is among the 22 villages in varied sizes under the administration of Lüzhuangzi township, the seat of a former people's commune. The township is located in Jixian county about 120 km from both Beijing and Tianjin, although administratively it is within the broad jurisdiction of the Tianjin municipal government. The per capita income of the village was 993 *yuan* in 1992, which ranked it medium as against the township's average of 1,000 *yuan* for that year [*Lüzhuangzi Township Council*, 1992: 13], but upper-middle compared with the national average of 784 *yuan* for the same year [*Qin*, 1993: 3].

In spite of its relatively high income level, Dongdatun was not deemed as particularly advantageous in resource endowment. It lies about 2 km to the southeast of a chain of hills, and its farmland becomes hilly as it extends in that direction. Furthermore, during the first half of the 1980s, a reservoir was built near Dongdatun in order to solve the problem of drinking water for Tianjin. According to the village officials, the reservoir submerged some 200 *mu* of Dongdatun's fertile land (1 *mu* = 1/15 hectare), about one-third of its total arable land. This further exacerbated the existing problem of land shortage, reducing its arable land to as little as 0.5 *mu* per person in 1992 [*Lüzhuangzi Township Council*, 1992: 1, 4]. Because of its typographical features and its land loss owing to the infrastructural project, Dongdatun was classified as a semi-mountainous, reservoir area and enjoyed some special treatment from the municipal government of Tianjin. As a compensatory measure for the village's shrunken land, the government exempted the villagers from agricultural tax.

For the past decade and more, Dongdatun's economic and social landscapes have been considerably reshaped by the post-Mao market reforms. When I visited the village, its economy was characterized by a marked diversification of rural livelihoods manifested in the rapid growth of rural industry, a diversification of ownership structure and development of sidelines. In these respects, Dongdatun can be viewed as reflecting the general trends of rural China since the late 1970s. In addition, livelihood diversification either in the form of migration or rural industrial development has had particular implications for social institutions, such as marriage, the family and intra-household gender relations, as well as welfare provision and outcomes. As will be shown in the following analysis, the more recent economic and societal changes witnessed in the village are gradually altering the bargaining leverage of men and women within rural households and village community with respect to transfer and redistribution of resources. In the meantime, new patterns of inclusion/exclusion and vulnerability in terms of security and welfare differentiated by, among other things, gender are emerging in the current transitional context.

It should be noted that the research methods used in my study share the inherent weaknesses of the qualitative approach as identified by many research methodologists – the limits in its representativeness and generalizability [*Burgess*, 1984/1993; *Creswell*, 1994: 158–9]. Such weaknesses are partly rectified by the use of other, more broad-based sources including government documents, statistics, newspapers, and relevant research findings and survey results at regional and national levels. These types of data are used as well both to compare with and to double-check the validity of this locally collected, detailed information. The utilization of such supplementary data, furthermore, represents an effort to bring in a wider social context in which the face-to-face interactions of the field research occurred, and to make linkage between this micro-study and its macro-implications.

DAUGHTERS' INHERITANCE RIGHTS: NATIONAL AND LOCAL SCENARIOS

As indicated above, the private dimension of intergenerational transfer of resources in the form of inheritance as a valued source of security and welfare for individuals within households is especially important in the development or transition context. This is largely due to the fact that in such economies public social provision has either been limited or underdeveloped owing to resource constraints, insufficient infrastructural building or withdrawal of the state from the domain. This is the case in rural China, where state, or collectively financed universal social security programmes have not been adequately established. As a result, most needs that have been met by socialized services in Western societies, and to a lesser degree, in Chinese urban settings, are still perceived as the responsibility of and shouldered by rural individuals, particularly their families [*Ahmad and Hussain*, 1991: 247–304; *Shi*, 1993: 468–80; *Wong*, 1998]. Furthermore, the bearings of inheritance on the welfare and financial security of individual members of rural families have increased considerably thanks to the growing personal wealth and family assets in rural households as a result of the quickened pace of economic development during the past couple of decades.

This directs attention to the transfer process occurring within the household. More recent studies on household income management and intra-household resource allocation have pointed to gender discrepancies in terms of access to, allocation and control of resources within the family or household [*Dasgupta*, 1997: 5–37; *Sen*, 1990: 123–49]. Informed by such studies, my research looks into the vertical processes of wealth flows within rural households, that is, between generations, in the form of inheritance, and examines gender differentiation, their dynamism, and the factors and forces underlying both the predominant patterns and their recent changes.[3] In fact, the question of women's inheritance rights in the Chinese countryside has involved several disparate issues, among which married daughters' inheritance to parental estates and remarried widows' inheritance rights in their previous married families have drawn most public attention and controversy. In this article, I focus discussion on the former issue, since it concerns more of 'vertical' than 'horizontal' flows of wealth within the household.

A national survey on Chinese women's status carried out jointly by the All-China Women's Federation and the State Statistical Bureau covering 11 provinces and major cities throughout the country in the early 1990s showed the Chinese public attitudes towards married daughters' inheritance to their parental property. Table 1 presents the survey results.

The survey results point to an acute gender asymmetry in attitudes held by the general public with respect to inheritance rights of sons and daughters. A couple of other interesting findings in relation to this observable asymmetry are also revealed, which may or may not be expected. One is the salient urban–rural gap in respect of people's attitudes towards married daughters' inheritance rights to their parental estates, with rural areas displaying greater gender bias. The other is the puzzling fact that, apparently, more women than men think unfavourably towards married daughters in terms of inheritance in their natal households. Important questions can be raised about the variables that have helped shape the different urban and rural perceptions of married daughters' equal inheritance rights, as well as about the complex factors behind the apparent female self-negating attitudes in respect of their own rights. To answer these

TABLE 1

ATTITUDES TOWARDS MARRIED DAUGHTERS' INHERITANCE TO
PARENTAL PROPERTY IN CHINA (%)

Attitudes	Urban			Rural		
	T	F	M	T	F	M
Equal share with brothers (yu xiongdi pingfen)	40.6	36.4	45.5	13.8	11.4	16.5
Smaller share than brothers (bi xiongdi shao xie)	7.9	7.2	8.6	9.7	9.4	10.1
Larger share than brothers (bi xiongdi duo xie)	0.6	0.6	0.6	0.5	0.6	0.4
Better not claim share (zuihao buyao)	10.1	12.0	7.9	15.6	16.0	15.2
Should not claim share (buyinggai yao)	10.6	11.8	9.2	40.5	44.0	36.7
Does not matter (wusuowei)	30.1	31.8	28.2	19.8	18.5	21.1

Source: ZFSDDK [1993: 307].

Note: T – Total; F – Female; M – Male. The 'does not matter' attitudes refer to those that regard
married daughters' entitlements to inheritance of parental property as 'context-dependent'
rather than universally eligible [ZFSDDK, 1993: 307–8].

questions requires an understanding of a set of institutions (urban–rural
differences in household structure, post-nuptial residence, female education
and employment opportunities, as well as the availability of public social
provisions), relationships (familial ties and kinship networks), the subtle
and intricate negotiating processes between the sexes and generations
within the household, and the complicated interactions between the existing
structure and the dynamics of societal processes. Discussions of the field
findings below are intended to shed some light on these aspects.

The figures presented in Table 1 have helped portray a general picture of
the public attitudinal orientation on the issue of gender equality in
inheritance. My fieldwork findings suggested a strong correlation between
people's attitudes and their social behaviour.

In Dongdatun, current inheritance practices varied in situations
involving different types of households. The most significant differences
appeared to be between all-daughter households (quan nü hu) and
households with both daughters and sons. Closely associated with this
distinction were marriage arrangements, which can be in conformity or in
discord with customs, norms and traditional familial ideals. The primary
marital arrangements in the village and its vicinity included the
predominant virilocal and the alternative uxorilocal post-nuptial
residences.[4] Here, the term of uxorilocal marriage refers to a particular

arrangement of post-nuptial residence, by which the groom moves into the bride's household at marriage, or, in the case of conjugal household, physically transfers to her native village, residing among her kin. This is in contrast with the dominant patrilineal organization in Chinese rural society manifested in, among other things, virilocal post-marital residence, by which the woman moves into the man's household, or into the man's village on marriage. It should be noted that although in many parts of today's rural China, including Dongdatun, many young couples form their own conjugal households either at, shortly or a few years after marriage, such a post-marital arrangement is distinct from the neo-locality of the nuclear family in its strict sense. This is because in most cases, women still have to move to their husbands' villages at marriage.

The dominant inheritance pattern in connection with the existing rural kinship organization and marriage institution can be detected from the following accounts of the village women:

> My parents paid for the wedding expenses and building the houses for my brothers. After their deaths, the family property was divided among my brothers. I didn't get any share of it [Interview with Wang Guifen, 52].

> Daughters don't inherit property after they are married. If a family has a son, daughters lose their inheritance rights to the son. Only when a family is sonless, do daughters have a chance to inherit [Interview with Wang Lifen, 22].

The inheritance practice revealed here is consistent with the findings of several researches on Chinese village life, the family and marriage. Gao [1999: 237], for instance, pointed out that in Gao village in southeast Jiangxi province, a married daughter was not entitled to any inheritance from her parents. Cohen's study on rural family management and family division in Hebei in the north, suburban Shanghai in the southeast and Sichuan in the southwest displayed a similar pattern [Cohen, 1992: 368]. In spite of the prevalent practice of excluding daughters from inheritance, spatial and temporal variations, particularly in relation to all-daughter households, were observed during my fieldwork.

In the years both before and after 1949 when the communists took power, transfers of wealth within rural households were strictly along the lineal line. It was the general practice in Dongdatun and the surrounding areas that daughters in sonless households were not deemed to be legal heirs by customs and norms, and the patrilineal negation of their inheritance rights were barely questioned. Moreover, inheritance by daughters in sonless households tended to be associated with uxorilocal marriage. Such marriage, however, was often looked down upon in the village community because of the Confucian cultural emphasis on patrilineage, sons and the centrality of parents–son relationships in the family.[5] The reality was that both uxorilocal marriage and the daughter's inheritance to the parental property in it met with strong resistance from agnate kin, who would otherwise inherit the deceased couple's estate. This had happened to 46-year-old Wang Guiying, who was one of the three daughters in an all-daughter household. When Guiying got married in the early 1960s, her unconventional uxorilocal marriage was strongly objected by her lineal cousin brother (*tangxiong*), who had coveted her parents' house. During the interview, Guiying recalled, 'I've been in a *zhaoxu* marriage, and when I got married, I was faced with huge social pressures and obstacles. It wasn't easy for me' [interview with Wang Guiying].

Owing to strong male opposition and the discrimination suffered by those involved in uxorilocal marriage, inheritance by daughters combined with such marriages were generally regarded as undesirable, and hence rare before post-Mao rural reforms. The adoption of a son from an agnate in the sonless household was normatively expected and practised whether or not the couple in question actually preferred such an arrangement. Although uxorilocal marriage and inheritance by a daughter in it were promoted and, to some extent, practised thanks to the government-launched campaigns known as 'transforming traditions and customs' (*yifeng yisu*) between the 1960s and 1970s, the actual effects of the official ideological propagation were limited. It is only during the past couple of decades that the number of uxorilocal marriages has started to increase significantly and inheritance by daughters in sonless families gradually become accepted norms. This is partly due to the fact that with the implementation of the family planning programme, more households than ever before have turned into all-daughter households. This scenario, in turn, has prompted the government at various levels to lay down regulations and laws that are considered favourable to daughters in such households in order to push ahead with its birth-control programme. A revised Marriage Law was introduced in 1980, which has affirmed in legal terms uxorilocal marriage and the unorthodox practice of adopting one's mother's surname (*suimuxing*) [ZHF, 1980: 64, 65].[6] The laws on inheritance and on protecting women's rights and interests enacted in 1985 and 1992, respectively, in response to the widened range of private property that has come into being with reforms and the increased disputes in connection with it, both state that women have the equal rights to property and inheritance with men [ZJ, 1985: 4; ZFQBF, 1992: 8, 9].[7]

Daughters' equal inheritance rights with sons are thus formally codified in the specific provisions of these laws. Such a legal framework plays an important role in empowering women through providing an instrument for women to claim their equal rights when faced with discrimination, and a basis for formal arbitration when property disputes involving a woman's rights arise. The influence of the legislation on the status of women in the family and the village community could be felt when the younger women in sonless households cited the laws and regulations either to justify their uxorilocal marriages, or to back their arguments for equal treatment of women and men with respect to inheritance:

> According to the law, a daughter has the same responsibility as a son does to support parents in their old age, therefore she should have the equal right to inherit the family's property. In my case, as I'm in a *zhaoxu* marriage, which has been encouraged by the government, I've been treated equally with men by the village policy in obtaining courtyard space (*fangjidi*) … [interview with Gu Weimin, 22].

> I've got my husband to move into my family. In the past the husband as well as the wife's family in a *zhaoxu* marriage would be looked down upon in the village. Nowadays such marriages are quite common. In recent years, there have been five girls in the village who have had their husbands married in … Now you won't be discriminated against for having a *zhaoxu* marriage [interview with Zhao Yuchun, 22].

The young women in uxorilocal marriage in the village today suffered less discrimination than their older counterparts thanks not only to the more recent extension of the legal framework to legitimate and protect their rights, but also to certain local regulations giving incentives to women in such households. According to the young village women and Lüzhuangzi township's family planning official Sun Hongmei, the encouraging measures formulated locally ranged from equal allocation of courtyard space, allowance of a second birth irrespective of the sex of the couple's first child,[8] to other special treatments to those all-daughter households that abide by the local family planning rules. Such treatments included preferences granted to all-daughter households in getting their contracted land watered during busy seasons when electricity and water were in short supply, in entrance by their children to the village nursery school when the number of openings was limited, and in their members being employed in the local rural enterprises.[9]

However, the practical recognition of daughters' rights in this respect as a more recent development has not extended beyond the all-daughter households, where intra-household competitions for resources between children of the opposite sexes are absent. When such competitions exist, most daughters then lose their rights to their vying brothers. As indicated in the interviews, daughters' loss in possible intra-household rivalries for inheritance is primarily due to the fact that the rural inheritance regime has been in the main sustained by the deep-ingrained concept of emphasizing men as the very root of the patriline:

> It is the custom. It isn't absolutely on the ground that sons rather than daughters support their aged parents. For example, if a family has three sons, the three sons will divide among themselves the property left over by their parents. Even if a daughter lives in the same village after marriage and shares the responsibility of taking care of the aged parents, she cannot join the sons to inherit the property. ... The practice is mainly based on the custom that values sons more than daughters [interview with Wang Guiying].

> It's old-fashioned ideas and tradition. A daughter's descendants wouldn't have the family's surname, and thus would be regarded as outsiders by the elderly. Now daughters can fulfil their duties to support parents as well. ... But people with old ideas still believe when daughters are married out, they are no longer members of the family, so they aren't entitled to inherit property [interview with Qi Sulan, 49].

VIRILOCAL MARRIAGE AND DAUGHTERS' LOSS OF INHERITANCE RIGHTS

The above observations of the women informants, together with the fact that gender inequality in inheritance is most notable in households with both daughters and sons, suggest a close association between the current rural inheritance regime and the prevalent custom of post-marital virilocality as pointed out by several studies on Chinese marriage, family and laws [*Buxbaum*, 1978: 19; *Cohen*, 1992: 368; *Ocko*, 1991: 330]. The distinction between urban and rural practices of post-nuptial residence may partly explain the marked urban–rural gap in public attitudes towards married daughters' inheritance rights as demonstrated in Table 1 above. In Chinese cities, young couples usually establish their own neo-local, nuclear families after marriage, whereas in the countryside, virilocal marriage has been the predominant norm. The following remarks by a village woman reflected the justification provided by the custom of virilocal marriage for the negation of daughters' inheritance rights:

> A married daughter is no longer seen as a member of her parents' family, but of her husband's family. ... A son has the duty to support the parents in old age, ... a daughter usually moves out of her natal village after marriage. ... The objective condition simply doesn't

allow her to stay by her parents' side and look after them for long [interview with Wang Guifen, 52].

When digging beneath the surface of a seemingly plausible duty-beneficiary argument for sons' exclusive inheritance, we can see that the virilocal marriage system has functioned to disadvantage women through its provision of a convenient justification for depriving women of their equal rights with their brothers. As sons stayed in their natal villages for life, it was seen as natural that the property of the parents was passed on to them. Moreover, the varied laws challenging the traditional practice in inheritance by emphasizing equal inheritance rights of sons and daughters have simultaneously conditioned such rights with the fulfilment of the duties that adult children should support their ageing parents. Such stipulations, however, have, in effect, helped relieve the modern state of its responsibilities for social provision by keeping in line with a cultural tradition, in which parents have relied on their grown-up children for old-age security. This contradiction built in the law with both the non-traditional elements in terms of daughters' inheritance rights and the more convention-oriented conditions for realizing such rights may be partly responsible for the ineffectiveness of the law in real life. As Ocko [1991: 330] pointed out, the premises prescribed by the law tended to be readily reinterpreted and accommodated in reality by the very custom of virilocality, since '… even some courts … held that "marrying out" should have the same effect (of forfeiting the obligation to care for one's elderly parents)'.

On the other hand, as shown earlier, although virilocal post-nuptial residence is still the convention in today's rural China, discursive norms like the uxorilocal one have been gaining greater visibility and significance since rural reforms. In addition, challenges to the deep-rooted custom of virilocality have come from the increase in rural women's mobility through, say rural–urban migration, their alternative employment opportunities and the new emphasis on rural women's education and training.

During my interviews with village women, Zhao Yuchun, who was a senior high school graduate and worked as a teacher in the village's nursery school, commented on the different educational policies and their impact on the parental attitudes towards daughters' education:

> Senior high school graduates today are different from their counterparts in the past. Before, the only occupation you could enter was agriculture, but now you have the chance and opportunity to find a more appropriate job. Qualifications and education are more stressed today. It'll be easier for people to find desirable jobs if they have senior high school graduation certificates. In the ads for employment or training programmes, it's often indicated that people with senior high school education are preferred. This has prompted

society to emphasize education and parents to pay more attention to their daughters' education. Now (off-farm) employment opportunities for girls have grown [interview with Zhao Yuchun].

Indeed, the trend of shifting perceptions on daughters' education thanks to increased possibilities for young women of gaining access to waged jobs either locally or away to the towns has been observed in many other parts of rural China. Gao's accounts of the social and cultural changes in Gao village, for instance, indicate that since the 1990s, Gao villagers' traditional attitudes towards daughters' education have been altered by rural–urban migration, and the greater demand on literacy and skills associated with better pay prospect in the urban labour market [*Gao*, 1999: 119–20].

Increased attention paid to daughters' education in response to the more recent changes in the structure and composition of the local economy in Dongdatun and its surrounding areas was visible from the higher level of education enjoyed by women in the youngest cohort in comparison with their older sisters and mothers. Among the village women informants aged 25 and younger, most were junior high school graduates, in contrast to the older women, of whom the majority were either illiterate or semi-literate with less than three years' schooling. In terms of employment, I was told by the village women representative that most unmarried girls and young wives in the village were now working in the nearby township- or village-run enterprises, such as garment factories and the brick kiln. The interplay between women's education and the waged employment opportunities induced changes in the convention of post-marital residence. Instead of moving into their husbands' villages upon marriage, many young village women with non-agricultural jobs now preferred staying in their natal village, if their husbands' villages were located in rather remote hilly regions, or less developed in rural industry and local economy. In this way, these women could keep their waged jobs in the non-farm sectors or continue enjoying the relative advantages of the village provided by its closer link with the city and the greater opportunities associated with it.[10]

This outcome of the economic and societal changes, however, did not receive much encouragement from the local arms of the state apparatus. According to the township and village officials, current local policies in this respect allowed young women who decided not to move out of their natal villages at marriage to stay and keep their waged jobs. However, the authorities refused to grant these women equal entitlements to the material benefits enjoyed by their fellow villagers, particularly married brothers, in the local redistribution of resources.[11] For instance, irrespective of a daughter's post-nuptial residence, her family would certainly lose the portion of land to the married daughter's name when the village government redivided the land once every few years.[12] She was also not to share the cash and other benefits, on top of her wages, distributed by local authorities from the village's collective income from varied sources, including those obtained from the profits of local enterprises and some one-off deals. One example was that the village sold some land in recent years to a Tianjin-based company seeking to explore local tourist resources, and part of the gains from the deal was distributed to the villagers. The staying-on married daughters from non-all-daughter households, however, were excluded from this type of local redistribution. Furthermore, the parents of a staying-on married daughter were denied extra courtyard space necessary for them to build a new house for the married daughter as they would be allowed for their married sons whether or not the sons still worked and lived in the village. The discriminative local policy against young staying-on married women in terms of allocation of courtyard space was highlighted by the contrast, favourable treatment granted to a household with five married sons. Although four of the sons had permanently migrated away from the village, the village authority still allocated sufficient courtyard spaces to allow the family to build one house in five separate courtyards for each of the sons.

Rapid economic and societal changes were taking place in Dongdatun, which were partly evidenced in such phenomena as increased number of marrying-in sons-in-law in all-daughter households, and staying-on married daughters or moving-out migrant sons in households with both daughters and sons. However, the previous rules for distribution of rights and entitlements of men and women, which had evolved on the basis of the conventional post-nuptial arrangements, seemed to stay intact. Negotiation over the rules and contestation about the norms and practices did occur, as suggested by the young women's unconventional marriage arrangements and their ability to retain their waged jobs in their natal village. However, the unbalanced gender power relations interacted with the existing structural constraints tended to produce new patterns of gendered exclusion, deprivation and vulnerability.

Studies conducted in other parts of the country have reported more serious problems concerning infringement of the rights and interests of rural married women who have refused to follow the conventions of virilocality. In her investigation into women's land use rights in connection with population mobility and demographic changes, such as marriages and births, in rural Sichuan province, Xu [1997: 32] noted that although uxorilocal marriage was legally recognized, and that there was a notable trend of increase in such marriages, local authorities tended to view the phenomenon as an unwelcome competition from women for the local scarce land resources. She found that such a view was often shared and backed by traditional customs and beliefs of the village community. As a result, various local regulations and policies were laid down to restrict uxorilocal marriages in the name of protecting the interests of the native villagers. In many localities, restrictions were put in place stipulating that only one daughter of a sonless household was allowed uxorilocal marriage. Other locally adopted constraints included prolonged delays in reallocating land to or even denial of land use rights of the marrying-in husband, and attempts to drive the staying-on married daughters out of their natal villages by demanding that they cancel their household registration there within short time limits after marriage [Xu, 1997: 32]. Such local policies have effectively produced and encouraged discrimination against uxorilocal marriages, or daughter-centred households.

In spite of the fact that married daughters who choose to reside in the natal village have made equal contributions to the locally accumulated resources, they have been excluded from the redistribution of resources by local regulations. This has shown the taken-for-grantedness of virilocal marriage as the established norm by local power holders as well as villagers. Underlying the local decisions are assumptions about the culturally defined spatial and social boundaries for a married daughter and the 'proper' gender relations regarding her: she is perceived as the Other and an outsider even if she does not move out of her natal village; and as a subordinate to her husband and property of him and his lineage in his village instead of an individual in her own right. This then brings out the non-material aspect of this exclusion: married daughters in their natal villages have been disenfranchised in terms of their membership (the local community) and citizenship (wider society), and effectively reduced to second-class citizens.

REVERSE FLOW OF FORTUNES PRIOR TO INHERITANCE

In addition to the problem of equating the fulfilment of one's duties to support elderly parents with virilocality as pointed out earlier, deprivation of daughters' rights to inheritance is based on the popular assumption of sons as one-way supporters of parents in old age. This assumption is typically expressed in an old saying *yanger fanglao*, which means to bear and rear sons for old-age security. However, as noted by many, intergenerational relations in China have been sustained on a more reciprocal than unilateral basis with respect to provisions of affection, assistance and finance [*Chen*, 1996; *Shi*, 1993: 468–80]. In line with such observations and contrary to the conventional assumption of sons as the one-way providers for parents, my field findings indicate that the intra-household, intergenerational resource transfers in Dongdatun were marked by a 'reverse flow of fortunes' from parents to adult sons occurring long before inheritance.

The marriage of a son and having heirs by a son are among the most important events in a rural household.[13] The parents often have to spend a major part of the household's pooled savings on the marriage, including paying for the increasingly expensive bride-wealth (caili), engagement (dingqin) and wedding ceremonies and banquets, and building a new house for the son.[14] As one village woman commented:

> ... But if I give you an itemized account, I wouldn't say with certainty that it (the practice of inheritance by sons only) is very fair. The parents build new houses and take care of the kids for the sons, but really don't need their sons to do much for them in return ... [interview with Yang Zhiying, 37].

Sometimes economic contributions by daughters to the household would be used for such purposes as well by the parents. In my contact with female migrant workers in Tianjin, I noticed that although some of these young women showed a greater individualistic tendency by disposing their wages at their own will, others tended to act more in conformity with the traditional requirements of performing filial duties [Zhang, 1999: 36]. The latter was achieved through remitting money (half to two-thirds of their income) back to their parents in the natal villages. With the parents acting as the redistributor, this money could find its way to the brother's pocket. The following account by Zhan Guifang, who worked in a joint venture factory producing cooking oil, is indicative:

> The money (the remainder of her wages that was sent back home, which represented some two-thirds of her income) will be used to build a new house for my younger brother in the future when he gets married. My dad says the priority is to build the house for my brother and after that, I'll be able to keep the money for myself [interview with Zhan Guifang, 21].

As the expenses born by the parents on bride-wealth, engagement and wedding ceremonies as well as house construction for the son can constitute a bulk of a rural household's pooled savings of the time, such expenditures are interpreted by some as a form of family partition before the deaths of parents, or 'pre-mortem inheritance' [Cohen, 1992: 368–70; Yan, 1997: 200]. In such cases, the property of the family based on the pooled contributions of its members, including those by the daughters, would be divided among the sons in a serial manner.

The parental support for the son usually continues after the son's marriage, ranging from helping with housework and looking after grandchildren, to attending domestic animals and contracted land for the son's family, as I observed in Dongdatun. This is also evident from the remarks by Yang Xuehong:

> He (the brother) hasn't given much money to my parents, because my parents still work themselves, and they've got enough money. My brother's family live with my parents. Economically they don't separate. So my parents have to subsidize them. What he has done is to buy some gifts for my parents during traditional festivals and holidays. We daughters have done the same thing. ... In fact, my younger sister is married into a household in the natal village. So when my parents get too old to work, my younger sister will take care of them as well. But even if my sister fulfils her duty to look after the aged parents, she cannot share with my brother in inheritance. ... I don't think this is fair [interview with Yang Xuehong, 25].

It was commonly acknowledged by the village women interviewees that daughters were closer to mothers, and compared with sons, they were more considerate, caring and thoughtful of their parents. Based on my understanding of the cultural heritage of a relatively competitive relationship between the mother-in-law and the daughter-in-law, I felt that the parents, particularly the mother, tended to view their daughter as more reliable than the married son as the possible source of emotional and material support in either need or old age. This perception of daughters as more 'loyal' to parents may also result from the cultural expectation of daughters as the more selfless and self-sacrificing members of the household in familial and intergenerational relations compared with their brothers. Moreover, daughters, even after marriage, tend to maintain strong emotional ties with their parents in natal families and continue providing care and support when needed [*Judd*, 1989: 541–3]. It has become particularly the case during the past decade and more when the daughter's economic contribution to her natal household has grown with the increasing possibility of her getting a paid job in either the rural enterprise or the urban industrial and tertiary sectors.

In addition, it is highly likely for a married daughter whose family by marriage is better off to make greater contributions, in terms of both cash and kind, than her brothers to the welfare of the parents and underage siblings. Development and expansion of modern transportation and communication networks in rural areas in the recent decades have significantly shortened the spatial and temporal distances between a married daughter and her natal village. This is especially so when intra-village, intra-surname marriages have become increasingly accepted and common in present-day rural society. Rural economic diversification and industrialization have also changed the scope of villagers' familial and social contacts: the traditional patrilineal ties within a natural village are extending to include more affinal relations in economic assistance and cooperation [*Judd*, 1989: 541–3; *Yang*, 1994: 157–79]. All this suggests married daughters' closer links with their natal families and undermines the cultural generalization of a son as the sole supporter of the parents in old age. And the roots of the prevailing inheritance regime in rural society were thus viewed by many women informants as the ideological centralization of sons stemming from the Confucian valuation of male descendants' exclusive role in continuing the family line (see the remarks in section three of the village women informants Wang Guiying and Qi Sulan).

Although many of the village women interviewees saw the current inheritance arrangements as the workings of a patriarchal ideology of valuing men but debasing women, and some showed disapproval, most of the women from families with sons neither did nor intended to claim their equal rights with their brothers to inheritance. Part of the reason for this seems to be associated with the cultural and social demand on women and the general socialization process internalizing the traditional criteria and expectations of a 'virtuous woman' (*xianhui*). Women were, and still are, expected not to assert their own interests in domestic settings, but to avoid intra-household disputes through persistently exercising forbearance and self-sacrifice [*Honig and Hershatter*, 1988]. As daughters and sisters in the natal household, women have been socially and culturally discouraged to claim their statutory rights to inheritance by such traditional values and requirements. On the other hand, there might be stakes for women in forfeiting their inheritance rights in their natal families. Indeed, despite the challenge to the traditional lineage organizations posed by the rapid industrialization and increased population mobility in rural China since the reforms, the power of the patrilineage are entrenched and still strong [*Gao*, 1999: 259–61]. Thus, it is vital for a woman to develop and forge strong links with her natal household including parents, brothers and lineal kin, in order to enhance her 'fallback position' in case her own marriage fails to work. In view of this, asserting her equal inheritance rights in the natal household may weaken the potential support that a woman expects to elicit from her natal lineage.

The general perception of the interests of a married woman as identical with those of her husband's and his family's, based largely on the traditional family as both an economic corporate unit and main social welfare agency, as well as women's subordinate position within it, also had a bearing upon the awareness of the village women about their own rights and interests. This was indicated by a few women interviewees' comments that although they did not enjoy equal inheritance rights with their brothers, they would inherit the property of their parents-in-law through their husbands. At first glance, there seems to be a balance, in terms of material benefits, between the inheritance rights that a woman loses to her brothers in the natal household and the property that her conjugal family may inherit from her husband's parents. However, a closer inspection reveals that the greater uncertainty and instability in marital relationships in the context of rapid socio-economic changes in present-day rural China has rendered more and more insecure women's indirect link to inheritance through conjugal ties.[15] Furthermore, the practice by which women gain access to inheritance only through their relationship with men has worked to deny women's equal inheritance rights in other ways, among which is the remarried widow's property and inheritance rights in her previous conjugal household. The existing inheritance regime stressing women's dependence on and subordination to men has had negative social and cultural implications for the position of women in the family and society. One such effect is on the consciousness of women as independent rights-bearing individuals, an effect that is discernible from the self-negating responses of rural women with respect to their own inheritance rights in the natal household as displayed in Table 1.

It seems that the internalized constraints (through socialization) that women carry with them combined with the external structural barriers (lineage organization, custom of virilocality, sons' exclusive inheritance rights and women's indirect association with inheritance) may provide a partial explanation for the largely negative attitudes of women themselves towards daughters' inheritance rights as shown earlier. Other explanations may be found in yet another set of structural constraints – the salient urban–rural gaps, which are often related to state social policy-making. These include, among other things, the division between urban and rural areas in welfare provision, particularly social security and support for the elderly. Unlike most people living in the cities who are entitled to basic state pensions and some old-age support services, rural people have long relied on themselves and their families, particularly sons in the dominant virilocal marital arrangement, for old-age security and support. Although during the past decade and more, pilot social security schemes jointly financed by local authorities and individual farmers, such as medical and old-age insurance, have emerged in the countryside, these have largely been confined to relatively better-off areas [*Ahmad and Hussain*, 1991: 247–304; *Feuchtwang*, 1987: 173–210; *Shi*, 1993: 468–80; *Yu*, 1995: 4]. This emerging trend and its current limitations were also observed in Dongdatun and its vicinity. Owing to the relative financial strength in conjunction with its higher development level, Lüzhuangzi township had been running a preliminary old-age insurance scheme since the early 1990s. However, the coverage of the scheme was not universal. Rather, it was operated on a selective hierarchical basis covering only the predominantly male village cadres of the 22 villages under the township's administration at the time of the fieldwork.

Lack of statutory mechanisms for old-age security has interacted with and reinforced the traditional emphasis on sons and patrilineage, customary denial of daughters' inheritance rights, as well as lineage organizations and their functions in providing security and protection within the structure. However, the traditional safety net built with extended and closely woven familial structures and kinship networks in subsistence agriculture is now faced with an imminent threat from greater rural industrialization, population mobility and the implementation of the official family planning programme. A provision vacuum may soon emerge in respect of social security and support during the transition from traditional to modern society. In this context, an active role of the government at various levels in introducing and extending rural social security programmes is deemed as a necessary and vital step to promote welfare for all, encourage alternative references as against the dominant male-centred norms and practices, and realize women's equal rights in inheritance in rural China.

CONCLUSION

A highly gendered pattern has emerged from this analysis of the process of intergenerational transfer of resources in the form of inheritance in rural China. The contrast between official legal recognition of women's equal rights with men and the *de facto* disenfranchizement of most rural women in inheritance represents a significant gap between legislation and social reality. Despite this general pattern, my research identifies a highly dynamic process characterized by not only continuity of, but also challenges to the patriarchal structures. Changes in rural economic structure and composition, greater urbanization and livelihood diversification, and the extension of the legal framework to the domain of women's equal rights in property and inheritance during the past couple of decades have contributed to a reshaping of social organizations, institutions and cultural perceptions. Improved opportunities for women to have waged jobs, education and training have increased their confidence in asserting their equal rights, as well as their bargaining power in intra- and extra-household transfer and redistribution of resources. This is evidenced in the young village women's unequivocal position on the legitimacy of uxorilocal marriage, the forceful claims by daughters in such marriages of their equal inheritance rights, as well as the increase in the number of staying-on married daughters in non-all-daughter households.

On the other hand, while the predominant norms and conventions of stressing men over women, virilocality and the customary denial of women's equal inheritance entitlements are being contested in varied ways, the possibility of fundamentally challenging the existing inheritance regime and the realization of women's full citizenship rights have been hampered by limitations of the laws and asymmetrical gender power relations. This is exemplified by the continued distribution of rights, benefits and risks between men and women in accordance with accepted patriarchal rules and conventions both within and outside the household. Furthermore, the conspicuous urban–rural differences in social provision marked, among other things, by the state inadequate action in establishing a basic universal system of social security and support have reinforced the structural constraints on the realization of women's equal entitlements to inheritance, as well as their membership and citizenship rights.

The traditional means by which women link to inheritance only indirectly through conjugal relations is now becoming less and less reliable in so far as women's welfare is concerned. This is largely due to the increasingly unstable marriage in a rapidly changing and uncertain environment emerging under market reforms. The prevailing perception of the interests of a married woman as identical with those of her husband and his family, expressed in common-sense understanding, relevant legislation and social policies has also negatively affected the consciousness of rural women as independent individuals and bearers of legal and social rights. The current patrilineal inheritance regime has redistributed and transferred resources horizontally and vertically. Interplaying with other structural arrangements, it has led to the emergence of new patterns of gendered exclusion, deprivation and vulnerability. This has affected women adversely not only in terms of their welfare and security, but also their position and power in both the private and public domains. While pluralist welfare provision is advocated in promoting the well-being of the rural population in China's current development situation, the problem of unequal entitlements and rights of men and women calls for more effective government interventions in the form of social policy-making to redress the balance and ensure more gender-equitable welfare outcomes.

NOTES

1. The term 'gender' is used in this article to refer to socially and culturally constructed categories based on individuals' biological differences. This is in contrast to the term 'sex', which refers to the biological characteristics by which human beings are categorized as male or female.
2. This model conceptualizes the household as a single unit with all its members having shared interests and preferences, which are represented by a benevolent or altruistic dictator, usually the male household head. For further discussions on the different household decision-making models, see Smith and Chavas [1999: 4]; Haddad et al. [1997].
3. The vertical dimension of intergenerational transfers should also include parental

investments in children's 'human capital', such as schooling, which are often differentiated by gender as well. The central concern of my research, however, is with processes of transfers that usually happen at the individual's later life stage.

4. The expressions in Chinese of uxorilocal marriage vary spatially as well as in different linguistic contexts. In some southern provinces such as Jiangxi, the term used is *zhaozhui* [*Gao*, 1999: 235], whereas in the area where I carried out fieldwork, it is called *zhaoxu*, which literally means a marriage involving a moving-in son-in-law. A more colloquial expression is *dao chu men*, which means a reversal of the conventional practice by a man marrying into a woman's house. The more traditionally used term is *ruzhui* and that for the moving-in son-in-law is *zhuixu*. Historically, however, these terms had discriminative meanings for both such households and the man involved [*Cihai Bianji Weiyuanhui*, 1979/1980: 309, 1439]. A written expression, which is adopted in academic writings and formal, legal documentation is *congqiju* (*congfuju* for virilocal marriage), which literally means that a man joins his wife in residence at marriage. In this article, I have adopted either the formal version of *congqiju* or the local expression of *zhaoxu* to refer to this type of post-marital arrangement.

5. For further analysis of both the traditional focus on parents–son relations within rural households and their being 'triumphed' by the rise of conjugal relationships in present-day village society, see Yan [1997: 191–212].

6. Articles 8 and 16 of the 1980 Marriage Law of the PRC.

7. Inheritance Law (1985): Articles 9 and 10. Law of the PRC on the Protection of Rights and Interests of Women (1992): Articles 28 and 31.

8. The local family planning regulations permit rural couples, except those in uxorilocal marriage, to have a second child only when their first birth is a girl. This finding confirms those of many other researches, which have criticized such family planning regulations for their cultural and gender implications. See Davin [1990: 81–91]; Greenhalgh and Li [1995: 601–41]; White [1994: 137–58] for more detailed discussions.

9. My interview with the township's family planning official indicated as well that the capacity of village authorities to deliver such beneficiary treatments varied considerably depending on the state of the village economy. The relative economic strength of Dongdatun was said to have enabled the village council to lend support for implementing such regulations.

10. In his study of rural industrialization and its effects on the socio-economic relations in rural Sichuan province in southwest China, Yang [1994: 159–79] observed a similar trend as discussed here. His focus, however, was on the expanded networks and social contact of the villagers with rural industrialization, which extended beyond familial and lineage relations in a natural village to include affinal ties and external market linkages.

11. The information was not provided by the local officials as an example to demonstrate gender inequality but to show their achievements in developing the local economy, hence the attraction of their locality.

12. According to the village women informants, division of land at the initial stage of decollectivization in the village was carried out in large measure on the basis of household size. Later, in order to keep pace with demographic changes in each household, local policies stipulated that readjustment to the division of land was to be made once every five years or so. During the intervals the households that had their sizes reduced should sell some of the grains at lower than market price to the households that had new members added.

13. Another routine major expenditure of rural households is on funerals for the older generation.

14. This trend of mounting expenses on a son's marriage has also been reported in many other researches on social and cultural changes in rural China [*Gao*, 1999: 232; *Harrel*, 1992: 325–6; *Yan*, 1997: 200].

15. This is manifest in the sharp rise in divorce rate since the enactment of the 1980 Marriage Law, which has granted greater freedom to divorce [*Chen*, 1993: 417–40; *Li*, 1995: 34–9; *Ocko*, 1991: 331].

REFERENCES

Ahmad, Ehtisham and Athar Hussain, 1991, 'Social Security in China: A Historical Perspective', in Ehtisham Ahmad, Jean Drèze, John Hills and Amartya Sen (eds.), *Social Security in Developing Countries*, Oxford: Clarendon Press, pp.247–304.

Barro, Robert J. and Martin S. Feldstein, 1978, *The Impact of Social Security on Private Saving: Evidence from Private Time Series*, Washington, DC: American Enterprise Institute.

Becker, Gary S., 1965, 'A Theory of the Allocation of Time', *Economic Journal*, Vol.75, pp.493–517.

Becker, Gary S., 1974, 'A Theory of Social Interactions', *Journal of Political Economy*, Vol.88, pp.1063–93.

Burgess, Robert G., 1984/1993, *In the Field: An Introduction to Field Research*, London and New York: Routledge.

Buxbaum, David C., 1978, 'Family Law and Social Change: A Theoretical Introduction', in David C. Buxbaum (ed.), *Chinese Family Law and Social Change in Historical and Comparative Perspective*, Seattle and London: University of Washington Press, pp.3–20.

Chen, Yiyun, 1993, 'Nüxing: zouchu hunyin kunjing – zhuanxingqi hunyin yu nüxing jueze' (Women: Out of the marriage dilemma – marriage and women's choice during economic transition), in Tianjin Shida Funü Yanjiu Zhongxin (Centre of Women's Studies, Tianjin Normal University) (ed.), *Zhongguo funü yu fazhan – diwei, jiankang, jiuye* (Women and development in China – status, health and employment), Zhengzhou: Henan renmin chubanshe, pp.417–40.

Chen, Sheying, 1996, *Social Policy and the Economic State and Community Care in Chinese Culture: Ageing, Family, Urban Change and the Socialist Welfare Pluralism*, Aldershot: Avebury.

Cihai Bianji Weiyuanhui (Editorial Board of Chinese Encyclopaedia) (condensed edition), 1979/1980, *Ci hai* (*Chinese encyclopaedia*), Shanghai: Shanghai cishu chubanshe.

Cohen, Myron, 1992, 'Family Management and Family Division in Contemporary China', *The China Quarterly*, No.130 (June), pp.357–77.

Creswell, John W., 1994, *Research Design, Qualitative & Quantitative Approaches*, Thousand Oaks and London: Sage.

Dasgupta, P., 1997, 'Nutritional Status, the Capacity for Work, and Poverty Traps, *Journal of Econometrics*, No.77, pp.5–37.

Davin, Delia, 1990, 'Never Mind if It's a Girl, You Can Have Another Try', in Jørgen Delman, Clemens Stubbe Østergaard and Flemming Christiansen (eds.), *Remaking Peasant China: Problems of Rural Development and Institutions at the Start of the 1990s*, Aarhus: Aarhus University Press, pp.81–91.

Denscombe, Martyn, 1998, *The Good Research Guide*, Buckingham and Philadelphia: Open University Press.

Erlandson, David, Edward Harris, Barbara Skipper and Steve Allen, 1993, *Doing Naturalistic Inquiry: A Guide to Methods*, Newbury Park and London: Sage.

Ermisch, John, 1989, 'Demographic Change and Intergenerational Transfers in Industrialized Countries', in Paul Johnson, Chritoph Conrad and David Thomson (eds.), *Workers versus Pensioners: Intergenerational Justice in an Ageing World*, Manchester and New York: Manchester University Press, pp.17–32.

Feuchtwang, Stephan, 1987, 'Changes in the System of Basic Social Security in the Countryside since 1979', in Ashwani Saith (ed.), *The Re-emergence of the Chinese Peasantry*, London, New York and Sydney: Croom Helm, pp.173–210.

Finch, J., 1996, 'Inheritance and Financial Transfer in Families', in Alan Walker (ed.), *The New Generational Contract: Intergenerational Relations, Old Age and Welfare*, London: UCL Press, pp.120–34.

Gao, Mobo C.F., 1999, *Gao Village: Rural Life in Modern China*, London: Hurst & Company.

Glaser, Barney G. and Anselm L. Strauss, 1967, *The Discovery of Grounded Theory*, Chicago: Aldine.

Greenhalgh, Susan and Li Jiali, 1995, 'Engendering Reproductive Policy and Practice in Peasant China: For a Feminist Demography of Reproduction', *Signs*, Vol.20, No.3, pp.601–41.

Haddad, Lawrence, John Hoddinott and Harold Alderman (eds.), 1997, *Intra-household Resource Allocation in Developing Countries: Models, Methods, and Policy*, Baltimore and London: The Johns Hopkins University Press.

Harding, Sandra (ed.), 1987, *Feminism and Methodology: Social Science Issues*, Bloomington and Milton Keynes: Indiana University Press and Open University Press.

Harrell, Stevan, 1992, 'Aspects of Marriage in Three South-western Villages', *The China Quarterly*, No.130 (June), pp.323–37.

Harriss, Barbara, 1990, 'The Intrafamily Distribution of Hunger in South Asia', in Jean Dreze and Amartya Sen (eds.), *The Political Economy of Hunger*, Vol.1, *Entitlement and Wellbeing*, Oxford: Clarendon Press, pp.351–424.

Honig, Emily and Gail Hershatter, 1988, *Personal Voices: Chinese Women in the 1980's*, Stanford: Stanford University Press.

Judd, Ellen R., 1989, '*Niangjia*: Chinese Women and Their Natal Families', *The Journal of Asian Studies*, Vol.48, No.3, pp.525–44.

Kessler, D., 1989, 'But Why Is There Social Security?', in Paul Johnson, Chritoph Conrad and David Thomson (eds.), *Workers versus Pensioners: Intergenerational Justice in an Ageing World*, Manchester and New York: Manchester University Press, pp.80–90.

Lee, R.D. and T. Miller, 1994, 'Population Age Structure, Intergenerational Transfer and Wealth – A New Approach, with Applications to the United States', *Journal of Human Resources*, Vol.29, No.4, pp.1027–63.

Li, L., 1995, 'Danshen muqin de fan yu you' (Difficulties and worries of single mothers), *Funü yanjiu luncong* (Collection of women's studies), No.4, pp.34–9.

Lüzhuangzi Township Council (ed.), 1992, *Lüzhuangzi xiang tongji ziliao huibian* (The collection of statistics of Lüzhuangzi township), mimeo.

Marshall, Catherine and Gretchen B. Rossman, 1989, *Designing Qualitative Research*, Newbury Park: Sage.

Mogey, J., 1991, 'Families: Intergenerational and Generational Connections – Conceptual Approaches to Kinship and Culture', in Susan K. Pfeifer and Marvin B. Sussman (eds.), *Families: Intergenerational and Generational Connections*, New York and London: The Haworth Press, pp.47–66.

Ocko, Jonathan K., 1991, 'Women, Property and Law in the People's Republic of China', in Rubie S. Watson and Patricia B. Ebrey (eds.), *Marriage and Inequality in Chinese Society*, Berkeley, Los Angeles and Oxford: University of California Press, pp.313–46.

Qin, Hongyu, 1993, 'Gaige shiwu nian, huaxia zhan xinyan' (Fifteen years of reform has brought China new face), *Renmin Ribao* (*People's Daily*) (overseas edition), 25 Sept., p.3.

Saith, Ruhi and Barbara Harriss-White, 1999, 'The Gender Sensitivity of Well-being Indicators', *Development and Change*, Vol.30, pp.465–97.

Sen, Amartya, 1990, 'Gender and Co-Operative Conflicts', in Irene Tinker (ed.), *Persistent Inequalities: Women and World Development*, New York and Oxford: Oxford University Press, pp.123–49.

Shi, L., 1993, 'Family Financial and Household Support Exchange between Generations: A Survey of Chinese Rural Elderly', *The Gerontologist*, Vol.33, No.4, pp.468–80.

Smith, Lisa C. and Jean-Paul Chavas, 1999, 'Supply Response of West African Agricultural Households: Implications of Intra-household Preference Heterogeneity', FCND Discussion Paper No.69, Washington, DC: International Food Policy Research Institute.

Warren, Carol, 1988, *Gender Issues in Field Research*, London: Sage.

White, T., 1994, 'Two Kinds of Production: The Evolution of China's Family Planning Policy in the 1980s', *Population and Development Review*, Vol.20, pp.137–58.

Wong, Linda, 1998, *Marginalisation and Social Welfare in China*, New York and London: Routledge.

Xu, Ping, 1997, 'Hunyin liudong yu nongcun funü de tudi shiyong quanyi' (Marriage mobility and the land use rights of rural women), *Funü yanjiu luncong* (Collection of women's studies) No.1, pp.29–34.

Yan, Yunxiang, 1997, 'The Triumph of Conjugality: Structural Transformation of Family Relations in a Chinese Village', *Ethnology*, Vol.36, No.3, pp.191–212.

Yang, M., 1994, 'Reshaping Peasant Culture and Community: Rural Industrialization in a Chinese Village', *Modern China*, Vol.20, No.2, pp.157–79.

Yu, Leiyan, 1995, 'Zhongguo wuqian duowan nongmin canjia shehui yanglao baoxian' (More than 50 million Chinese farmers joining old-age insurance schemes), *Renmin Ribao* (*People's Daily*) (overseas edition), 20 March, p.4.

ZFQBF (Zhonghuarenmingongheguo Funü Quanyi Baozhang Fa) (Law of the PRC on the Protection of Rights and Interests of Women), 1992, Beijing: Falü chubanshe.

ZFSDDK (Zhongguo Funü Shehui Diwei Diaocha Ketizu) (Survey on Chinese Women's Status Project Team), 1993, *Zhongguo funü shehui diwei gaiguan* (General situation of Chinese women's status), Beijing: Zhongguo funü chubanshe.

Zhang, Heather Xiaoquan, 1999, 'Female Migration and Urban Labour Markets in Tianjin', *Development and Change*, Vol.30, No.1, pp.21–41.

ZHF (Zhonghuarenmingongheguo Hunyin Fa) (Marriage Law of the PRC), 1980, in Quanguofulian Funüganbuxuexiao (School of Women Cadres, All-China Women's Federation) (ed.), 1983, *Zhonghuarenmingongheguo youguan baohu funü ertong hefa quanyi fagui xuanbian* (Laws and regulations on the protection of rights and interests of women and children of the PRC), Beijing: Falü chubanshe, pp.63–7.

ZJ (Zhonghuarenmingongheguo Jichengfa) (Inheritance Law of the People's Republic of China), 1985, *Renmin Ribao* (*People's Daily*), 15 May, p.4.

Local State Corporatism and Private Business

MARIA EDIN

INTRODUCTION

The important role played by the Chinese local state in promoting economic development is by now well established. It has been shown by a number of scholars how local governments use their administrative control to further the growth of township and village enterprises (TVEs) within their locality. The phenomenon of local governments doing business has been variously described as the 'developmental state' [*Blecher*, 1991; *Blecher and Shue*, 1996], 'local governments as firms' [*Walder*, 1995], 'local market socialism' [*Lin*, 1995], 'village conglomerates' [*Chen*, 1998], 'entrepreneurial state' [*Duckett*, 1998] and 'bureaucratic entrepreneurs' [*Gore*, 1998 and 1999]. Jean Oi [1992, 1995 and 1999] has written extensively on rural industrialization and she coined the concept of local state corporatism, where local governments are viewed as business corporations. Officials are literally acting as board of directors of their collective enterprises, over which they exercise control. Oi's model of local state corporatism has been the most influential to describe rural economic development and analyse the role of the local state. With the rapid changes taking place in rural China, it can be asked what parts of the model of local state corporatism are still applicable and what parts of the model need to be modified. The notion of local state corporatism defined the field of China rural studies in the 1990s, and the question is what relevance the model holds in the coming decades. This study links up with the ongoing debate on TVE development and the role of the local state in rich and poor areas, and points to which new issues must be addressed.

Maria Edin, Postdoctoral Fellow, Swedish School of Advanced Asia Pacific Studies (SSAAPS), Uppsala University, Department of Government, Box 514, SE-751 20 Uppsala, Sweden. Email: maria.edin@statsvet.uu.se. The author is grateful to Jacob Eyferth and Li Xiande for inspiring discussions and helpful comments, and to Wen Tiejun, Cai Fang and Bai Gang for invaluable help in China. This project was financed by the Swedish International Development Agency (Sida) between the years 1995 and 1998.

One intriguing question, which still begs a satisfactory answer, is why local cadres have furthered the growth of rural industry rather than engage in rent-seeking to a larger extent than has actually been the case. What drives cadre behaviour? The dominant explanation in the China field as to why officials have promoted economic development is that local cadres were granted fiscal incentives by economic reforms. Fiscal reforms granted incentives to officials since those reforms provided local governments with residual claimant rights over enterprise profit. Oi writes that the benefits to township and villages to be gained from developing their own enterprises are fairly obvious: 'the reasons center on revenue' [1998a: 106]. Walder conceives government officials as solely economic actors, whose incentives and constraints must be understood as surely as those of firms. He poses the question as to what incentives drive local officials to play such an active role in the development of local public industry and provides the reply: 'the answer, in a word, is revenue' [1998: 69]. In this interpretation, local governments and their township enterprises are viewed as firms that, like any other private actor, are driven by the profit motive.

It is crucial, however, to ask how the revenue controlled by the local state is used. In Oi's analysis of the local state as a business corporation, it takes money from one of its enterprises to invest in some other of their enterprises. In the literature on rent-seeking of government officials, on the other hand, it is simply assumed that rents are used by officials to enrich themselves (see, for example, Buchanan [1980]). Levi [1988: 10] states that leaders are predatory since they will always try to maximize revenue. Levi and others state that leaders will always try to maximize revenue, but they omit the most interesting aspect of the question: how do leaders and bureaucrats use the revenue? The point is that in both cases local governments take illicit fees but use them in different ways. In accounts of TVE development, it has perhaps too often been taken for granted that local governments use rents for reinvestment. Accounts from poor areas show that sometimes rents are indeed used for benefits of the cadres themselves. The heavy peasant burden is well captured by Li Xiande in his contribution to this volume. Illicit fees can be used to buy expensive cars at the expense of peasants but they can also be used to finance infrastructure in industrial parks, and we must ask which has been the case and what explains the different behaviour.

To answer the question what explains cadre behaviour, we need to redirect our attention to the political institutions, usually treated as given, that underlie the economic behaviour of the state. I argue that non-economic incentives drive the economic behaviour of local cadres to a larger extent than has previously been assumed. The first part of this article focuses on the political institutions that structure the incentives of local officials in

China. It thereby highlights the political incentive structure, generated by the cadre responsibility system, at the micro-level, which has prompted local cadres to promote growth. The notion of local state corporatism refers foremost to local governments assisting collective township and village enterprises (*xiangzhen qiye*), which are set up and controlled by local governments. Most accounts of TVE development have therefore looked at the development of collective enterprises. Similarly, the literature on the private sector in China does not sufficiently emphasize the economic coordinating role of local governments.[1] Oi [1998b: 94] herself wrote that while her concept of local state corporatism captures the experience of those areas that have industrialized through collectively owned industry, some modifications will no doubt be necessary when it is applied to areas where there is a strong private sector.[2] As ownership reform of enterprises is speeded up, the relationship between the local state and private enterprises becomes central to any assessment of the subsequent relevance of the local state corporatist model. The second part of the article examines how the local state has coordinated the development of private business. It is shown that local state corporatism also encompasses the private sector, and I argue that ownership is of subordinate importance for local governments when selecting enterprises for preferential treatment. The finding that local governments promote the growth of private enterprises, whose profits they are able to control to a much lesser extent, strengthens the argument that political incentives are more important than fiscal incentives as the motivating force behind cadre behaviour.

The research reported here was carried out during a number of sojourns in rural China, all in all seven months of field research at the county level and below, between the years 1996 and 1999. A total of 153 interviews were conducted with local cadres and local entrepreneurs in southern Jiangsu, Shandong, Zhejiang and Shanxi province.[3] I was also fortunate enough to be able to stay at the home of a township mayor and his family for three weeks, which provided invaluable insights into the working of township government. The field research has almost exclusively been carried out in the rich coastal areas where the local state has been particularly active in promoting township and village enterprises. It can therefore not be representative of poor areas but the findings from the developed areas are utilized to pose questions about cadre behaviour in less developed areas. With regard to how the local state promotes economic development, the focus of the presentation is exclusively on private enterprises. Material on how the local state supports private industry was collected in five different counties in Zhejiang.

POLITICAL INCENTIVES AT THE MICRO-LEVEL[4]

In China, market reforms have been introduced into the state administration itself. Reforms have attempted to refine the old cadre management system to make it more effective. The leading cadres (*lingdao ganbu*) of each level of local government are held accountable for their work performance to higher levels, as part of the cadre responsibility system (*gangwei zerenzhi*). The focus of this project is on the township leading cadres, namely the party secretary and the township mayor. The basis for the evaluation system is the nomenklatura, a list of leading positions over which the party controls appointments [*Burns*, 1987 and 1994]. Higher levels are able to conduct evaluation of lower levels precisely because they are part of a hierarchical structure. At the end of each year, it is assessed whether township leaders have attained their work targets, and rewards and punishments are based on the result of assessment [*Whiting*, 2001].

The most novel feature of the cadre responsibility system is the performance contracts (*gangwei mubiao zerenshu*), which party secretaries and mayors sign with the county level.[5] Township cadres pledge to attain certain targets laid down by higher levels for whose attainment they are held personally responsible. At the same time, there are overlapping responsibilities. There are two types of contracts: collective and individual. Collective contracts are drawn up between the county and the township level, and are signed either by the party secretary or the township mayor, depending on the content of the contract. Individual contracts are drawn up between the county line department and their equivalent at the township. The township cadre in charge, for example, of industrial development signs a contract with the county level township enterprise bureau, but he or she will be evaluated by the township. Only the party secretary and the mayor are then directly accountable to the county level. As a result of the shift towards comprehensive evaluation, they are held ultimately responsible also in the cases where work has been delegated to department heads or vice-heads.

One official in charge of evaluation describes how county leaders compete to have their area of responsibility included in the performance contracts of township leaders as the probability of attainment is greatly increased.[6] Under the new system, performance targets are internally ranked in importance. There are soft targets (*yiban zhibiao),* hard targets (*ying zhibiao*) and priority targets or those with veto power (*yipiao fojue*). Nowadays, targets derived from the plan are no longer mandatory (*zhilingxing*) but ought to be regarded as targets for guidance (*yindaoxing*) or aspiration. Economic incentives have been integrated into the old planning system, and bonuses are linked to the attainment of targets. With regard to economic rewards the three categories of targets may be of equal worth while hard targets and priority targets constitute the basis for appointment decisions and the granting of political rewards. Although hard targets vary depending on what higher levels choose to emphasize at the time, they are typically drawn from the economic and social development plan. Tax revenues submitted to the county, industrial output and economic growth are defined as hard targets specified in the performance contract with the township government. Priority targets or targets with veto power may also vary between areas but they are exclusively used for key priority policies of higher levels. Failure to attain these priority targets cancels out all other work performance, however successful, in the comprehensive evaluation at the end of the year.

There are two priority targets that are enforced nationwide, mirroring the importance that the Communist Party places on these policies: family planning and social order (*shehui zhi'an*). The target to uphold social order is intimately linked with evaluation by lower levels, and the absence of citizen complaints and social disturbances in particular. The Chinese system is so constructed that the assessment by local society is made an integrated part of the evaluation by higher levels of the state. A democratic appraisal meeting (*minzhu pingyi*), where colleagues and lower levels rate the work performance of the party secretary and the township mayor, is held in junction with the annual evaluation. If many people express dissatisfaction with a leader at the meeting, the party organization department must initiate an investigation.[7] Both client rating and citizen complaints function as channels of information to higher levels. Citizen complaints mostly target local leaders and are launched by groups of an average 20–30 members. Excessive fees and embezzlement of public funds by local cadres are common causes of complaints. If township and county levels are not sympathetic, community members may then appeal to higher levels and they may subsequently gain a positive hearing. There is thus a risk involved if township leaders ignore complaints as this may lead to reprimands from higher levels. In recent years, citizen complaints are having a direct effect on the evaluation of cadres [*O'Brien and Li*, 1995]. Citizen complaints, moreover, take on a special importance in evaluation since higher levels are very sensitive to any situation that might develop into social disturbances. With this risky potential, citizen complaints fall under the priority target social order. Township government is, in a limited way, accountable to local society members, who can exercise their influence through established channels.

When the comprehensive evaluation at the end of each year is brought to an end, a total score is calculated for each township government, as well as for each leading cadre, and on the basis of these scores townships and their leaders are placed in an internal ranking order. There are thus collective and individual rankings, which seem to be interrelated in the case of township leading cadres. Townships are ranked on the basis of total scores and bonuses are paid to all township state cadres in accordance with the collective ranking of their township. Economic rewards are in this way pegged to work performance. In a southern Jiangsu county, an ordinary state cadre in a middle-ranking township received Rmb 4,600 by way of bonus in 1995.[8] In a Zhejiang county, the average bonus for township cadres amounted to more than Rmb 2,500 in 1997.[9] Bonus payment appears to be a conscious strategy on the part of local governments to supplement, through legal means, the basic salary for cadres. It is important to note that bonuses are not financed out of the state budget but paid from the township's own collective funds, that is to say, funds from income from local projects such as township enterprises. In this way, bonus payment is dependent on the condition of local finances, which reduces its organizational incentive. The township leading cadres in a given county are also ranked on the basis of the outcome of the evaluation. Top-ranking offices and individual leading cadres will be awarded the title of advanced work units (*xianjin danwei*) or advanced leader (*xianjin lingdao*). If a township leader has failed to attain the priority targets, namely those targets that cancel out other work performance (*yipiao fojue*), it disqualifies the township government from becoming an advanced unit and the responsible cadre from becoming an advanced leader. For those township leaders who are awarded the title of advanced leader it is easier to receive preferential treatment, with regard to both promotion and other forms of assistance. There is a striking similarity between the way cadres and enterprises are ranked, as we will see.

The cadre responsibility system, to sum up, provides the institutional context in which local cadres operate, and structures the incentives and constraints that cadres have to deal with. Accountability to higher levels of the party state prompts township leading cadres to promote growth in the following ways. First, economic development is one of the most important targets in cadre evaluation. Tax revenues, industrial output and growth figures are all part and parcel of this target. Second, the development of township enterprises enables local cadres to perform many other work functions, such as building infrastructure, improving living standards, providing social welfare, maintaining the standard of education, supporting agriculture, and so on, which also are targets of higher levels. Budgetary funds are insufficient, and without income from the TVEs and other local projects, it is difficult for township governments to attain also the other targets. Township leaders, as middlemen in between higher levels of the party state and the local community, work under strong pressure in an uncertain bureaucratic environment. They risk either being targeted by the county in one of their campaign drives or being targeted by dissatisfied local community members. How can township leaders cope with this uncertainty? To avoid being targeted in a campaign by higher levels, local officials of course use their political connections. But there are also indications that it is easier to avoid being targeted if cadres have been successful in furthering economic growth. Being economically successful certainly also helps to make good connections. Furthermore, local citizens may be less inclined to submit complaints to higher levels concerning their grievances and local distortions of national policies if township leaders have been successful in promoting growth. To date, the majority of peasant protests and demonstrations have occurred in poor areas.

In short, economic development is an asset, or insurance, that reduces the risk of being targeted in a politically uncertain environment. I argue that promoting economic development is a way for township leaders to cope with uncertainty. According to this interpretation, township leaders promote growth not only because it is rewarded by higher levels but also because it is a means to survive in a system and gain some control over their work situation. In some coastal areas, the political institutions have prompted local cadres to promote the development of private business.

PROMOTING DEVELOPMENT OF PRIVATE BUSINESS

Market reforms in the post-Mao period have blurred the distinction between government and enterprise in such a way that public institutions have come to resemble business corporations and public officials have been induced to act as entrepreneurs. A number of China scholars have simply regarded local governments together with their enterprises as a single firm [*Oi*, 1992, 1995 and 1999; *Walder*, 1995 and 1998; *Che and Qian*, 1998; *Pei*, 1996].[10] To counter this view of local governments as solely business corporations, the political incentives that drive the economic behaviour of local cadres are emphasized below. Local cadres have set up, and continue to support, township enterprises, partly with political objectives in sight.

The fact that cadres are motivated by non-economic incentives does not automatically mean that the outcome of their decisions is economically irrational. There is no irreconcilable contradiction between political rationality and market-driven development. To be sure, the outcome has often been economically irrational as Eyferth in his contribution to this volume shows, but depending on the context it can likewise be economically rational. The local state in China has followed in the footsteps of the East Asian developmental state. In Japan, Taiwan and South Korea, economic bureaucrats selected industries that they regarded to be of importance for future development and directed capital into these industries, whereby they gained a competitive advantage [*Johnson*, 1982; *Wade*, 1990; *Amsden*, 1989).[11] The state in East Asia picked the winners. In China, the local state has also targeted certain sectors, enterprises and projects for promotion. But while economic bureaucrats in East Asia picked projects that they believed had future potential, Chinese local cadres supported those sectors and enterprises that had already demonstrated good performance.[12] One official of the planning commission said that they target enterprises that have a good basis and have already shown a successful development trend.[13] In this way, local state-led development has been more in conformity with market forces than it has been in East Asia.

This holds true also for areas where private industry dominates. It is necessary at this point to define more clearly the difference between collective and private enterprises.[14] The term 'TVE' has come to serve as an umbrella term for different categories of enterprises in rural areas, including collective and private enterprises. The first category includes township-run (*xiangban/zhenban*) and village-run (*cunban*), the second category includes household (*lianhu*), partnership (*hehuo*) and individual and private (*geti* or *siying*). To simplify, local governments have very often invested in township-run and village-run enterprises, which continue to submit part of the profits to their initial investors (also in the case where they are contracted out, leased and transformed into shareholding cooperatives) who are dependent on them to finance social and economic projects laid upon them by higher levels of the party state. This contributes to the general feeling among local cadres that 'their enterprises' ought to contribute to the collective whenever public expenditure requires it. Private enterprises, in theory, only pay local and national taxes (and perhaps management fees) but also they may have to contribute to local projects, either by paying an earmarked fee or giving a 'donation'. It is usually agreed that the burden of collective enterprises to contribute to local projects is heavier than that of private enterprises.

Even though local cadres have a stronger fiscal incentive to promote collective enterprises, they do assist the development of private industry. The political logic of local state-led development also applies to promoting private enterprises. Promoting the growth of private industry enables local cadres to carry out their government work and score high in the evaluation of work performance. At the same time, economic development, regardless of whether it is based on collective or private enterprises, serves as an insurance against unpredictable situations, as we have seen. In addition, there are specific reasons for assisting private industry. First of all, as growth of collective enterprises is generally declining, the private sector is becoming more important for township governments as an instrument to fulfil state goals, although they do not benefit financially in the same direct way as from collective enterprises. Second, the development of private enterprises has in many areas become a separate work target of township governments. Even in Jiangsu where collective industry dominates, the target to assist the development of private enterprises was added in the first half of the 1990s.

Like in the East Asian countries, the local state takes upon itself the role as promoter and protector of selected enterprises and projects. The planning process in China is however driven from the bottom-up: enterprises that have already proved to be successful are targeted for preferential treatment. Local enterprises and projects selected for preferential treatment are included in the plans drawn up by the county-level planning commission. Such plans contain special sections on key industrial and construction projects (*zhongdian xiangmu*) in the area.[15] In areas where private industry dominates, key projects typically involve infrastructural projects and the construction of industrial zones, where enterprises are invited to establish themselves. The two are related, as one of the main purposes in setting up industrial parks is to facilitate infrastructure construction. If a project is not listed in the county plan, it becomes much more difficult to obtain either bank loans or government assistance. All relevant government departments are urged to pay due attention to the key projects listed in the plan, and are expected to grant them highest priority.

Even as banks are becoming increasingly commercialized and are no longer under the thumb of government, township-level bank directors could, at least until recently, only be nominated with approval of the township leaders. Moreover, township leaders exercise authority over bank leaders through party channels [*Whiting*, 1995: 240]. In one county in Zhejiang, the county government convenes a meeting where the leaders express the hope that banks will support the key project and a support scheme is drawn up, which the banks, in principle, agree to follow.[16] Enterprises are ranked on the basis of their economic performance and these ranking lists are given to the bank. Township governments are thereby able to create internal competition, just as firms were exposed to international competition in East Asia. Collective assets are much more limited in extent in areas where private industry dominates, so the local state has less control over capital in these areas. It is common that private persons invest in infrastructure projects and public welfare projects in return for profits. However, building infrastructure and setting up industrial parks in private areas is also a means for local governments to enter into business themselves.

In one Zhejiang county, all of the 26 key projects were important construction projects such as building state highways, power stations, and so on. These projects will receive preferential treatment and the local government will assist in all possible ways to complete the projects on time.[17] Some infrastructure projects are financed through bank loans while some are reportedly financed by private persons.[18] According to one vice-director of the planning commission in another county, more than 80 per cent of all projects are financed by investments from non-state institutions (*feiguo touzi*). As collective assets are small, the township government relies on 'farmers' to invest in new projects, according to its representatives. But in fact, it is enterprises on behalf of collective institutions that buy shares, rather than farmers. The construction of the Keyun Zhongxin (a passenger transport centre) is a case in point: the bureau of communication was an investor and held 45 per cent of total shares through its company (*qiche yunshu gongsi*). Another 45 per cent of total shares were held by the wealthiest village in the county through one of its collective companies (*yunshu gongsi*). The village used their collective funds to establish this company. The third shareholder is another village that contributed land as an investment.[19] Here, the enterprises or, more correctly, the government bureaux through their companies, choose to invest in infrastructure rather than industrial projects. This pattern of investment is encouraged, furthermore, by local government leaders. In short, various government institutions do business while at the same time coordinating development.

Another important coordinating function of local governments is the establishment of industrial parks or industrial development zones (*gongyequ*). Preferential treatment, in the form of limited tax concessions and waiving of fees, are offered to enterprises that move into the park.[20] The setting up of parks is intimately linked today to the question of leasing land. Typically, the township government coordinates land use, builds access roads to the park and provides electricity and water supplies. Factory buildings are usually constructed by the enterprises themselves. According to an official in charge of industrial development, setting up one such park involved a total investment of Rmb 100 million. However, there was no 'direct investment' by the township government from its own funds but funds derived from profits made through leasing land and providing infrastructure.[21] In another Zhejiang township, the government set up a company (*kaifa gongsi*) with the specific purpose of investing in infrastructure. This company, in other words, invests on behalf of the township government, as it is a legal entity (*qiye faren*).[22]

The government, in the name of the company, is granted bank loans that are used to construct infrastructure in the park and, when profits are earned from leasing land to enterprises that have moved into the park, the bank loans are repaid. Today only key backbone enterprises at the district level and large-scale enterprises are invited to move in.[23] In this particular area, farmers were paid Rmb 30,000 per *mu* in compensation but industry leased land from Rmb 90,000 per *mu* (and commerce for much more). Unger [2000: 82] writes that land is expropriated from farmers and handed over to semi-private 'development companies' that the officials themselves own, and the land is immediately resold at a very high price for use as industrial sites, causing farmer riots. While it is clear that the low prices paid to farmers in compensation for land is a form of land expropriation, Unger's observation is only partly correct. The 'development companies' are not semi-private, but the economic arm of township government enabling them to take bank loans. The example above well illustrates how government carries on business but at the same time reinvests (part of) its profits in facilities for private enterprises. A second rational for establishing industrial zones, it can be suspected, is that it is one of the few ways to go around strict national regulations on land.[24]

Apart from coordinating overall development, local governments in areas where private industry dominates also target selected enterprises for preferential treatment. All areas I visited in Zhejiang had adopted a policy of publishing official lists of selected enterprises, which they distributed to relevant government departments and financial institutions to signal that everything should be done to help these enterprises. One such list contained 36 enterprises, categorized as key enterprises.[25] Moreover, the local state in private areas has drawn up special programmes to promote the growth in scale of enterprises. Since the 1990s, the Chinese authorities have emphasized the importance of encouraging the development of enterprise groups (*qiye jituan*), modelled on the Korean *chaebols* [*Yang*, 1996; *Nolan*, 2001]. In Zhejiang, in the late 1990s, the provincial government recommended that preferential treatment should be provided to 'small giant projects' (*xiaojuren*).[26] This strategy takes the form of emphasizing large-scale enterprises, at least at the lower levels. In one county, a list of 21 small giant enterprises was publicized and these enterprises were to be given special attention by government departments at different levels.[27]

As we see, enlarging the scale of private enterprises is a top priority of local governments. They also encourage mergers between enterprises, but use indirect methods since they do not own the enterprises.[28] One township set up three industrial parks, each specialized in a particular industrial sector. Total investments for the plastic industrial park, which was set up jointly with the village upon whose land it was built, were Rmb 30 million.[29] More than 200 enterprises in the plastic industry have decided to move into the park. There had been far-reaching plans to form one single enterprise conglomerate on the basis of the enterprises established in the park. The industrial park would then become one large enterprise group. However, enterprise assets would not be merged, according to the township official in charge. The main motive behind creating an enterprise group was no doubt to increase the scale of the existing small-scale private enterprises as well as to improve the reputation of the plastic products from this area. The official of the industrial office in charge of the plastic industry will be the general manager of the enterprise group.[30]

That scale of enterprise is very important for township governments is also clear from looking at the criteria for listing enterprises to receive preferential treatment. Scale of project and financial indicators are the main criteria. In the county where 36 key enterprises were listed, the three criteria were: production output, tax contribution and profit. In one county, the government assists enterprises listed as 'small giants' to be granted bank loans and, moreover, pays the interest on the loans on behalf of the enterprises. For enterprises listed as key backbone enterprises, on the other hand, the county-level tax and local fees are reduced.[31] One village-run enterprise group, which was listed as both a 'small giant' and a key backbone enterprise received an income tax reduction of Rmb 10 million in 1999.[32] In rich areas, local governments are able to afford to grant their enterprises tax concessions and to waive local fees. This stands in sharp contrast with the reality in poor regions, where local governments have to tax their enterprises at maximum, in order to meet tax revenue targets and to meet government expenditure.

CONCLUDING REMARKS

Above, it has been described how the local state coordinates the development of private enterprises in its region – a case of successful local state-led development. It has been argued here that political incentives drive the economic behaviour of local cadres to a greater extent than has previously been assumed. Fiscal and political incentives both lead to the same economic behaviour of cadres: promoting the growth of township enterprises. In that sense, the two explanations are mutually reinforcing. I view the fiscal incentive explanation as an integral component of the reformed political institution, the cadre responsibility system.[33] As part of the decentralization drive, fiscal incentives were made available to local governments who were granted greater autonomy with regard to operation. At the same time, higher levels strengthened their control over appointment and evaluation [*Edin*, 2003]. But political incentives also explain additional cadre behaviour, which fiscal incentives cannot. First, an approach that centres on political incentives can shed light on why local cadres use collective funds not only to invest in new development projects that benefit them financially, but also to finance other government activities that are made work targets by higher levels. Second, local governments also promote the development of private enterprises, whose profit they do not directly control.

There are two dominant images of local party and state cadres in the China field today, which stand in sharp contrast to each other. One portrays local party leaders as developmental oriented and the engine behind China's rapid growth. The other characterizes local party leaders as inherently corrupt and whose actions only serve to reinforce poverty in rural areas [*Lu*, 1997 and 2000; *Bernstein and Lu*, 2000]. These two contrasting images mirror the opposite stands taken in the general debate on the economic role of the state.[34] How can we combine these two images? To go to the bottom with the two contrasting images, we need to examine the political institutions behind. Areas in the central and inland provinces were certainly at great economic disadvantage from the outset. But there are indications that the bureaucratic structure only aggravates the situation. One brief visit to an officially designated poor county in Shanxi suggests that the tax revenue target was more heavily emphasized than was the case in the developed coastal regions. The township government had little choice than to shift the tax burden downwards to enterprises and households. Peng [1996] has shown how two county governments in poor Guizhou province forced farmers to grow tobacco on their individual land as tobacco is taxed more heavily than other products. The same picture is provided by Eyferth in this volume. In his village in Sichuan, the leaders set out on reckless industrial expansion instead of supporting the papermaking industry. This stands in contrast to one of my areas in Shandong, where the local state could afford to upgrade and diversify the traditional papermaking industry.[35] Poor areas are also at a disadvantage since the condition of local finance does not permit that bonuses are paid in reward for good performance.

It is apparent to us that similar political institutions have not led to the same positive effects in all areas, in particular, but not exclusively, in poor areas. The mechanism behind the economic behaviour of local cadres needs to be further refined in order to find out under which conditions the political institutions in question have a positive effect on cadre behaviour, and under which conditions they have a negative effect. In conclusion, the notion of local state corporatism needs to be modified in a number of ways. The local state does not confine itself to promoting collective enterprises but it is found here that ownership is not significant. Because political incentives guide local cadre behaviour, the local state has in some coastal areas also promoted the development of private business whose profits it is able to control to a much lesser extent. Consequently, our attention should be directed to the political institutions at the local level that underpin local state corporatism. Modifications aside, the question for the future is whether the model can stay relevant in the field after a flooding of reports of predatory behaviour, reckless industrial expansion, duplicate construction, increasing peasant burden, and rising social unrest in the countryside. To test its relevance, the model has to be tried out in the inland and central provinces of China, just as the predatory state model has to be applied in the rich areas of the coast, thereby allowing for different types of outcomes. Very similar cadre behaviour has been described as developmental and predatory, owing to inadequate operationalization. It is conceivable that the political foundation of the model will prove useful to understand the role of the local state in poor areas. Yet, the different conditions under which it is implemented may help to contribute to theory development and increase our understanding of the contrasting images of the state.

NOTES

1. One exception is a recent study by Unger and Chan [1999], which explores the role of different levels of local governments in promoting the development of private industry.
2. In her most recent book, Oi [1999] finds that local governments in collective areas have now started to promote the development of private enterprises.
3. These 153 interviews consisted of the following: 105 interviews were carried out with local cadres and 48 interviews with local entrepreneurs; 49 interviews were carried out at the county level, 95 interviews at township level and nine interviews at the village level; 49 interviews took place in southern Jiangsu province, seven interviews in a rural county under Beijing municipality, 49 interviews in Shandong, 38 interviews in Zhejiang and 11 interviews in Shanxi province. See Edin [2000] for a more detailed account of the fieldwork.
4. The text of this section draws largely from my article 'State Capacity and Local Agent Control: CCP Cadre Management from a Township Perspective', *The China Quarterly*, No.173 (March) 2003.
5. As yet, there is little information available about cadre performance contracts. The only sources in English that mentions this type of contract that I am aware of are Brown [1998: 32] and O'Brien and Li [1999: 172].
6. Interview ZC5 with the vice-director in charge of evaluation in the party bureau of rural affairs in a Zhejiang county (1998).
7. The outcome of the investigation still depends on the will of the organization department, but it gives the cadre under investigation undesirable attention; see interview SCA1 with the village party secretary cum chairman of the board of the village corporation in Shandong village (1998) and interview ZCa1 with the vice-mayor cum director of the industrial office and the vice-director of the industrial office in a Zhejiang township (1998).
8. Interview JAa4 with the general manager of the industrial corporation in a southern Jiangsu township (1996).
9. Interview ZC5 with the vice-director in charge of evaluation in the party bureau of rural affairs in a Zhejiang county (1998).
10. Che and Qian view the entire three-tier structure of communist residents, local government and individual enterprises as a firm. This is even more obvious at the village level, where some village committees have been turned into village conglomerates [*Lin*, 1995; *Pei*, 1996; *Chen*, 1998].
11. For the view that industrial policy in Japan was less a well thought-out *ex ante* strategy than an *ex post* compromise between the economic bureaucracy and business firms, see Aoki, Kim and Okuno-Fujiwara [1997].
12. See chapter 4 in Edin [2000] for a longer and more systematic comparison between the East Asian developmental state and the Chinese local developmental state.
13. Interview ZB2 with personnel from the planning commission in a Zhejiang county (1998).
14. A TVE is formally a collectively owned enterprise located in a township or village in the

rural areas of China. All residents in the township or village are thus co-owners where they are represented, as residents, by their township or village committee. Local governments are thereby the *de facto* owners of township enterprises while community residents are mainly beneficiaries [*Weitzman and Xu*, 1994: 128].

15. Industrial planning in terms of channelling funds into a particular sector is almost exclusively practised in areas where collective industry dominates.

16. Interview ZC4 with a section chief of the planning economic committee in a Zhejiang county (1998).

17. Interview ZB2 with personnel from the planning commission in a Zhejiang county (1998); and from document *X shi 1997 nian guomin jingji he shehui fazhan jihua zhixing qinkuang, 1998 nian guomin jingji he shuhui fazhan jihua* (Report of implementation of the 1997 national economic and social development, the 1998 national economic and social development plan of X municipality), pp.19–20. It is a county level municipality.

18. In some areas, private persons invested in schools and kindergartens, water reservoirs and power stations, toll roads and other such projects in order to earn a profit.

19. Interview ZE2 with the vice-director and the section chief in charge of investment of the planning economic committee in a Zhejiang county (1999). I did not interview representatives of the transportation bureau or the villages who had invested. See also document *Jiuwu qijian woqu guding zichan touzi gongzuo qingkuang huiba'* (Report of the situation of fixed assets investment in the period of the Ninth Five Year Plan) issued by the planning economic committee.

20. Until recently, national tax was waived for the first year or the first two years after entry. Today, tax concessions only concern county-level tax. Typically, payment of management fees is waived or reduced for the first years the enterprises are operating in the industrial park.

21. Interview ZBa2 with the director of the township management service station in a Zhejiang township (1998).

22. The director of the industrial office is also the head of the company.

23. Interview ZEb1 with the vice-mayor in charge of industry and the director of the industrial office cum enterprise management station cum manager of the investment company, in a Zhejiang township (1999). The majority of enterprises – most of them small-scale – had moved into the park in 1992 when the park was built. In a neighbouring township, where an industrial park is under construction, the main criterion for entering into the park is an output value above Rmb 10 million; see interview ZEa1 with the vice-director in charge of industry of the street committee in a Zhejiang township (1999). So far, six enterprises had been cleared to enter, all with output value above Rmb 10 million. These six enterprises were not in the same industrial sector.

24. It can not be denied that it is not always economically rational to set up an industrial park, but the point made here is that township governments do not necessarily expropriate farm land in order to put the money into private pockets or to subsidize administrative expenditure, including salaries, for which there are not sufficient budgetary funds, but to build infrastructure used for private industry.

25. From document *Guanyu gongbu 1998 niandu shi zhongdian gongye qiye de tongzhi* (Circular publicly announcing 1998 key industrial enterprises of X municipality). It is a county-level municipality.

26. This is basically a strategy to support small and middle enterprises that have captured a large share of a market, along the lines of the Taiwan model. See interview with Zhang Renshou, vice-president of Zhejiang Academy of Social Science (1998). It would appear to me that it is, at the same time, a method for upgrading the status of enterprises in Zhejiang, which are on the whole relatively small-scale.

27. See document *Zhonggong X xianwei wenjian: Guanyu gongbu X xian 1998 ninadu 'xiaoxing juren' qiye de tongzhi* (Document by the Communist Party committee: Circular publicly announcing the small giant type enterprises in 1998 of X county).

28. Sometimes the local government can be very active in assisting enterprises to merge. One promising private enterprise was to form an enterprise group and needed other enterprises with which to merge. The local government assisted this enterprise to find several partners

around which it could form a group, see interview ZAb2 with the enterprise manager in a Zhejiang township (1997). Altogether there were 23 enterprises merging, with the first enterprise forming the core of the group.

29. Interview ZBb1 with the vice-mayor in charge of industry in a Zhejiang township (1998). The farmers were thus not paid compensation for land but the village held shares in the park.

30. Interview ZBb2 with the vice-director of the industrial office cum enterprise management station in a Zhejiang township (1998). The forerunner of the enterprise group was an administrative company whose head was to become the manager of the group. The more than 200 private enterprises that chose to move into the park accounted for around 60 per cent of the total number of enterprises in the plastic industry, so enterprises voluntarily joined this government initiative. There were similar plans to form an enterprise group on the basis of enterprises that produce water pumps. It is quite common for areas to earn a reputation for specific products. In Wenzhou, ten market towns each specialize in a particular kind of manufacturing [Liu, 1992: 701]. Liushi is, for example, famous for its low voltage products.

31. Interview ZD1 with the director of the planning commission, vice-director of the economic committee and vice-director of the township enterprise bureau in a Zhejiang county (1999).

32. Interview ZDa2 with the general manager of the village corporation cum village party secretary in a Zhejiang village (1999). It was granted when he imported expensive machinery.

33. The political incentive explanation encompasses the fiscal incentive explanation: political incentives are capable of explaining the same result as the fiscal incentive explanation.

34. The theory of the developmental state highlights how states have governed markets and promoted development in East Asia. The theory of the rent-seeking state, in contrast, perceives the state as hindering economic development and itself constituting the problem of underdevelopment.

35. Interview SAc2 with the chairman of the board of a village-run enterprise group cum village party secretary in a Shandong village (1997).

REFERENCES

Amsden, Alice H., 1989, *Asian's Next Giant: South Korea and Late Industrialization*, New York: Oxford University Press.

Aoki, Masahiko, Kim Hyung-ki and Okuno-Fujiwara Masahiro, 1997, *The Role of Government in East Asian Economic Development: Comparative Institutional Analysis*, Oxford: Clarendon Press.

Bernstein, Thomas P. and Lu Xiaobo, 2000, 'Taxation without Representation: Peasants, the Central and the Local States in Reform China', *The China Quarterly*, No.163 (September).

Blecher, Marc, 1991, 'Development State, Entrepreneurial State: The Political Economy of Socialist Reform in Xinju Municipality and Guanghan County', in G. White (ed.), *The Chinese State in the Era of Economic Reform: The Road to Crisis*, London: Macmillan.

Blecher, Marc and Vivienne Shue, 1996, *Tethered Deer: Government & Economy in a Chinese County*, Stanford: Stanford University Press.

Brown, George P., 1998, 'Budgets, Cadres and Local State Capacity in Rural Jiangsu', in F. Christiansen and Zhang Junzuo (eds.), *Village Inc. Chinese Rural Society in the 1990s*, Richmond: Curzon Press.

Buchanan, James M., 1980, 'Rent Seeking and Profit Seeking', in J. Buchanan, R. Tollison and G. Tullock (eds.), *Toward a Theory of the Rent-Seeking Society*, Texas: A & M University Press.

Burns, John P., 1987, 'China's Nomenklatura System', *Problems of Communism*, Vol.36, No.5.

Burns, John P., 1994, 'Strengthening Central CCP Control of Leadership Selection: The 1990 Nomenklatura', *The China Quarterly*, No.138 (June).

Che, Jiahua and Qian Yingyi, 1998, 'Institutional Environment, Community Government, and Corporate Governance: Understanding China's Township-Village Enterprises', *Journal of Law, Economics and Organization*, Vol.14, No.1.

Chen, Weixing, 1998, 'The Political Economy of Rural Industrialization in China: Village Conglomerates in Shandong Province', *Modern China*, Vol.24, No.1.

Duckett, Jane, 1998, *The Entrepreneurial State in China*, London: Routledge.

Edin, Maria, 2000, *Market Forces and Communist Power: Local Political Institutions and Economic Development in China*, Uppsala: Uppsala University Printers.

Edin, Maria, 2003, 'State Capacity and Local Agent Control: CCP Cadre Management from a Township Perspective', forthcoming in *The China Quarterly*, No.173 (March).

Gore, Lance L.P., 1998, *Market Communism: The Institutional Foundations of China's Post-Mao Hyper-Growth*, Hong Kong: Oxford University Press.

Gore, Lance L.P., 1999, 'The Communist Legacy in Post-Mao Economic Growth', *The China Journal*, No.41 (January).

Johnson, Chalmers, 1982, *MITI and the Japanese Miracle: The Growth of Industrial Policy, 1925–1975*, Stanford: Stanford University Press.

Levi, Margaret, 1988, *Of Rule and Revenue*, Berkeley, CA: University of California Press.

Lin, Nan, 1995, 'Local Market Socialism: Local Corporatism in Action in Rural China', *Theory and Society*, Vol.24, No.3.

Liu, Alan P.L., 1992, 'The 'Wenzhou Model' of Development and China's Modernization', *Asian Survey*, Vol.32, No.8.

Lu, Xiaobo, 1997, 'The Politics of Peasant Burden in Reform China', *The Journal of Peasant Studies*, Vol.25, No.1.

Lu, Xiaobo, 2000, *Cadres and Corruption: The Organizational Involution of the Chinese Communist Party*, Stanford: Stanford University Press.

Nolan, Peter, 2001, *China and the Global Economy: National Champions, Industrial Policy and the Big Business Revolution*, Houndsmill, Basingstoke: Palgrave.

O'Brien, Kevin J. and Li Lianjiang, 1995, 'The Politics of Lodging Complaints in Rural China', *The China Quarterly*, No.143 (September).

O'Brien, Kevin J. and Li Lianjiang, 1999, 'Selective Policy Implementation in Rural China', *Comparative Politics*, Vol.31, No.2.

Oi, Jean C., 1992, 'Fiscal Reform and the Economic Foundations of Local State Corporatism in China', *World Politics*, Vol.45, No.1.

Oi, Jean C., 1995, 'The Role of the Local State in China's Transitional Economy', *The China Quarterly*, No.144 (December).

Oi, Jean C., 1998a, 'The Evolution of Local State Corporatism', in A. Walder (ed.), *Zouping in Transition: The Process of Reform in Rural North China*, Cambridge, MA: Harvard University Press.

Oi, Jean C., 1998b, 'The Collective Foundation for Rapid Rural Industrialization', in E. Vermeer, F. Pieke and W.L. Chong (eds.), *Cooperative and Collective in China's Rural Development: Between State and Private Interests*, London: M.E. Sharpe.

Oi, Jean C., 1999, *Rural China Takes Off: Institutional Foundations of Economic Reform*, Berkeley, CA: University of California Press.

Pei, Xiaolin, 1996, 'Township-Village Enterprises, Local Governments and Rural Communities: The Chinese Village as a Firm During Economic Transition', *Economics of Transition*, Vol.4, No.1.

Peng, Yali, 1996, 'The Politics of Tobacco: Relations between Farmers and Local Governments in China's Southwest', *The China Journal*, No.36 (July).

Unger, Jonathan, 2000, 'Power, Patronage, and Protest in Rural China', in T. White (ed.), *China Briefing 2000: The Continuing Transformation*, Armonk, New York: M.E. Sharpe.

Unger, Jonathan and Anita Chan, 1999, 'Inheritors of the Boom: Private Enterprise and the Role of Local Government in a Rural South China Township', *The China Journal*, No.42 (July).

Wade, Robert, 1990, *Governing the Market: Economic Theory and the Role of Government in East Asian Industrialization*, Princeton, NJ: Princeton University Press.

Walder, Andrew G., 1995, 'Local Governments as Industrial Firms: An Organizational Analysis of China's Transitional Economy', *American Journal of Sociology*, Vol.101, No.2.

Walder, Andrew G., 1998, 'The County Government as an Industrial Corporation', in A. Walder (ed.), *Zouping in Transition: The Process of Reform in Rural North China*, Cambridge, MA: Harvard University Press.

Weitzman, Martin L. and Xu Chenggang, 1994, 'Chinese Township-Village Enterprises as Vaguely Defined Cooperatives', *Journal of Comparative Economics*, Vol.18.

Whiting, Susan Hayes, 1995, 'The Micro-Foundations of Institutional Change in Reform China: Property Rights and Revenue Extraction in the Rural Industrial Sector', unpublished dissertation, University of Michigan.

Whiting, Susan H., 2001, *Power and Wealth in Rural China: The Political Economy of Institutional Change*, Cambridge: Cambridge University Press.

Yang, Dali L., 1996, 'Governing China's Transition to the Market: Institutional Incentives, Politicians' Choices and Unintended Outcomes', *World Politics*, Vol.48.

Abstracts

Regional Differences in Chinese Agriculture: Results from the 1997 First National Agricultural Census
ROBERTO FANFANI AND CRISTINA BRASILI

The knowledge of agriculture and rural areas in China was incomplete and fragmented until recently. The First National Agricultural Census in China overcame the lack of information. In this article, we first underline the wide differences that exist in farm typologies (households and non-households) after the extensive application of agrarian reform. In the second part of the article we will apply cluster analysis to Census data at the province and county level in order to redefine the geography of Chinese agriculture. The new reality of agriculture often differs from the economic and geographic regions previously utilized for the representation of Chinese economy.

Rethinking the Peasant Burden: Evidence from a Chinese Village
LI XIANDE

In the past years, the 'peasant burden' has become a very serious problem in the Chinese countryside, with farmers paying heavy taxes and levies. The government took many measures and regulations to tackle this issue. But, based on a village survey, this article shows that these regulations are largely ineffective. Most of the taxes, especially the various levies and funds paid to the local governmental agencies, escape the controls. The author argues that the dysfunction of local administrations is, among others, the main cause of the peasant burden. The problem is not a new one in China and reflects still the subordinate status of the peasantry. Therefore, any solution should imply active participation of the farmers in the management of public affairs and the implementation of democracy at grassroots level.

How Not to Industrialize: Observations from a Village in Sichuan
JACOB EYFERTH

Throughout the 1980s and 1990s, township and village enterprises (TVEs) were the main motor of development in rural China. This article looks at the mechanisms of industrial expansion in a single village and examines its associated costs. It finds that industrialization was narrowly conceived as a concerted mobilization effort in the pursuit of 'projects' that were not embedded in the local economy, produced few benefits for the local population, and burdened the village with crippling debts. Alternative pathways to industrialization, in the form of well-established handicrafts, were not explored. TVE privatization since 1998 has not fundamentally altered the mobilizational approach to industrialization.

Determinants of Income from Wages in Rural Wuxi and Baoding: A Survey of 22 Villages
EDUARD B. VERMEER

Opportunities and propensity to work for wages differ greatly between villages in China, depending on administrative position, urban proximity, economic development and cultural factors. A 1998 survey of over 3,000 households in 22 villages in two regions highlights the varying importance of personal attributes such as gender, age, education and political affiliation. Both in Wuxi in the rich, industrialized lower Yangtze delta and in agricultural Baoding on the North China Plain gender and education are critical factors for wage income, but differently so for younger and older generations. Political affiliation, if corrected for other factors, has less effect. Individual attributes appear to be important determinants of wage labour decisions, and socio-economic change has had different effects on the income position of households and individuals.

The Wasteland Auction Policy in Northwest China: Solving Environmental Degradation and Rural Poverty?
PETER HO

In order to relieve rural poverty and solve the problem of soil and water erosion on marginal land, various provinces and regions throughout China proclaimed a new policy in the late 1980s and early 1990s. This 'Four Wastelands Auction Policy' attempts to boost the development of land of low economic value through the auction of land leases, not only to the rural but also to the non-rural population. In this sense, the policy forms a double break with the past. First, it was initiated at the grassroots and thus signifies a larger manoeuvring space for local cadres to launch new – sensitive – policies. Second, access to rural (marginal) land is no longer restricted to farmers but has also become available to officials, urban entrepreneurs and citizens. By relying on concepts of institution building, two village case studies provide a detailed overview of the implementation of the wasteland auction policy in the Ningxia Hui Muslim autonomous region in northwest China, and its implications for poverty alleviation and soil and water conservation.

Ningxia's Third Road to Rural Development: Resettlement Schemes as a Last Means to Poverty Reduction?
RITA MERKLE

From the perspective of policy effectiveness and economic performance, this article evaluates government-directed resettlement projects in rural Ningxia, which had begun already in 1983. This will make it possible to reassess China's main approach to poverty reduction after the year 2000. The different policies are described and poverty indices are discussed. The article examines in particular the case of one cross-county resettlement project that was based on voluntary participation, illustrating its implementation characteristics and its outcomes. Finally, the findings are put into the broader context again and implications for policy-making are pointed out.

A Comparative Study of Projection Models on China's Food Economy
XIAOYONG ZHANG

During the last two decades, China's food supply and demand has been a hot topic for both politicians and academics given China's rapid economic development and its sheer market size. Accordingly, researchers are trying to project the future development of China's food economy. This article reviews several influential projection models and compares their model structure, major assumptions and projection results. In addition, the author tries to pinpoint the most significant factors that could influence the projection results. Several emerging issues, such as the projection validity, livestock structure changes and data reliability are discussed at the end.

Social Welfare in Rural China: Suggestions for a Comprehensive Approach
JUTTA HEBEL

Post-Mao China has seen a rapid restructuring of social welfare. In contrast to urban residents, China's rural population never received much state support. Rural welfare in China is best understood as a 'welfare mix', in which different actors – state agencies, intermediate organizations, and the market – supply goods and services to rural households, which are the ultimate producers of welfare and well-being. To understand how welfare works in rural China, we need to move away from a narrow focus on insurance schemes to a broader perspective that includes the everyday production of welfare in the household and the complex interaction between various institutional actors.

Gender Difference in Inheritance Rights: Observations from a
Chinese Village
HEATHER XIAOQUAN ZHANG

This article analyses inheritance in Chinese village society within a broad notion of welfare and social policy research. Its central concern is with the gendered dimension of inheritance. Based on fieldwork, the study reveals a significant gap between legislation and reality with daughters losing their statutory rights to their brothers in rural households and the village community despite the legal recognition of equal rights between women and men in property and inheritance. The article argues that while pluralist welfare provision is emphasized in promoting well-being in rural China, the problem of unequal entitlements and rights of men and women calls for more effective government actions in the form of social policy-making to combat gender discrimination and gendered exclusion, and to ensure more gender-equitable welfare outcomes.

Local State Corporatism and Private Business
MARIA EDIN

This article examines the role of the local state in promoting the development of private business in China, and the political institutions behind local state-led development. It argues that political incentives are more important than fiscal incentives to understand why local leaders have assisted the growth of rural industry. It also shows that local cadres not only promote collective enterprises, but also the private sector whose profits they are able to control to a much lesser extent, which reinforces the finding that political incentives guide cadre behaviour. The study applies the notion of local state corporatism but also asks what relevance the model, so dominant in the 1990s, holds for rural China studies in the coming years.

Author Index

Subject Index

Latin American Peasants
Tom Brass (Ed)

The essays in this collection examine current agrarian transformation in Latin America, and the role in this of peasants, with particular reference to Bolivia, Peru, Chile, Brazil and Central America. Among the issues covered are the impact of globalization and neoliberal economic policies and on peasant economy and rural labour, the historical and contemporary nature of peasant/state relations, debates over Amazonian peasantries, forms taken by local/regional/national peasant ideology/agency, and political disputes over agrarian reform. Land still remains on the agenda of most Latin American peasants, who continue to be politically active, not just in Chiapas (Mexico), nor in ways stipulated by post-modern, post-colonial, and post-development theory. The international group of scholars contributing to this volume include Tom Brass, James Petras, Henry Veltmeyer, Willem Assies, John Crabtree, Stephen Nugent, Warwick E Murray, John McNeish, Kees Jansen, Esther Roquas and José de Souza Martins.

400 pages illus 2003
0 7146 5384 5 cloth £45.00/$62.50
0 7146 8319 1 paper £18.50/$26.50
A special issue of the Journal of Peasant Studies
Library of Peasant Studies No. 21

UK: Crown House, 47 Chase Side, Southgate, London N14 5BP
Tel: +44 (0)20 8920 2100 Fax: +44 (0)20 8447 8548

North America: 920 NE 58th Avenue Suite 300, Portland, OR 97213-3786 USA
Tel: 800 944 6190 Fax: 503 280 8832

Website: www.frankcass.com E-mail: sales@frankcass.com

Publishers

FrankCass

Peasants, Populism and Postmodernism

The Return of the Agrarian Myth

Tom Brass

'hard-hitting ... the richness of the work, in terms of
historical depth, geographical span, and disciplinary
and thematic variety cannot fail to impress.'
The European Journal of Development Research

After an initial consideration of nineteenth and early
twentieth century versions of the agrarian myth, the
first part of the book examines the respective roles of
the agrarian myth, populism, socialism and
nationalism in a number of grassroots rural
mobilizations which occurred in Latin America and
India during the latter part of the twentieth century.
The second part charts the rise of the 'new' populism
and the 'new' right over the same period, together
with the reasons for this, its implications for
development theory in general, and the analysis of
agrarian change in particular, while the final section
analyses the different forms taken by the agrarian
myth in the domain of popular change (literature,
film).

392 pages 1999
0 7146 4940 6 cloth £45.00/$62.50
0 7146 8000 1 paper £18.50/$27.50
Library of Peasant Studies No. 17

UK: Crown House, 47 Chase Side, Southgate, London N14 5BP
Tel: +44 (0)20 8920 2100 Fax: +44 (0)20 8447 8548

North America: 920 NE 58th Avenue Suite 300, Portland, OR 97213-3786 USA
Tel: 800 944 6190 Fax: 503 280 8832

Website: www.frankcass.com E-mail: sales@frankcass.com

FrankCass publishers

An Apartheid Oasis?

Agriculture and Rural Livelihoods in Venda

Edward Lahiff
Nkuzi Development Association, South Africa

This study includes a review of micro-studies of agriculture and livelihoods from the ten former homelands. A range of unpublished materials and original field research are also used to provide an overview of society and economy in Venda, one of the black South African homelands, at the end of apartheid and to highlight the problems faced by households attempting to secure a livelihood from the land.

320 pages maps 2000
0 7146 5137 0 cloth £37.50/$52.50
Library of Peasant Studies No. 20

UK: Crown House, 47 Chase Side, Southgate, London N14 5BP
Tel: +44 (0)20 8920 2100 Fax: +44 (0)20 8447 8548

North America: 920 NE 58th Avenue Suite 300, Portland, OR 97213-3786 USA
Tel: 800 944 6190 Fax: 503 280 8832

Website: www.frankcass.com E-mail: sales@frankcass.com

Frank Cass
publishers